Volume 1

Story & Art by Emura

W Juliet
Volume 1

Story and Art by Emura

Translation & English Adaptation/William Flanagan
Touch-up Art & Lettering/Mark McMurray
Graphic Design/Hidemi Sahara
Editor/Megan Bates

Managing Editor/Annette Roman
Director of Production/Noboru Watanabe
Editorial Director/Alvin Lu
Sr. Director of Licensing & Acquisitions/Rika Inouye
Vice President of Sales & Marketing/Liza Coppola
Executive Vice President/Hyoe Narita
Publisher/Seiji Horibuchi

Printed in the U.S.A.

Published by VIZ, LLC
P.O. Box 77010
San Francisco, CA 94107

10 9 8 7 6 5 4 3 2 1
First printing, October 2004

www.viz.com

store.viz.com

PARENTAL ADVISORY
W JULIET is rated T for teens. Contains mild sexual situations/humor and tobacco usage. Recommended for ages 13 and up.

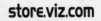

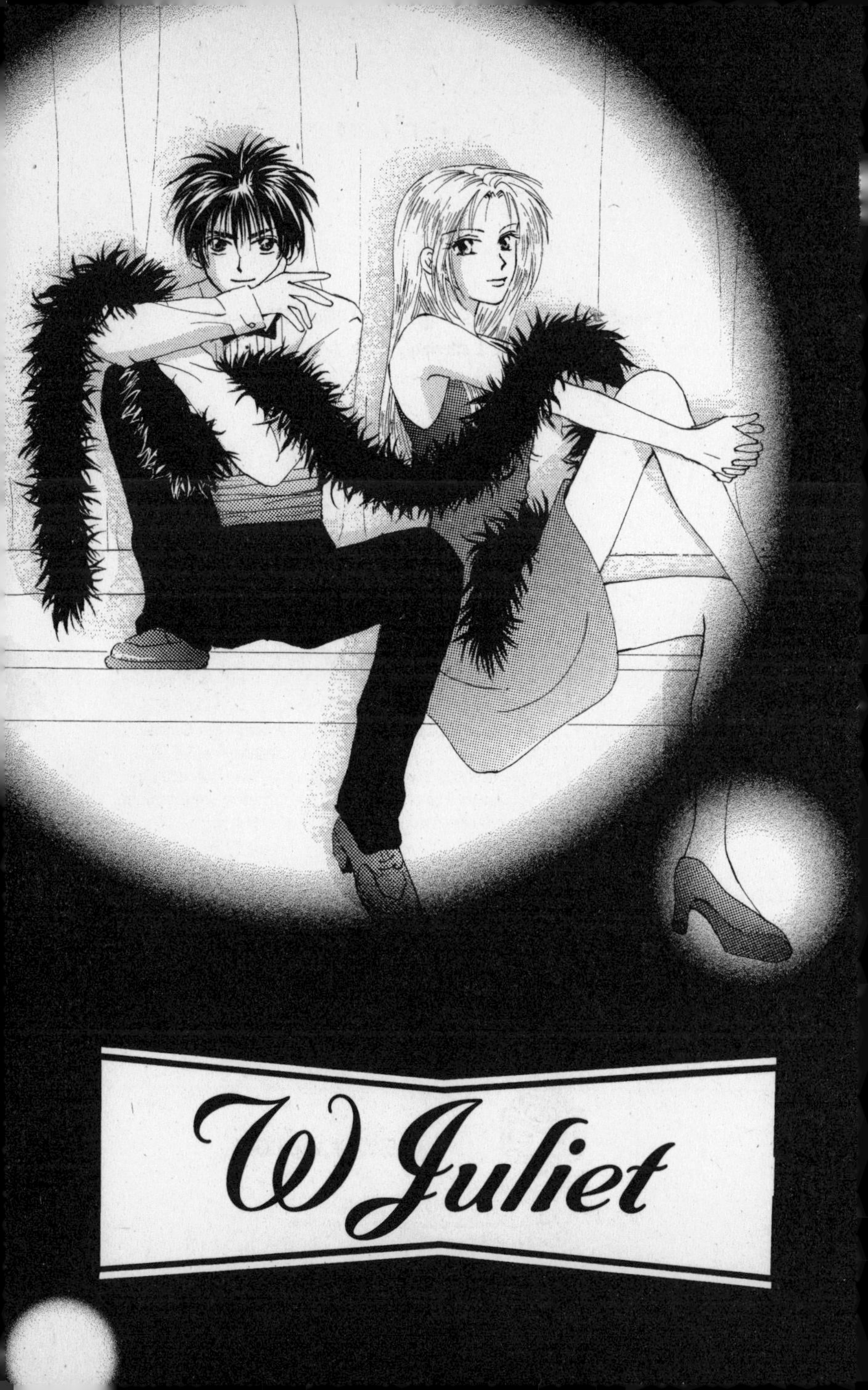
W Juliet

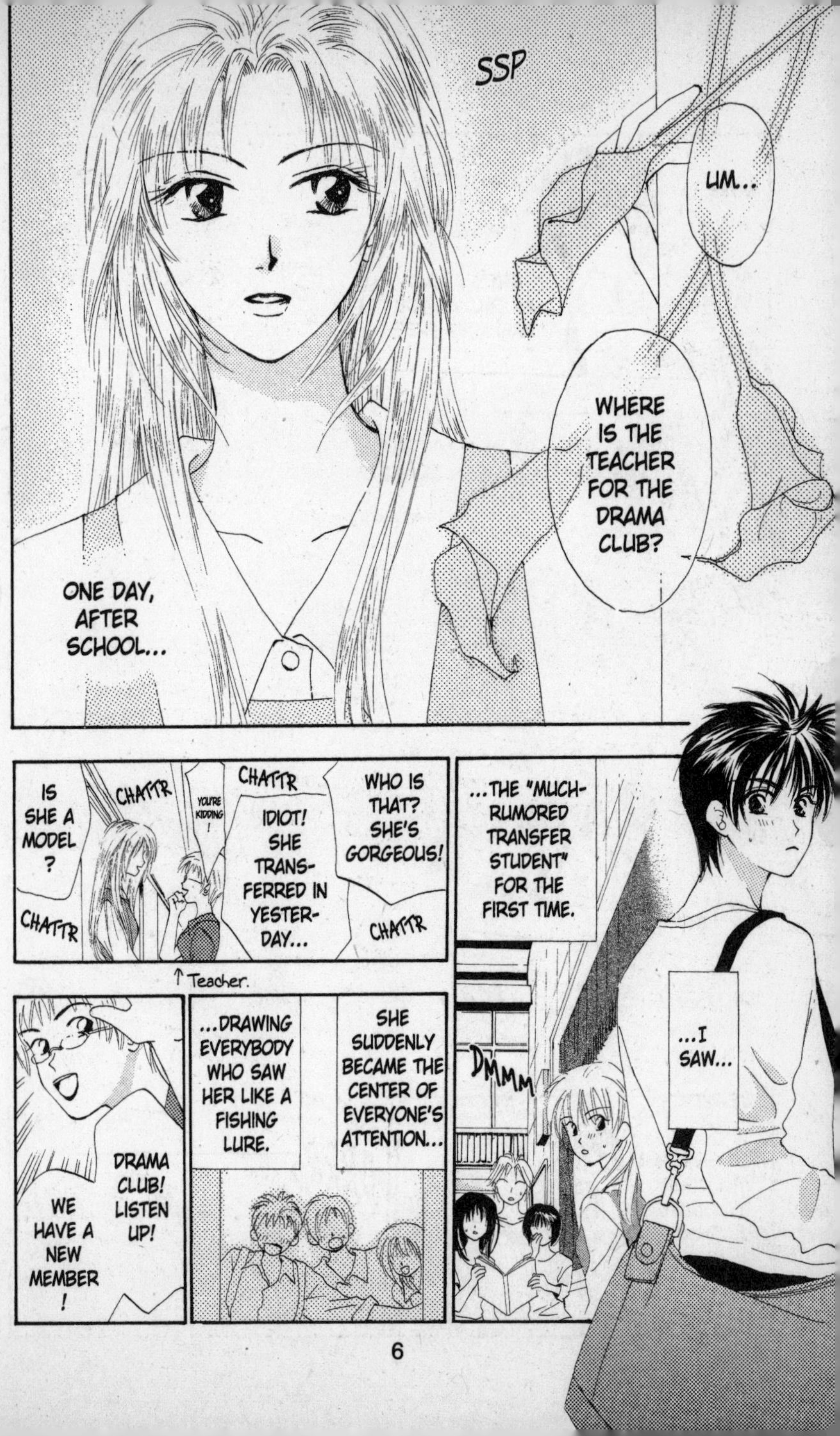
SSP
UM...
WHERE IS THE TEACHER FOR THE DRAMA CLUB?
ONE DAY, AFTER SCHOOL...
...I SAW...
...THE "MUCH-RUMORED TRANSFER STUDENT" FOR THE FIRST TIME.
WHO IS THAT? SHE'S GORGEOUS!
CHATTR
IDIOT! SHE TRANSFERRED IN YESTERDAY...
CHATTR
YOU'RE KIDDING!
CHATTR
IS SHE A MODEL?
CHATTR
↑Teacher.
DMMM
SHE SUDDENLY BECAME THE CENTER OF EVERYONE'S ATTENTION...
...DRAWING EVERYBODY WHO SAW HER LIKE A FISHING LURE.
DRAMA CLUB! LISTEN UP!
WE HAVE A NEW MEMBER!

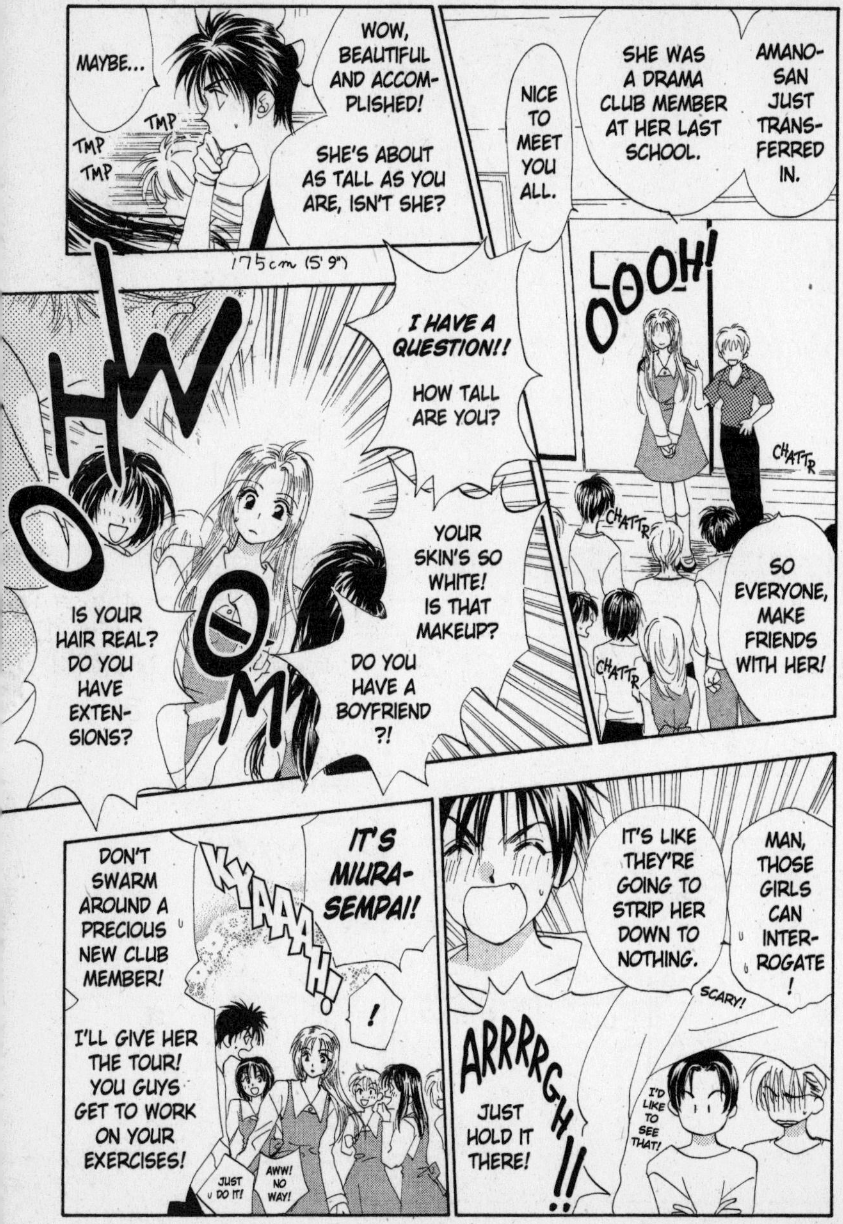
AMANO-SAN JUST TRANSFERRED IN.
SHE WAS A DRAMA CLUB MEMBER AT HER LAST SCHOOL.
NICE TO MEET YOU ALL.
WOW, BEAUTIFUL AND ACCOMPLISHED!
SHE'S ABOUT AS TALL AS YOU ARE, ISN'T SHE?
MAYBE...
TMP
TMP
TMP
175cm (5'9")
OOOH!
CHATTR
CHATTR
CHATTR
SO EVERYONE, MAKE FRIENDS WITH HER!
I HAVE A QUESTION!!
HOW TALL ARE YOU?
YOUR SKIN'S SO WHITE! IS THAT MAKEUP?
DO YOU HAVE A BOYFRIEND?!
IS YOUR HAIR REAL? DO YOU HAVE EXTENSIONS?
MAN, THOSE GIRLS CAN INTERROGATE!
IT'S LIKE THEY'RE GOING TO STRIP HER DOWN TO NOTHING.
SCARY!
ARRRRGH!!
I'D LIKE TO SEE THAT!
JUST HOLD IT THERE!
IT'S MIURA-SEMPAI!
KYAAAAH!
DON'T SWARM AROUND A PRECIOUS NEW CLUB MEMBER!
I'LL GIVE HER THE TOUR! YOU GUYS GET TO WORK ON YOUR EXERCISES!
!
AWW! NO WAY!
JUST DO IT!

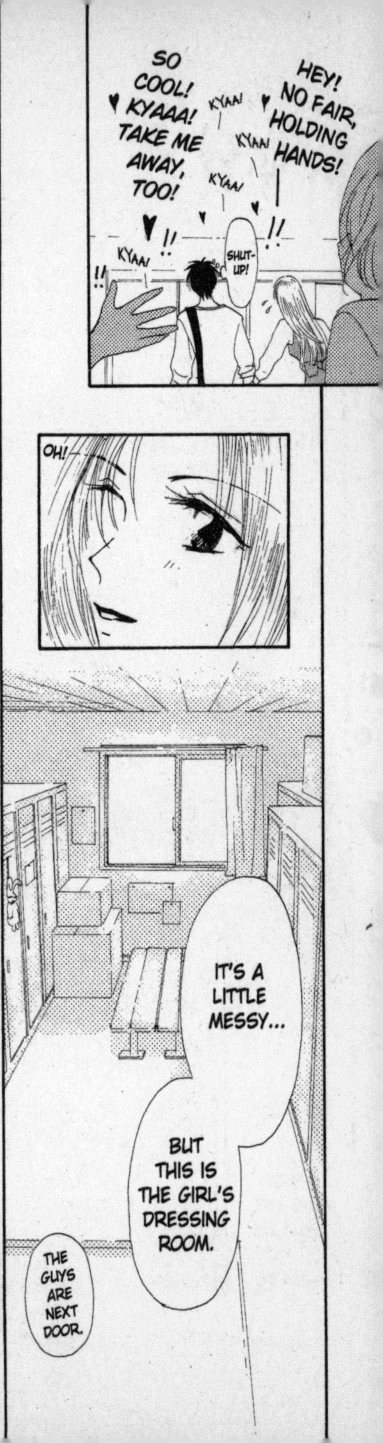
HEY! NO FAIR, HOLDING HANDS!
KYAA!
KYAA!
SHUT-UP!
KYAA!
SO COOL! KYAAA! TAKE ME AWAY, TOO!
KYAA!
OH!
IT'S A LITTLE MESSY...
BUT THIS IS THE GIRL'S DRESSING ROOM.
THE GUYS ARE NEXT DOOR.

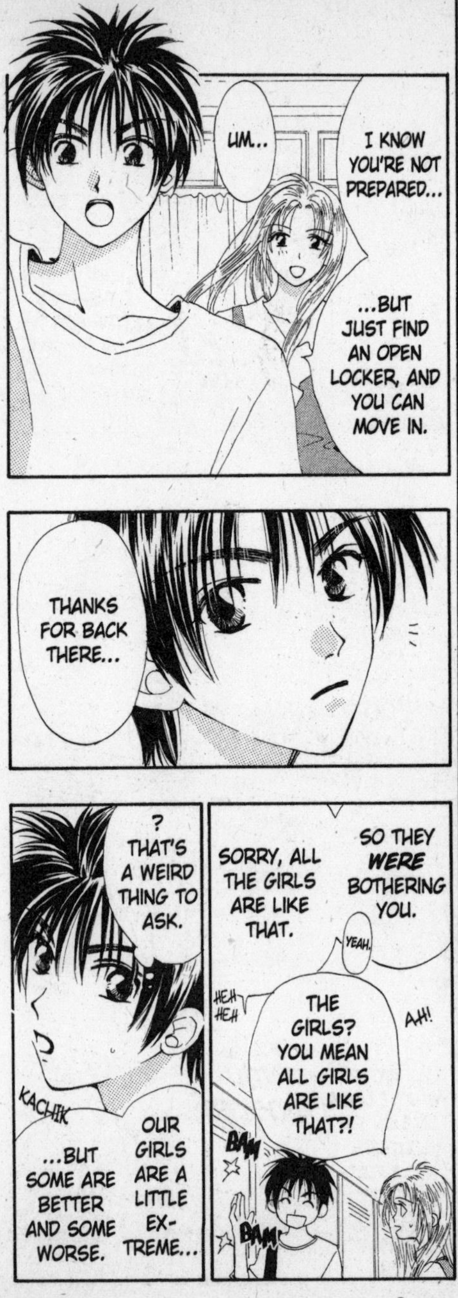
I KNOW YOU'RE NOT PREPARED...
...BUT JUST FIND AN OPEN LOCKER, AND YOU CAN MOVE IN.
UM...
THANKS FOR BACK THERE...
SO THEY *WERE* BOTHERING YOU.
SORRY, ALL THE GIRLS ARE LIKE THAT.
YEAH.
AH!
THE GIRLS? YOU MEAN ALL GIRLS ARE LIKE THAT?!
HEH HEH
BAM
BAM
? THAT'S A WEIRD THING TO ASK.
KACHIK
OUR GIRLS ARE A LITTLE EX-TREME...
...BUT SOME ARE BETTER AND SOME WORSE.

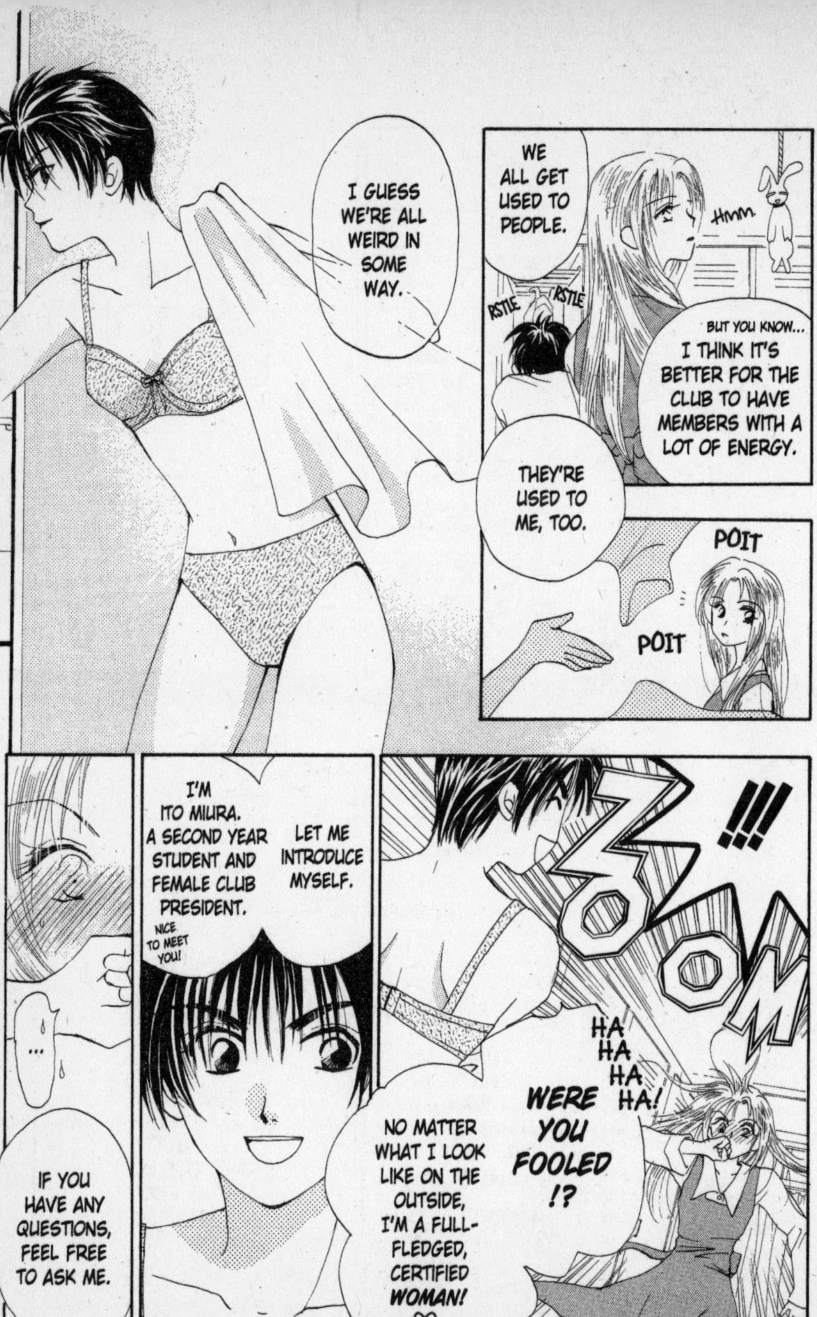
WE ALL GET USED TO PEOPLE.
Hmm.
RSTLE
RSTLE
BUT YOU KNOW... I THINK IT'S BETTER FOR THE CLUB TO HAVE MEMBERS WITH A LOT OF ENERGY.
THEY'RE USED TO ME, TOO.
POIT
POIT
I GUESS WE'RE ALL WEIRD IN SOME WAY.
ZOOM
!!!
HA HA HA HA!
WERE YOU FOOLED !?
LET ME INTRODUCE MYSELF.
I'M ITO MIURA. A SECOND YEAR STUDENT AND FEMALE CLUB PRESIDENT.
NICE TO MEET YOU!
NO MATTER WHAT I LOOK LIKE ON THE OUTSIDE, I'M A FULL-FLEDGED, CERTIFIED WOMAN! ♡
...
IF YOU HAVE ANY QUESTIONS, FEEL FREE TO ASK ME.

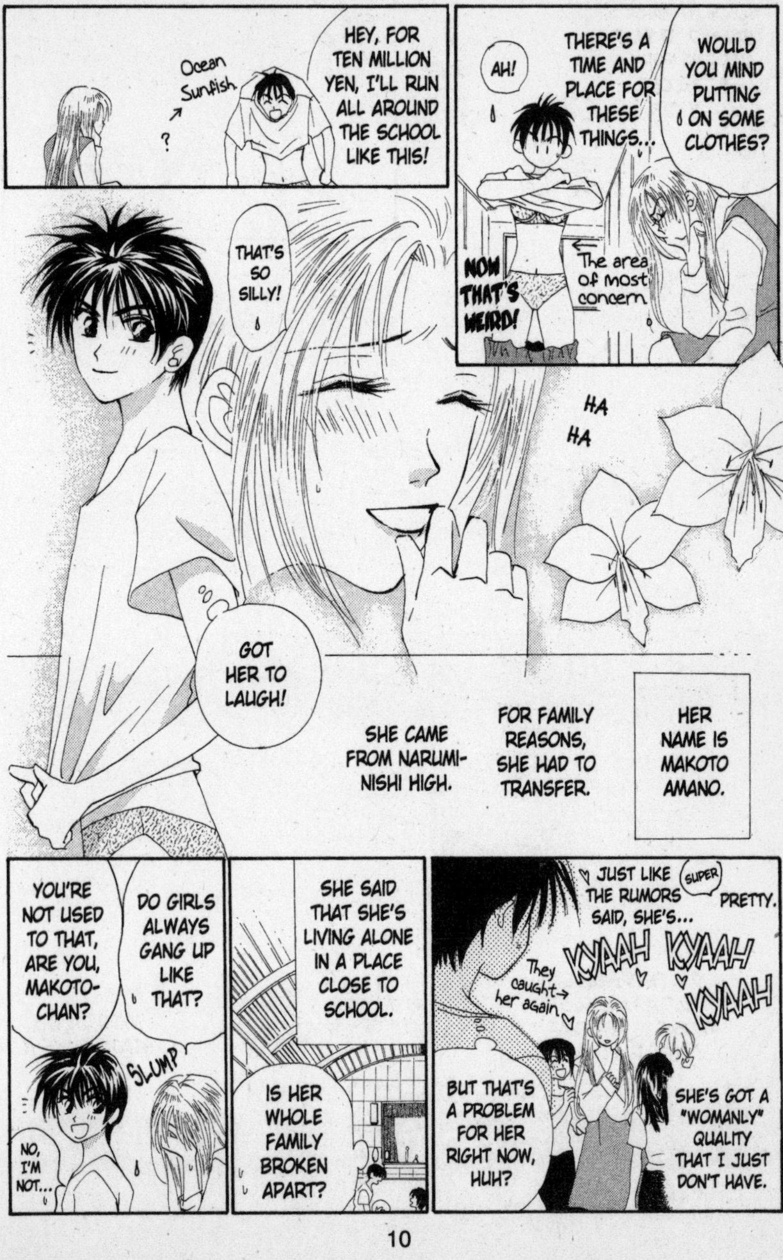
WOULD YOU MIND PUTTING ON SOME CLOTHES?
THERE'S A TIME AND PLACE FOR THESE THINGS...
AH!
The area of most concern
NOW THAT'S WEIRD!
HEY, FOR TEN MILLION YEN, I'LL RUN ALL AROUND THE SCHOOL LIKE THIS!
Ocean Sunfish
?
HA HA
THAT'S SO SILLY!
GOT HER TO LAUGH!
HER NAME IS MAKOTO AMANO.
FOR FAMILY REASONS, SHE HAD TO TRANSFER.
SHE CAME FROM NARUMI-NISHI HIGH.
JUST LIKE THE RUMORS SAID, SHE'S... SUPER PRETTY.
KYAAH KYAAH KYAAH
They caught her again.
SHE'S GOT A "WOMANLY" QUALITY THAT I JUST DON'T HAVE.
BUT THAT'S A PROBLEM FOR HER RIGHT NOW, HUH?
SHE SAID THAT SHE'S LIVING ALONE IN A PLACE CLOSE TO SCHOOL.
IS HER WHOLE FAMILY BROKEN APART?
DO GIRLS ALWAYS GANG UP LIKE THAT?
YOU'RE NOT USED TO THAT, ARE YOU, MAKOTO-CHAN?
SLUMP
NO, I'M NOT...

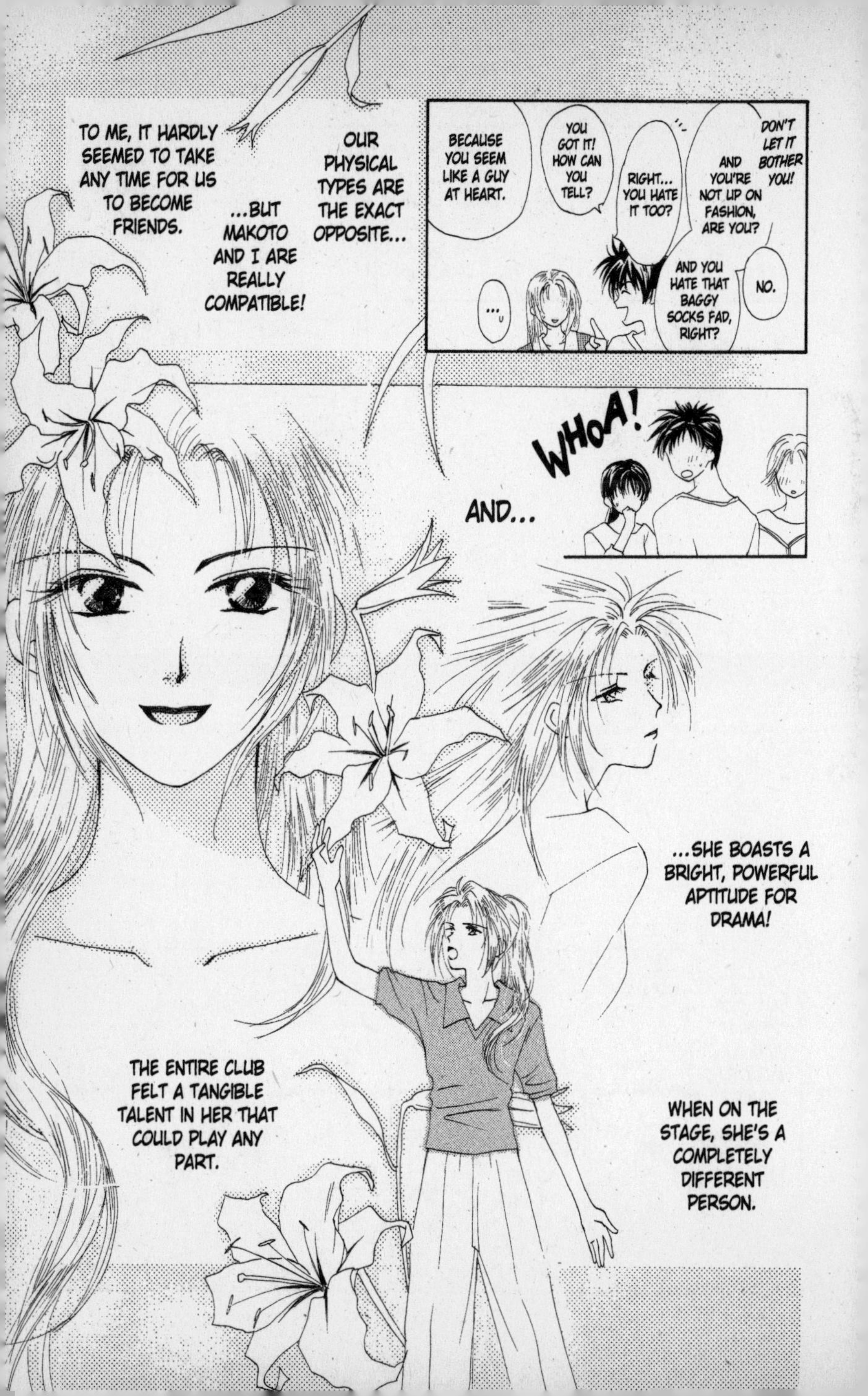
DON'T LET IT BOTHER YOU!
AND YOU'RE NOT UP ON FASHION, ARE YOU?
NO.
AND YOU HATE THAT BAGGY SOCKS FAD, RIGHT?
RIGHT... YOU HATE IT TOO?
YOU GOT IT! HOW CAN YOU TELL?
BECAUSE YOU SEEM LIKE A GUY AT HEART.
...
OUR PHYSICAL TYPES ARE THE EXACT OPPOSITE...
...BUT MAKOTO AND I ARE REALLY COMPATIBLE!
TO ME, IT HARDLY SEEMED TO TAKE ANY TIME FOR US TO BECOME FRIENDS.
WHOA!
AND...
...SHE BOASTS A BRIGHT, POWERFUL APTITUDE FOR DRAMA!
WHEN ON THE STAGE, SHE'S A COMPLETELY DIFFERENT PERSON.
THE ENTIRE CLUB FELT A TANGIBLE TALENT IN HER THAT COULD PLAY ANY PART.

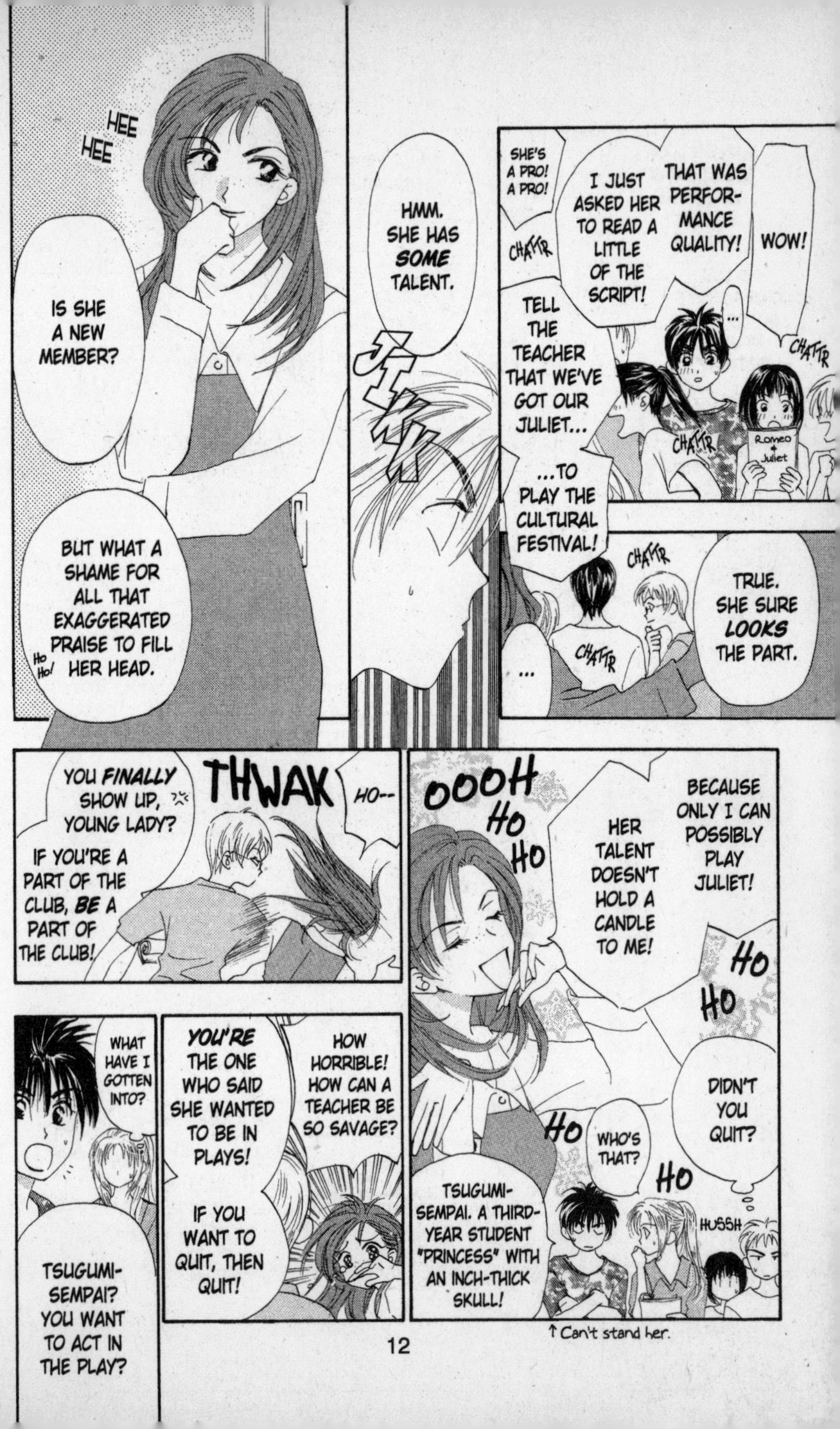
WOW!
THAT WAS PERFORMANCE QUALITY!
I JUST ASKED HER TO READ A LITTLE OF THE SCRIPT!
SHE'S A PRO! A PRO!
CHATTR
...
CHATTR
Romeo + Juliet
CHATTR
TELL THE TEACHER THAT WE'VE GOT OUR JULIET...
...TO PLAY THE CULTURAL FESTIVAL!
TRUE. SHE SURE LOOKS THE PART.
CHATTR
CHATTR
...
HMM. SHE HAS SOME TALENT.
JINK
HEE HEE
IS SHE A NEW MEMBER?
BUT WHAT A SHAME FOR ALL THAT EXAGGERATED PRAISE TO FILL HER HEAD.
Ho Ho!
OOOH HO HO
BECAUSE ONLY I CAN POSSIBLY PLAY JULIET!
HER TALENT DOESN'T HOLD A CANDLE TO ME!
HO HO
DIDN'T YOU QUIT?
HO
WHO'S THAT?
HO
TSUGUMI-SEMPAI. A THIRD-YEAR STUDENT "PRINCESS" WITH AN INCH-THICK SKULL!
HUSSH
↑Can't stand her.
HO--
THWAK
YOU FINALLY SHOW UP, YOUNG LADY?
IF YOU'RE A PART OF THE CLUB, BE A PART OF THE CLUB!
HOW HORRIBLE! HOW CAN A TEACHER BE SO SAVAGE?
YOU'RE THE ONE WHO SAID SHE WANTED TO BE IN PLAYS!
IF YOU WANT TO QUIT, THEN QUIT!
WHAT HAVE I GOTTEN INTO?
TSUGUMI-SEMPAI? YOU WANT TO ACT IN THE PLAY?

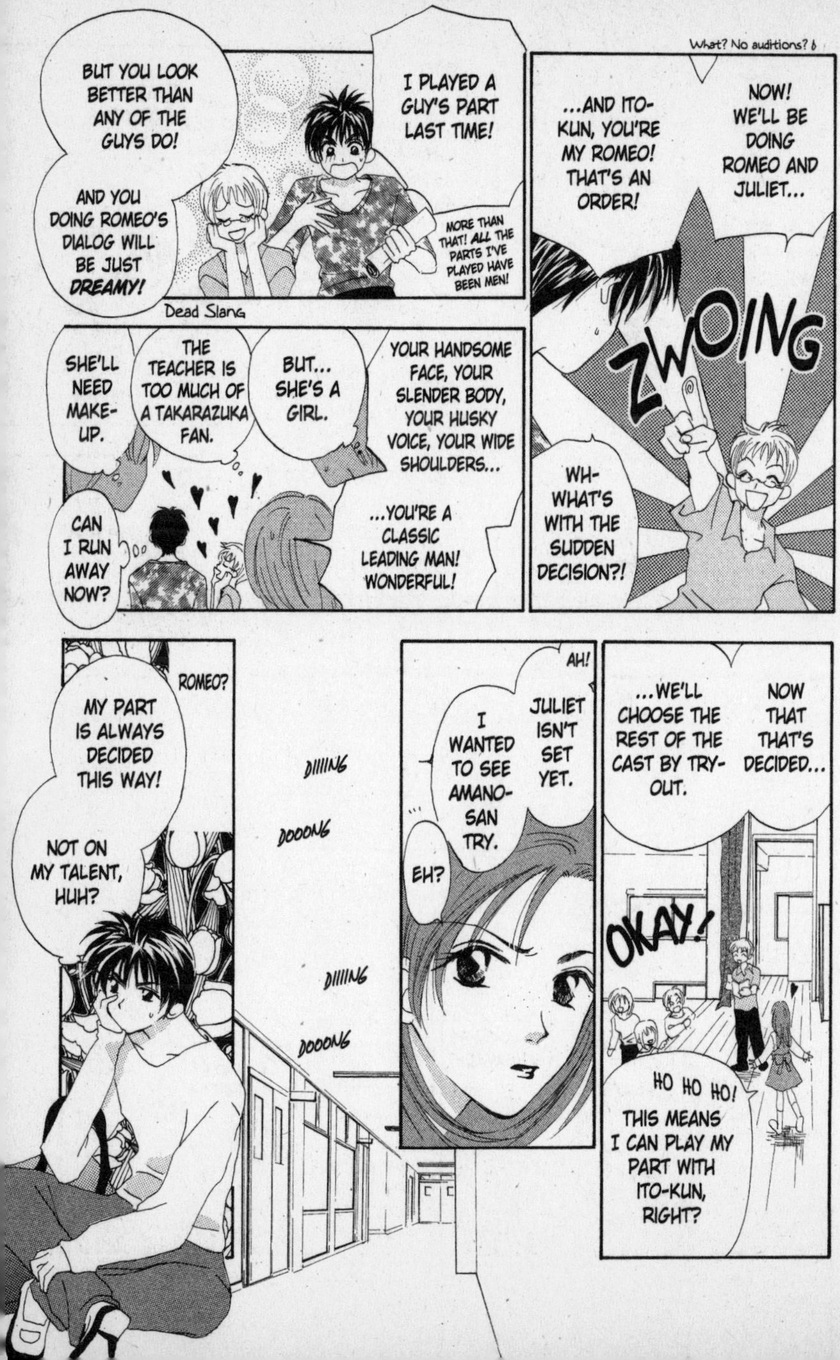
What? No auditions?
NOW! WE'LL BE DOING ROMEO AND JULIET...
...AND ITO-KUN, YOU'RE MY ROMEO! THAT'S AN ORDER!
ZWOING
WH-WHAT'S WITH THE SUDDEN DECISION?!
I PLAYED A GUY'S PART LAST TIME!
MORE THAN THAT! ALL THE PARTS I'VE PLAYED HAVE BEEN MEN!
BUT YOU LOOK BETTER THAN ANY OF THE GUYS DO!
AND YOU DOING ROMEO'S DIALOG WILL BE JUST DREAMY!
Dead Slang
YOUR HANDSOME FACE, YOUR SLENDER BODY, YOUR HUSKY VOICE, YOUR WIDE SHOULDERS...
...YOU'RE A CLASSIC LEADING MAN! WONDERFUL!
BUT... SHE'S A GIRL.
THE TEACHER IS TOO MUCH OF A TAKARAZUKA FAN.
SHE'LL NEED MAKE-UP.
CAN I RUN AWAY NOW?
NOW THAT THAT'S DECIDED...
...WE'LL CHOOSE THE REST OF THE CAST BY TRY-OUT.
OKAY!
HO HO HO! THIS MEANS I CAN PLAY MY PART WITH ITO-KUN, RIGHT?
AH!
JULIET ISN'T SET YET.
I WANTED TO SEE AMANO-SAN TRY.
...
EH?
ROMEO?
MY PART IS ALWAYS DECIDED THIS WAY!
NOT ON MY TALENT, HUH?
DIIIING
DOOONG
DIIIING
DOOONG

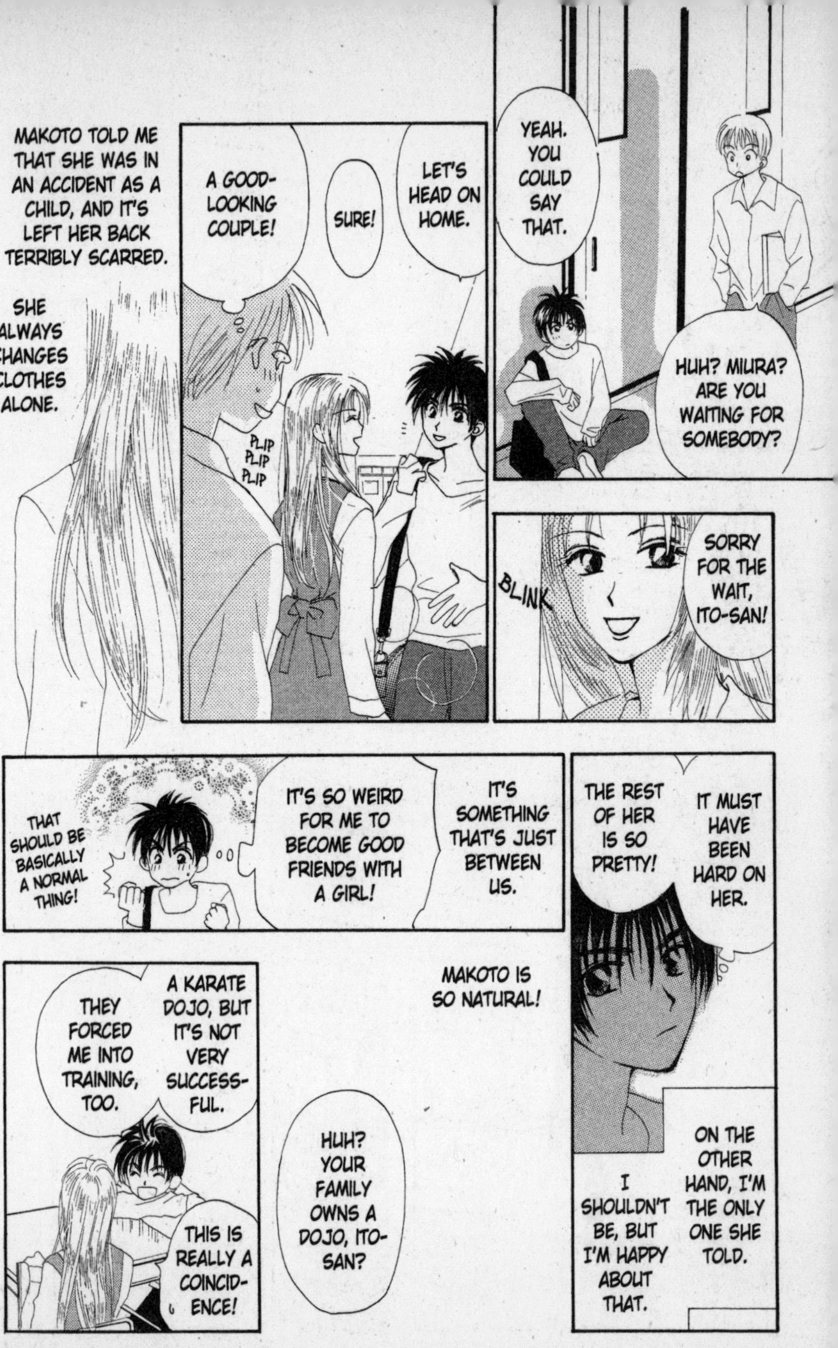

HUH? MIURA? ARE YOU WAITING FOR SOMEBODY?
YEAH. YOU COULD SAY THAT.
SORRY FOR THE WAIT, ITO-SAN!
BLINK
LET'S HEAD ON HOME.
SURE!
A GOOD-LOOKING COUPLE!
PLIP PLIP PLIP
MAKOTO TOLD ME THAT SHE WAS IN AN ACCIDENT AS A CHILD, AND IT'S LEFT HER BACK TERRIBLY SCARRED.
SHE ALWAYS CHANGES CLOTHES ALONE.
IT MUST HAVE BEEN HARD ON HER.
THE REST OF HER IS SO PRETTY!
ON THE OTHER HAND, I'M THE ONLY ONE SHE TOLD.
I SHOULDN'T BE, BUT I'M HAPPY ABOUT THAT.
IT'S SOMETHING THAT'S JUST BETWEEN US.
IT'S SO WEIRD FOR ME TO BECOME GOOD FRIENDS WITH A GIRL!
THAT SHOULD BE BASICALLY A NORMAL THING!
MAKOTO IS SO NATURAL!
HUH? YOUR FAMILY OWNS A DOJO, ITO-SAN?
A KARATE DOJO, BUT IT'S NOT VERY SUCCESSFUL.
THEY FORCED ME INTO TRAINING, TOO.
THIS IS REALLY A COINCIDENCE!

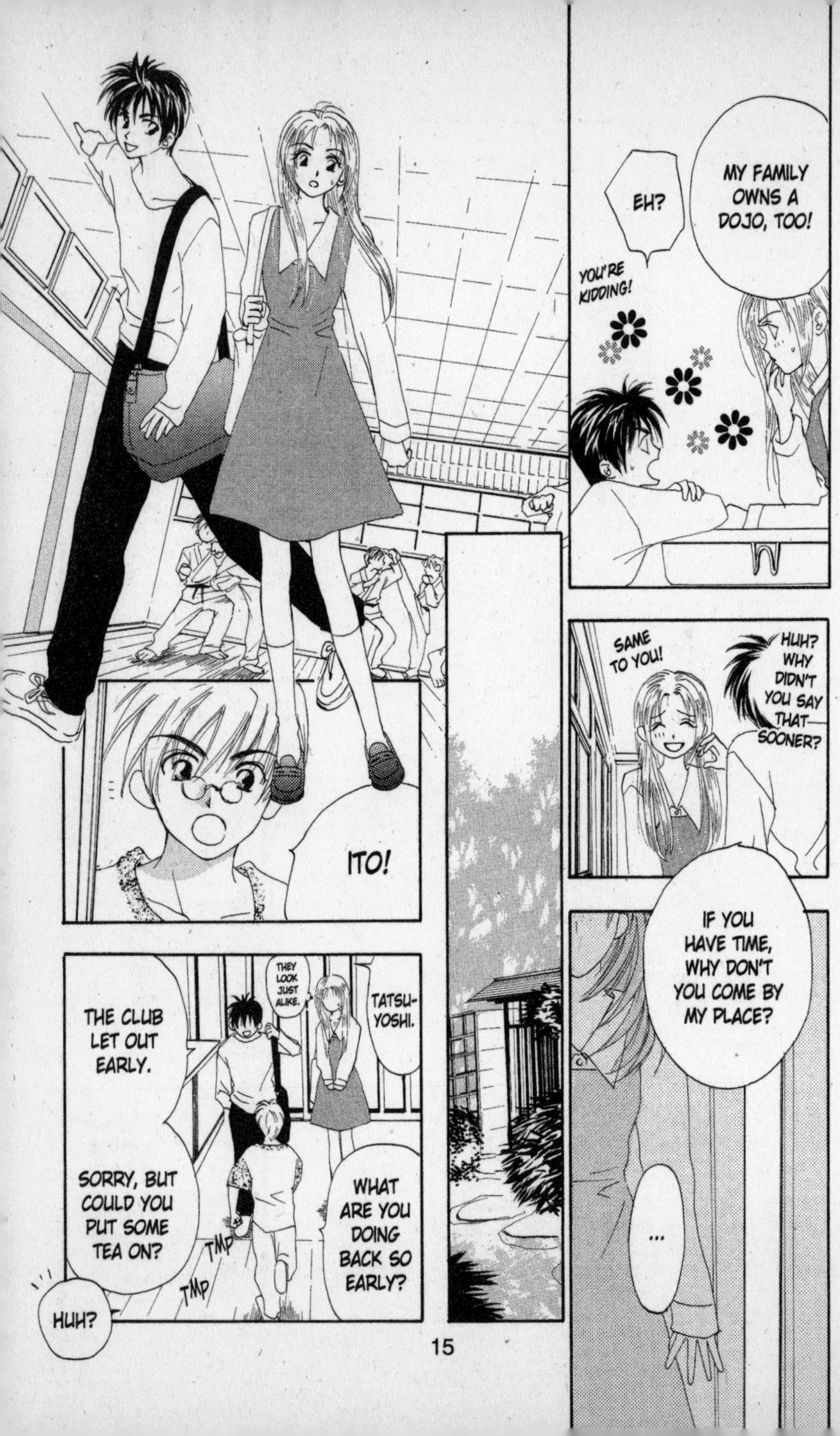
MY FAMILY OWNS A DOJO, TOO!
EH?
YOU'RE KIDDING!
HUH? WHY DIDN'T YOU SAY THAT SOONER?
SAME TO YOU!
IF YOU HAVE TIME, WHY DON'T YOU COME BY MY PLACE?
...
ITO!
TATSU-YOSHI.
THEY LOOK JUST ALIKE.
WHAT ARE YOU DOING BACK SO EARLY?
THE CLUB LET OUT EARLY.
SORRY, BUT COULD YOU PUT SOME TEA ON?
TMP
TMP
HUH?

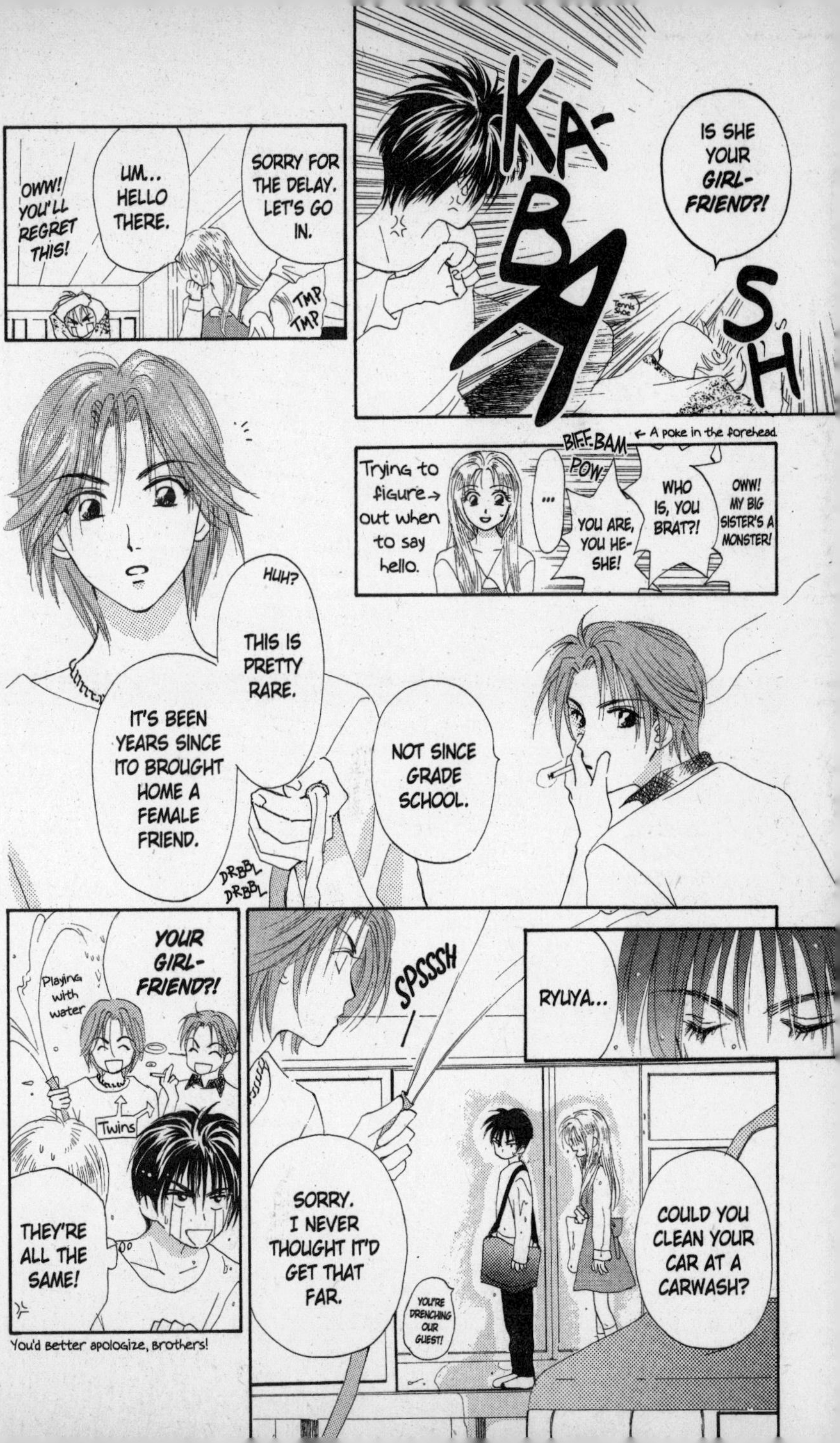
IS SHE YOUR GIRL-FRIEND?!
KA-BA-SH
Tennis Shoe
SORRY FOR THE DELAY. LET'S GO IN.
TMP TMP
UM... HELLO THERE.
OWW! YOU'LL REGRET THIS!
← A poke in the forehead.
OWW! MY BIG SISTER'S A MONSTER!
WHO IS, YOU BRAT?!
BIFF BAM POW
YOU ARE, YOU HE-SHE!
...
Trying to figure → out when to say hello.
HUH?
THIS IS PRETTY RARE.
IT'S BEEN YEARS SINCE ITO BROUGHT HOME A FEMALE FRIEND.
NOT SINCE GRADE SCHOOL.
DRBBL DRBBL
RYUYA...
SPSSSH
COULD YOU CLEAN YOUR CAR AT A CARWASH?
SORRY. I NEVER THOUGHT IT'D GET THAT FAR.
YOU'RE DRENCHING OUR GUEST!
YOUR GIRL-FRIEND?!
Playing with water
Twins
THEY'RE ALL THE SAME!
You'd better apologize, brothers!

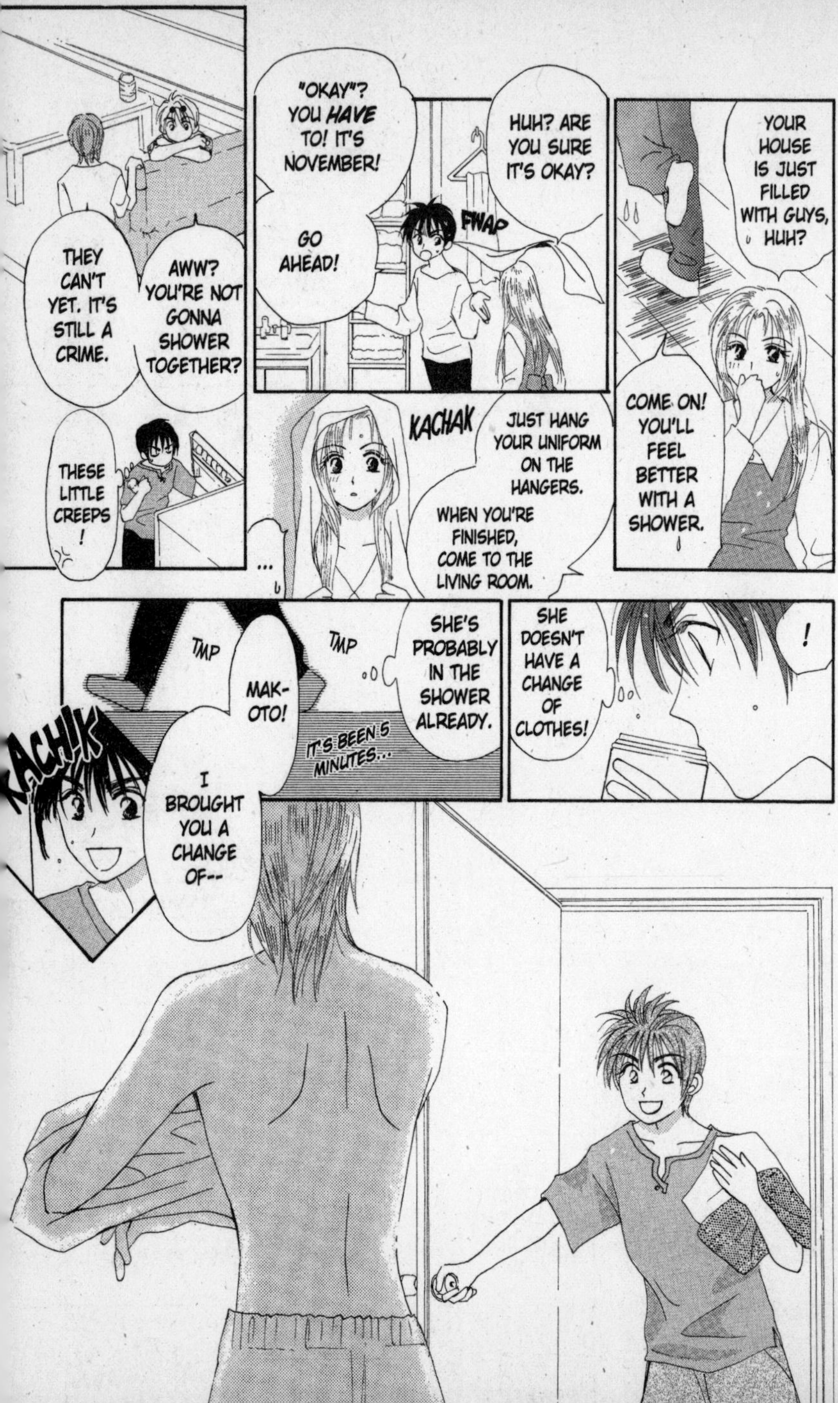
YOUR HOUSE IS JUST FILLED WITH GUYS, HUH?
COME ON! YOU'LL FEEL BETTER WITH A SHOWER.
HUH? ARE YOU SURE IT'S OKAY?
"OKAY"? YOU *HAVE* TO! IT'S NOVEMBER!
FWAP
GO AHEAD!
KACHAK
JUST HANG YOUR UNIFORM ON THE HANGERS.
WHEN YOU'RE FINISHED, COME TO THE LIVING ROOM.
...
AWW? YOU'RE NOT GONNA SHOWER TOGETHER?
THEY CAN'T YET. IT'S STILL A CRIME.
THESE LITTLE CREEPS!
!
SHE DOESN'T HAVE A CHANGE OF CLOTHES!
SHE'S PROBABLY IN THE SHOWER ALREADY.
TMP
TMP
IT'S BEEN 5 MINUTES...
MAK-OTO!
KACHIK
I BROUGHT YOU A CHANGE OF--

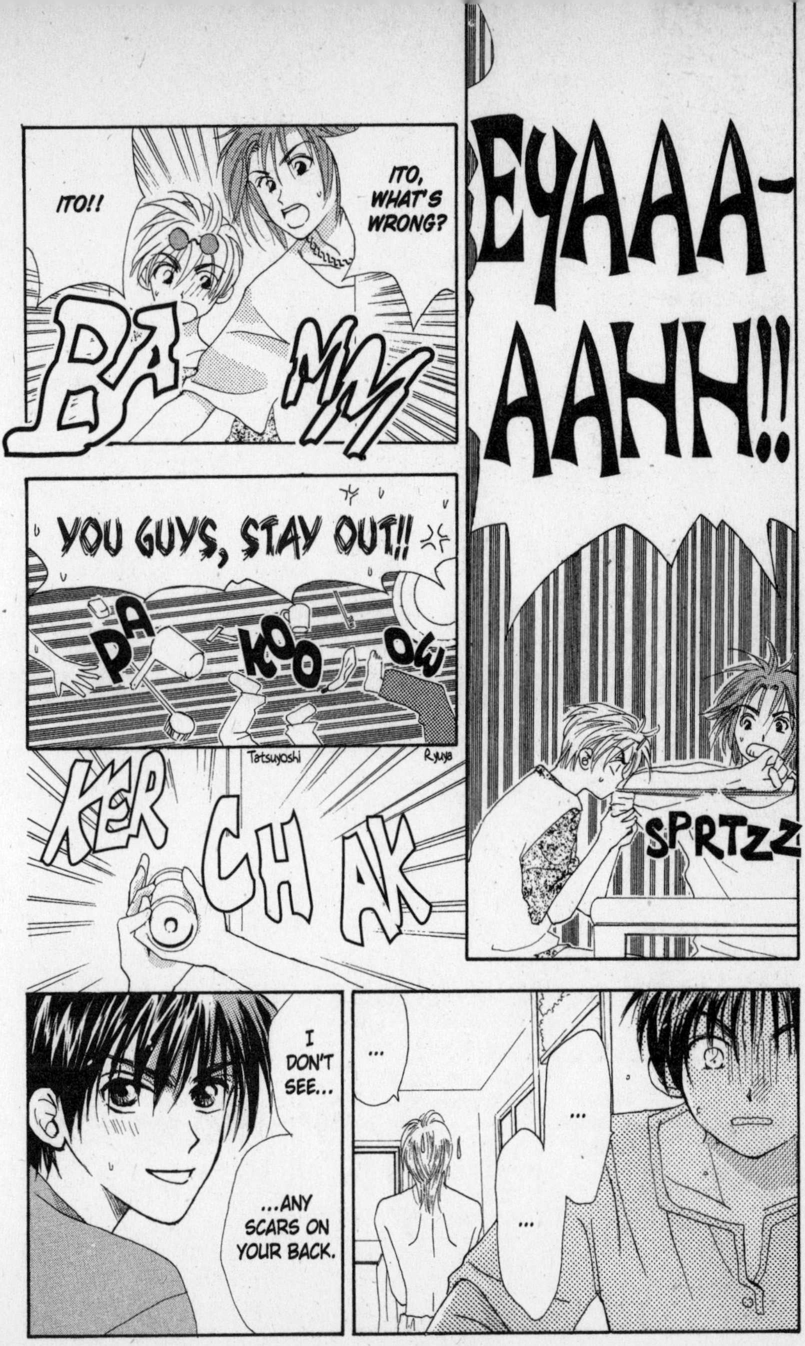
EYAAA-AAHH!!
SPRTZZ
ITO, WHAT'S WRONG?
ITO!!
BAMM
YOU GUYS, STAY OUT!!
PA
KOO
OW
Ryuya
Tatsuyoshi
KER CH AK
...
...
...
I DON'T SEE...
...ANY SCARS ON YOUR BACK.

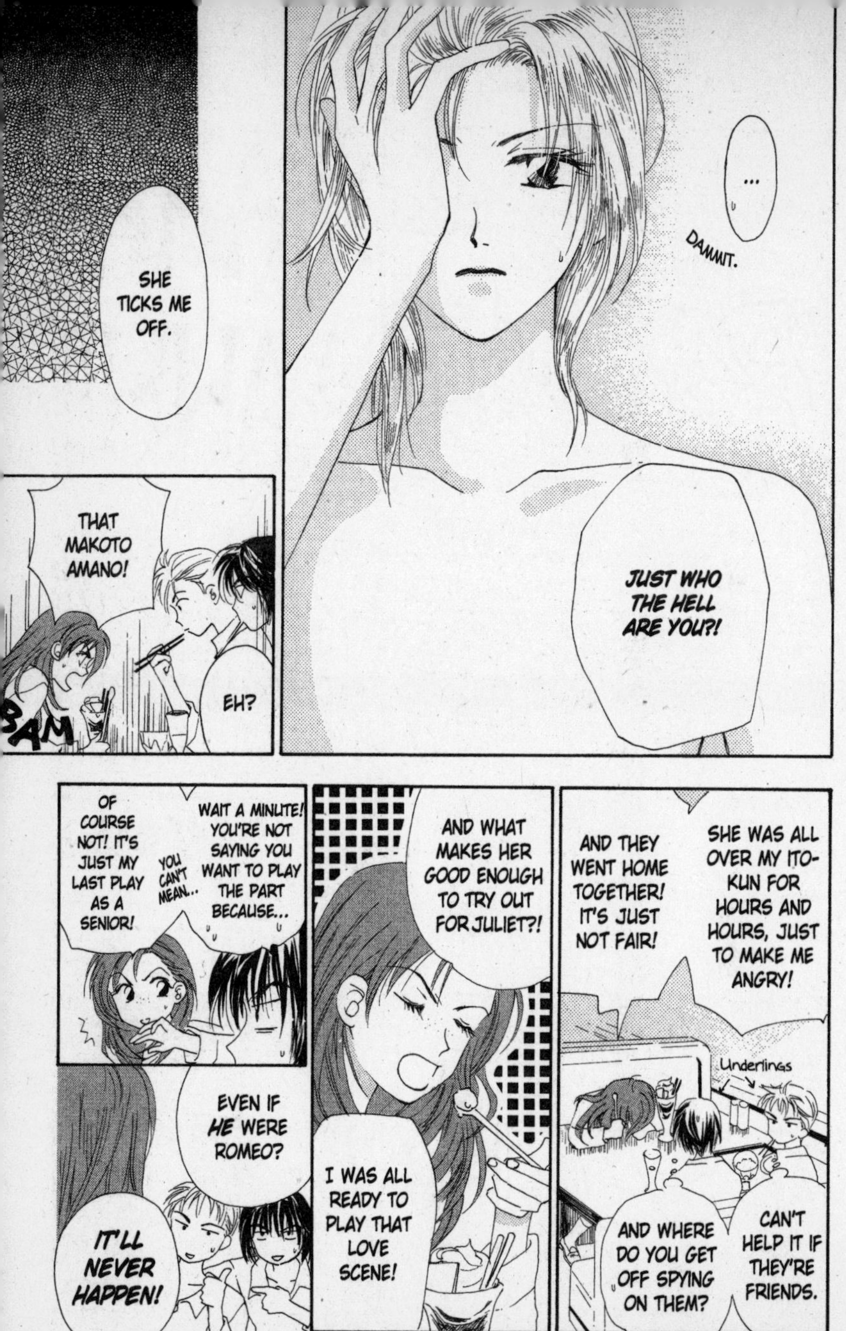
...
DAMMIT.
JUST WHO THE HELL ARE YOU?!
SHE TICKS ME OFF.
THAT MAKOTO AMANO!
EH?
BAM
SHE WAS ALL OVER MY ITO-KUN FOR HOURS AND HOURS, JUST TO MAKE ME ANGRY!
AND THEY WENT HOME TOGETHER! IT'S JUST NOT FAIR!
Underlings
CAN'T HELP IT IF THEY'RE FRIENDS.
AND WHERE DO YOU GET OFF SPYING ON THEM?
AND WHAT MAKES HER GOOD ENOUGH TO TRY OUT FOR JULIET?!
I WAS ALL READY TO PLAY THAT LOVE SCENE!
WAIT A MINUTE! YOU'RE NOT SAYING YOU WANT TO PLAY THE PART BECAUSE...
YOU CAN'T MEAN...
OF COURSE NOT! IT'S JUST MY LAST PLAY AS A SENIOR!
EVEN IF *HE* WERE ROMEO?
IT'LL NEVER HAPPEN!

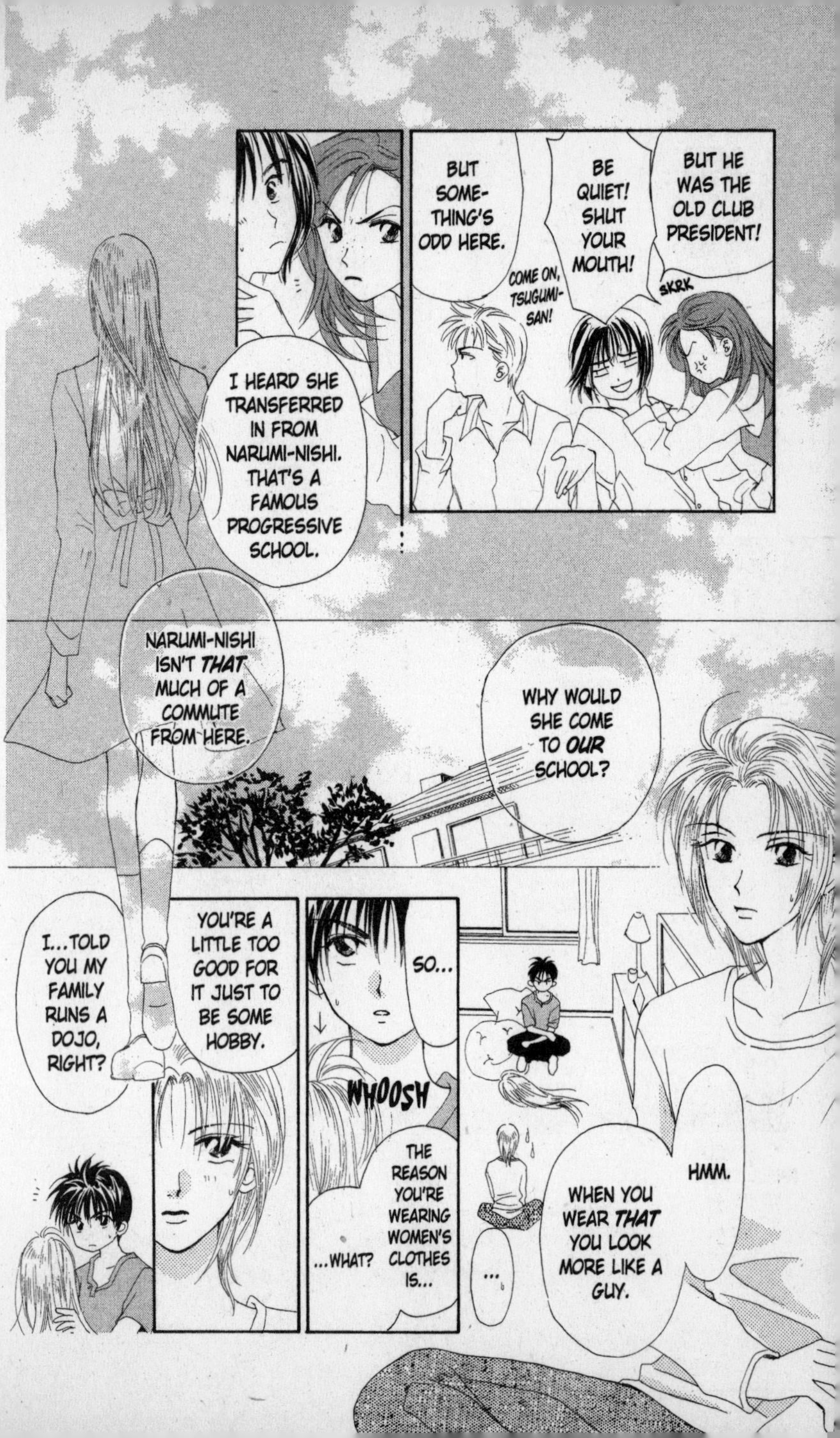
BUT HE WAS THE OLD CLUB PRESIDENT!
BE QUIET! SHUT YOUR MOUTH!
BUT SOME-THING'S ODD HERE.
SKRK
COME ON, TSUGUMI-SAN!
I HEARD SHE TRANSFERRED IN FROM NARUMI-NISHI. THAT'S A FAMOUS PROGRESSIVE SCHOOL.
NARUMI-NISHI ISN'T *THAT* MUCH OF A COMMUTE FROM HERE.
WHY WOULD SHE COME TO *OUR* SCHOOL?
HMM.
WHEN YOU WEAR *THAT* YOU LOOK MORE LIKE A GUY.
...
SO...
WHOOSH
THE REASON YOU'RE WEARING WOMEN'S CLOTHES IS...
...WHAT?
YOU'RE A LITTLE TOO GOOD FOR IT JUST TO BE SOME HOBBY.
I...TOLD YOU MY FAMILY RUNS A DOJO, RIGHT?

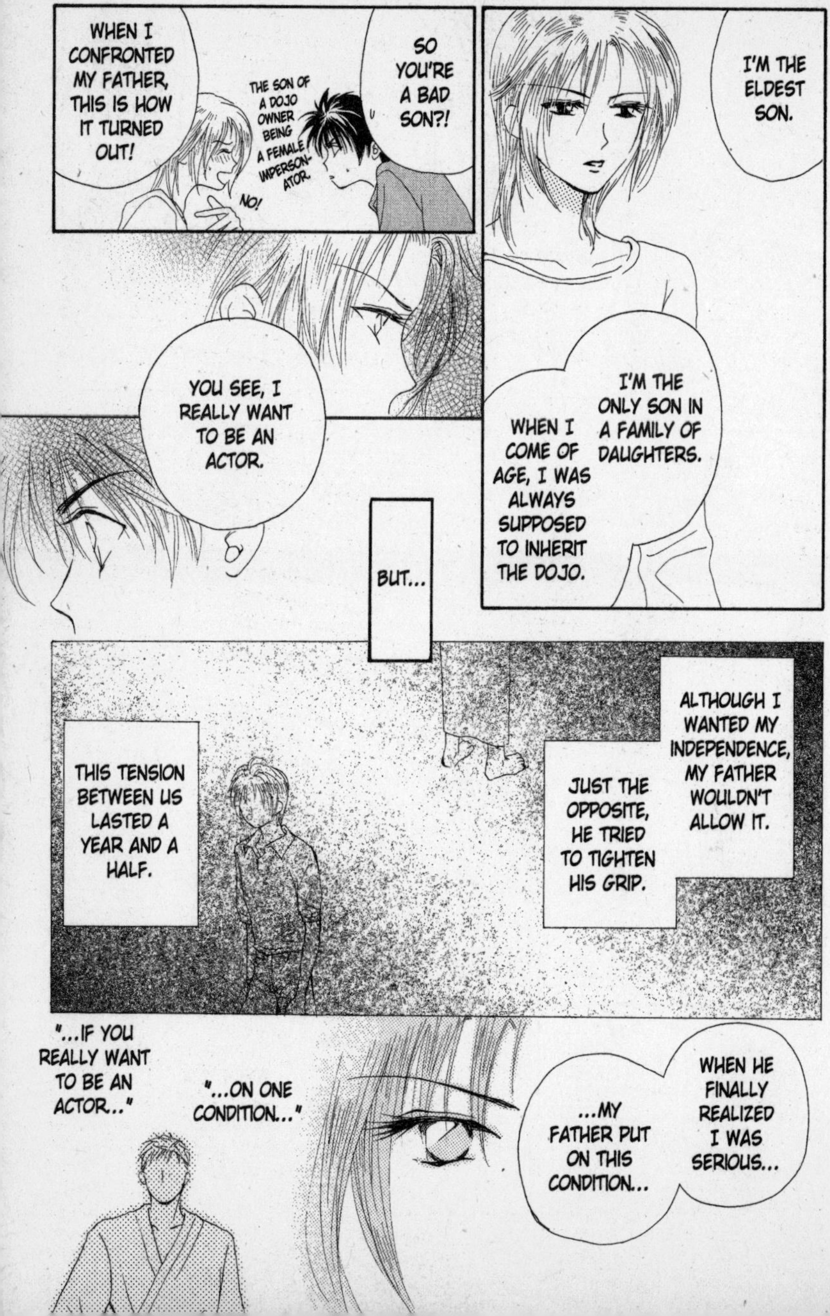
I'M THE ELDEST SON.
I'M THE ONLY SON IN A FAMILY OF DAUGHTERS.
WHEN I COME OF AGE, I WAS ALWAYS SUPPOSED TO INHERIT THE DOJO.
SO YOU'RE A BAD SON?!
THE SON OF A DOJO OWNER BEING A FEMALE IMPERSON-ATOR.
WHEN I CONFRONTED MY FATHER, THIS IS HOW IT TURNED OUT!
NO!
BUT...
YOU SEE, I REALLY WANT TO BE AN ACTOR.
ALTHOUGH I WANTED MY INDEPENDENCE, MY FATHER WOULDN'T ALLOW IT.
JUST THE OPPOSITE, HE TRIED TO TIGHTEN HIS GRIP.
THIS TENSION BETWEEN US LASTED A YEAR AND A HALF.
WHEN HE FINALLY REALIZED I WAS SERIOUS...
...MY FATHER PUT ON THIS CONDITION...
"...ON ONE CONDITION..."
"...IF YOU REALLY WANT TO BE AN ACTOR..."

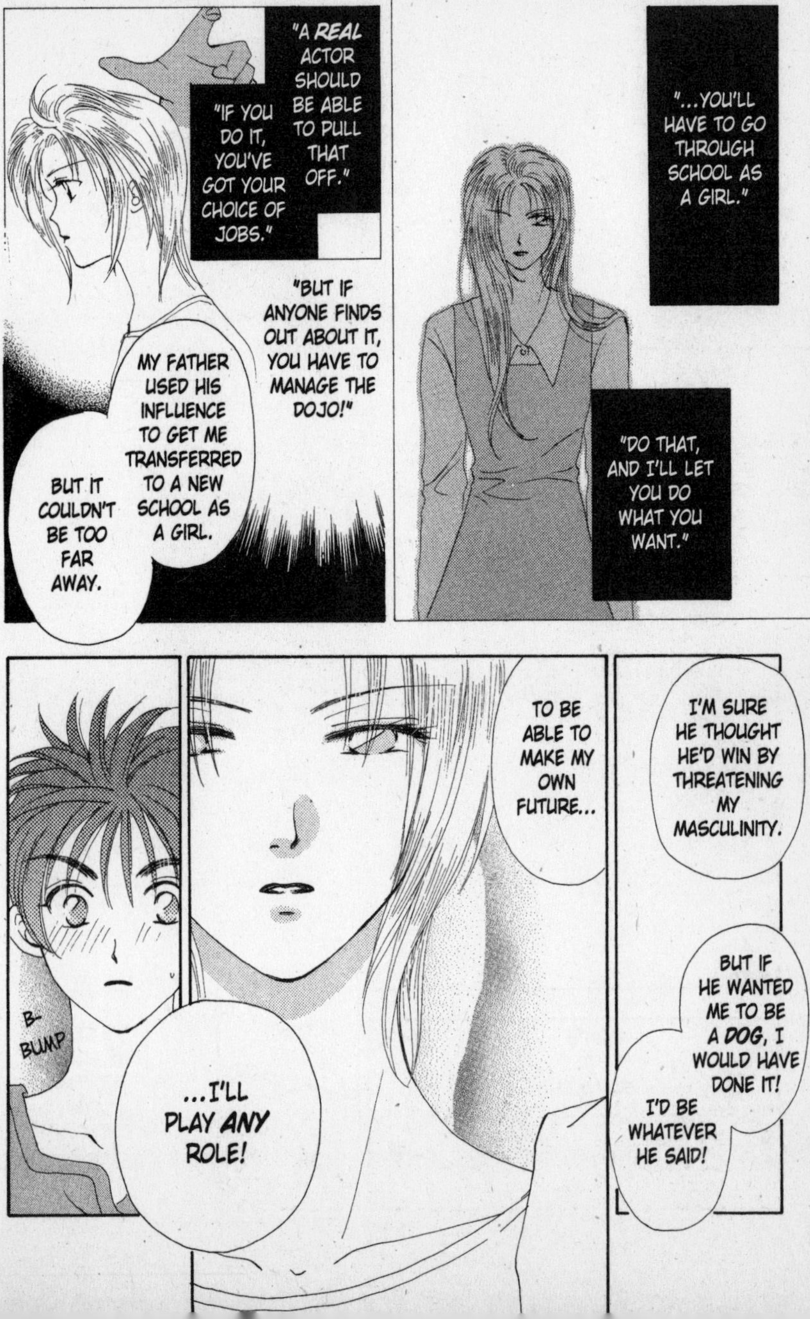
"...YOU'LL HAVE TO GO THROUGH SCHOOL AS A GIRL."
"DO THAT, AND I'LL LET YOU DO WHAT YOU WANT."
"A *REAL* ACTOR SHOULD BE ABLE TO PULL THAT OFF."
"IF YOU DO IT, YOU'VE GOT YOUR CHOICE OF JOBS."
"BUT IF ANYONE FINDS OUT ABOUT IT, YOU HAVE TO MANAGE THE DOJO!"
MY FATHER USED HIS INFLUENCE TO GET ME TRANSFERRED TO A NEW SCHOOL AS A GIRL.
BUT IT COULDN'T BE TOO FAR AWAY.
I'M SURE HE THOUGHT HE'D WIN BY THREATENING MY MASCULINITY.
BUT IF HE WANTED ME TO BE A *DOG*, I WOULD HAVE DONE IT!
I'D BE WHATEVER HE SAID!
TO BE ABLE TO MAKE MY OWN FUTURE...
...I'LL PLAY *ANY* ROLE!
B-BUMP

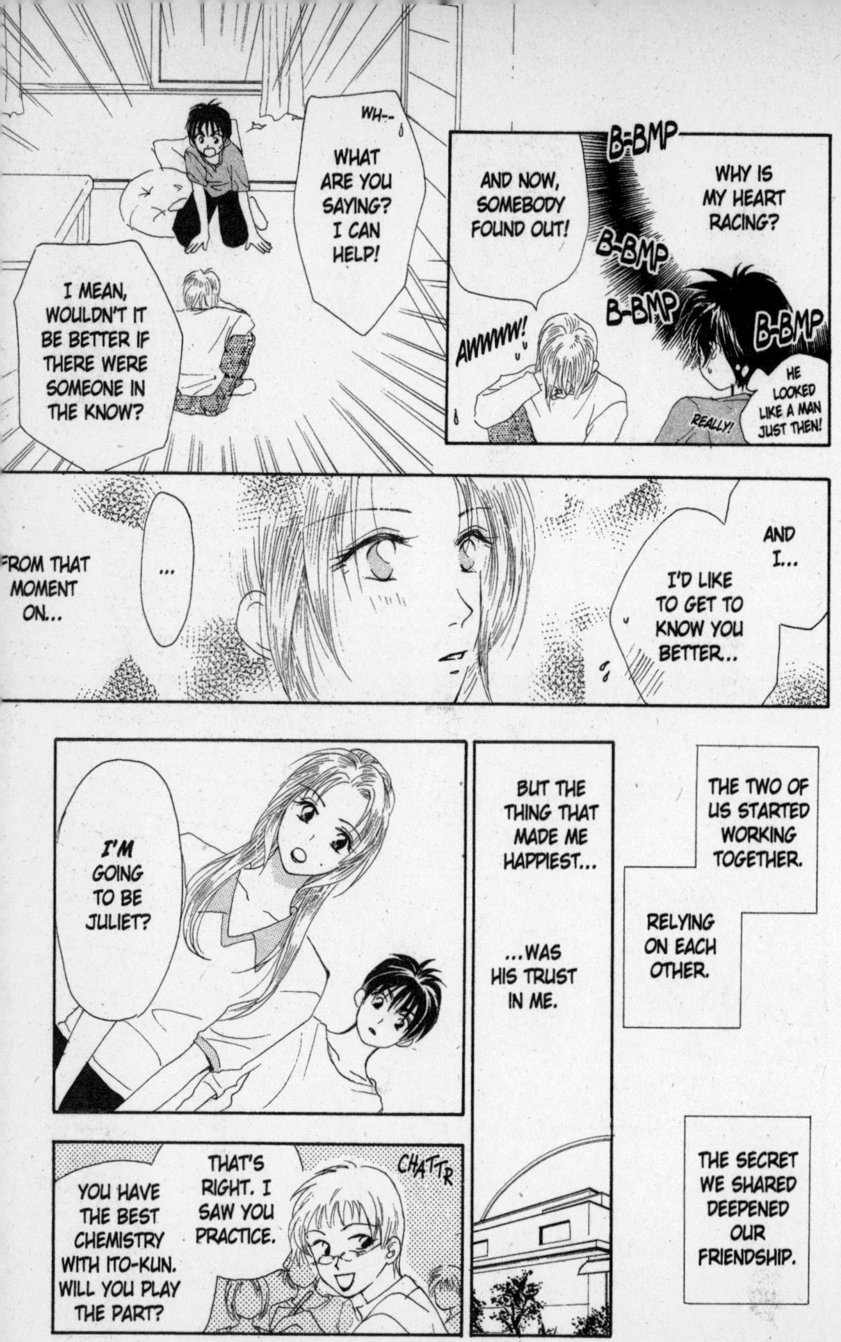
WHY IS MY HEART RACING?
B-BMP
AND NOW, SOMEBODY FOUND OUT!
B-BMP
B-BMP
B-BMP
HE LOOKED LIKE A MAN JUST THEN!
REALLY!
AWWWW!
WH--
WHAT ARE YOU SAYING? I CAN HELP!
I MEAN, WOULDN'T IT BE BETTER IF THERE WERE SOMEONE IN THE KNOW?
AND I...
I'D LIKE TO GET TO KNOW YOU BETTER...
...
FROM THAT MOMENT ON...
THE TWO OF US STARTED WORKING TOGETHER.
RELYING ON EACH OTHER.
THE SECRET WE SHARED DEEPENED OUR FRIENDSHIP.
BUT THE THING THAT MADE ME HAPPIEST...
...WAS HIS TRUST IN ME.
I'M GOING TO BE JULIET?
CHATTR
THAT'S RIGHT. I SAW YOU PRACTICE.
YOU HAVE THE BEST CHEMISTRY WITH ITO-KUN. WILL YOU PLAY THE PART?

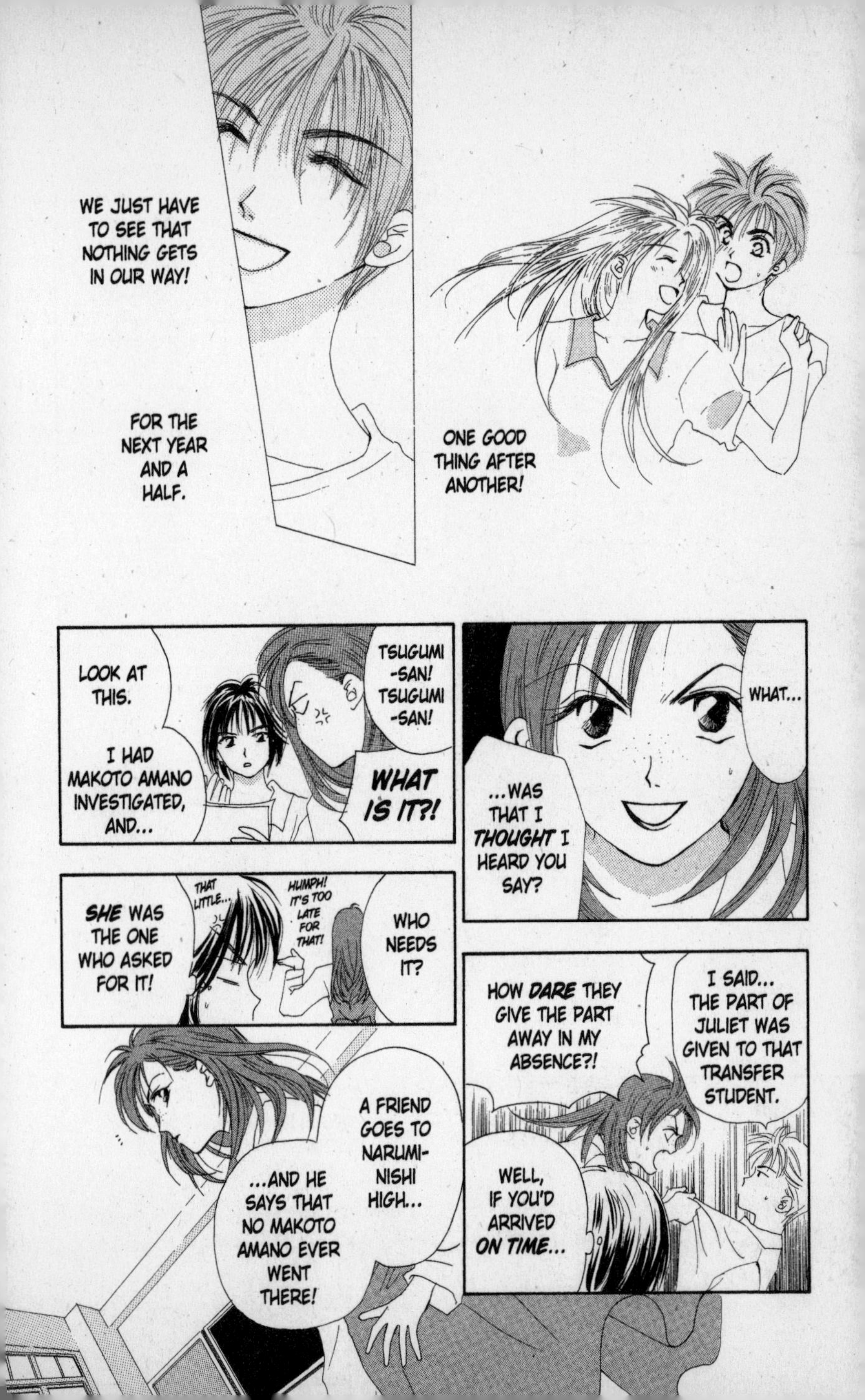

ONE GOOD THING AFTER ANOTHER!
WE JUST HAVE TO SEE THAT NOTHING GETS IN OUR WAY!
FOR THE NEXT YEAR AND A HALF.
WHAT...
...WAS THAT I THOUGHT I HEARD YOU SAY?
I SAID... THE PART OF JULIET WAS GIVEN TO THAT TRANSFER STUDENT.
HOW DARE THEY GIVE THE PART AWAY IN MY ABSENCE?!
WELL, IF YOU'D ARRIVED ON TIME...
TSUGUMI-SAN! TSUGUMI-SAN!
WHAT IS IT?!
LOOK AT THIS.
I HAD MAKOTO AMANO INVESTIGATED, AND...
WHO NEEDS IT?
HUMPH! IT'S TOO LATE FOR THAT!
THAT LITTLE...
SHE WAS THE ONE WHO ASKED FOR IT!
A FRIEND GOES TO NARUMI-NISHI HIGH...
...AND HE SAYS THAT NO MAKOTO AMANO EVER WENT THERE!

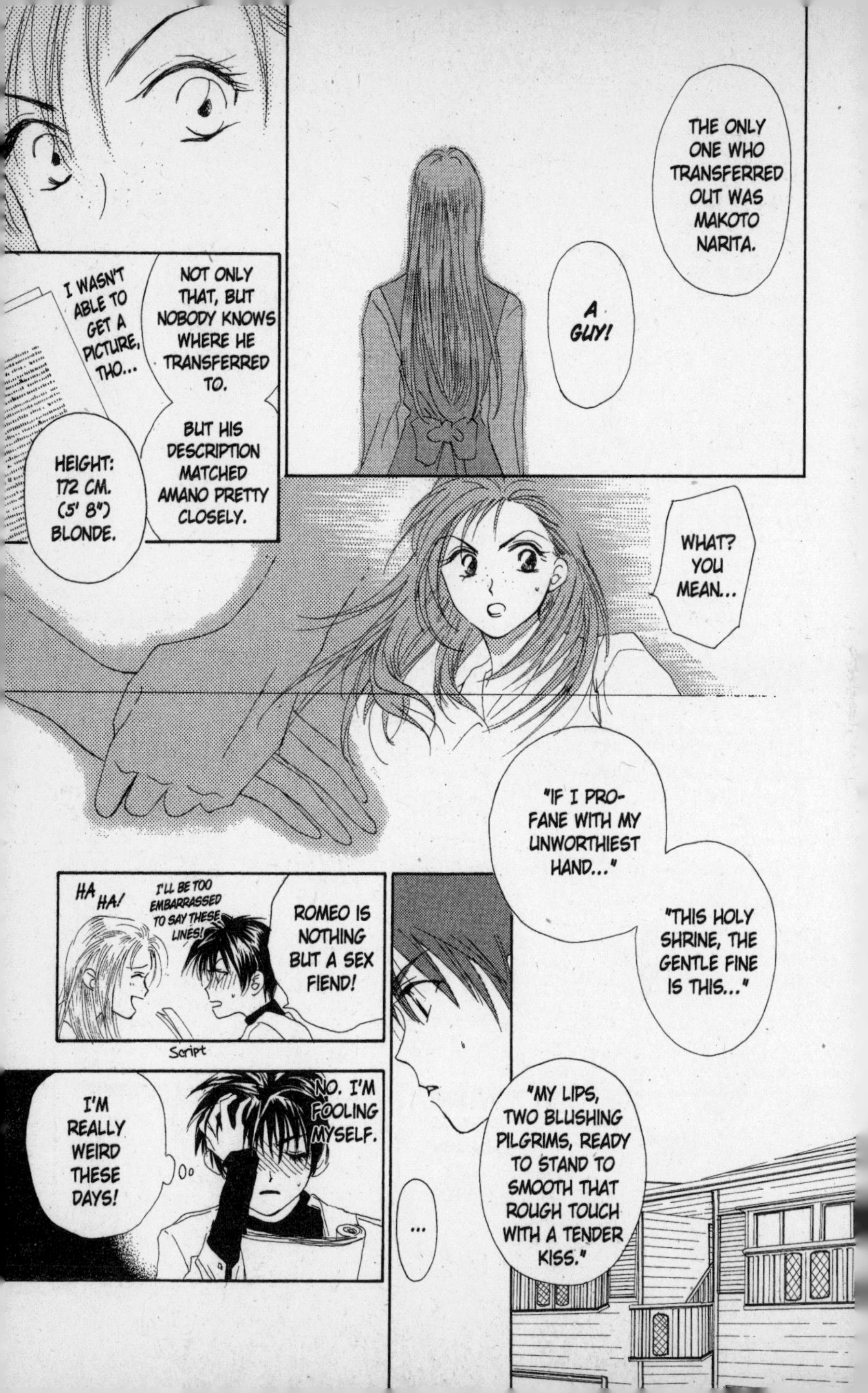
THE ONLY ONE WHO TRANSFERRED OUT WAS MAKOTO NARITA.
A GUY!
NOT ONLY THAT, BUT NOBODY KNOWS WHERE HE TRANSFERRED TO.
I WASN'T ABLE TO GET A PICTURE, THO...
BUT HIS DESCRIPTION MATCHED AMANO PRETTY CLOSELY.
HEIGHT: 172 CM. (5' 8") BLONDE.
WHAT? YOU MEAN...
"IF I PRO-FANE WITH MY UNWORTHIEST HAND..."
"THIS HOLY SHRINE, THE GENTLE FINE IS THIS..."
"MY LIPS, TWO BLUSHING PILGRIMS, READY TO STAND TO SMOOTH THAT ROUGH TOUCH WITH A TENDER KISS."
...
ROMEO IS NOTHING BUT A SEX FIEND!
I'LL BE TOO EMBARRASSED TO SAY THESE LINES!
HA HA!
Script
NO. I'M FOOLING MYSELF.
I'M REALLY WEIRD THESE DAYS!

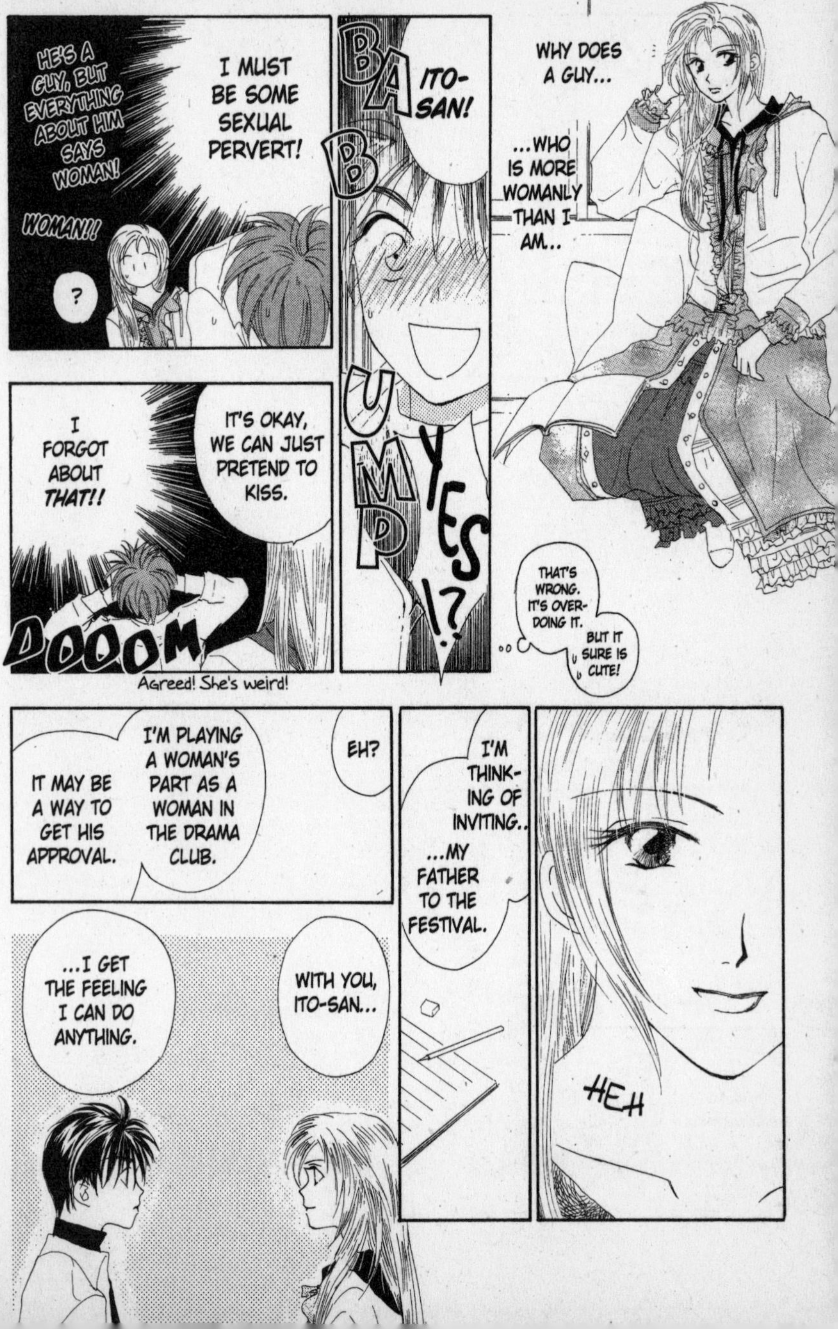
WHY DOES A GUY...
...WHO IS MORE WOMANLY THAN I AM...
THAT'S WRONG. IT'S OVER-DOING IT.
BUT IT SURE IS CUTE!
ITO-SAN!
BA-BUMP
YES!?
I MUST BE SOME SEXUAL PERVERT!
HE'S A GUY, BUT EVERYTHING ABOUT HIM SAYS WOMAN!
WOMAN!!
?
IT'S OKAY, WE CAN JUST PRETEND TO KISS.
I FORGOT ABOUT THAT!!
DOOOM
Agreed! She's weird!
HEH
I'M THINKING OF INVITING...
...MY FATHER TO THE FESTIVAL.
EH?
I'M PLAYING A WOMAN'S PART AS A WOMAN IN THE DRAMA CLUB.
IT MAY BE A WAY TO GET HIS APPROVAL.
WITH YOU, ITO-SAN...
...I GET THE FEELING I CAN DO ANYTHING.

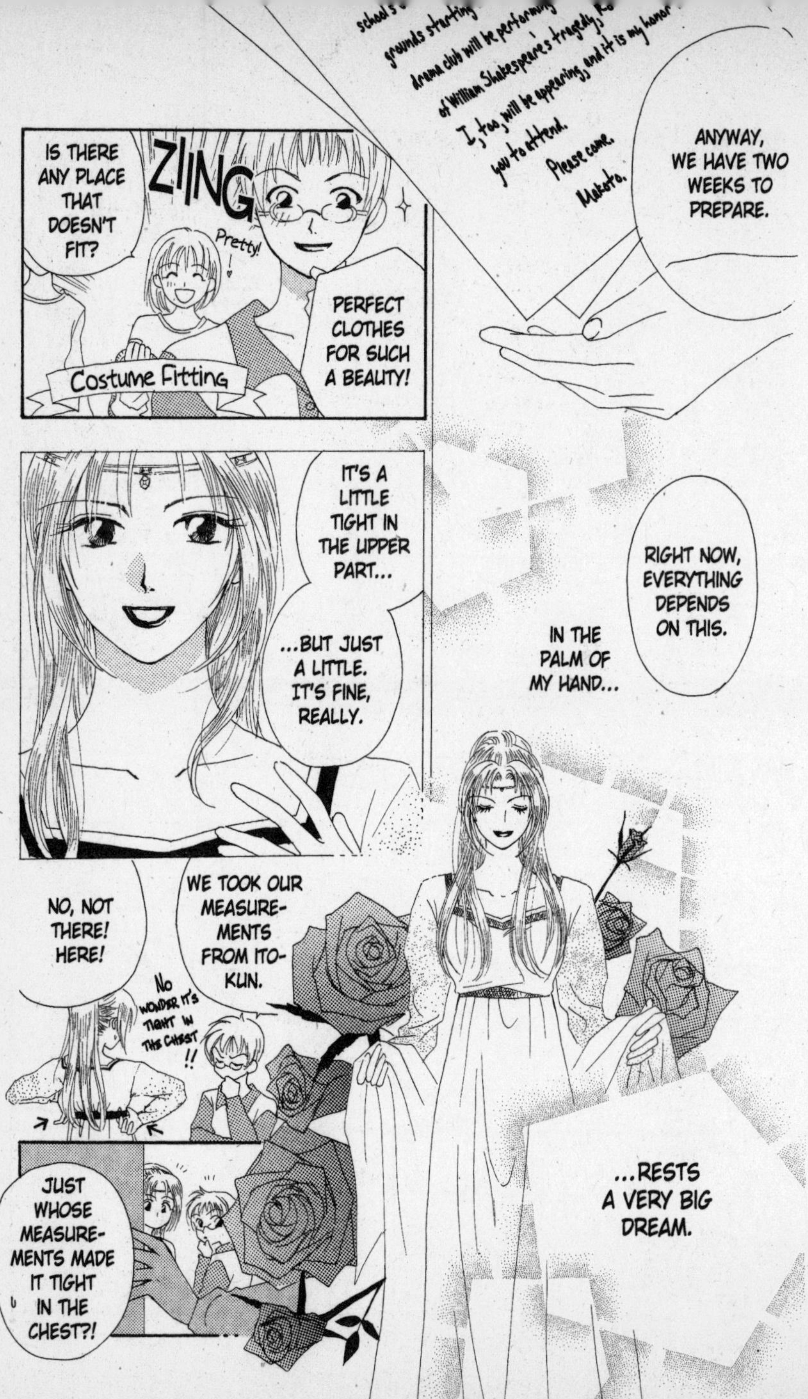

school's
grounds starting
drama club will be performing
of William Shakespeare's tragedy, Ro
I, too, will be appearing, and it is my honor
you to attend.
Please come.
Makoto.
ANYWAY, WE HAVE TWO WEEKS TO PREPARE.
RIGHT NOW, EVERYTHING DEPENDS ON THIS.
IN THE PALM OF MY HAND...
...RESTS A VERY BIG DREAM.
IS THERE ANY PLACE THAT DOESN'T FIT?
ZIING
PERFECT CLOTHES FOR SUCH A BEAUTY!
Pretty! !
Costume Fitting
IT'S A LITTLE TIGHT IN THE UPPER PART...
...BUT JUST A LITTLE. IT'S FINE, REALLY.
WE TOOK OUR MEASUREMENTS FROM ITO-KUN.
NO, NOT THERE! HERE!
No wonder it's tight in the chest!!
JUST WHOSE MEASUREMENTS MADE IT TIGHT IN THE CHEST?!

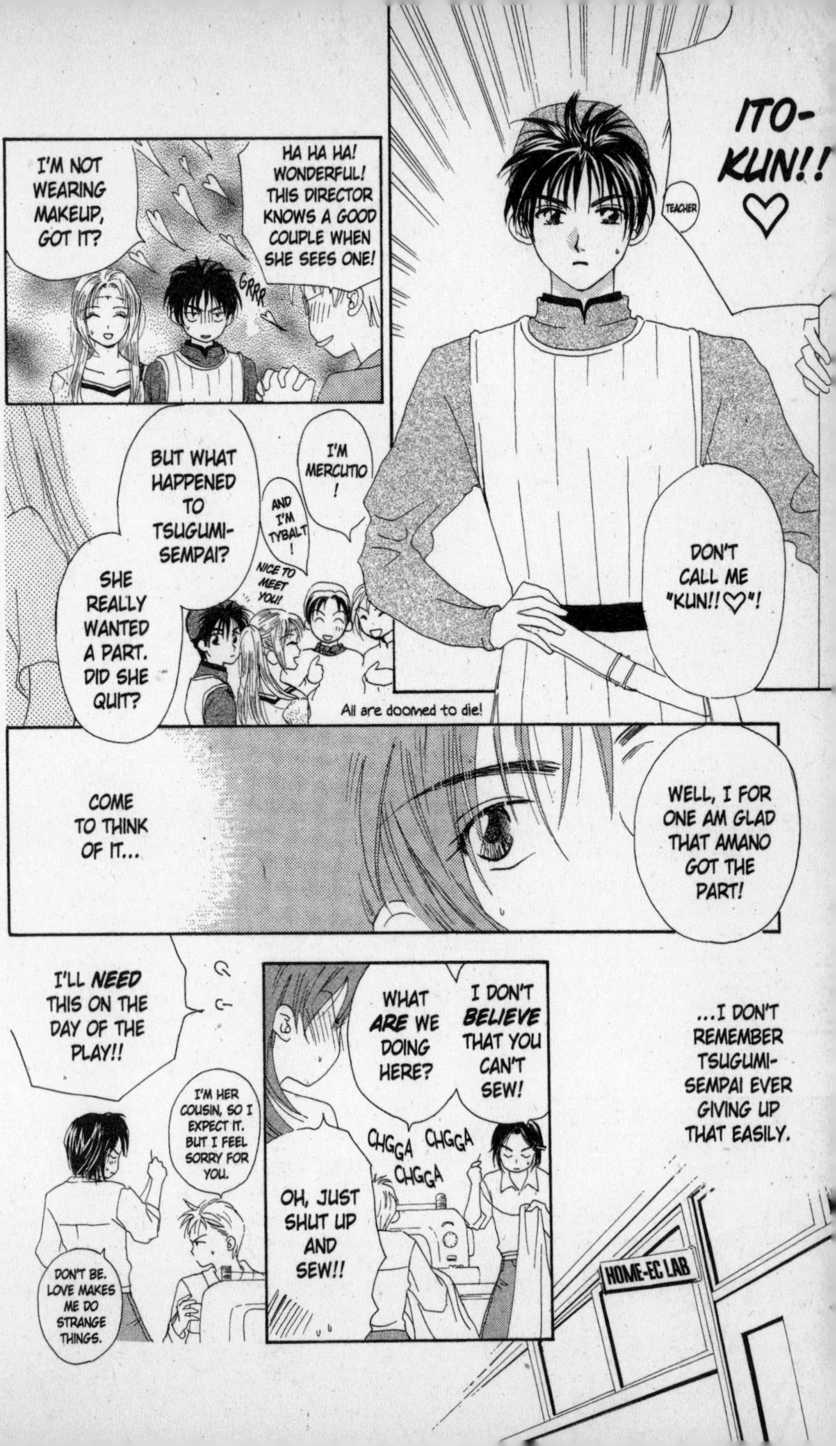
ITO-KUN!! ♡
TEACHER
DON'T CALL ME "KUN!! ♡"!
HA HA HA! WONDERFUL! THIS DIRECTOR KNOWS A GOOD COUPLE WHEN SHE SEES ONE!
I'M NOT WEARING MAKEUP, GOT IT?
GRRR
I'M MERCUTIO!
AND I'M TYBALT!
NICE TO MEET YOU!
BUT WHAT HAPPENED TO TSUGUMI-SEMPAI?
SHE REALLY WANTED A PART. DID SHE QUIT?
All are doomed to die!
WELL, I FOR ONE AM GLAD THAT AMANO GOT THE PART!
COME TO THINK OF IT...
...I DON'T REMEMBER TSUGUMI-SEMPAI EVER GIVING UP THAT EASILY.
HOME-EC LAB
I DON'T BELIEVE THAT YOU CAN'T SEW!
WHAT ARE WE DOING HERE?
CHGGA CHGGA CHGGA
OH, JUST SHUT UP AND SEW!!
I'LL NEED THIS ON THE DAY OF THE PLAY!!
I'M HER COUSIN, SO I EXPECT IT. BUT I FEEL SORRY FOR YOU.
DON'T BE. LOVE MAKES ME DO STRANGE THINGS.

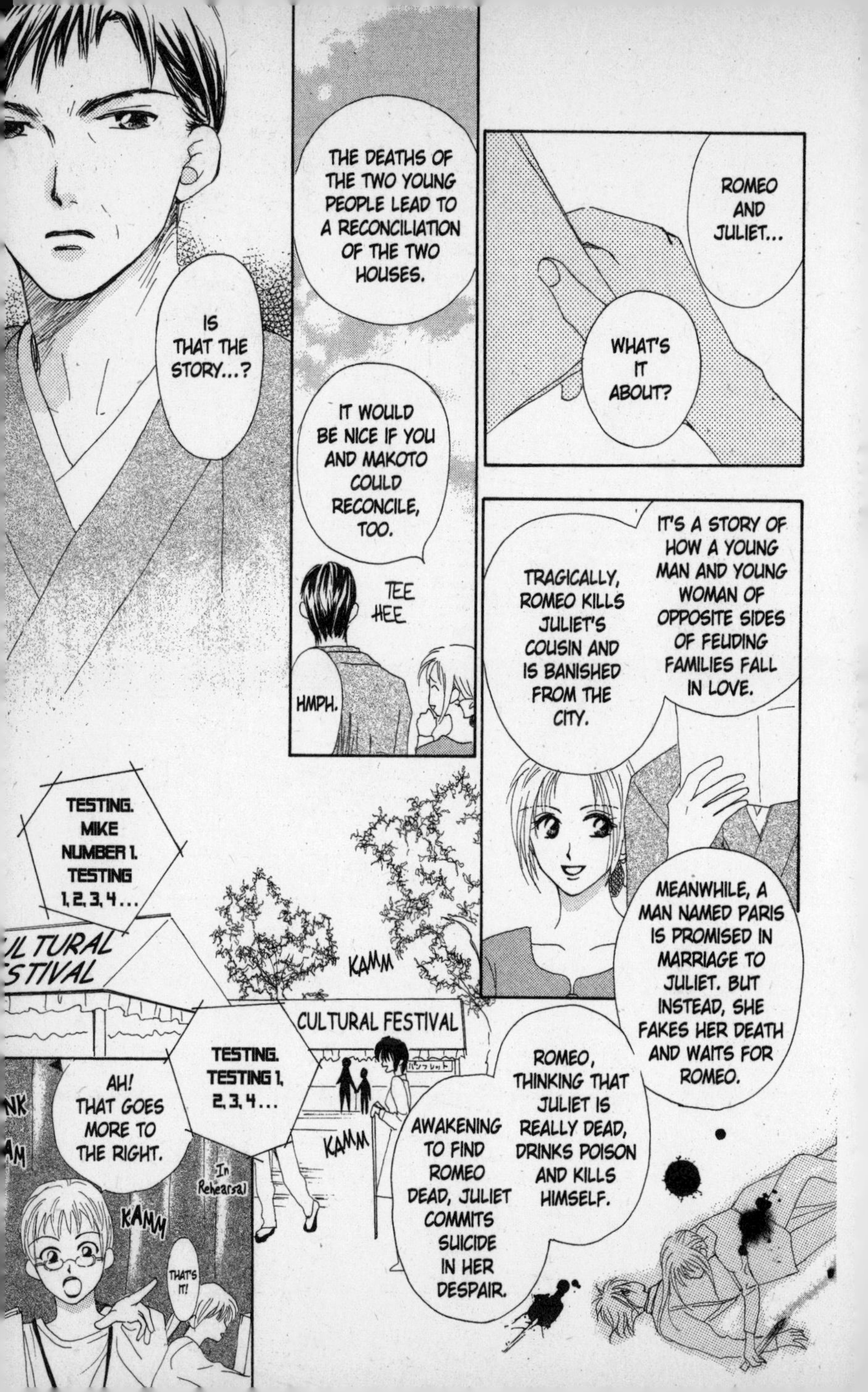
ROMEO AND JULIET...
WHAT'S IT ABOUT?
IT'S A STORY OF HOW A YOUNG MAN AND YOUNG WOMAN OF OPPOSITE SIDES OF FEUDING FAMILIES FALL IN LOVE.
TRAGICALLY, ROMEO KILLS JULIET'S COUSIN AND IS BANISHED FROM THE CITY.
MEANWHILE, A MAN NAMED PARIS IS PROMISED IN MARRIAGE TO JULIET. BUT INSTEAD, SHE FAKES HER DEATH AND WAITS FOR ROMEO.
ROMEO, THINKING THAT JULIET IS REALLY DEAD, DRINKS POISON AND KILLS HIMSELF.
AWAKENING TO FIND ROMEO DEAD, JULIET COMMITS SUICIDE IN HER DESPAIR.
THE DEATHS OF THE TWO YOUNG PEOPLE LEAD TO A RECONCILIATION OF THE TWO HOUSES.
IT WOULD BE NICE IF YOU AND MAKOTO COULD RECONCILE, TOO.
TEE HEE
HMPH.
IS THAT THE STORY...?
TESTING. MIKE NUMBER 1. TESTING 1, 2, 3, 4...
KAMM
CULTURAL FESTIVAL
TESTING. TESTING 1, 2, 3, 4...
KAMM
AH! THAT GOES MORE TO THE RIGHT.
In Rehearsal
KAMM
THAT'S IT!

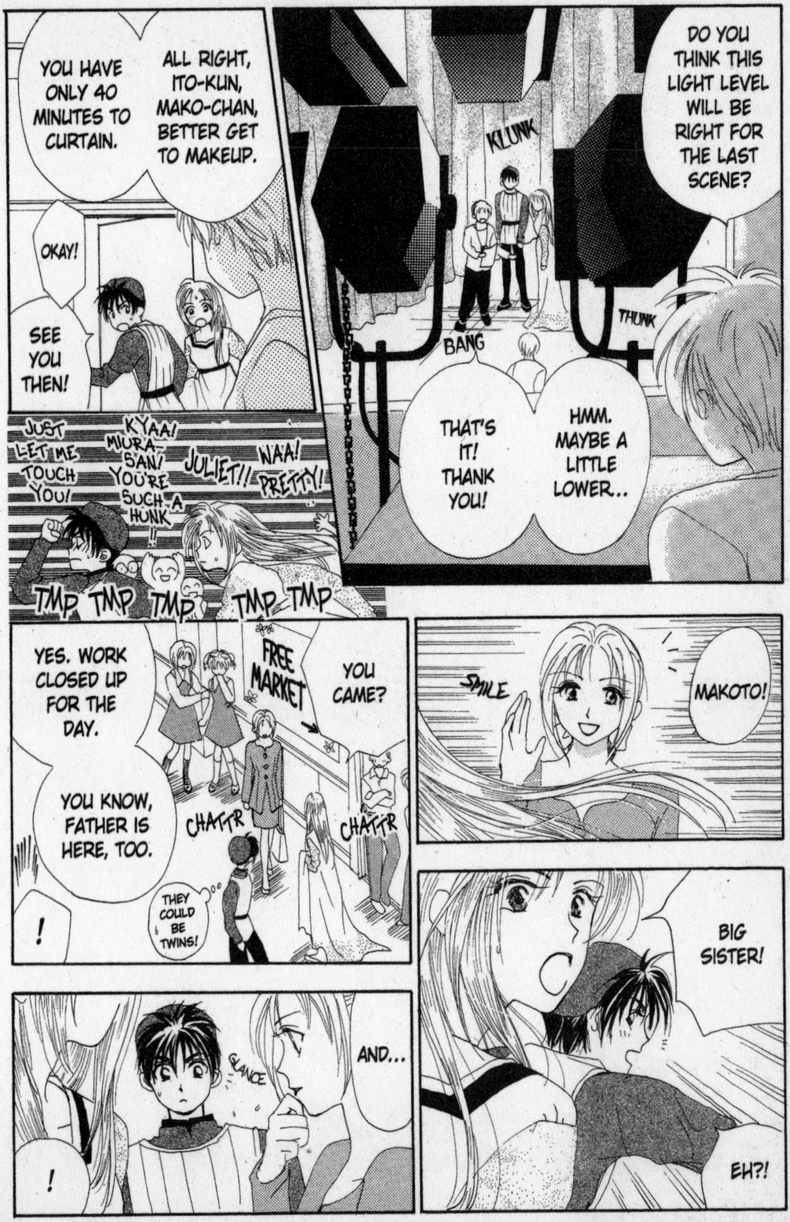
DO YOU THINK THIS LIGHT LEVEL WILL BE RIGHT FOR THE LAST SCENE?
KLUNK
THUNK
BANG
HMM. MAYBE A LITTLE LOWER...
THAT'S IT! THANK YOU!
ALL RIGHT, ITO-KUN, MAKO-CHAN, BETTER GET TO MAKEUP.
YOU HAVE ONLY 40 MINUTES TO CURTAIN.
OKAY!
SEE YOU THEN!
WAA! PRETTY!
JULIET!!
KYAA! MIURA-SAN! YOU'RE SUCH A HUNK!!
JUST LET ME TOUCH YOU!
TMP TMP TMP TMP TMP
SMILE
MAKOTO!
YOU CAME?
FREE MARKET
YES. WORK CLOSED UP FOR THE DAY.
CHATTR
CHATTR
YOU KNOW, FATHER IS HERE, TOO.
THEY COULD BE TWINS!
!
BIG SISTER!
EH?!
AND...
GLANCE
!

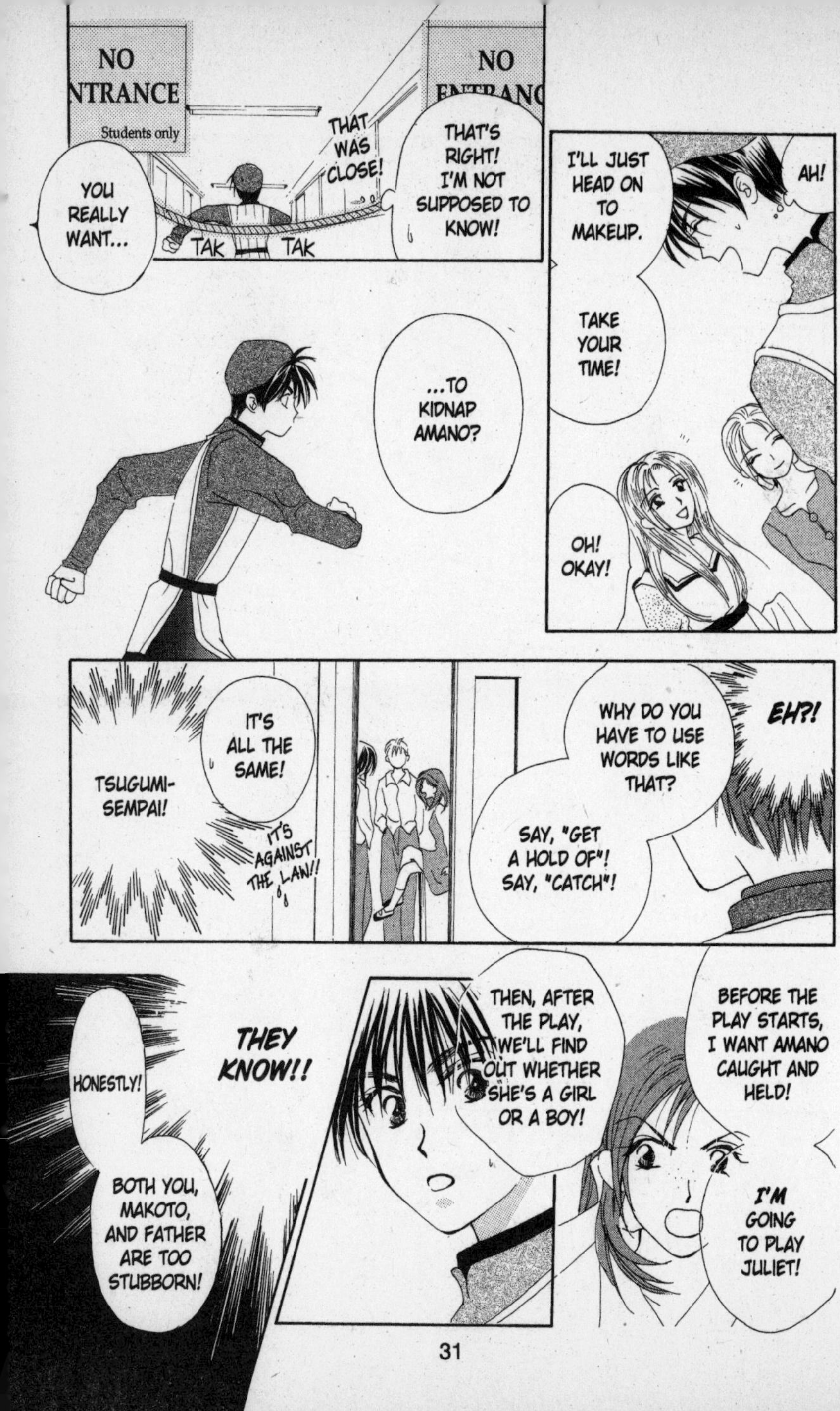
AH!
I'LL JUST HEAD ON TO MAKEUP.
TAKE YOUR TIME!
OH! OKAY!
NO
NO
NTRANCE
Students only
THAT'S RIGHT! I'M NOT SUPPOSED TO KNOW!
THAT WAS CLOSE!
TAK TAK
YOU REALLY WANT...
...TO KIDNAP AMANO?
EH?!
WHY DO YOU HAVE TO USE WORDS LIKE THAT?
SAY, "GET A HOLD OF"! SAY, "CATCH"!
IT'S ALL THE SAME!
IT'S AGAINST THE LAW!!
TSUGUMI-SEMPAI!
BEFORE THE PLAY STARTS, I WANT AMANO CAUGHT AND HELD!
I'M GOING TO PLAY JULIET!
THEN, AFTER THE PLAY, WE'LL FIND OUT WHETHER SHE'S A GIRL OR A BOY!
THEY KNOW!!
HONESTLY!
BOTH YOU, MAKOTO, AND FATHER ARE TOO STUBBORN!

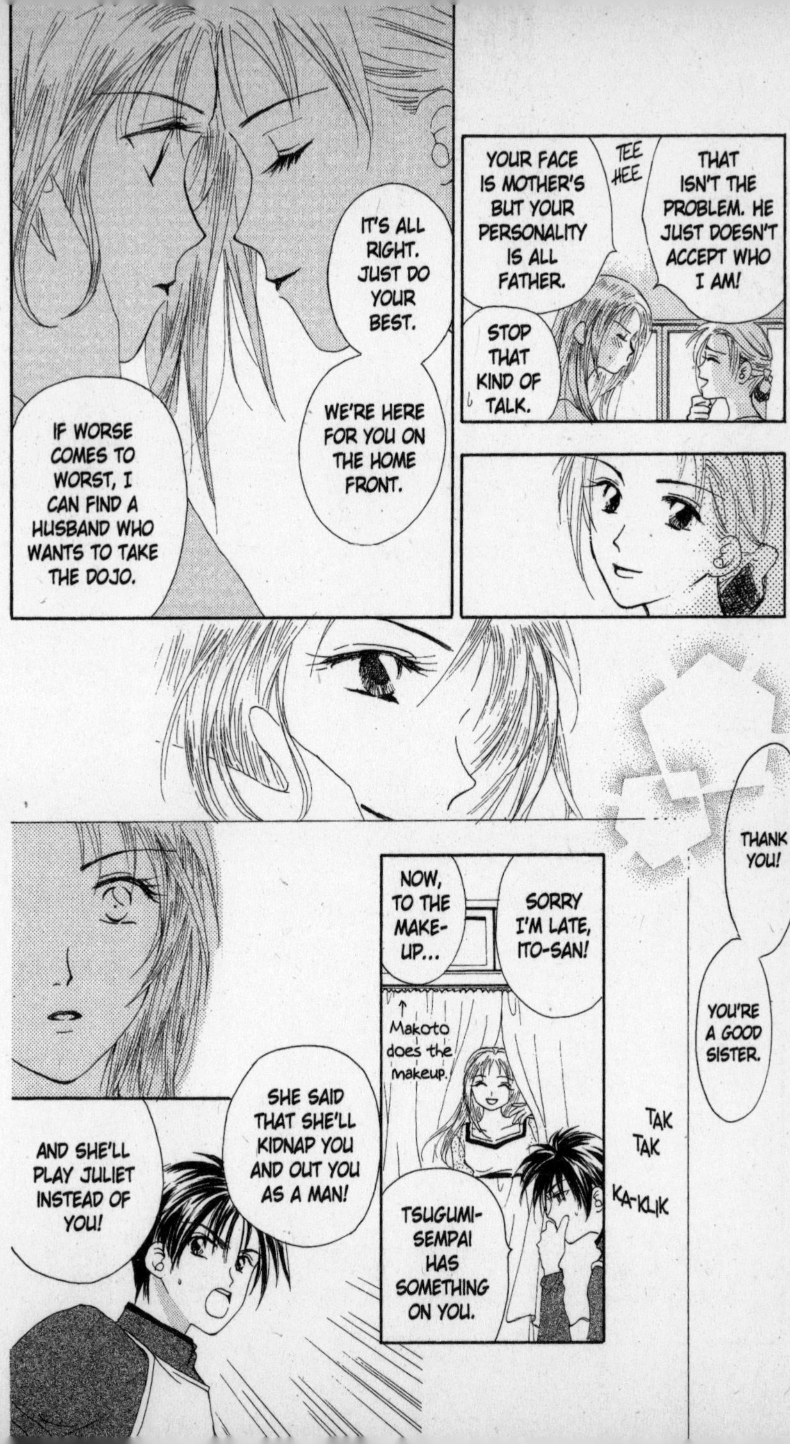
THAT ISN'T THE PROBLEM. HE JUST DOESN'T ACCEPT WHO I AM!
TEE HEE
YOUR FACE IS MOTHER'S BUT YOUR PERSONALITY IS ALL FATHER.
STOP THAT KIND OF TALK.
IT'S ALL RIGHT. JUST DO YOUR BEST.
WE'RE HERE FOR YOU ON THE HOME FRONT.
IF WORSE COMES TO WORST, I CAN FIND A HUSBAND WHO WANTS TO TAKE THE DOJO.
THANK YOU!
YOU'RE A GOOD SISTER.
TAK TAK
KA-KLIK
SORRY I'M LATE, ITO-SAN!
NOW, TO THE MAKE-UP...
↑ Makoto does the makeup.
TSUGUMI-SEMPAI HAS SOMETHING ON YOU.
SHE SAID THAT SHE'LL KIDNAP YOU AND OUT YOU AS A MAN!
AND SHE'LL PLAY JULIET INSTEAD OF YOU!

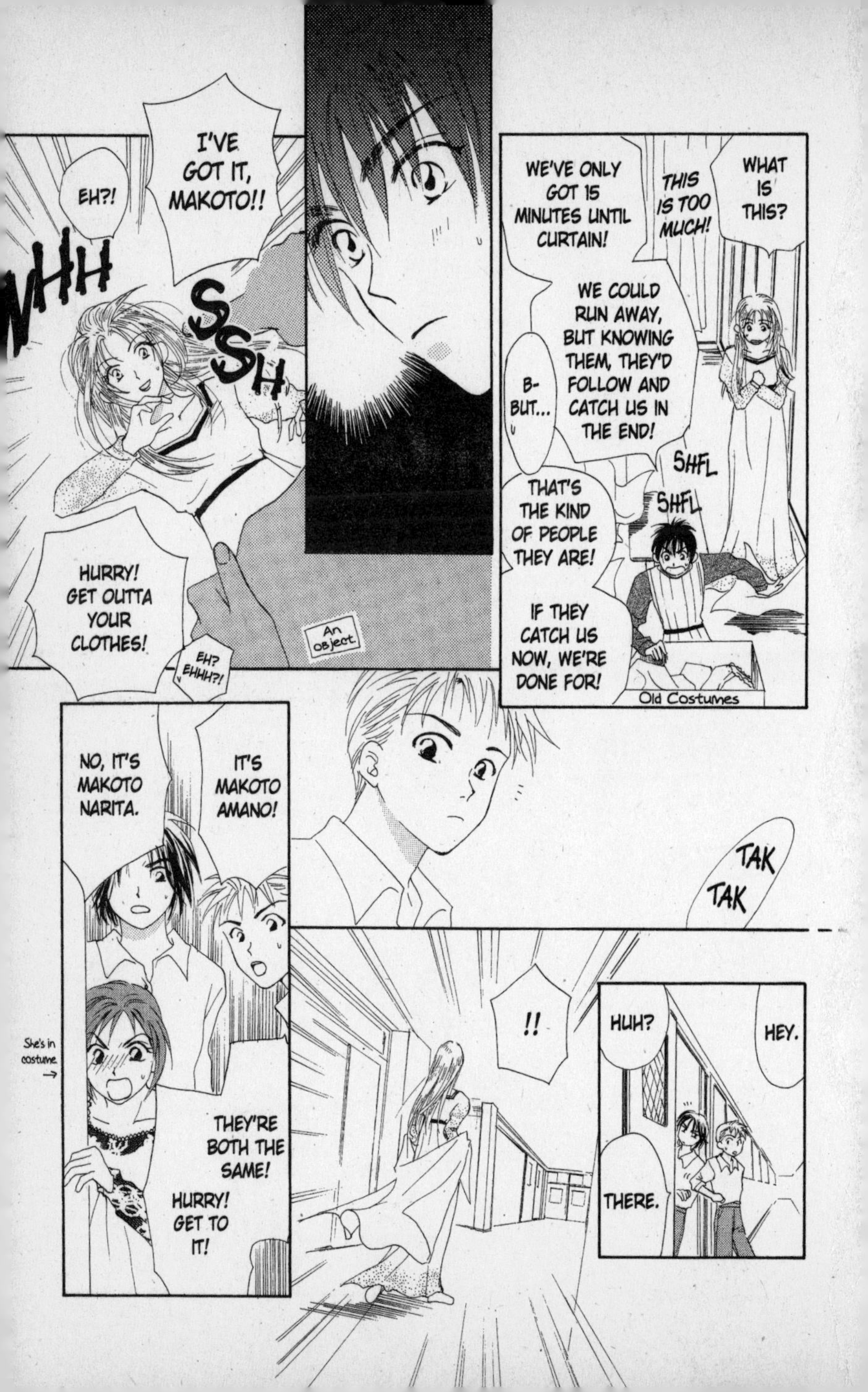
WHAT IS THIS?
THIS IS TOO MUCH!
WE'VE ONLY GOT 15 MINUTES UNTIL CURTAIN!
WE COULD RUN AWAY, BUT KNOWING THEM, THEY'D FOLLOW AND CATCH US IN THE END!
B-BUT...
SHFL
SHFL
THAT'S THE KIND OF PEOPLE THEY ARE!
IF THEY CATCH US NOW, WE'RE DONE FOR!
Old Costumes
An object.
I'VE GOT IT, MAKOTO!!
EH?!
SSSH
WHH
HURRY! GET OUTTA YOUR CLOTHES!
EH? EHHH?!
TAK
TAK
HEY.
HUH?
THERE.
!!
IT'S MAKOTO AMANO!
NO, IT'S MAKOTO NARITA.
She's in costume
THEY'RE BOTH THE SAME!
HURRY! GET TO IT!

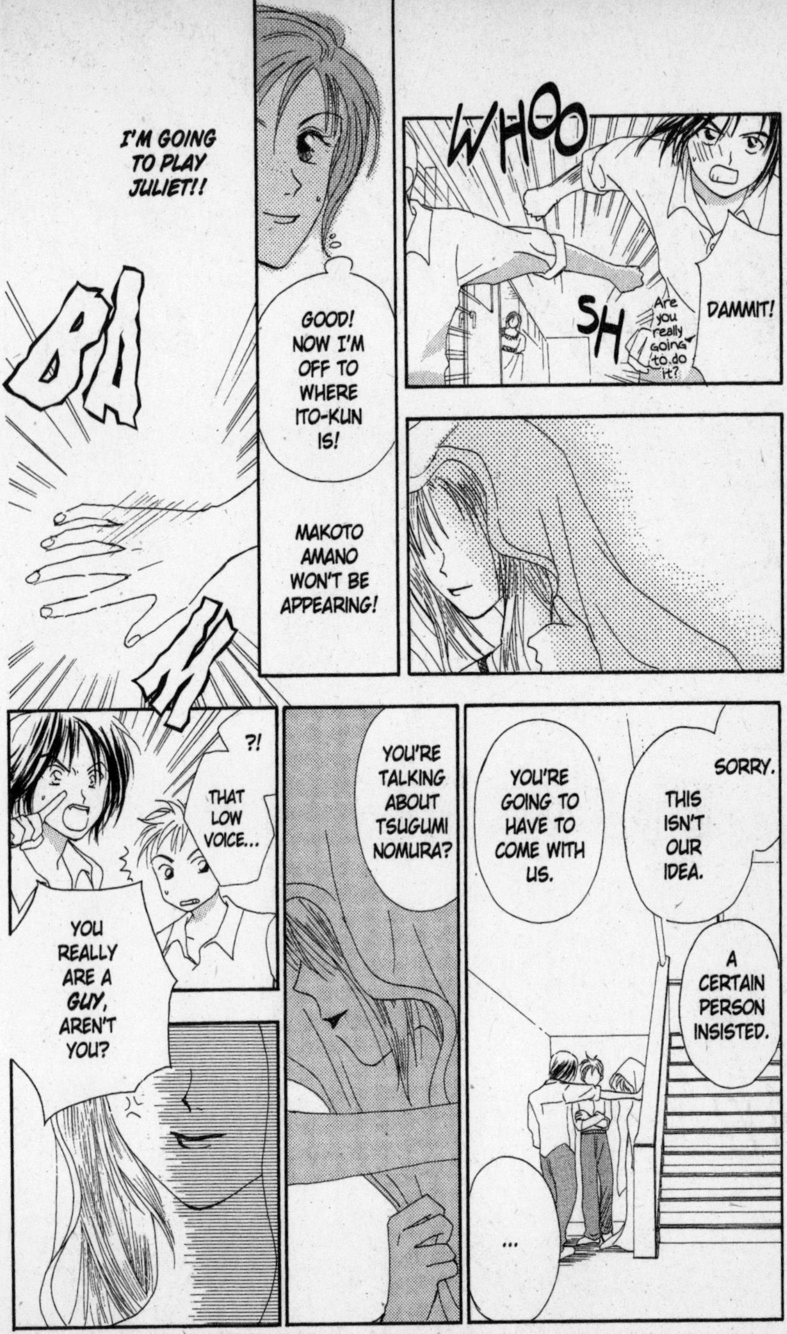
WHOO
DAMMIT!
Are you really going to do it?
SH
GOOD! NOW I'M OFF TO WHERE ITO-KUN IS!
MAKOTO AMANO WON'T BE APPEARING!
I'M GOING TO PLAY JULIET!!
BA
M
SORRY.
THIS ISN'T OUR IDEA.
YOU'RE GOING TO HAVE TO COME WITH US.
A CERTAIN PERSON INSISTED.
...
YOU'RE TALKING ABOUT TSUGUMI NOMURA?
?!
THAT LOW VOICE...
YOU REALLY ARE A GUY, AREN'T YOU?

!!

WHUOOSH

MIURA?!

?!

WOOM

YOU FELL FOR IT!

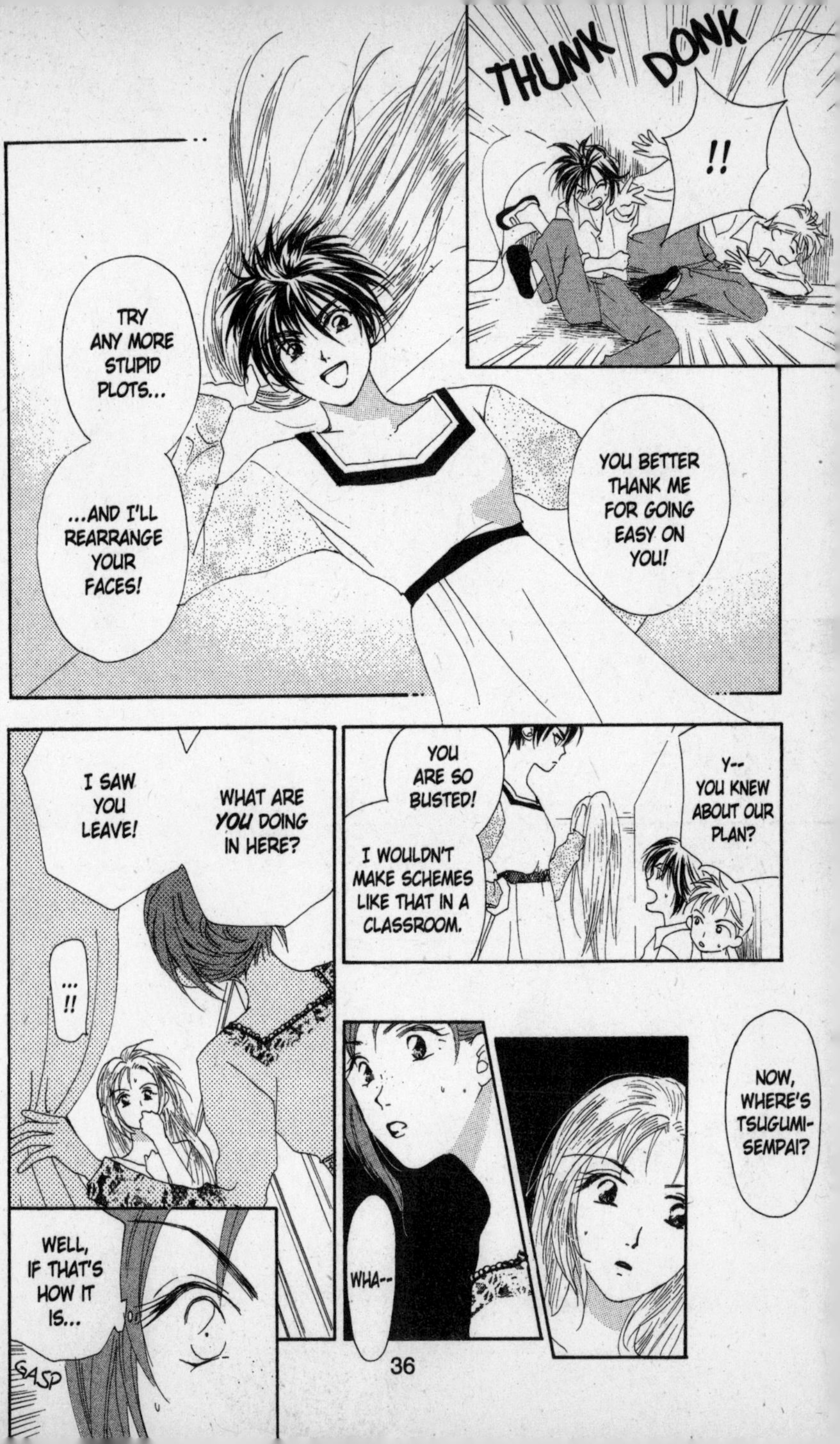
THUNK
DONK
!!
TRY ANY MORE STUPID PLOTS...
...AND I'LL REARRANGE YOUR FACES!
YOU BETTER THANK ME FOR GOING EASY ON YOU!
Y-- YOU KNEW ABOUT OUR PLAN?
YOU ARE SO BUSTED!
I WOULDN'T MAKE SCHEMES LIKE THAT IN A CLASSROOM.
WHAT ARE *YOU* DOING IN HERE?
I SAW YOU LEAVE!
...!!
NOW, WHERE'S TSUGUMI-SEMPAI?
WHA--
WELL, IF THAT'S HOW IT IS...
GASP

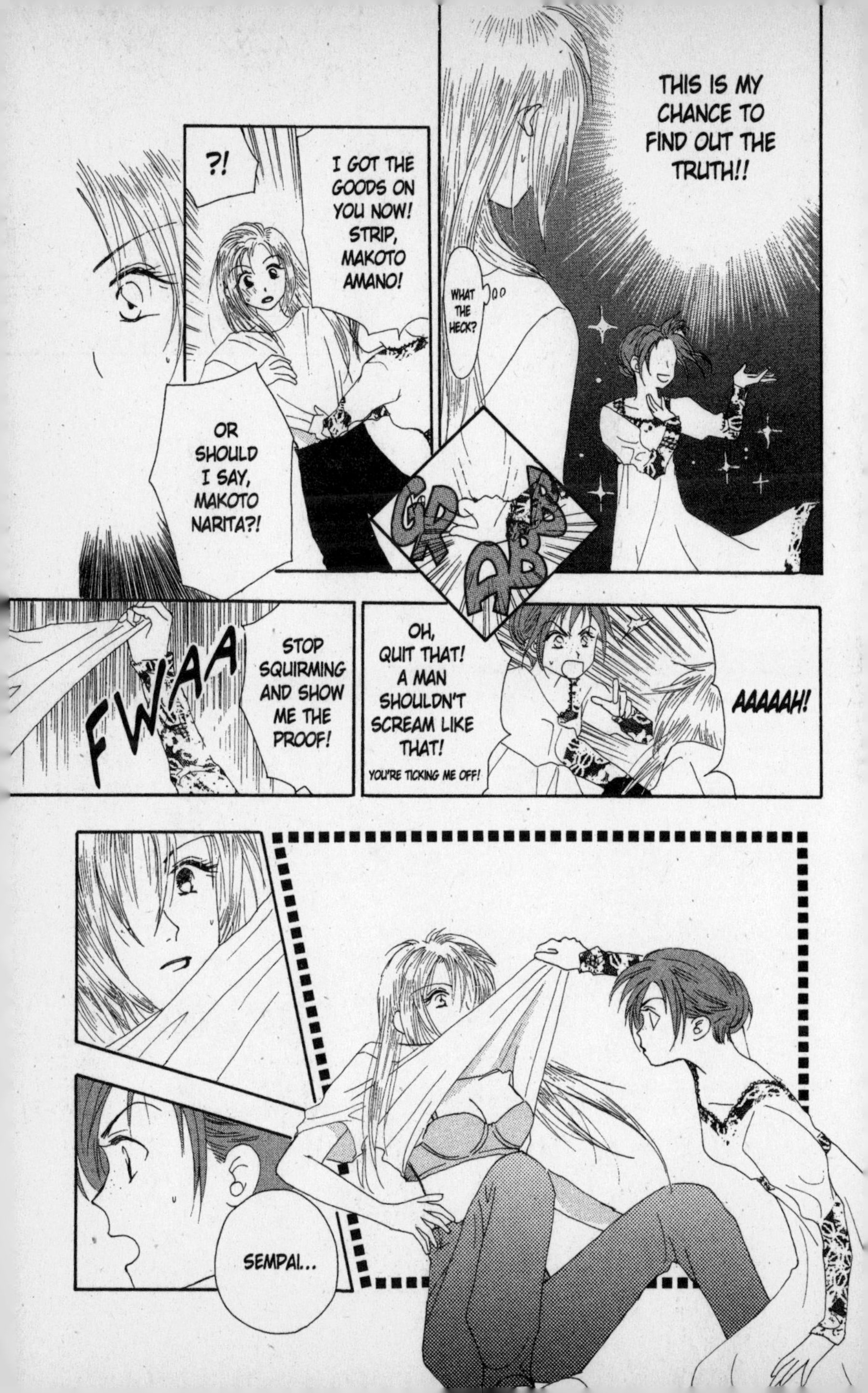
THIS IS MY CHANCE TO FIND OUT THE TRUTH!!
WHAT THE HECK?
GRAB
I GOT THE GOODS ON YOU NOW! STRIP, MAKOTO AMANO!
?!
OR SHOULD I SAY, MAKOTO NARITA?!
AAAAAH!
OH, QUIT THAT! A MAN SHOULDN'T SCREAM LIKE THAT!
YOU'RE TICKING ME OFF!
STOP SQUIRMING AND SHOW ME THE PROOF!
FWAA
SEMPAI...

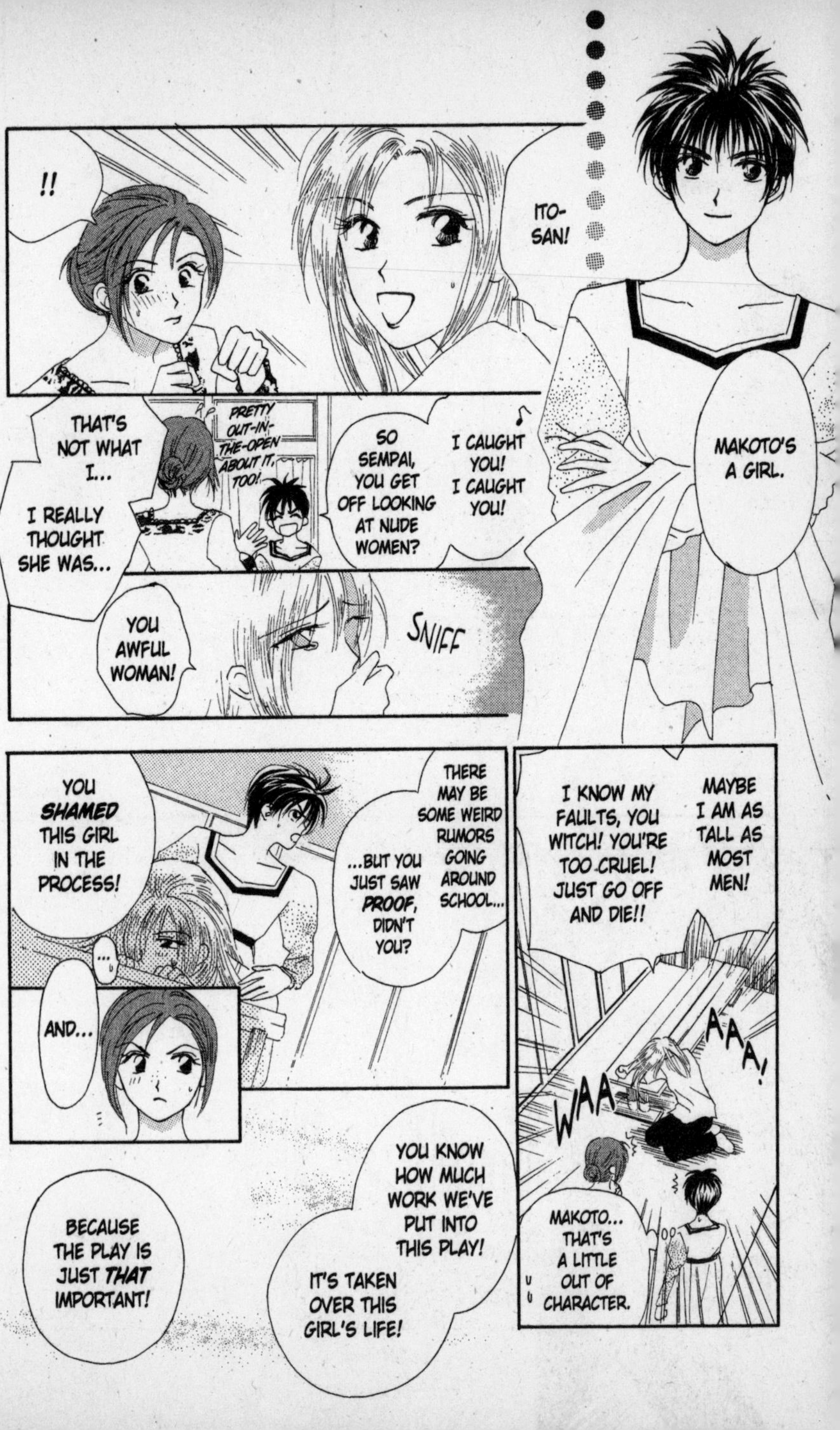
ITO-SAN!
MAKOTO'S A GIRL.
!!
I CAUGHT YOU! I CAUGHT YOU!
SO SEMPAI, YOU GET OFF LOOKING AT NUDE WOMEN?
PRETTY OUT-IN-THE-OPEN ABOUT IT, TOO!
THAT'S NOT WHAT I...
I REALLY THOUGHT SHE WAS...
SNIFF
YOU AWFUL WOMAN!
MAYBE I AM AS TALL AS MOST MEN!
I KNOW MY FAULTS, YOU WITCH! YOU'RE TOO CRUEL! JUST GO OFF AND DIE!!
WAA AAA!
MAKOTO... THAT'S A LITTLE OUT OF CHARACTER.
THERE MAY BE SOME WEIRD RUMORS GOING AROUND SCHOOL...
...BUT YOU JUST SAW *PROOF*, DIDN'T YOU?
YOU *SHAMED* THIS GIRL IN THE PROCESS!
...
AND...
YOU KNOW HOW MUCH WORK WE'VE PUT INTO THIS PLAY!
IT'S TAKEN OVER THIS GIRL'S LIFE!
BECAUSE THE PLAY IS JUST *THAT* IMPORTANT!

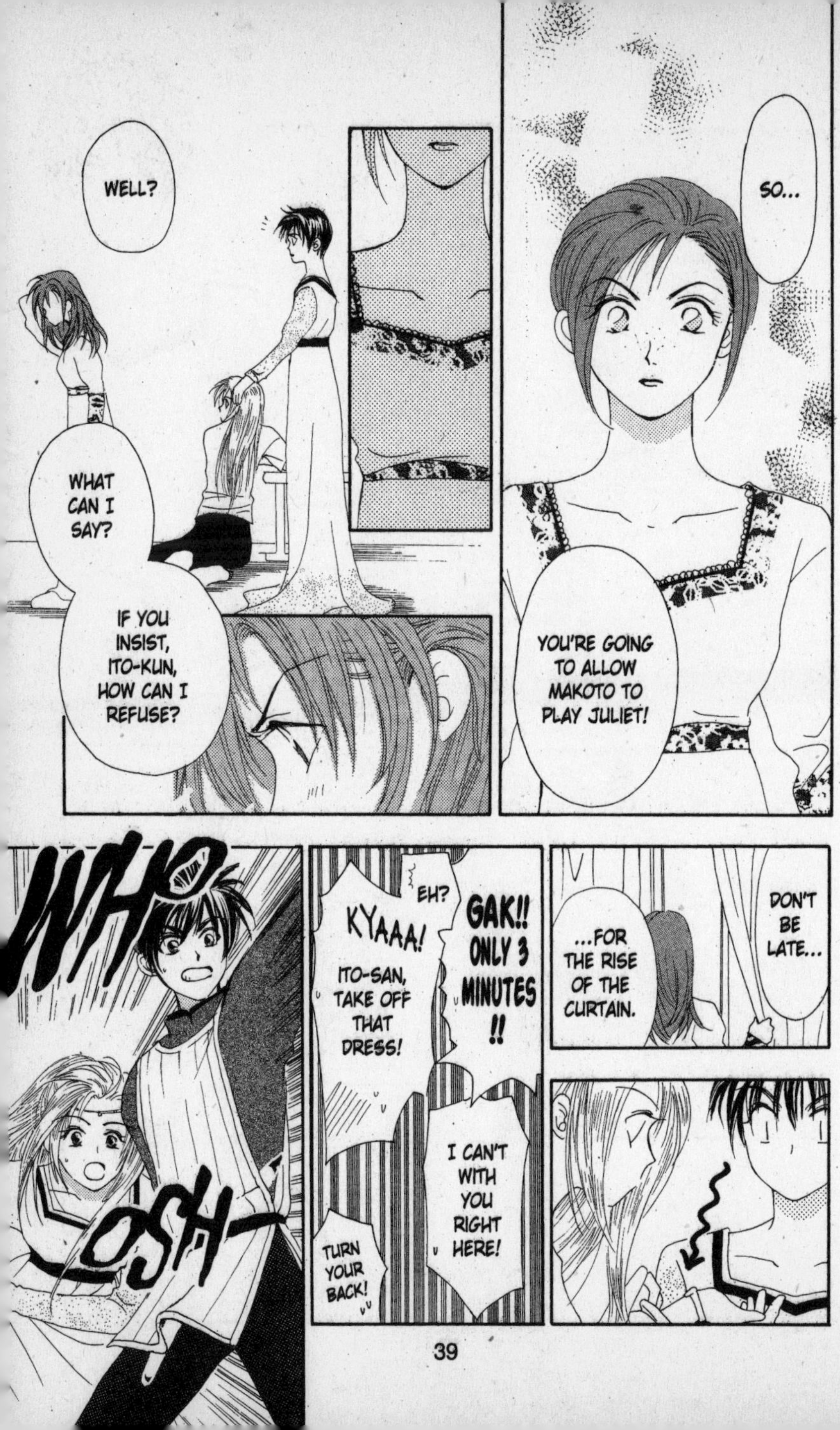
SO...
YOU'RE GOING TO ALLOW MAKOTO TO PLAY JULIET!
WELL?
WHAT CAN I SAY?
IF YOU INSIST, ITO-KUN, HOW CAN I REFUSE?
DON'T BE LATE...
...FOR THE RISE OF THE CURTAIN.
EH?
GAK!! ONLY 3 MINUTES!!
KYAAA!
ITO-SAN, TAKE OFF THAT DRESS!
I CAN'T WITH YOU RIGHT HERE!
TURN YOUR BACK!
WHOOSH

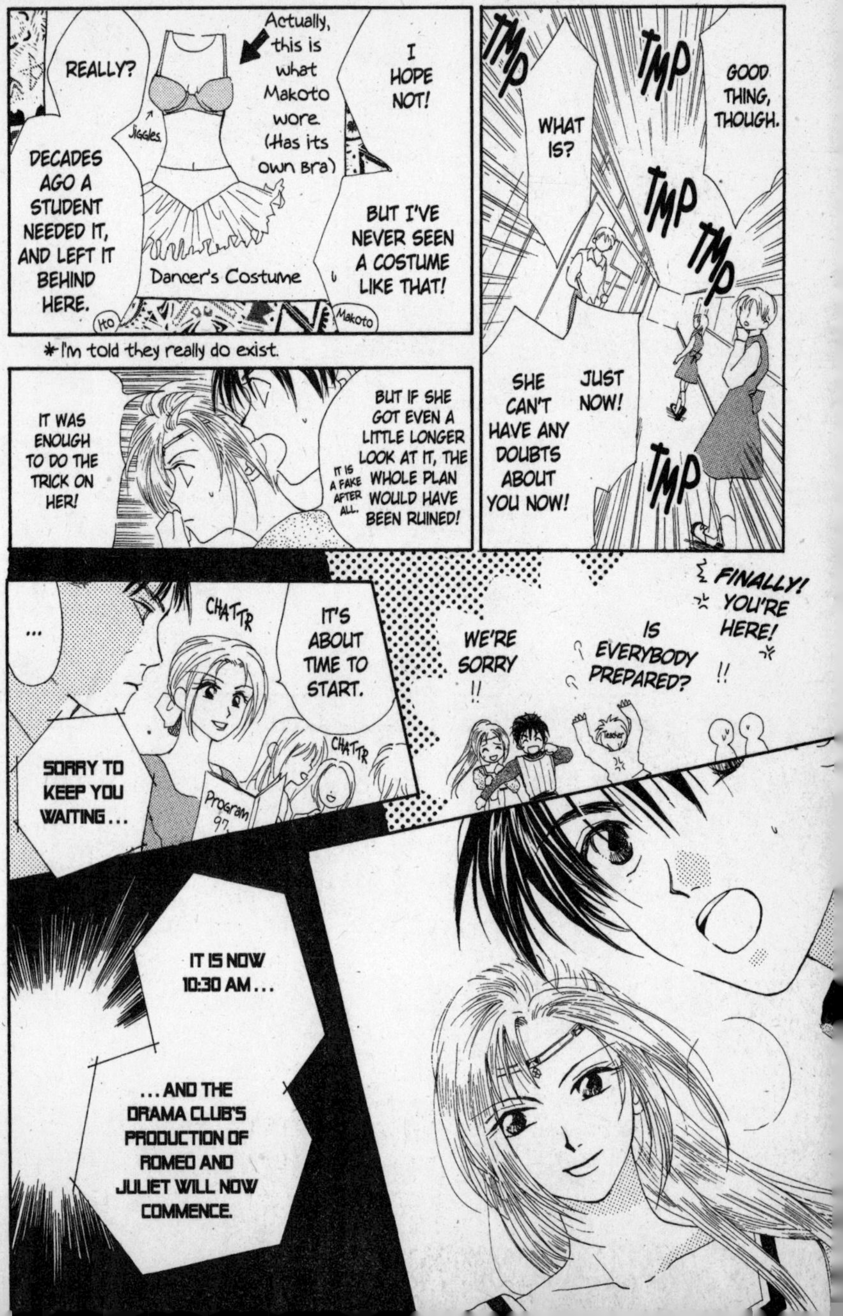
TMP
GOOD THING, THOUGH.
TMP
WHAT IS?
TMP
TMP
JUST NOW!
SHE CAN'T HAVE ANY DOUBTS ABOUT YOU NOW!
TMP
I HOPE NOT!
BUT I'VE NEVER SEEN A COSTUME LIKE THAT!
Makoto
Actually, this is what Makoto wore (Has its own Bra)
Jiggles
Dancer's Costume
REALLY?
DECADES AGO A STUDENT NEEDED IT, AND LEFT IT BEHIND HERE.
Ito
*I'm told they really do exist.
BUT IF SHE GOT EVEN A LITTLE LONGER LOOK AT IT, THE WHOLE PLAN WOULD HAVE BEEN RUINED!
IT IS A FAKE AFTER ALL.
IT WAS ENOUGH TO DO THE TRICK ON HER!
FINALLY! YOU'RE HERE!
IS EVERYBODY PREPARED?
Teacher
WE'RE SORRY!!
IT'S ABOUT TIME TO START.
CHATTR
CHATTR
...
SORRY TO KEEP YOU WAITING...
Program 97
IT IS NOW 10:30 AM...
...AND THE DRAMA CLUB'S PRODUCTION OF ROMEO AND JULIET WILL NOW COMMENCE.

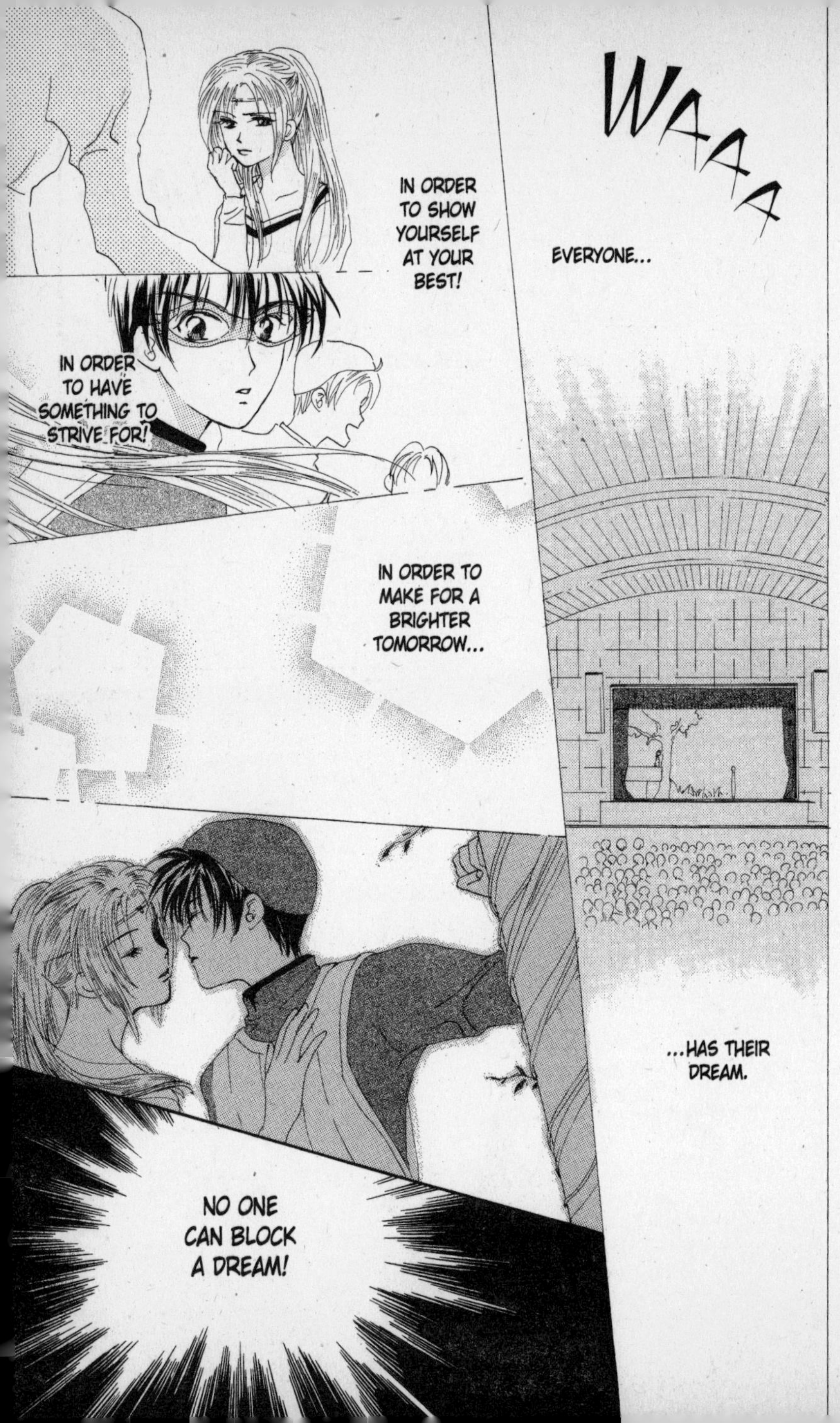
WAAAA
EVERYONE...
...HAS THEIR DREAM.
IN ORDER TO SHOW YOURSELF AT YOUR BEST!
IN ORDER TO HAVE SOMETHING TO STRIVE FOR!
IN ORDER TO MAKE FOR A BRIGHTER TOMORROW...
NO ONE CAN BLOCK A DREAM!

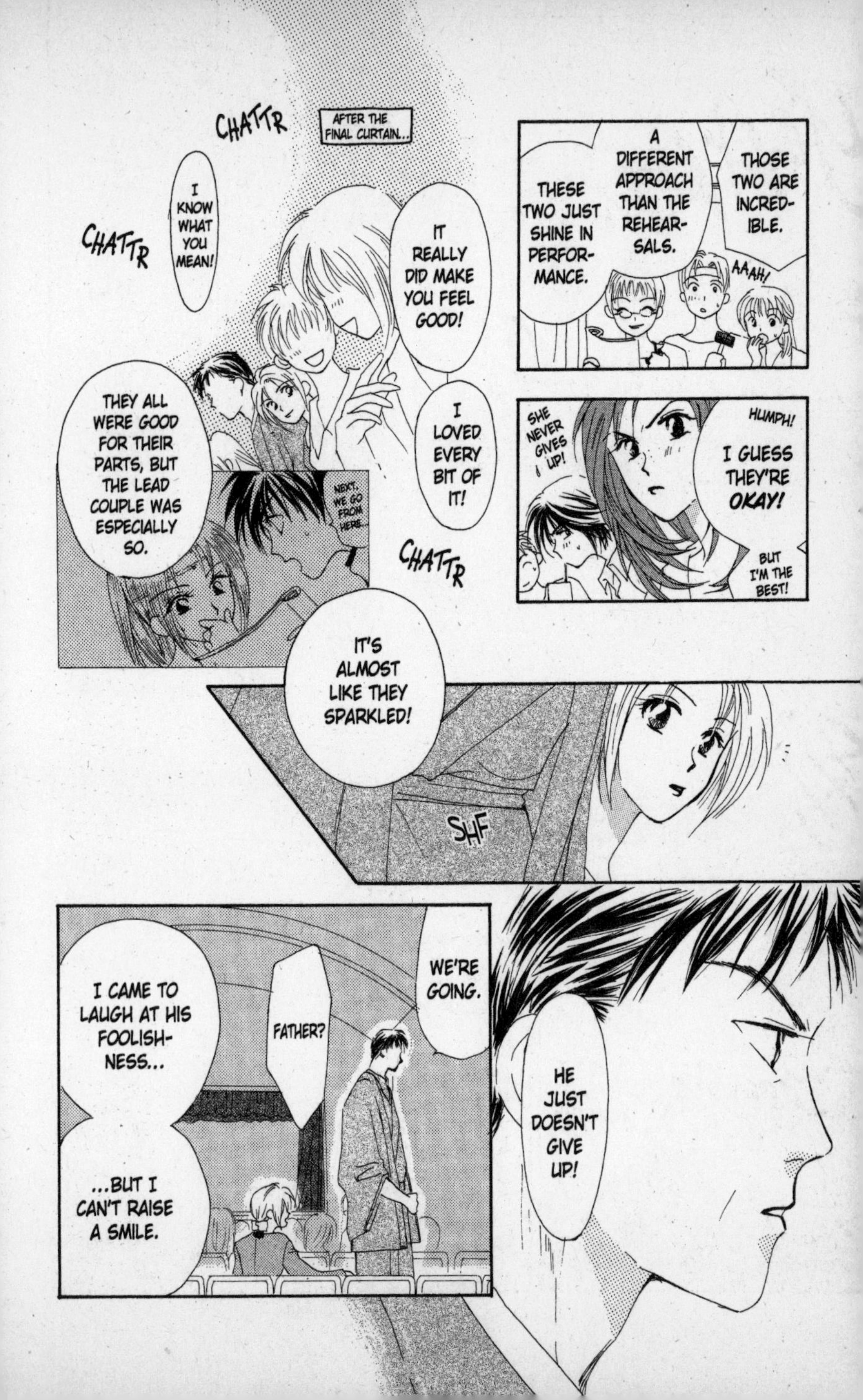
THOSE TWO ARE INCRED-IBLE.
AAAH!
A DIFFERENT APPROACH THAN THE REHEAR-SALS.
THESE TWO JUST SHINE IN PERFOR-MANCE.
HUMPH!
I GUESS THEY'RE *OKAY!*
BUT I'M THE BEST!
SHE NEVER GIVES UP!
AFTER THE FINAL CURTAIN...
CHATTR
IT REALLY DID MAKE YOU FEEL GOOD!
I KNOW WHAT YOU MEAN!
CHATTR
I LOVED EVERY BIT OF IT!
THEY ALL WERE GOOD FOR THEIR PARTS, BUT THE LEAD COUPLE WAS ESPECIALLY SO.
NEXT, WE GO FROM HERE...
CHATTR
IT'S ALMOST LIKE THEY SPARKLED!
SHF
HE JUST DOESN'T GIVE UP!
WE'RE GOING.
FATHER?
I CAME TO LAUGH AT HIS FOOLISH-NESS...
...BUT I CAN'T RAISE A SMILE.

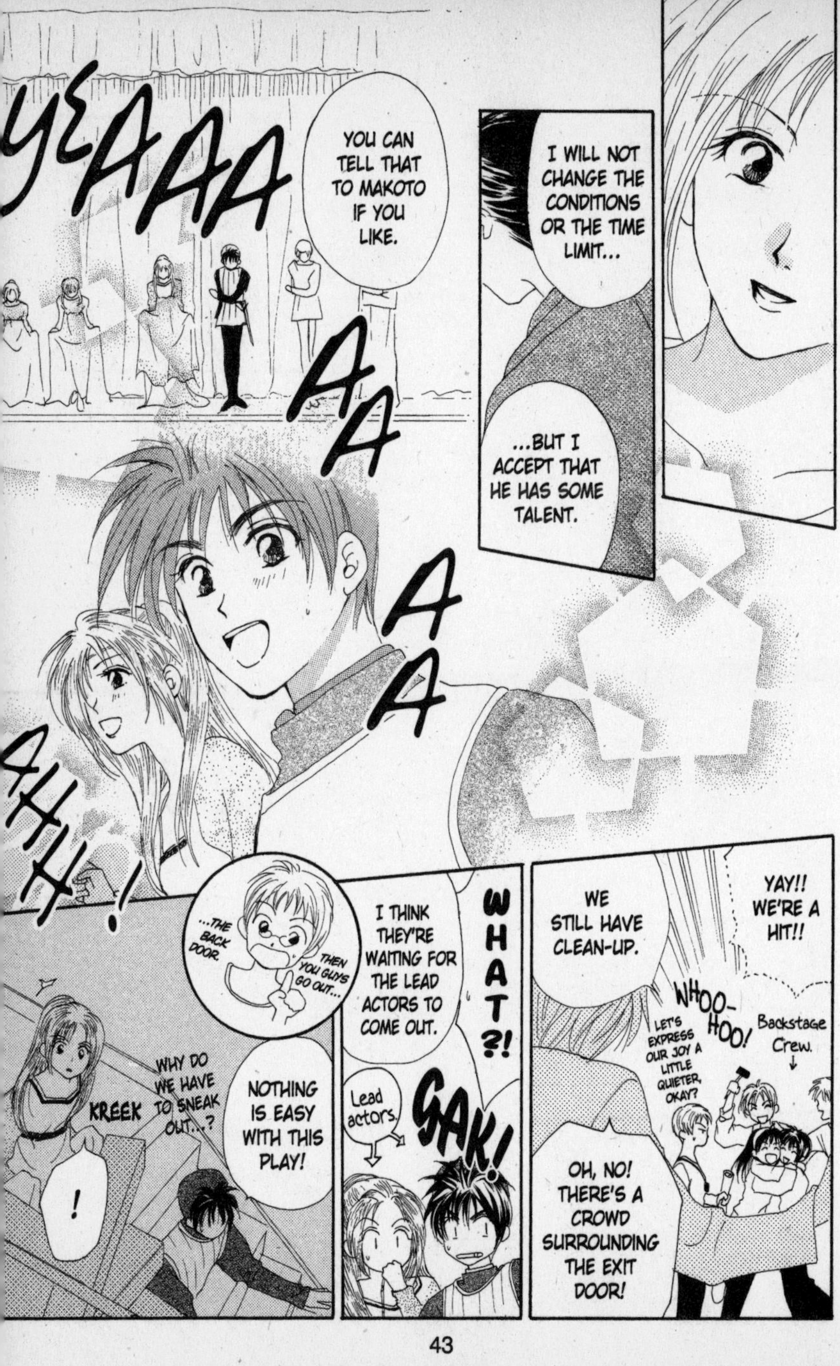
I WILL NOT CHANGE THE CONDITIONS OR THE TIME LIMIT...
...BUT I ACCEPT THAT HE HAS SOME TALENT.
YOU CAN TELL THAT TO MAKOTO IF YOU LIKE.
YEAAAAAAAAHH!
YAY!! WE'RE A HIT!!
WE STILL HAVE CLEAN-UP.
WHOO-HOO!
LET'S EXPRESS OUR JOY A LITTLE QUIETER, OKAY?
Backstage Crew.
OH, NO! THERE'S A CROWD SURROUNDING THE EXIT DOOR!
WHAT?!
I THINK THEY'RE WAITING FOR THE LEAD ACTORS TO COME OUT.
Lead actors.
SAK!
THEN YOU GUYS GO OUT...
...THE BACK DOOR.
NOTHING IS EASY WITH THIS PLAY!
WHY DO WE HAVE TO SNEAK OUT...?
KREEK
!

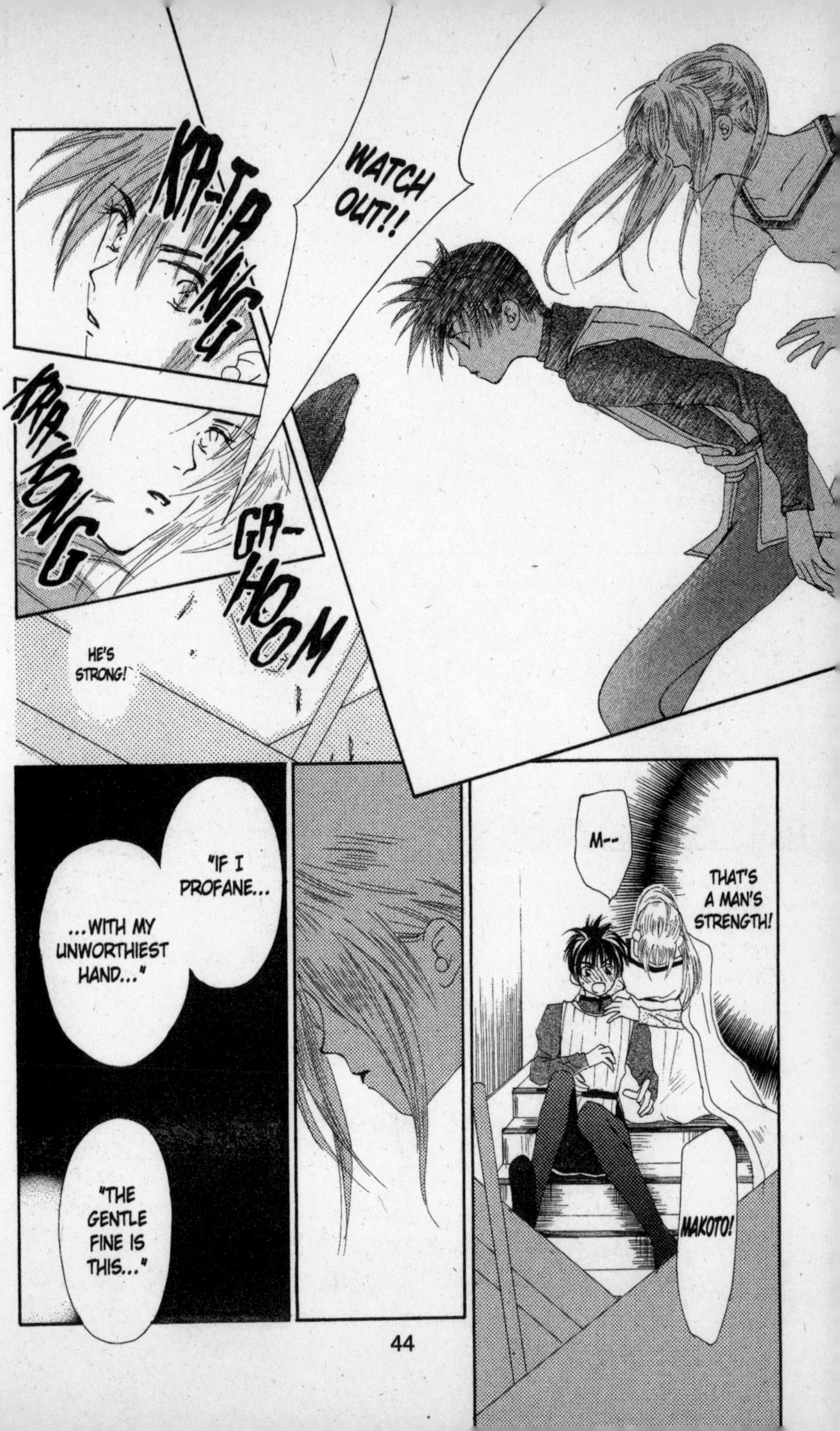
WATCH OUT!!
KA-TANG
KRA-KONG
GA-HOOM
HE'S STRONG!
M--
THAT'S A MAN'S STRENGTH!
MAKOTO!
"IF I PROFANE...
...WITH MY UNWORTHIEST HAND..."
"THE GENTLE FINE IS THIS..."

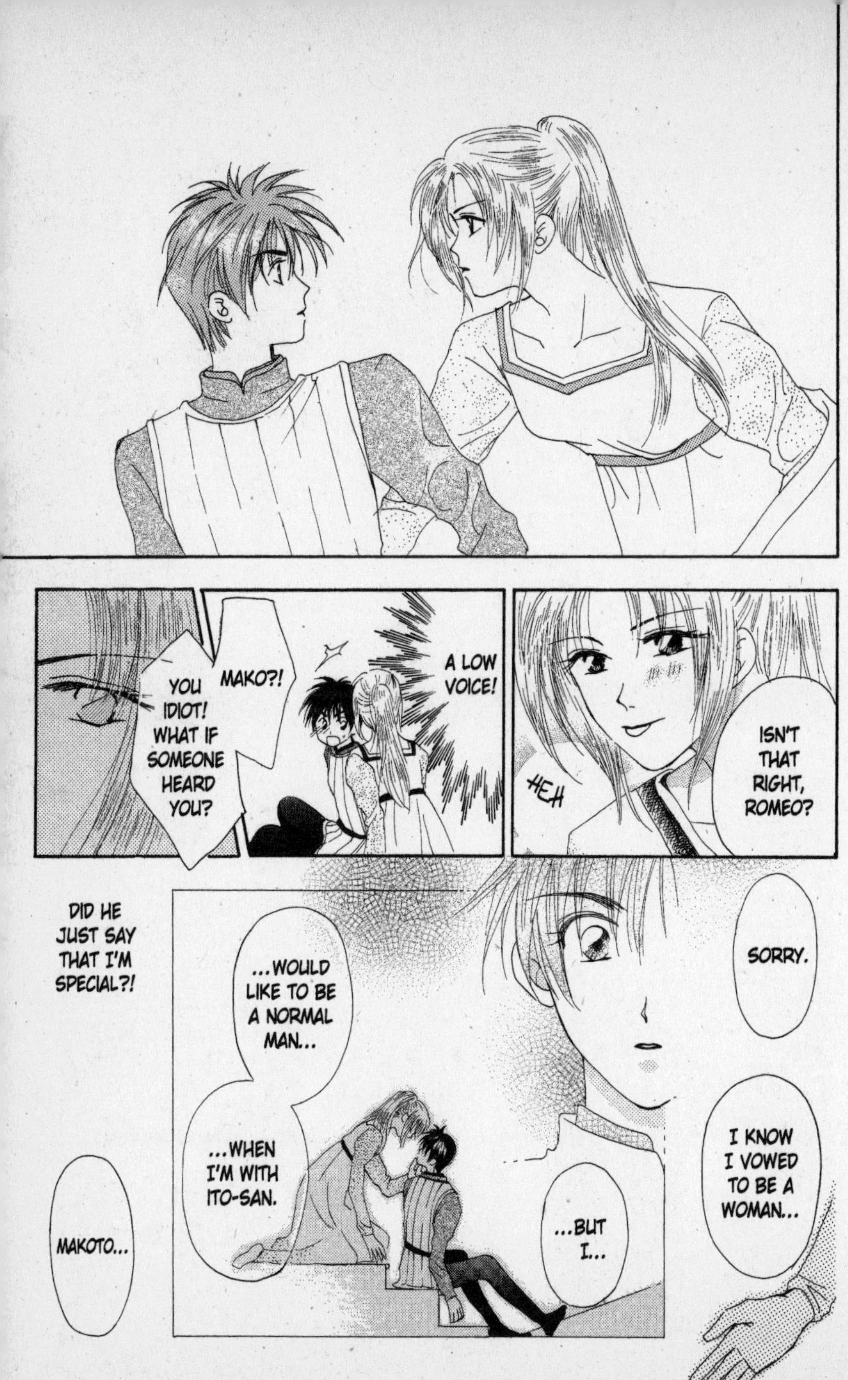

ISN'T THAT RIGHT, ROMEO?
HEH
A LOW VOICE!
MAKO?!
YOU IDIOT! WHAT IF SOMEONE HEARD YOU?
SORRY.
I KNOW I VOWED TO BE A WOMAN...
...BUT I...
...WOULD LIKE TO BE A NORMAL MAN...
...WHEN I'M WITH ITO-SAN.
DID HE JUST SAY THAT I'M SPECIAL?!
MAKOTO...

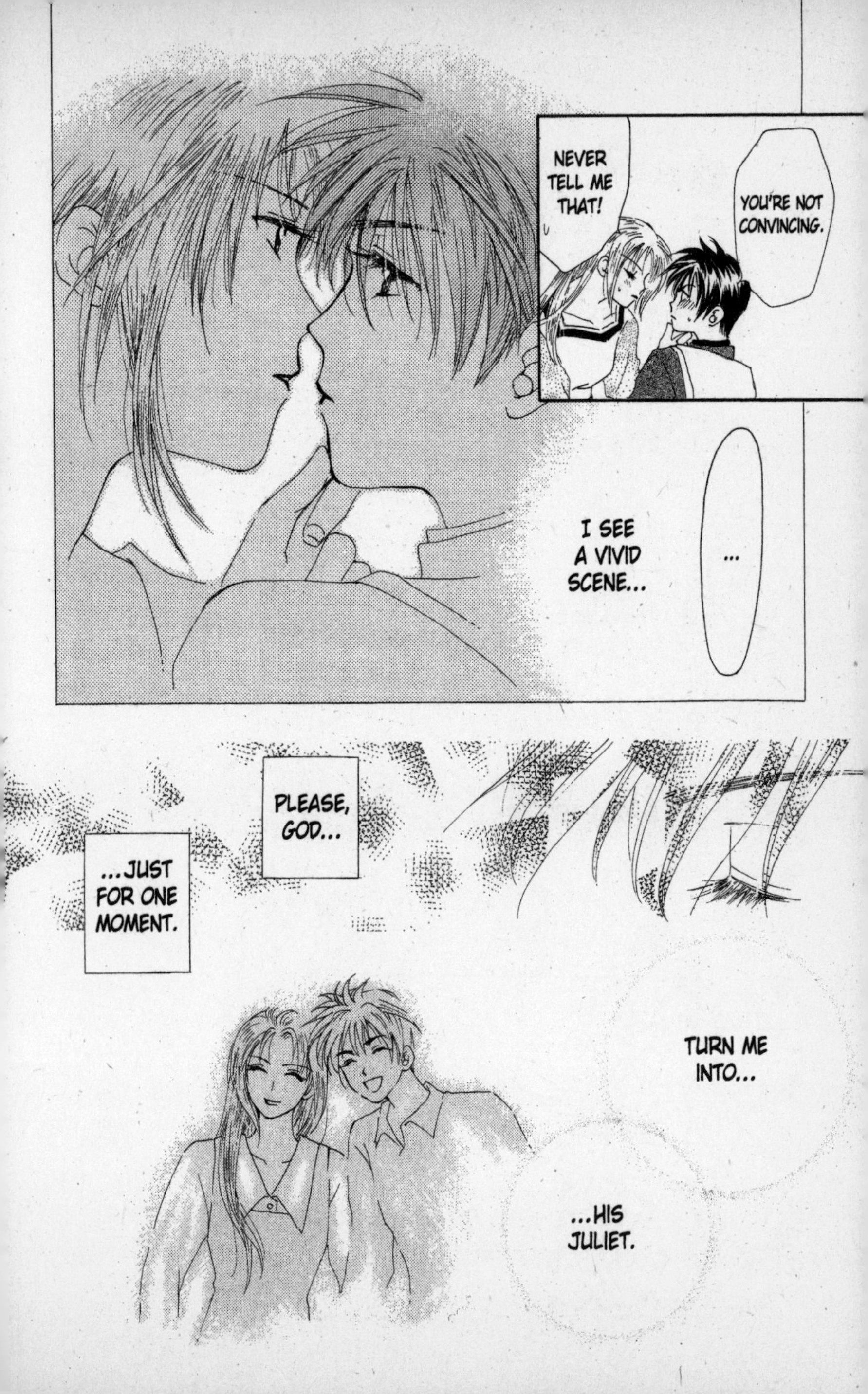
YOU'RE NOT CONVINCING.
NEVER TELL ME THAT!
...
I SEE A VIVID SCENE...
PLEASE, GOD...
...JUST FOR ONE MOMENT.
TURN ME INTO...
...HIS JULIET.

HELLO. GOOD DAY. NICE TO MEET YOU.

...a quick sketch. (笑)

I just tried...

I'm always wearing these kinds of clothes...

I'm Emura. My first comic is finally published! It's a little scary isn't it... my early artwork.
I tried to put some effort into cleaning up my artwork before publication, but it was just too terrible to do much with.
I'm as satisfied as I can be with the new work, but some may think, "I liked the artwork that was in the original magazine publication," and to you, I can only say, I'm sorry. I, personally, think it came out better this way.
I'm going to cover my thoughts on the work itself in an afterword page or two, so for now, I'd ask you to just enjoy the read.

'99. 4. 11.

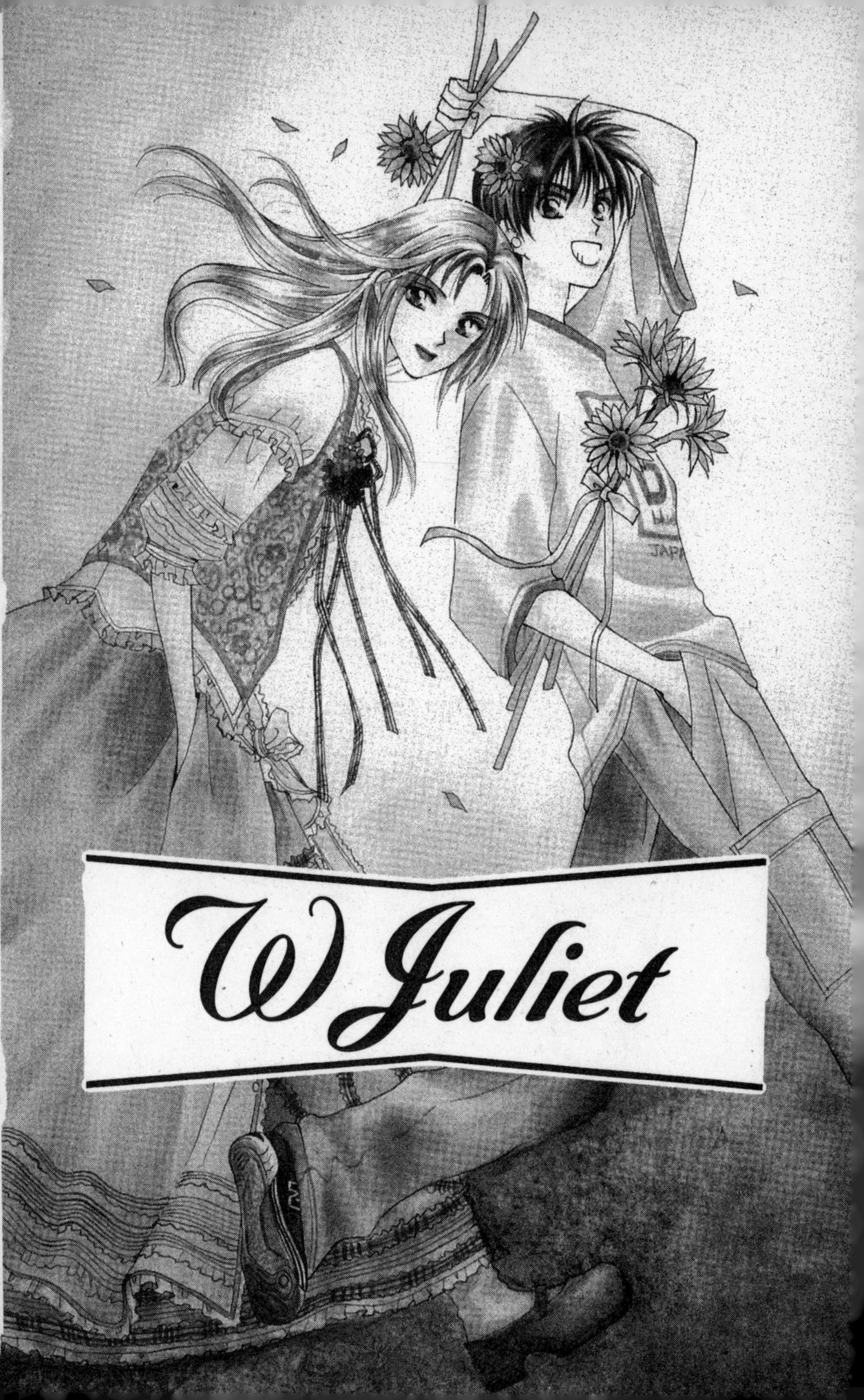
W Juliet

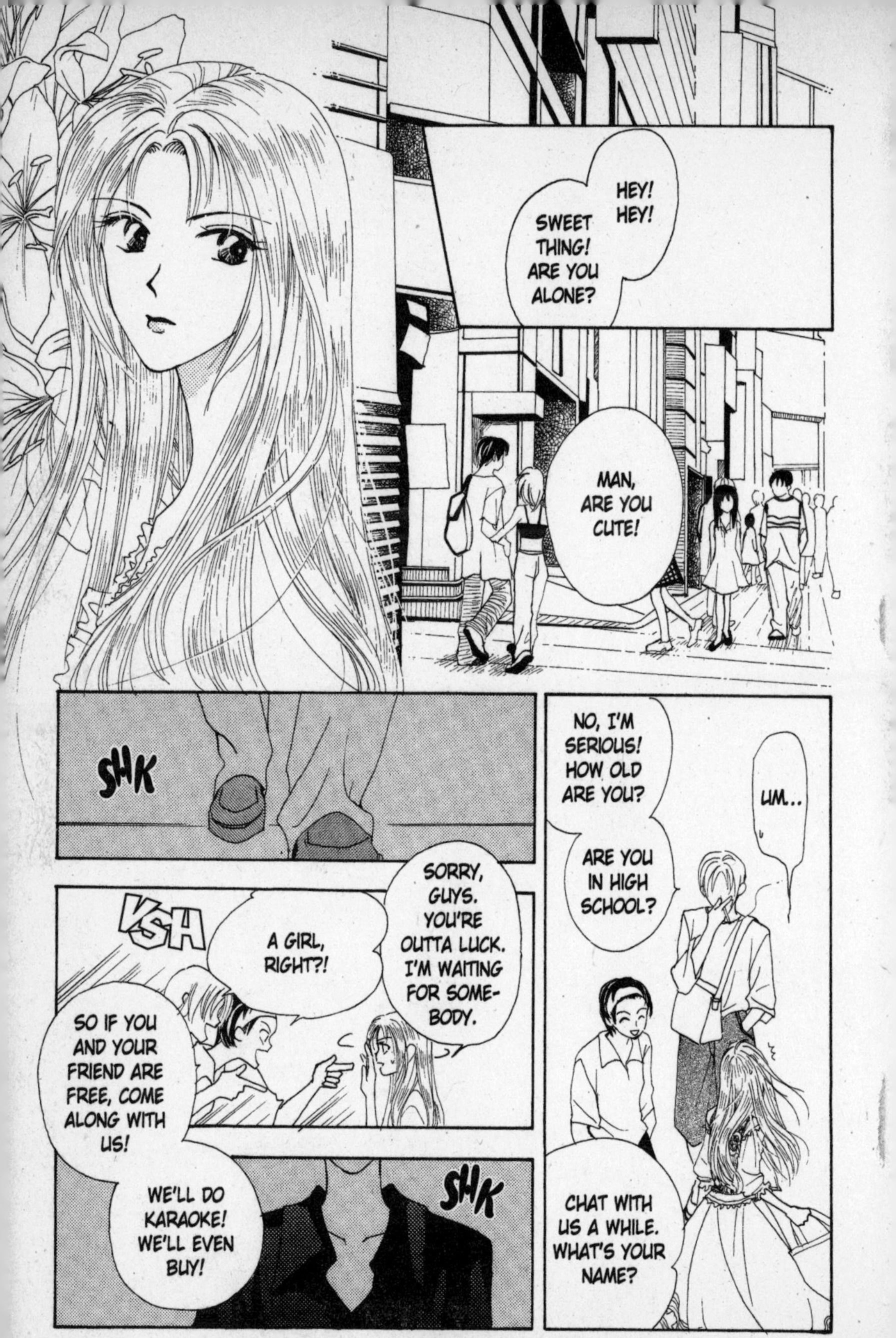

HEY! HEY!
SWEET THING! ARE YOU ALONE?
MAN, ARE YOU CUTE!
NO, I'M SERIOUS! HOW OLD ARE YOU?
ARE YOU IN HIGH SCHOOL?
UM...
CHAT WITH US A WHILE. WHAT'S YOUR NAME?
SHK
VSH
SORRY, GUYS. YOU'RE OUTTA LUCK. I'M WAITING FOR SOME-BODY.
A GIRL, RIGHT?!
SO IF YOU AND YOUR FRIEND ARE FREE, COME ALONG WITH US!
WE'LL DO KARAOKE! WE'LL EVEN BUY!
SHK

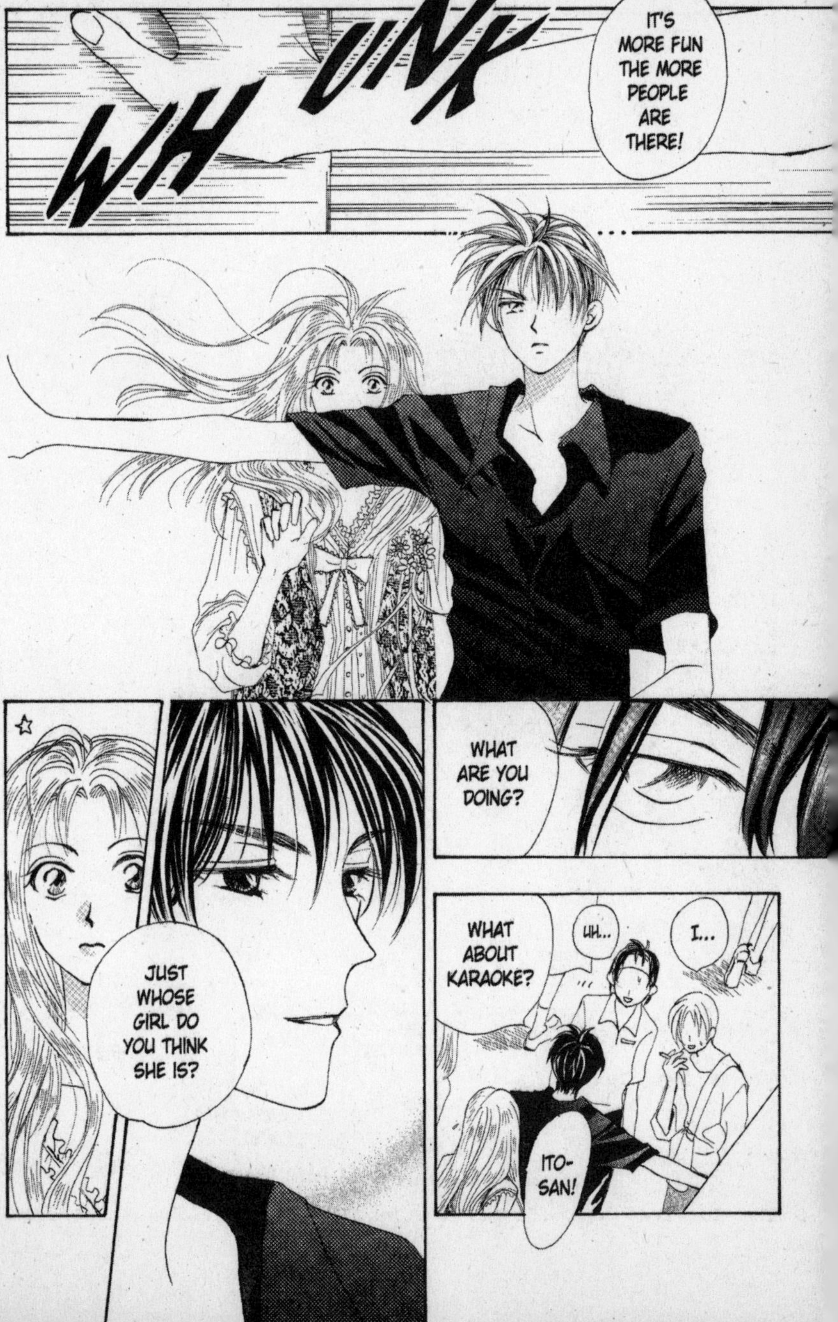
IT'S MORE FUN THE MORE PEOPLE ARE THERE!
WHUNK
...
WHAT ARE YOU DOING?
I...
UH...
WHAT ABOUT KARAOKE?
ITO-SAN!
JUST WHOSE GIRL DO YOU THINK SHE IS?

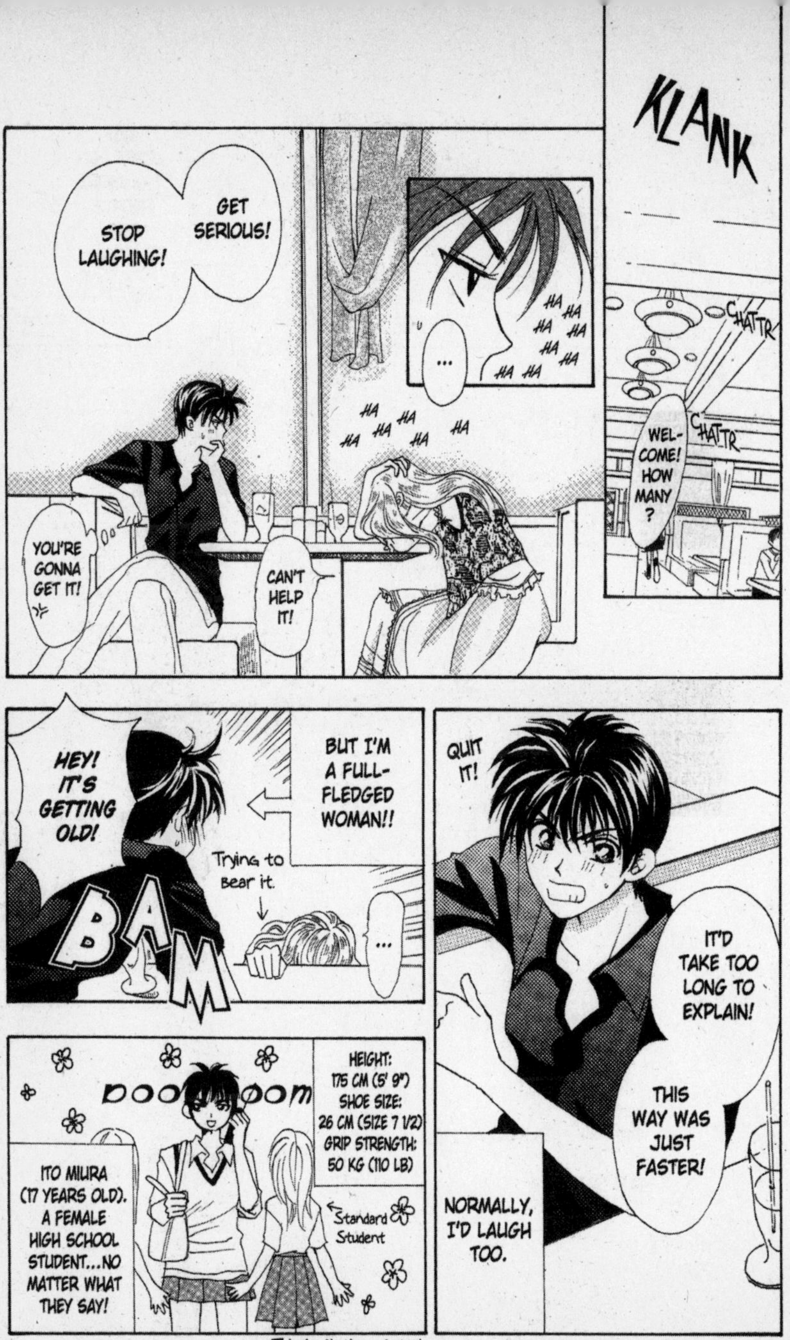
KLANK
CHATTR
CHATTR
WELCOME! HOW MANY?
...
HA HA HA HA HA HA HA HA HA
GET SERIOUS!
STOP LAUGHING!
HA HA HA HA HA HA
CAN'T HELP IT!
YOU'RE GONNA GET IT!
QUIT IT!
IT'D TAKE TOO LONG TO EXPLAIN!
THIS WAY WAS JUST FASTER!
NORMALLY, I'D LAUGH TOO.
BUT I'M A FULL-FLEDGED WOMAN!!
Trying to Bear it.
...
HEY! IT'S GETTING OLD!
BAM
HEIGHT: 175 CM (5' 9") SHOE SIZE: 26 CM (SIZE 7 1/2) GRIP STRENGTH: 50 KG (110 LB)
Standard Student
DOOM DOOM
ITO MIURA (17 YEARS OLD). A FEMALE HIGH SCHOOL STUDENT...NO MATTER WHAT THEY SAY!

This is fiction, folks!

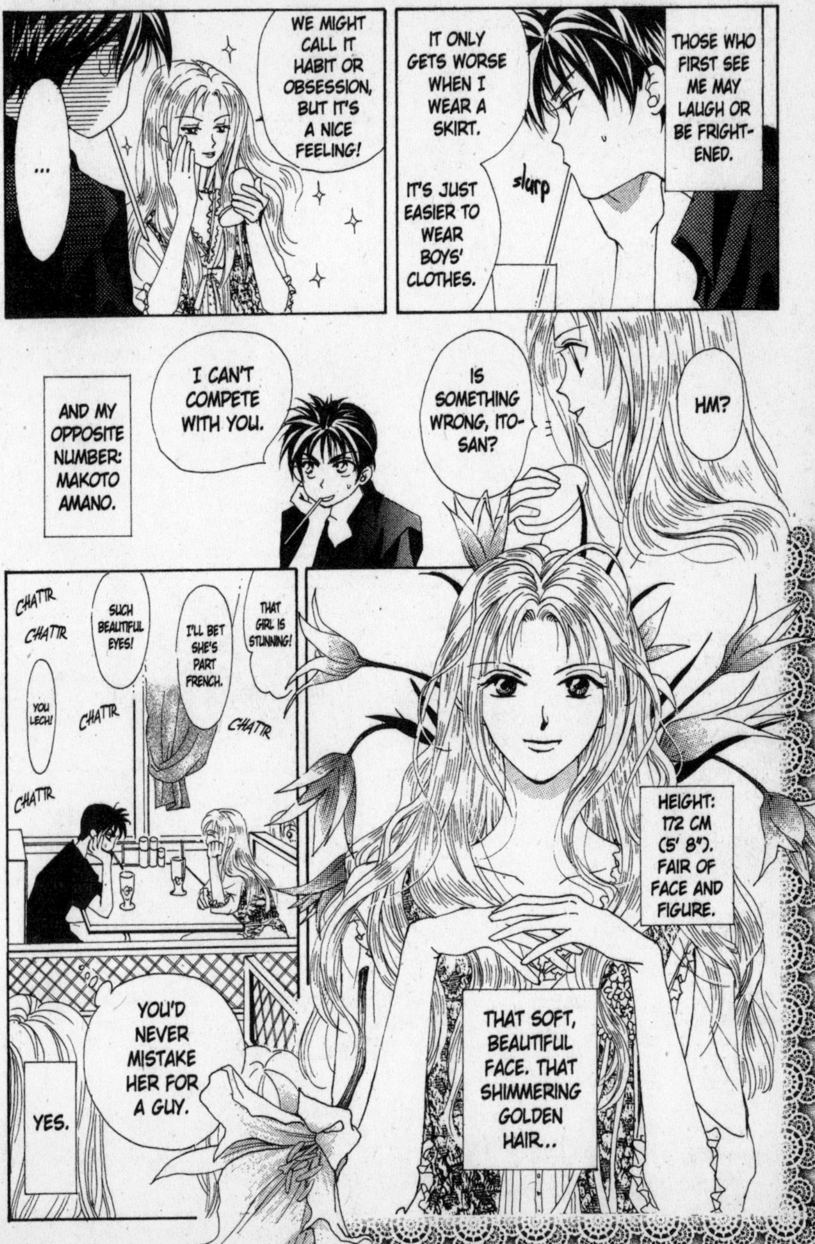
THOSE WHO FIRST SEE ME MAY LAUGH OR BE FRIGHT-ENED.
IT ONLY GETS WORSE WHEN I WEAR A SKIRT.
slurp
IT'S JUST EASIER TO WEAR BOYS' CLOTHES.
WE MIGHT CALL IT HABIT OR OBSESSION, BUT IT'S A NICE FEELING!
...
HM?
IS SOMETHING WRONG, ITO-SAN?
I CAN'T COMPETE WITH YOU.
AND MY OPPOSITE NUMBER: MAKOTO AMANO.
HEIGHT: 172 CM (5' 8"). FAIR OF FACE AND FIGURE.
THAT SOFT, BEAUTIFUL FACE. THAT SHIMMERING GOLDEN HAIR..
THAT GIRL IS STUNNING!
I'LL BET SHE'S PART FRENCH.
SUCH BEAUTIFUL EYES!
CHATTR
CHATTR
CHATTR
YOU LECH!
CHATTR
CHATTR
YOU'D NEVER MISTAKE HER FOR A GUY.
YES.

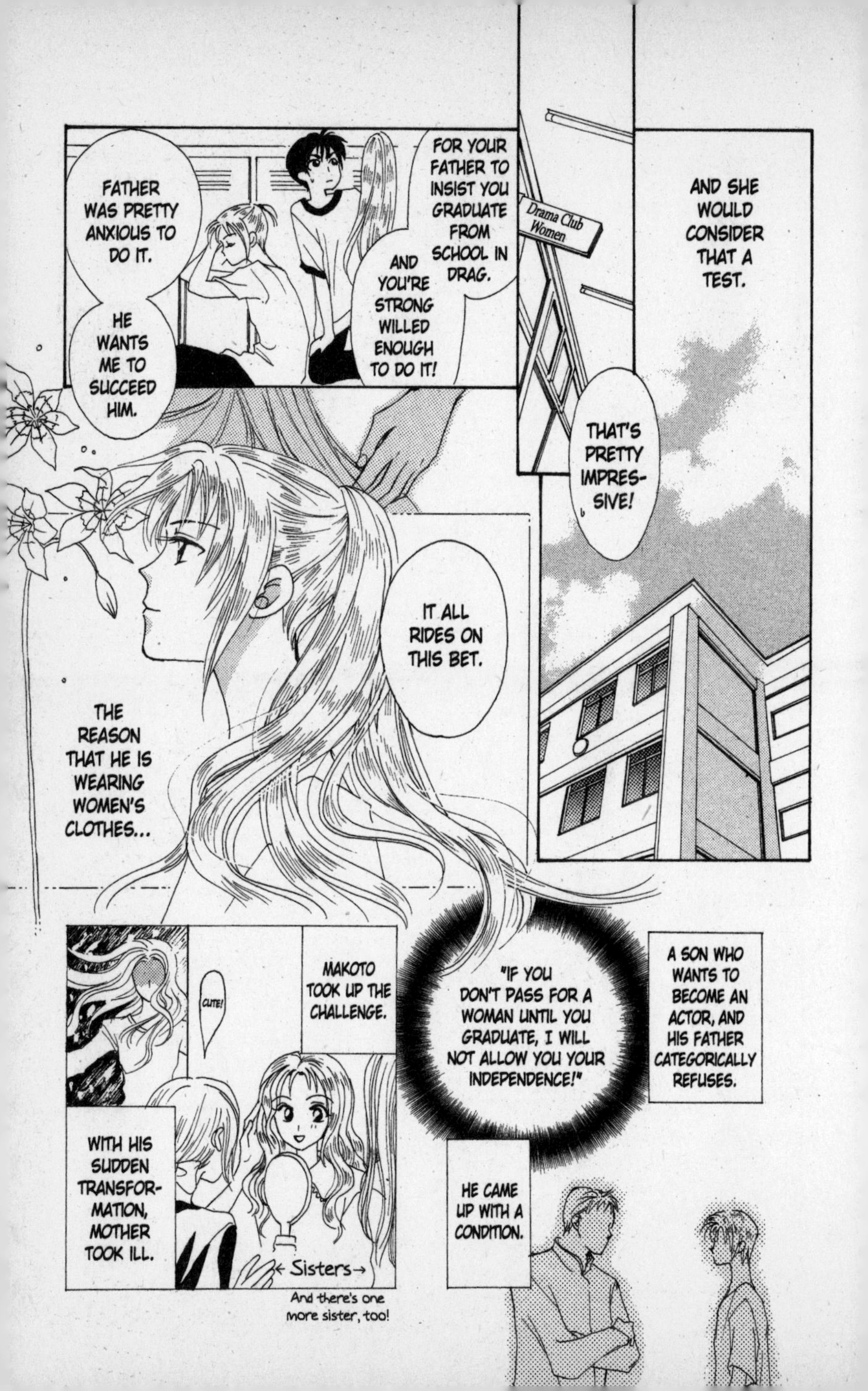
AND SHE WOULD CONSIDER THAT A TEST.
Drama Club Women
THAT'S PRETTY IMPRES-SIVE!
FOR YOUR FATHER TO INSIST YOU GRADUATE FROM SCHOOL IN DRAG.
AND YOU'RE STRONG WILLED ENOUGH TO DO IT!
FATHER WAS PRETTY ANXIOUS TO DO IT.
HE WANTS ME TO SUCCEED HIM.
IT ALL RIDES ON THIS BET.
THE REASON THAT HE IS WEARING WOMEN'S CLOTHES...
A SON WHO WANTS TO BECOME AN ACTOR, AND HIS FATHER CATEGORICALLY REFUSES.
HE CAME UP WITH A CONDITION.
"IF YOU DON'T PASS FOR A WOMAN UNTIL YOU GRADUATE, I WILL NOT ALLOW YOU YOUR INDEPENDENCE!"
MAKOTO TOOK UP THE CHALLENGE.
CUTE!
WITH HIS SUDDEN TRANSFOR-MATION, MOTHER TOOK ILL.
← Sisters →
And there's one more sister, too!

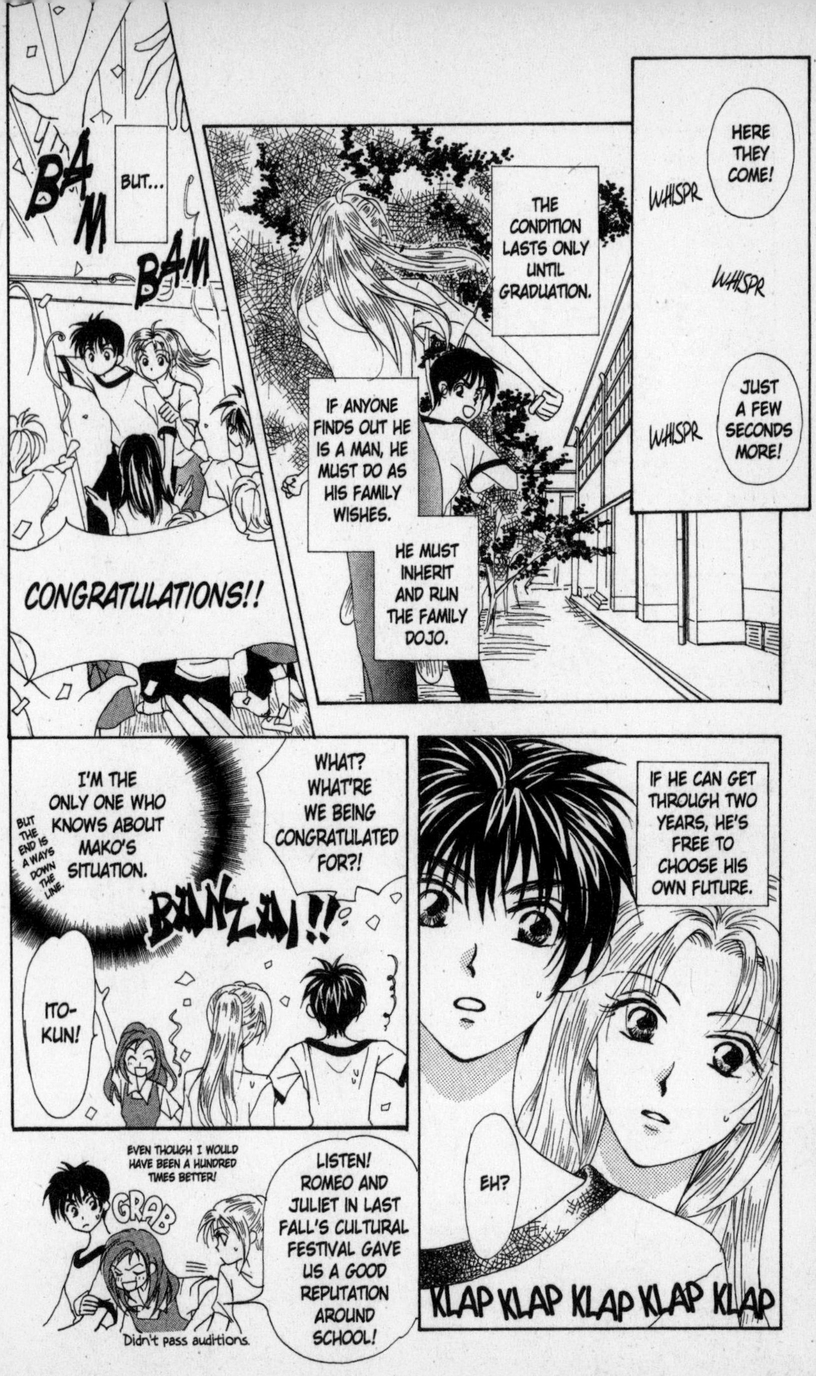
HERE THEY COME!
WHISPR
WHISPR
WHISPR
JUST A FEW SECONDS MORE!
THE CONDITION LASTS ONLY UNTIL GRADUATION.
IF ANYONE FINDS OUT HE IS A MAN, HE MUST DO AS HIS FAMILY WISHES.
HE MUST INHERIT AND RUN THE FAMILY DOJO.
BUT...
BAM
BAM
CONGRATULATIONS!!
IF HE CAN GET THROUGH TWO YEARS, HE'S FREE TO CHOOSE HIS OWN FUTURE.
EH?
KLAP KLAP KLAP KLAP KLAP
WHAT? WHAT'RE WE BEING CONGRATULATED FOR?!
I'M THE ONLY ONE WHO KNOWS ABOUT MAKO'S SITUATION.
BUT THE END IS A WAYS DOWN THE LINE.
BANZAI!!
ITO-KUN!
LISTEN! ROMEO AND JULIET IN LAST FALL'S CULTURAL FESTIVAL GAVE US A GOOD REPUTATION AROUND SCHOOL!
EVEN THOUGH I WOULD HAVE BEEN A HUNDRED TIMES BETTER!
GRAB
Didn't pass auditions.

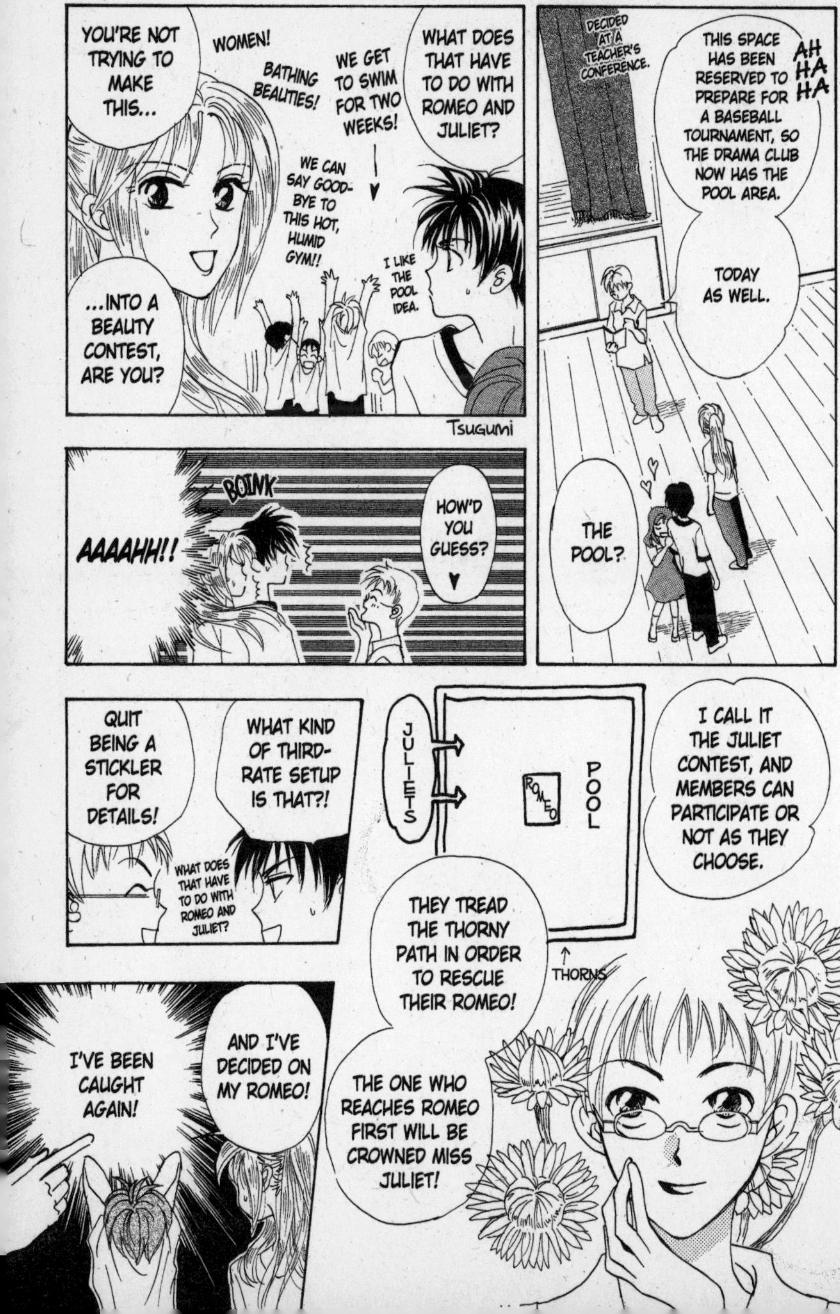
DECIDED AT A TEACHER'S CONFERENCE.
THIS SPACE HAS BEEN RESERVED TO PREPARE FOR A BASEBALL TOURNAMENT, SO THE DRAMA CLUB NOW HAS THE POOL AREA.
AH HA HA
TODAY AS WELL.
THE POOL?
WHAT DOES THAT HAVE TO DO WITH ROMEO AND JULIET?
WE GET TO SWIM FOR TWO WEEKS!
BATHING BEAUTIES!
WOMEN!
YOU'RE NOT TRYING TO MAKE THIS...
WE CAN SAY GOOD-BYE TO THIS HOT, HUMID GYM!!
I LIKE THE POOL IDEA.
...INTO A BEAUTY CONTEST, ARE YOU?
Tsugumi
HOW'D YOU GUESS? ♥
BOINK
AAAAHH!!
I CALL IT THE JULIET CONTEST, AND MEMBERS CAN PARTICIPATE OR NOT AS THEY CHOOSE.
JULIETS
ROMEO
POOL
THORNS
THEY TREAD THE THORNY PATH IN ORDER TO RESCUE THEIR ROMEO!
THE ONE WHO REACHES ROMEO FIRST WILL BE CROWNED MISS JULIET!
WHAT KIND OF THIRD-RATE SETUP IS THAT?!
QUIT BEING A STICKLER FOR DETAILS!
WHAT DOES THAT HAVE TO DO WITH ROMEO AND JULIET?
AND I'VE DECIDED ON MY ROMEO!
I'VE BEEN CAUGHT AGAIN!

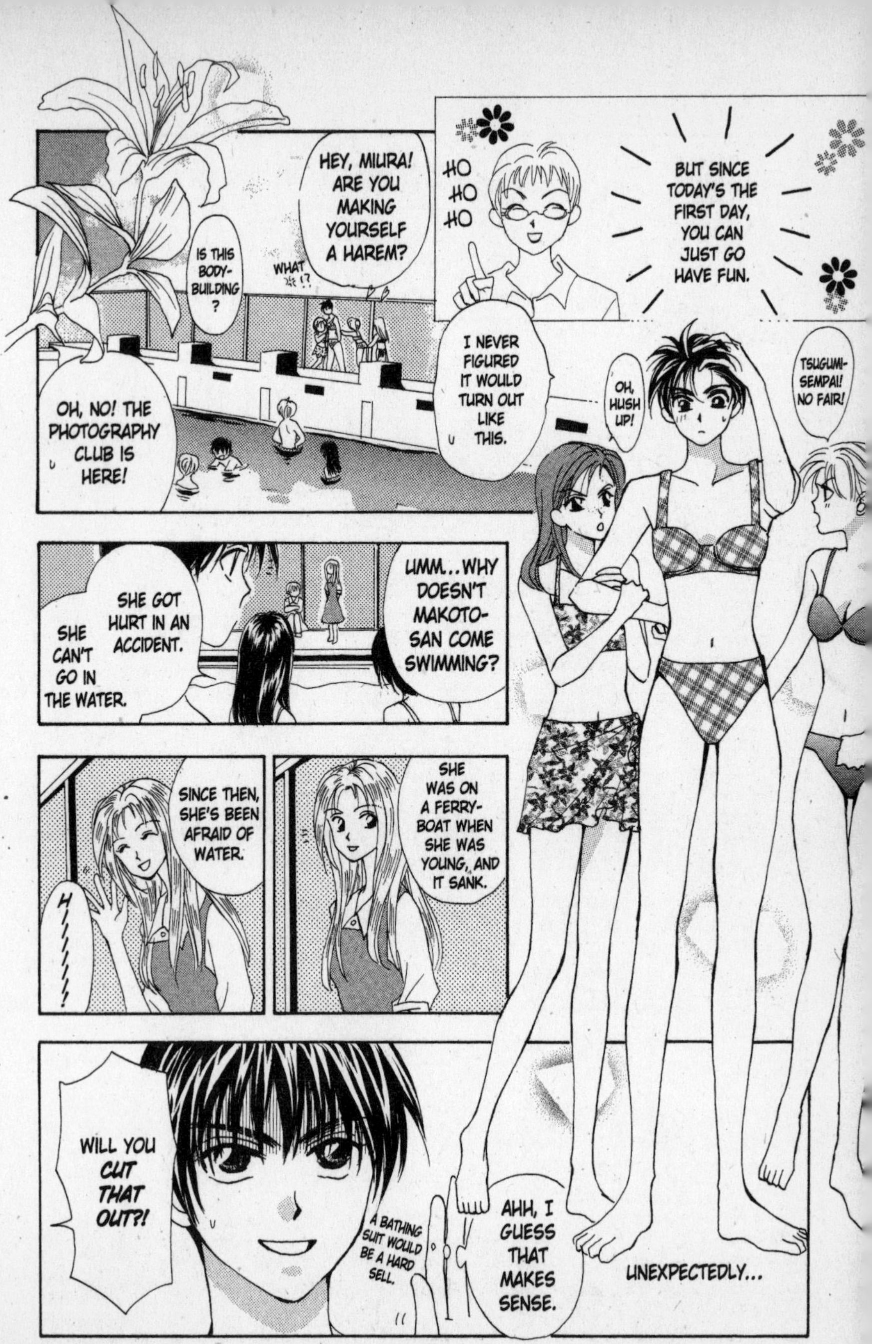
HO HO HO
BUT SINCE TODAY'S THE FIRST DAY, YOU CAN JUST GO HAVE FUN.
HEY, MIURA! ARE YOU MAKING YOURSELF A HAREM?
WHAT!?
IS THIS BODY-BUILDING?
OH, NO! THE PHOTOGRAPHY CLUB IS HERE!
I NEVER FIGURED IT WOULD TURN OUT LIKE THIS.
TSUGUMI-SEMPAI! NO FAIR!
OH, HUSH UP!
UMM...WHY DOESN'T MAKOTO-SAN COME SWIMMING?
SHE GOT HURT IN AN ACCIDENT.
SHE CAN'T GO IN THE WATER.
SHE WAS ON A FERRY-BOAT WHEN SHE WAS YOUNG, AND IT SANK.
SINCE THEN, SHE'S BEEN AFRAID OF WATER.
HI!!!!!!!
AHH, I GUESS THAT MAKES SENSE.
A BATHING SUIT WOULD BE A HARD SELL.
WILL YOU CUT THAT OUT?!
UNEXPECTEDLY...

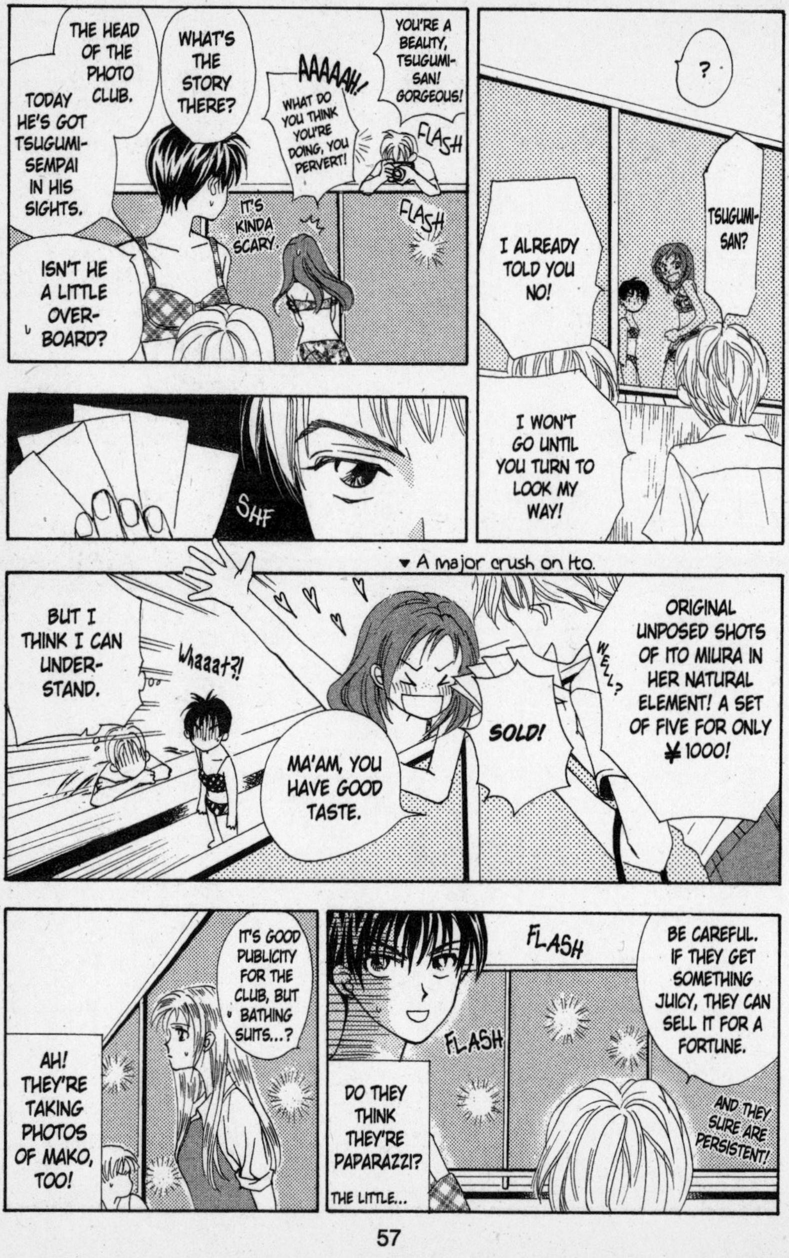
?
TSUGUMI-SAN?
I ALREADY TOLD YOU NO!
I WON'T GO UNTIL YOU TURN TO LOOK MY WAY!
YOU'RE A BEAUTY, TSUGUMI-SAN! GORGEOUS!
FLASH
AAAAAH!
WHAT DO YOU THINK YOU'RE DOING, YOU PERVERT!
FLASH
WHAT'S THE STORY THERE?
THE HEAD OF THE PHOTO CLUB.
TODAY HE'S GOT TSUGUMI-SEMPAI IN HIS SIGHTS.
IT'S KINDA SCARY.
ISN'T HE A LITTLE OVER-BOARD?
SHF
▼ A major crush on Ito.
ORIGINAL UNPOSED SHOTS OF ITO MIURA IN HER NATURAL ELEMENT! A SET OF FIVE FOR ONLY ¥1000!
WELL?
SOLD!
MA'AM, YOU HAVE GOOD TASTE.
Whaaat?!
BUT I THINK I CAN UNDER-STAND.
BE CAREFUL. IF THEY GET SOMETHING JUICY, THEY CAN SELL IT FOR A FORTUNE.
FLASH
AND THEY SURE ARE PERSISTENT!
FLASH
DO THEY THINK THEY'RE PAPARAZZI?
THE LITTLE...
IT'S GOOD PUBLICITY FOR THE CLUB, BUT BATHING SUITS...?
AH! THEY'RE TAKING PHOTOS OF MAKO, TOO!

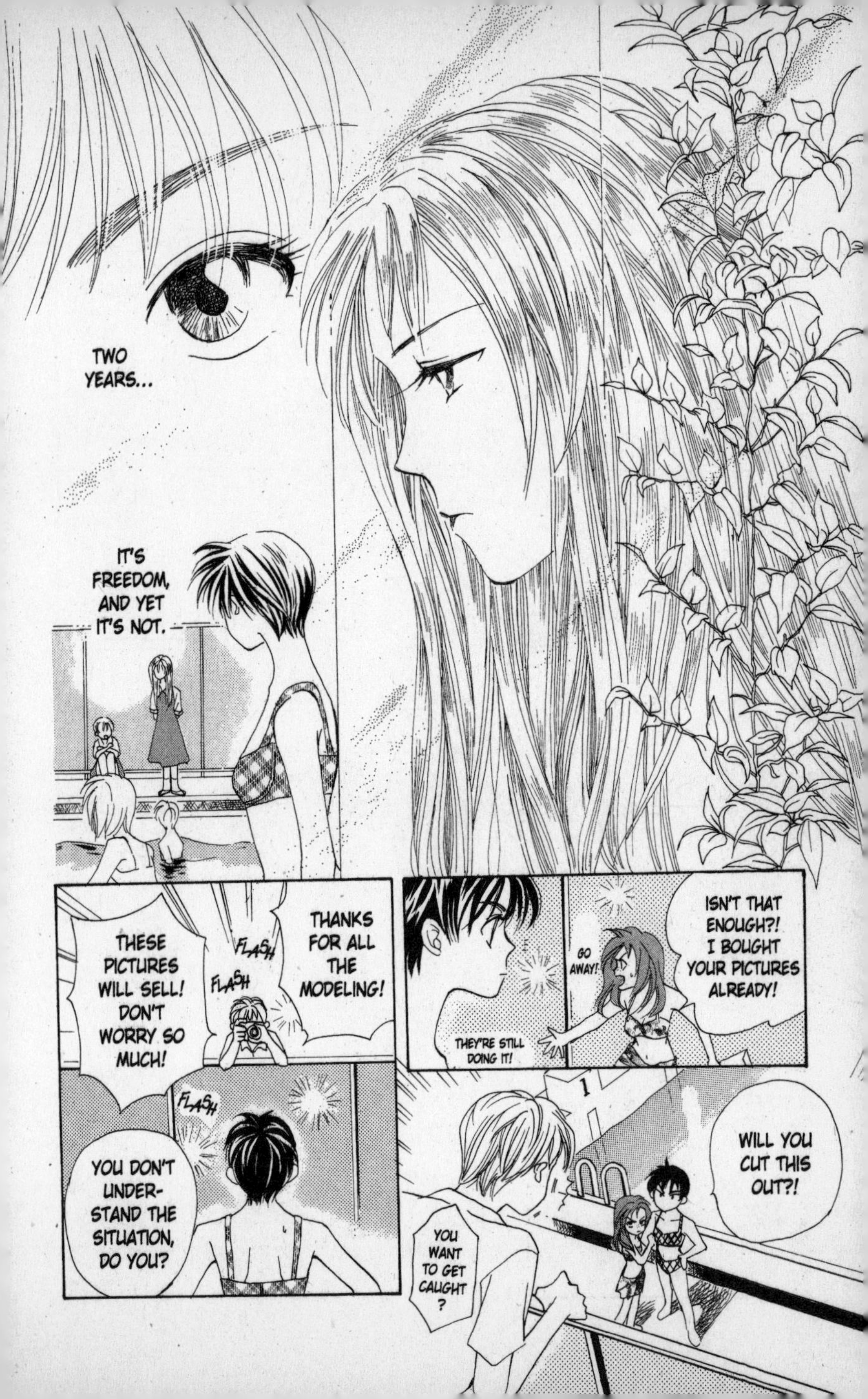
TWO YEARS...
IT'S FREEDOM, AND YET IT'S NOT.
ISN'T THAT ENOUGH?! I BOUGHT YOUR PICTURES ALREADY!
GO AWAY!
THEY'RE STILL DOING IT!
THANKS FOR ALL THE MODELING!
FLASH
FLASH
THESE PICTURES WILL SELL! DON'T WORRY SO MUCH!
WILL YOU CUT THIS OUT?!
YOU WANT TO GET CAUGHT?
FLASH
YOU DON'T UNDER-STAND THE SITUATION, DO YOU?

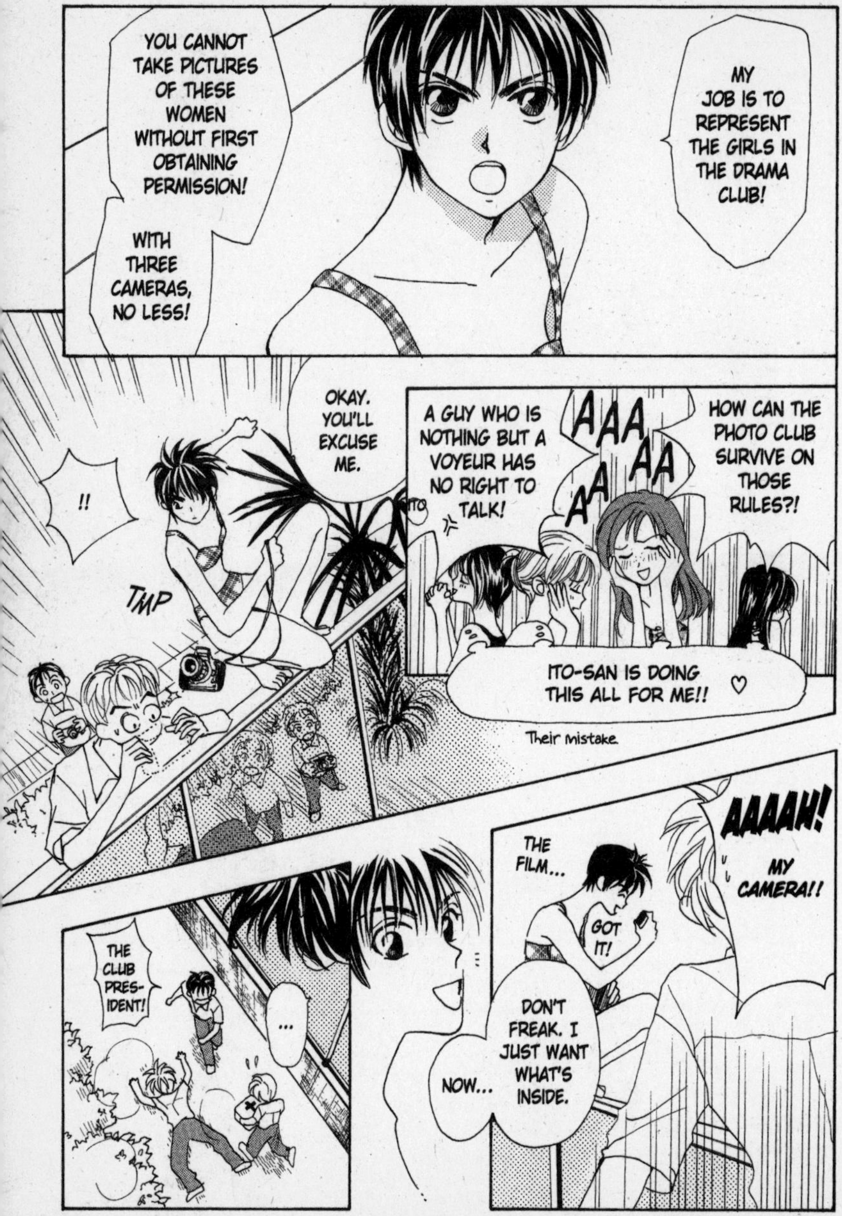
MY JOB IS TO REPRESENT THE GIRLS IN THE DRAMA CLUB!
YOU CANNOT TAKE PICTURES OF THESE WOMEN WITHOUT FIRST OBTAINING PERMISSION!
WITH THREE CAMERAS, NO LESS!
HOW CAN THE PHOTO CLUB SURVIVE ON THOSE RULES?!
AAAAAAA
A GUY WHO IS NOTHING BUT A VOYEUR HAS NO RIGHT TO TALK!
ITO
ITO-SAN IS DOING THIS ALL FOR ME!! ♡
Their mistake.
OKAY. YOU'LL EXCUSE ME.
!!
TMP
AAAAH!
MY CAMERA!!
THE FILM...
GOT IT!
DON'T FREAK. I JUST WANT WHAT'S INSIDE.
NOW...
THE CLUB PRESIDENT!
...

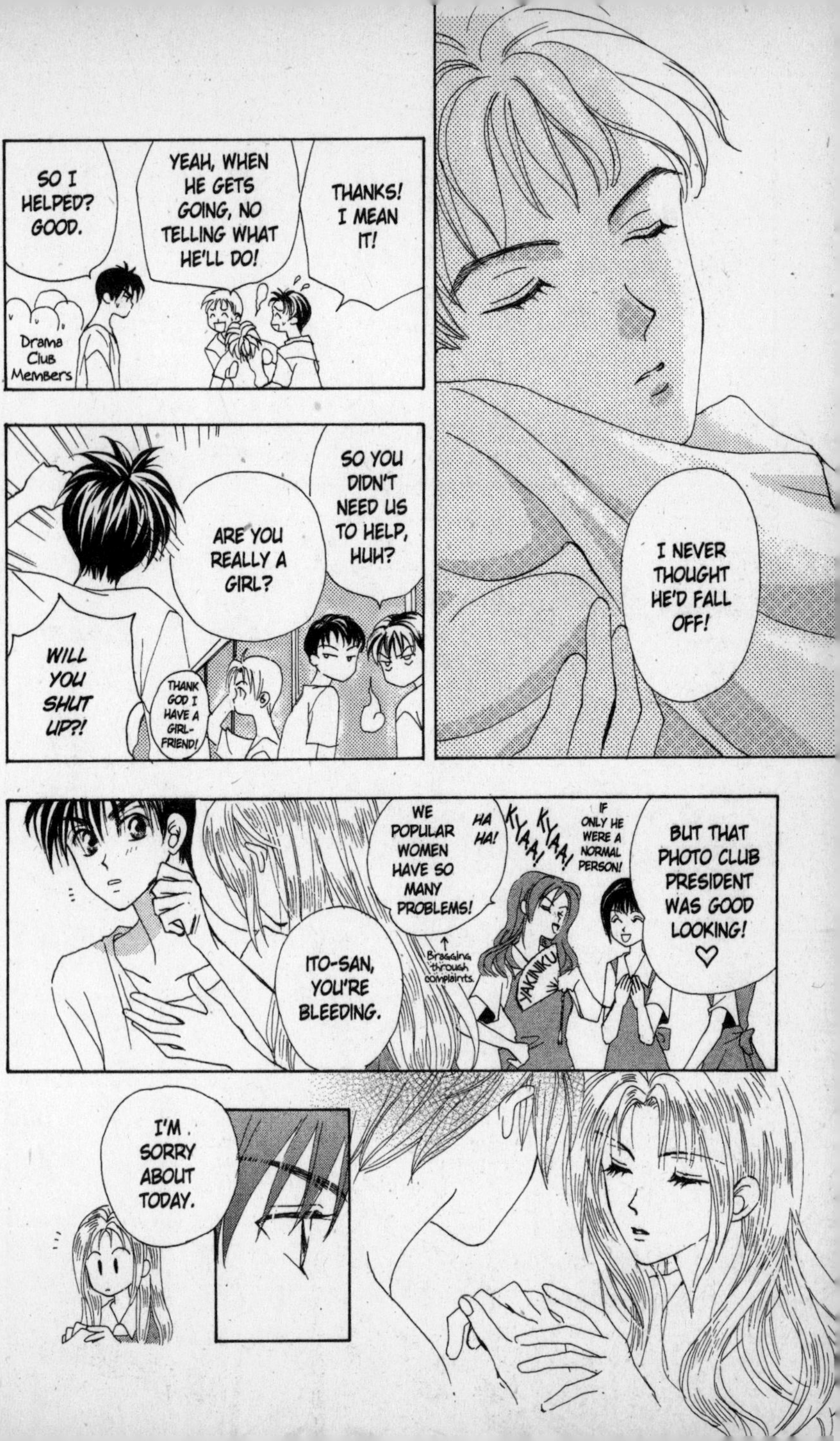
I NEVER THOUGHT HE'D FALL OFF!
THANKS! I MEAN IT!
YEAH, WHEN HE GETS GOING, NO TELLING WHAT HE'LL DO!
SO I HELPED? GOOD.
Drama Club Members
SO YOU DIDN'T NEED US TO HELP, HUH?
ARE YOU REALLY A GIRL?
THANK GOD I HAVE A GIRL-FRIEND!
WILL YOU SHUT UP?!
BUT THAT PHOTO CLUB PRESIDENT WAS GOOD LOOKING! ♡
IF ONLY HE WERE A NORMAL PERSON!
KYAA! KYAA!
HA HA!
WE POPULAR WOMEN HAVE SO MANY PROBLEMS!
Bragging through complaints.
YAKINIKU
ITO-SAN, YOU'RE BLEEDING.
I'M SORRY ABOUT TODAY.

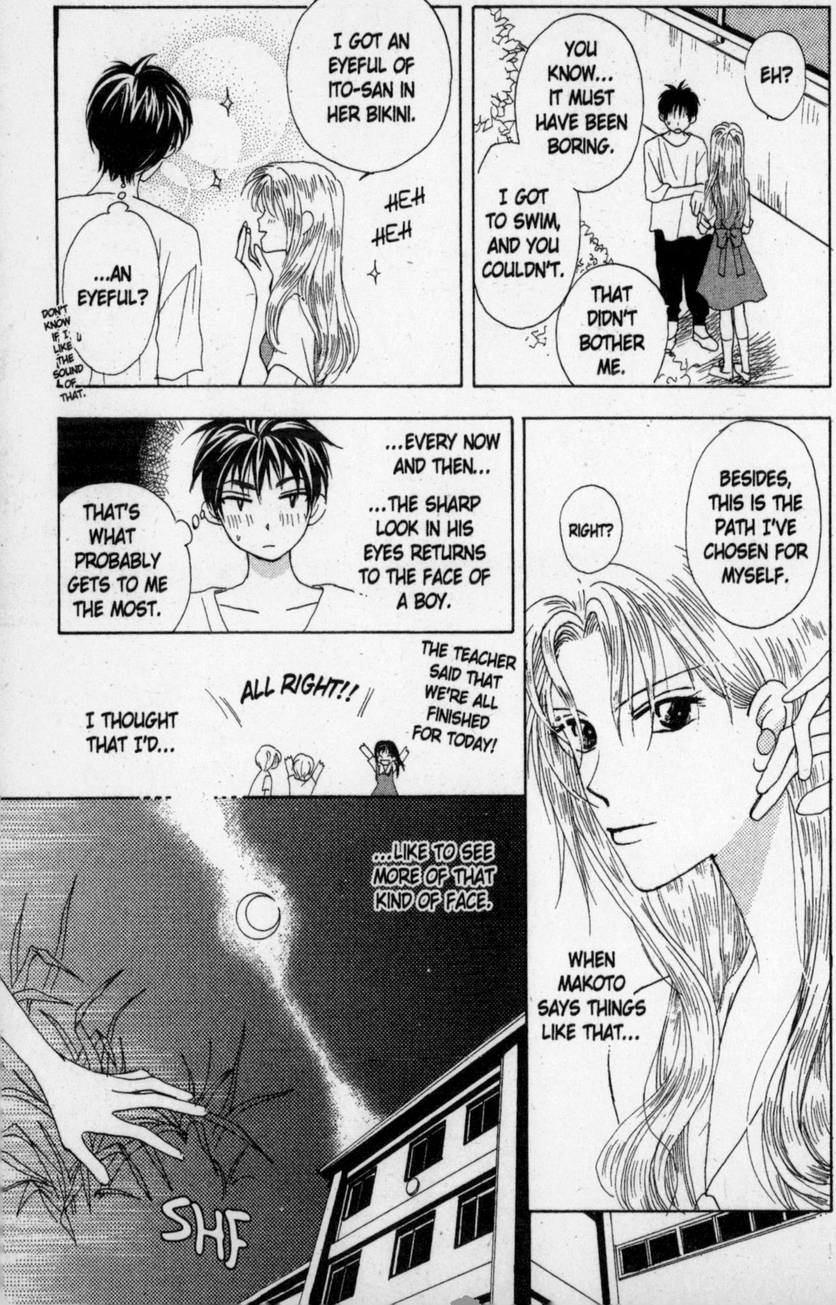
EH?
YOU KNOW... IT MUST HAVE BEEN BORING.
I GOT TO SWIM, AND YOU COULDN'T.
THAT DIDN'T BOTHER ME.
I GOT AN EYEFUL OF ITO-SAN IN HER BIKINI.
HEH HEH
...AN EYEFUL?
DON'T KNOW IF I LIKE THE SOUND OF THAT.
BESIDES, THIS IS THE PATH I'VE CHOSEN FOR MYSELF.
RIGHT?
WHEN MAKOTO SAYS THINGS LIKE THAT...
...EVERY NOW AND THEN...
...THE SHARP LOOK IN HIS EYES RETURNS TO THE FACE OF A BOY.
THAT'S WHAT PROBABLY GETS TO ME THE MOST.
THE TEACHER SAID THAT WE'RE ALL FINISHED FOR TODAY!
ALL RIGHT!!
I THOUGHT THAT I'D...
...LIKE TO SEE MORE OF THAT KIND OF FACE.
SHF

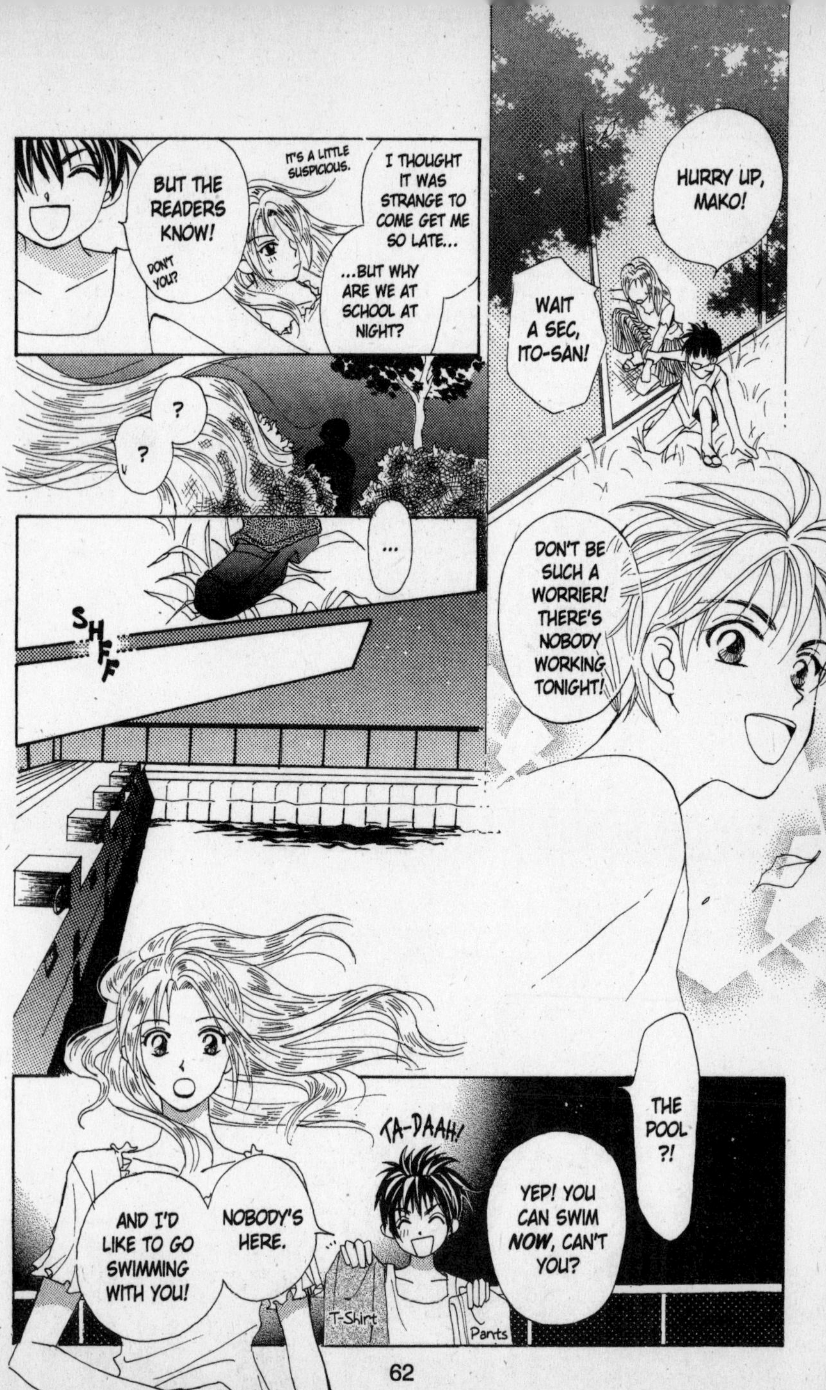
HURRY UP, MAKO!
WAIT A SEC, ITO-SAN!
DON'T BE SUCH A WORRIER! THERE'S NOBODY WORKING TONIGHT!
I THOUGHT IT WAS STRANGE TO COME GET ME SO LATE...
IT'S A LITTLE SUSPICIOUS.
...BUT WHY ARE WE AT SCHOOL AT NIGHT?
BUT THE READERS KNOW!
DON'T YOU?
?
?
...
SHFF
THE POOL ?!
YEP! YOU CAN SWIM NOW, CAN'T YOU?
TA-DAAH!
NOBODY'S HERE.
AND I'D LIKE TO GO SWIMMING WITH YOU!
T-Shirt
Pants

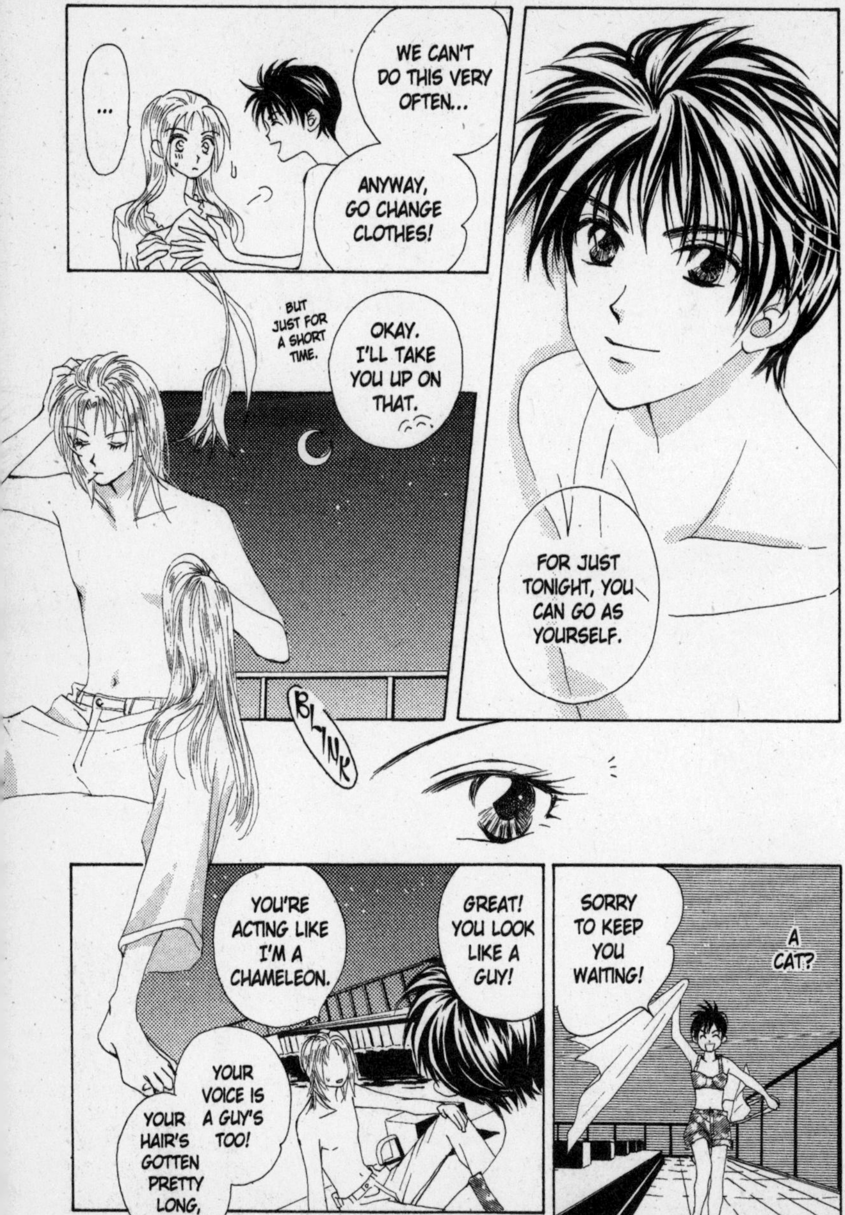
FOR JUST TONIGHT, YOU CAN GO AS YOURSELF.
WE CAN'T DO THIS VERY OFTEN...
ANYWAY, GO CHANGE CLOTHES!
...
OKAY. I'LL TAKE YOU UP ON THAT.
BUT JUST FOR A SHORT TIME.
BLINK
A CAT?
SORRY TO KEEP YOU WAITING!
GREAT! YOU LOOK LIKE A GUY!
YOU'RE ACTING LIKE I'M A CHAMELEON.
YOUR VOICE IS A GUY'S TOO!
YOUR HAIR'S GOTTEN PRETTY LONG, HUH?

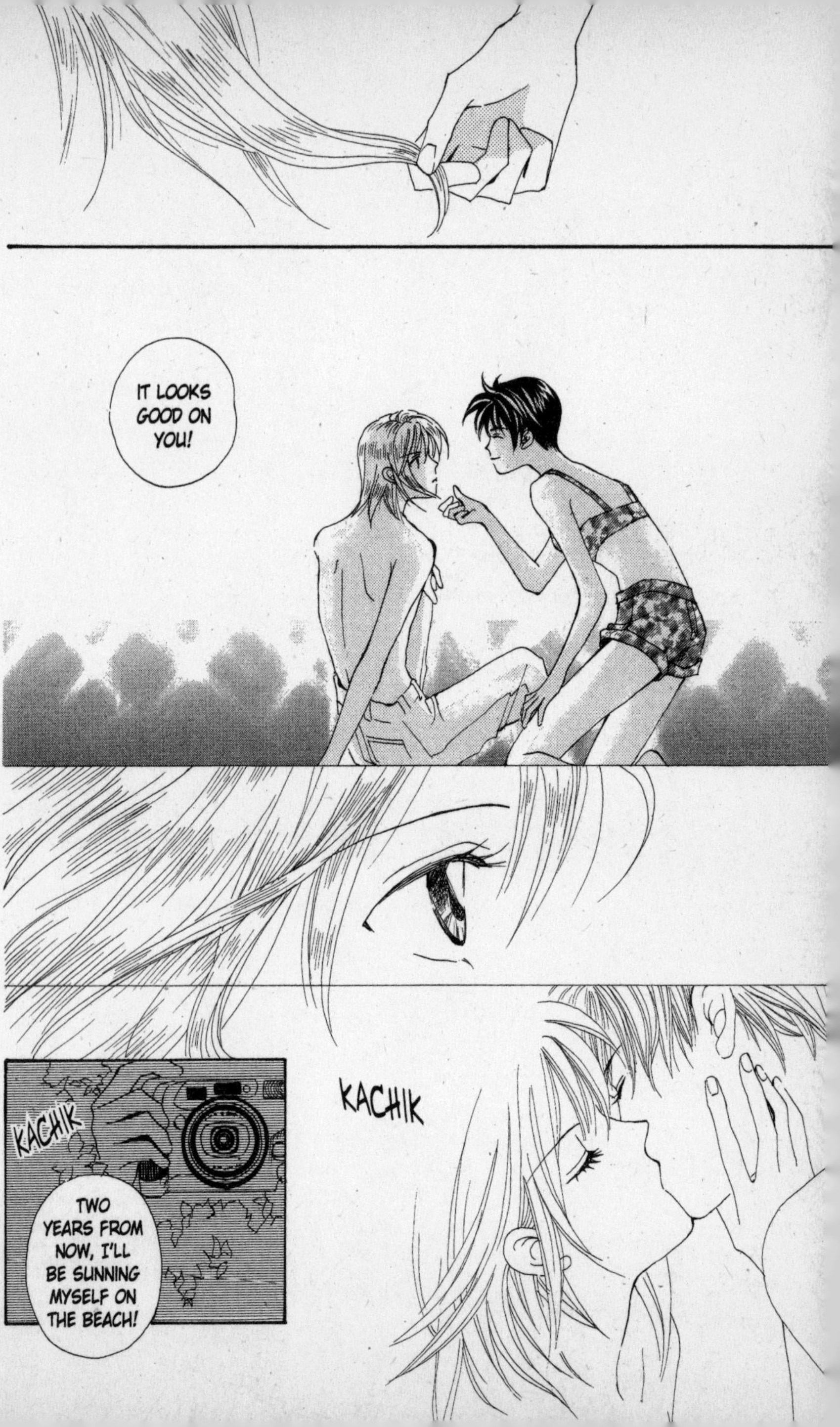
IT LOOKS GOOD ON YOU!
KACHIK
KACHIK
TWO YEARS FROM NOW, I'LL BE SUNNING MYSELF ON THE BEACH!

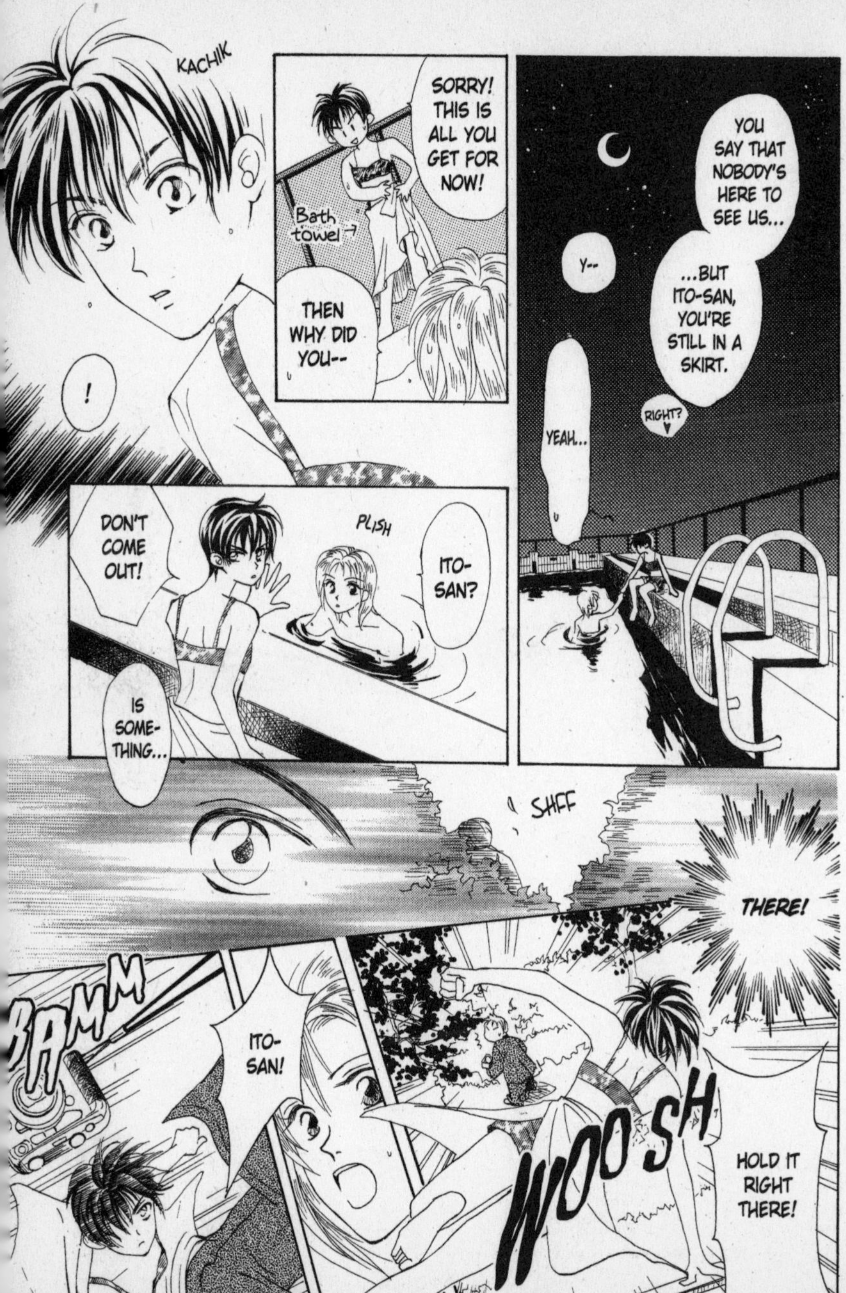
YOU SAY THAT NOBODY'S HERE TO SEE US...
Y--
...BUT ITO-SAN, YOU'RE STILL IN A SKIRT.
RIGHT?
YEAH...
SORRY! THIS IS ALL YOU GET FOR NOW!
Bath towel →
THEN WHY DID YOU--
KACHIK
!
ITO-SAN?
PLISH
DON'T COME OUT!
IS SOME-THING...
SHFF
THERE!
HOLD IT RIGHT THERE!
WOOSH
ITO-SAN!
BAMM

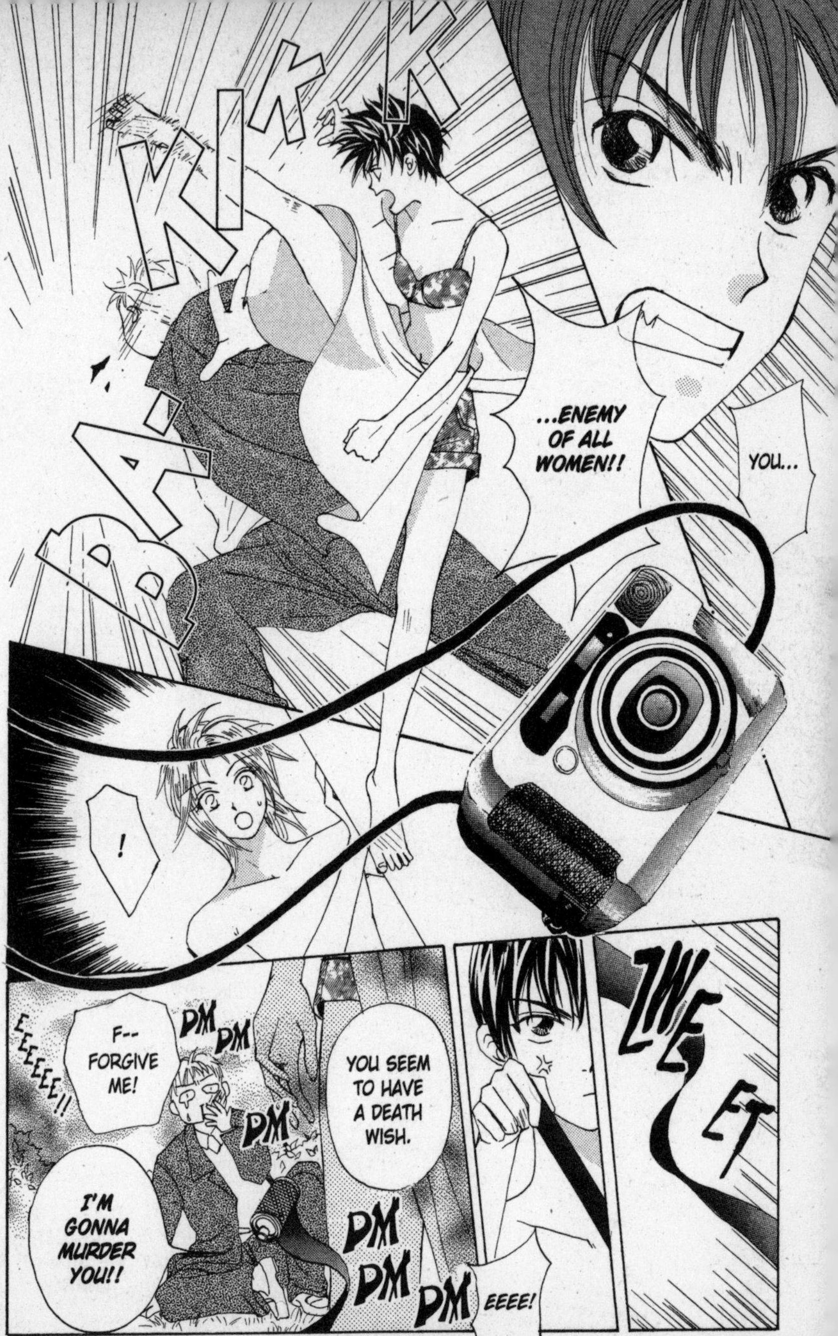

YOU...
...ENEMY OF ALL WOMEN!!
BA-KIKK
!
ZWEET
EEEE!
YOU SEEM TO HAVE A DEATH WISH.
DM DM DM DM DM DM
F-- FORGIVE ME!
I'M GONNA MURDER YOU!!
EEEEEE!!

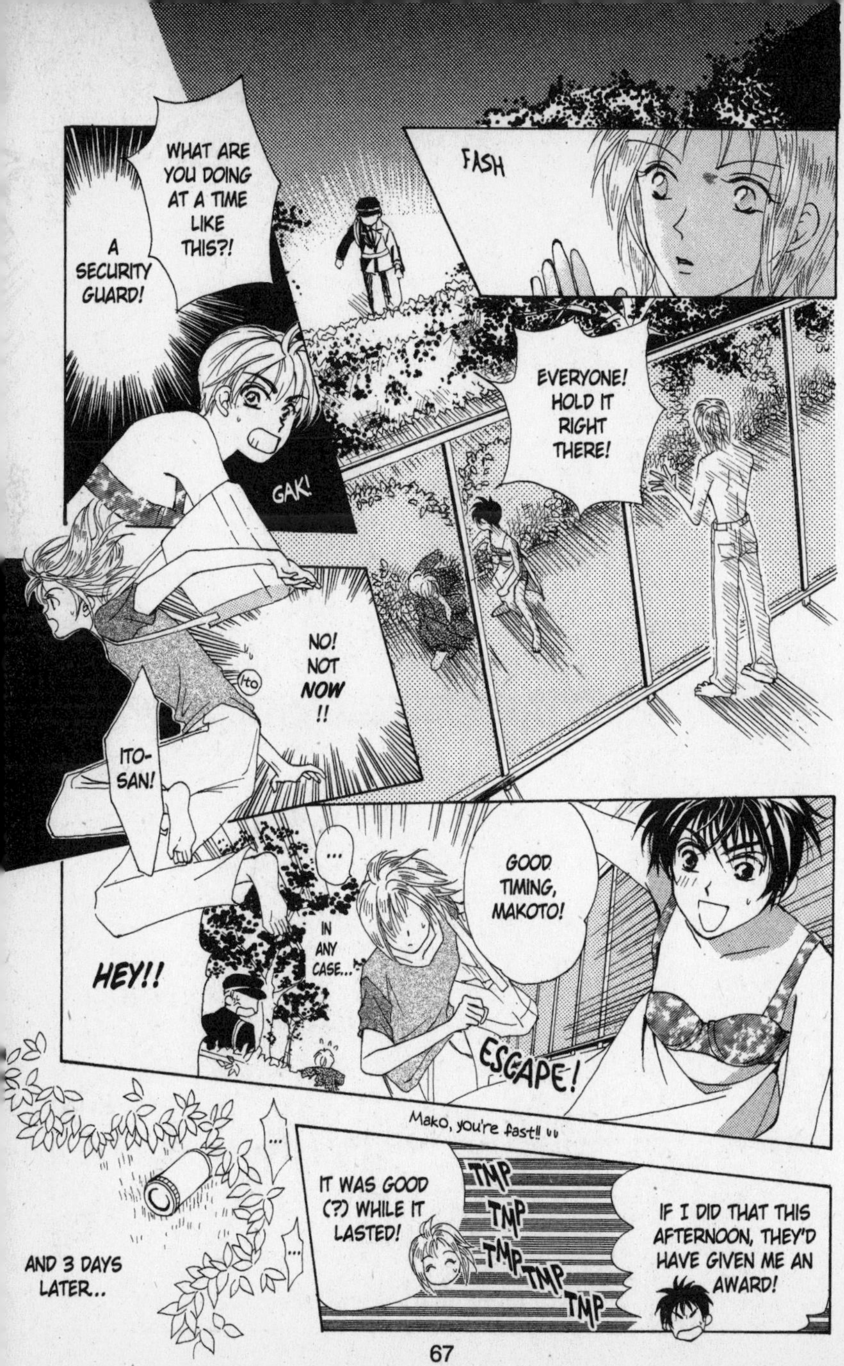
FASH
EVERYONE! HOLD IT RIGHT THERE!
WHAT ARE YOU DOING AT A TIME LIKE THIS?!
A SECURITY GUARD!
GAK!
NO! NOT NOW!!
Ito
ITO-SAN!
GOOD TIMING, MAKOTO!
ESCAPE!
...
IN ANY CASE...
HEY!!
Mako, you're fast!!
IF I DID THAT THIS AFTERNOON, THEY'D HAVE GIVEN ME AN AWARD!
TMP TMP TMP TMP TMP
IT WAS GOOD (?) WHILE IT LASTED!
...
...
AND 3 DAYS LATER...

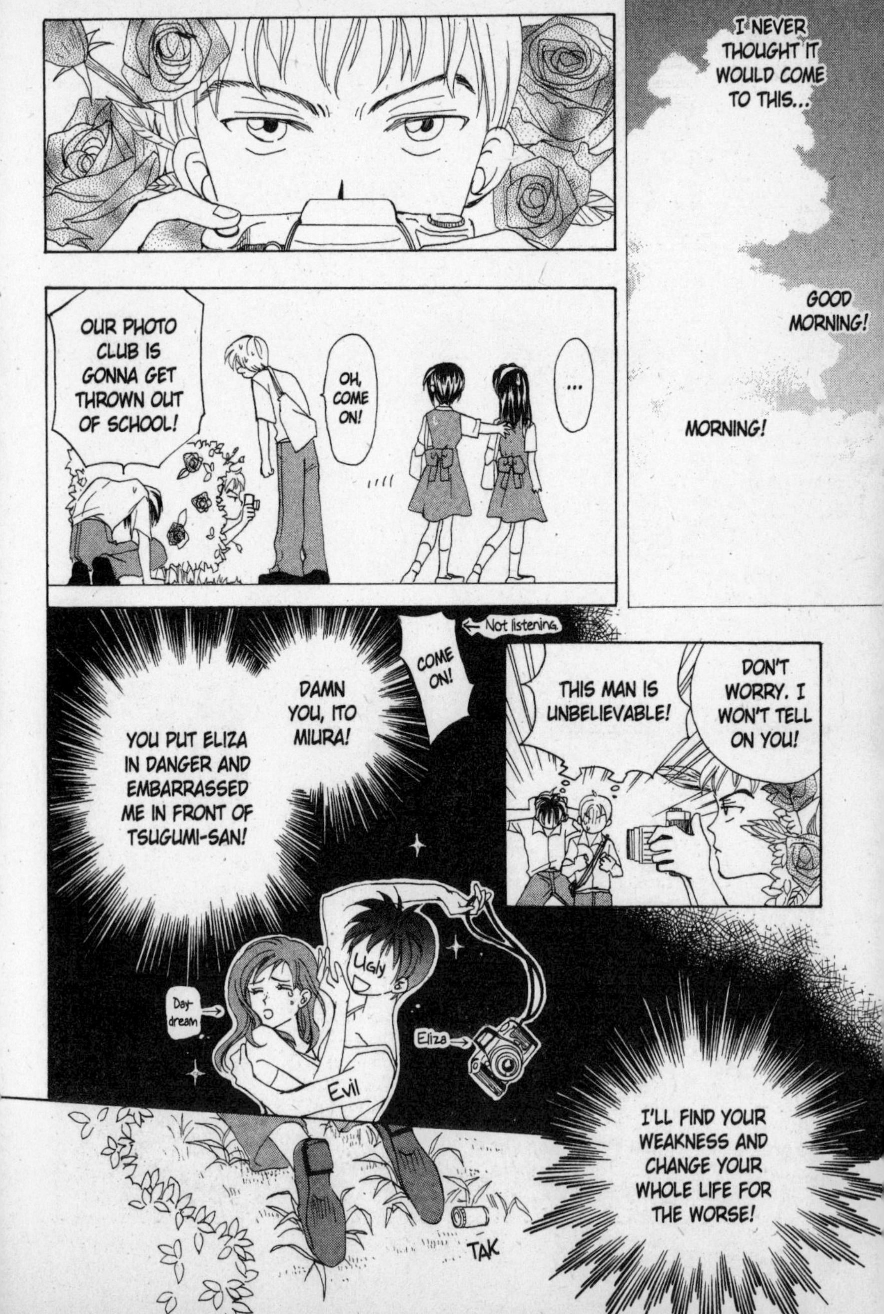

I NEVER THOUGHT IT WOULD COME TO THIS...
GOOD MORNING!
MORNING!
...
OH, COME ON!
OUR PHOTO CLUB IS GONNA GET THROWN OUT OF SCHOOL!
DON'T WORRY. I WON'T TELL ON YOU!
THIS MAN IS UNBELIEVABLE!
COME ON!
Not listening.
DAMN YOU, ITO MIURA!
YOU PUT ELIZA IN DANGER AND EMBARRASSED ME IN FRONT OF TSUGUMI-SAN!
Ugly
Day-dream
Eliza
Evil
I'LL FIND YOUR WEAKNESS AND CHANGE YOUR WHOLE LIFE FOR THE WORSE!
TAK

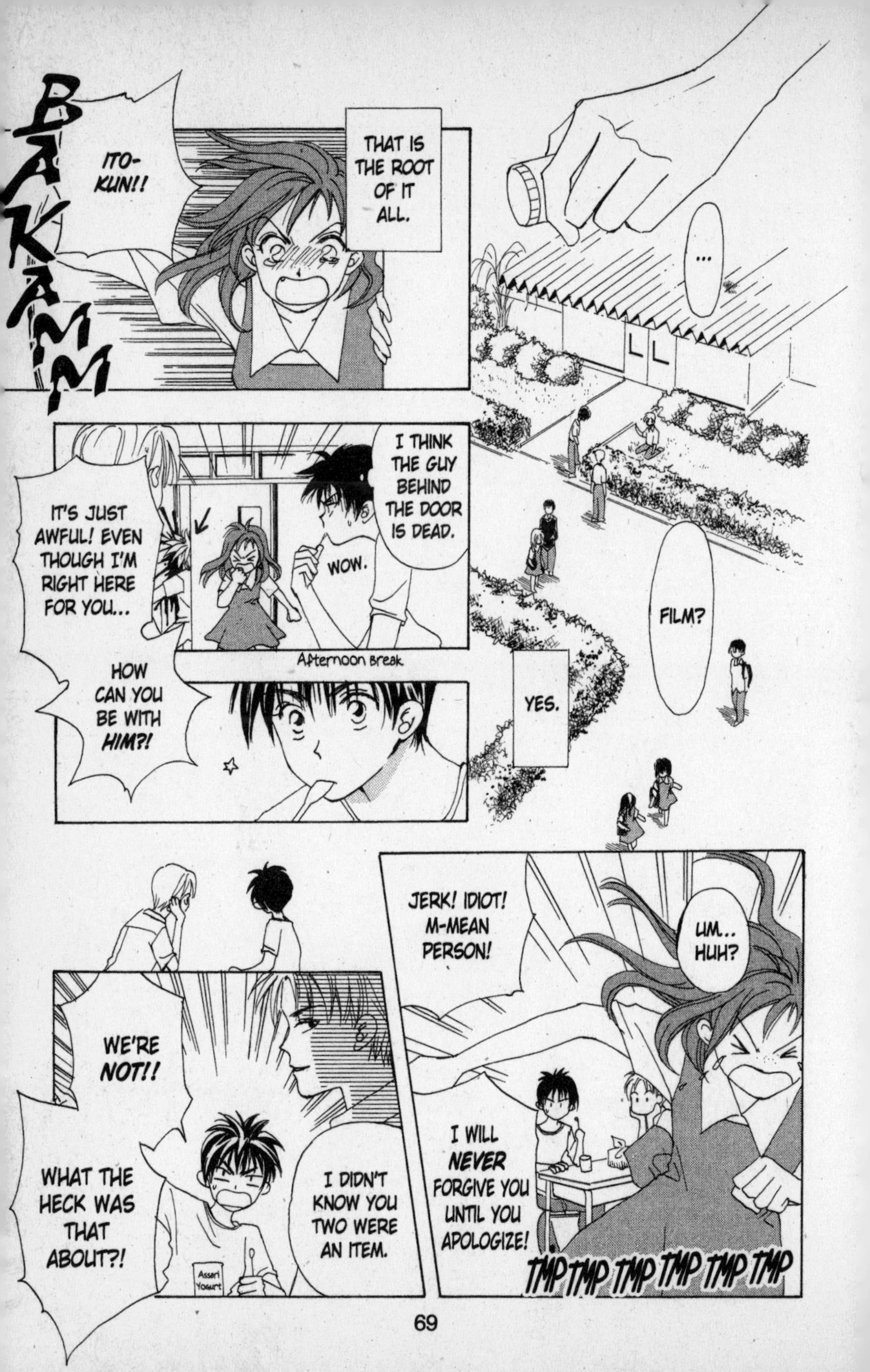
...
FILM?
YES.
THAT IS THE ROOT OF IT ALL.
ITO-KUN!!
BAKAMM
I THINK THE GUY BEHIND THE DOOR IS DEAD.
WOW.
Afternoon Break
IT'S JUST AWFUL! EVEN THOUGH I'M RIGHT HERE FOR YOU...
HOW CAN YOU BE WITH *HIM?!*
UM.. HUH?
JERK! IDIOT! M-MEAN PERSON!
I WILL *NEVER* FORGIVE YOU UNTIL YOU APOLOGIZE!
TMP TMP TMP TMP TMP TMP
WE'RE *NOT!!*
I DIDN'T KNOW YOU TWO WERE AN ITEM.
WHAT THE HECK WAS THAT ABOUT?!
Assari Yogurt

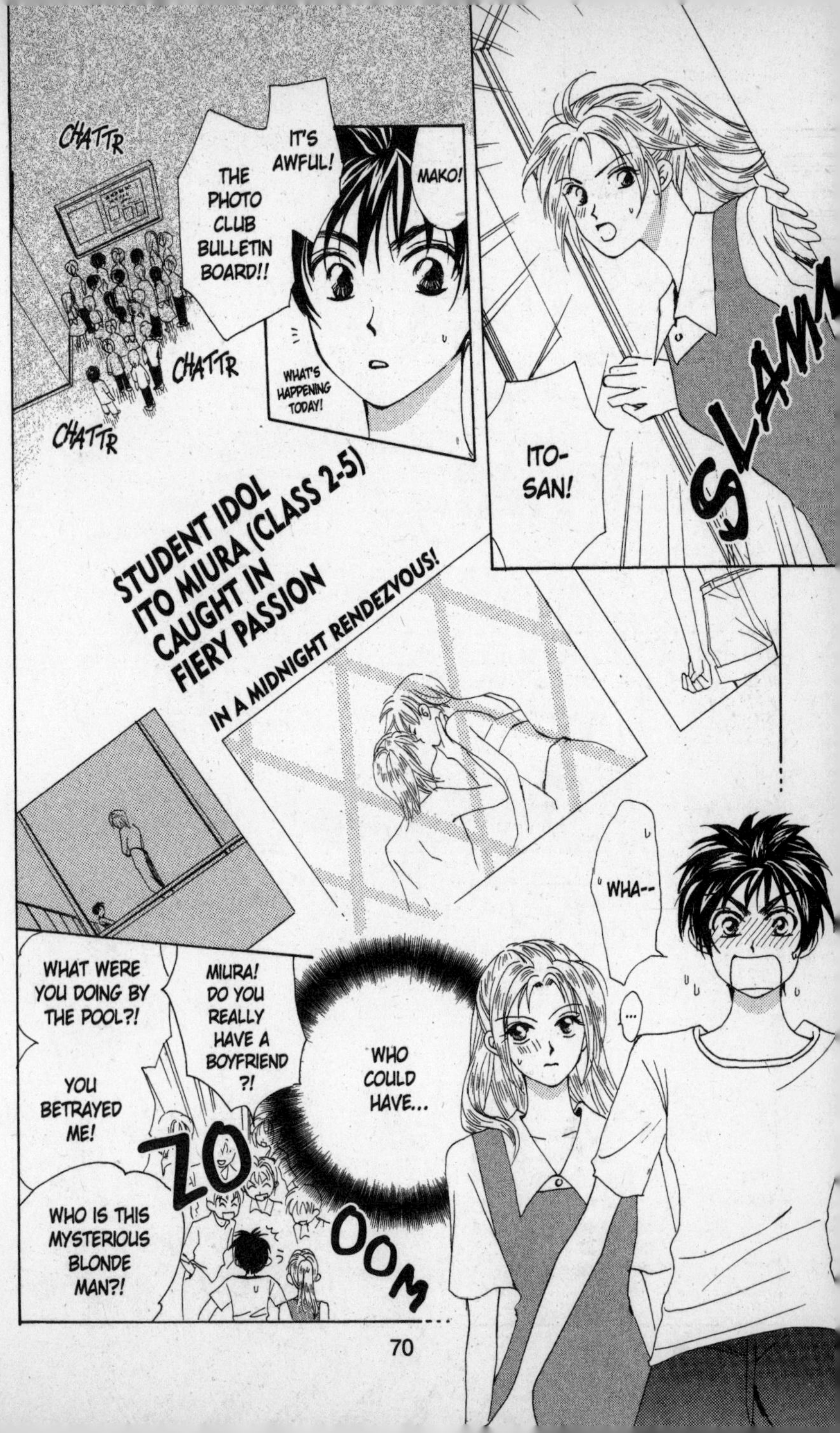
SLAM
ITO-SAN!
MAKO!
IT'S AWFUL!
THE PHOTO CLUB BULLETIN BOARD!!
WHAT'S HAPPENING TODAY!
CHATTR
CHATTR
CHATTR
STUDENT IDOL ITO MIURA (CLASS 2-5) CAUGHT IN FIERY PASSION
IN A MIDNIGHT RENDEZVOUS!
WHA--
...
WHO COULD HAVE...
MIURA! DO YOU REALLY HAVE A BOYFRIEND ?!
WHAT WERE YOU DOING BY THE POOL?!
YOU BETRAYED ME!
ZOOOM
WHO IS THIS MYSTERIOUS BLONDE MAN?!

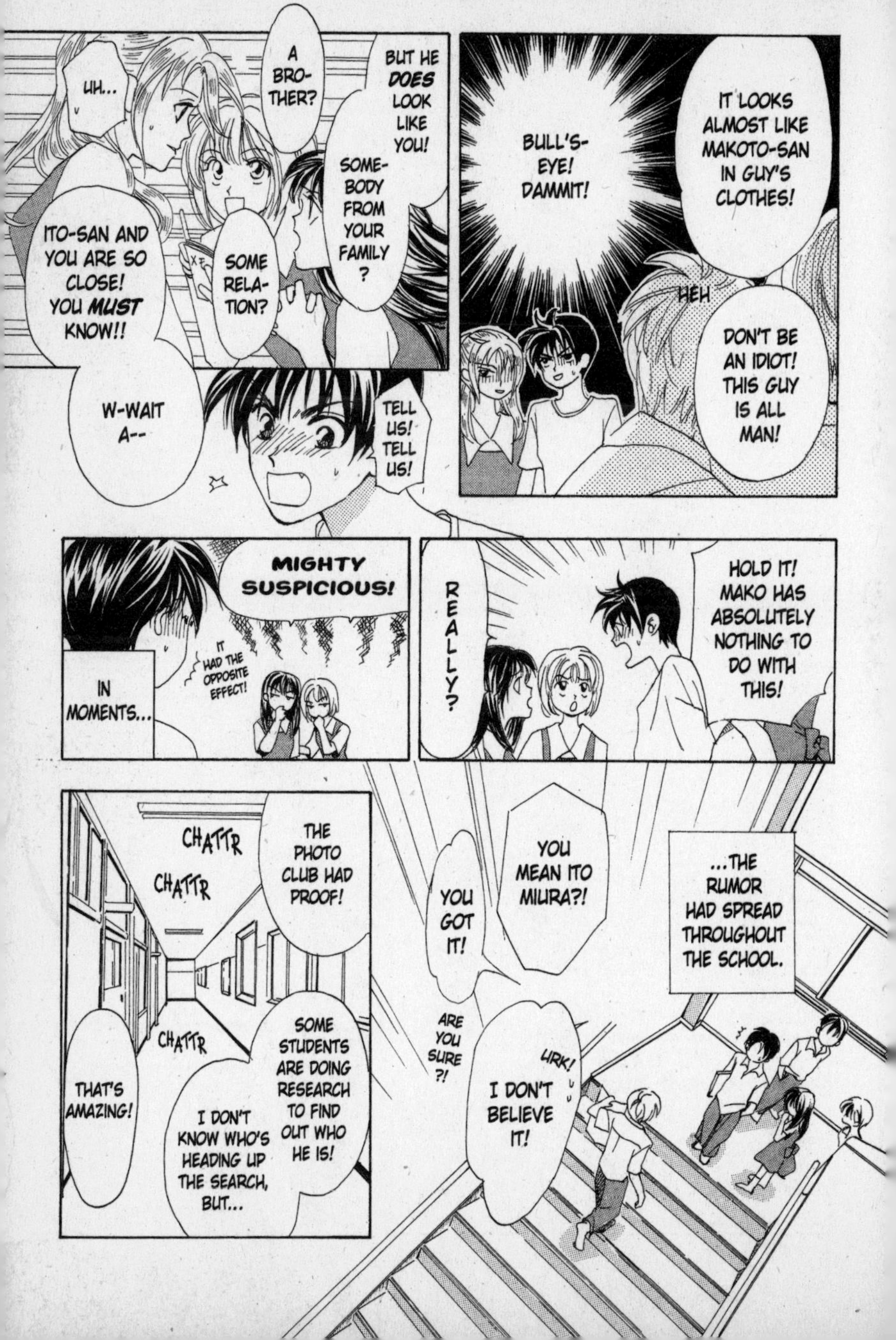
IT LOOKS ALMOST LIKE MAKOTO-SAN IN GUY'S CLOTHES!
BULL'S-EYE! DAMMIT!
HEH
DON'T BE AN IDIOT! THIS GUY IS ALL MAN!
BUT HE *DOES* LOOK LIKE YOU!
A BRO-THER?
SOME-BODY FROM YOUR FAMILY?
UH...
SOME RELA-TION?
ITO-SAN AND YOU ARE SO CLOSE! YOU *MUST* KNOW!!
TELL US! TELL US!
W-WAIT A--
HOLD IT! MAKO HAS ABSOLUTELY NOTHING TO DO WITH THIS!
REALLY?
MIGHTY SUSPICIOUS!
IT HAD THE OPPOSITE EFFECT!
IN MOMENTS...
...THE RUMOR HAD SPREAD THROUGHOUT THE SCHOOL.
YOU MEAN ITO MIURA?!
YOU GOT IT!
URK!
I DON'T BELIEVE IT!
ARE YOU SURE?!
THE PHOTO CLUB HAD PROOF!
CHATTR
CHATTR
CHATTR
SOME STUDENTS ARE DOING RESEARCH TO FIND OUT WHO HE IS!
I DON'T KNOW WHO'S HEADING UP THE SEARCH, BUT...
THAT'S AMAZING!

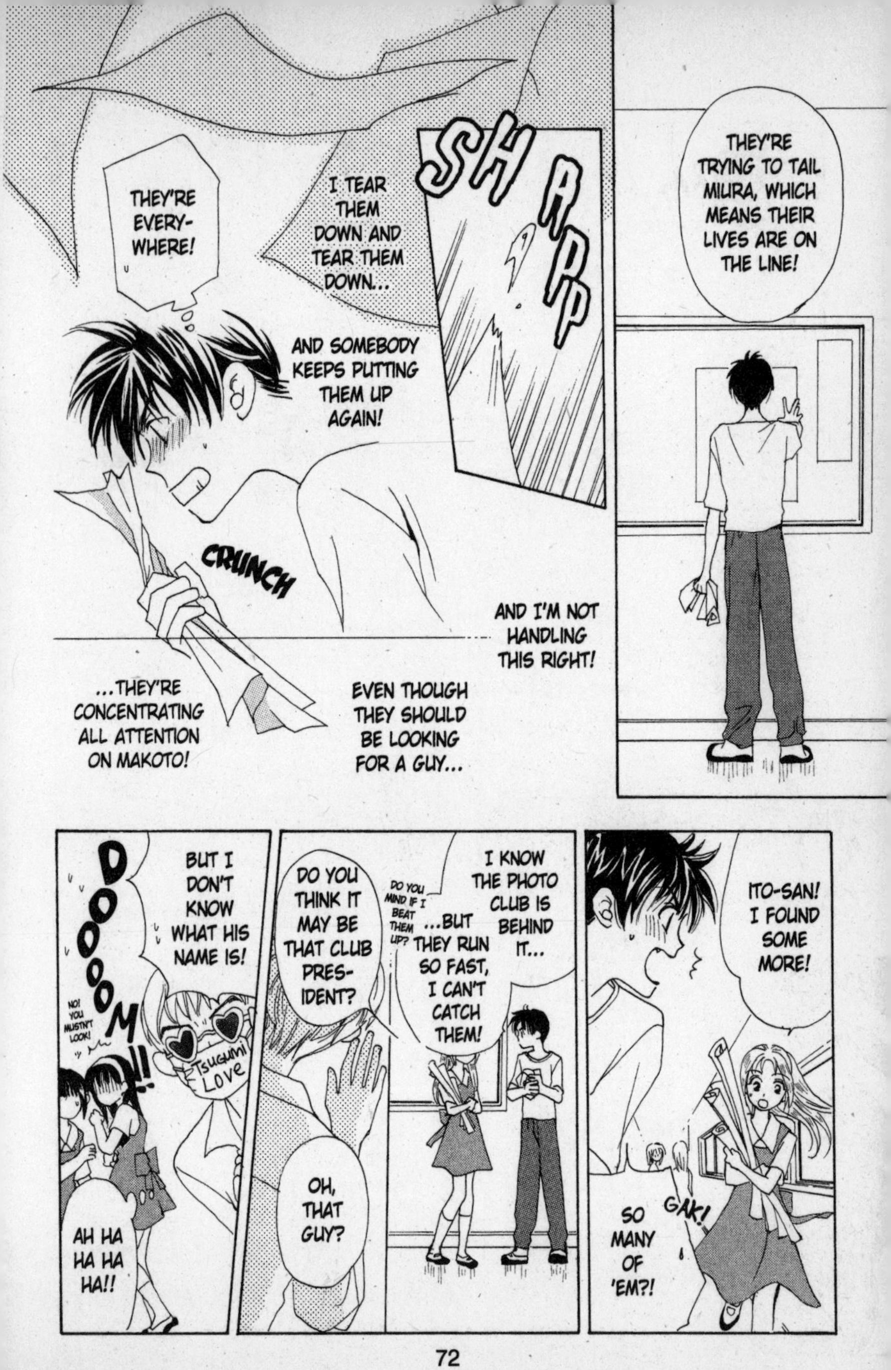
THEY'RE TRYING TO TAIL MIURA, WHICH MEANS THEIR LIVES ARE ON THE LINE!
SHAPP
I TEAR THEM DOWN AND TEAR THEM DOWN...
THEY'RE EVERY-WHERE!
AND SOMEBODY KEEPS PUTTING THEM UP AGAIN!
CRUNCH
AND I'M NOT HANDLING THIS RIGHT!
EVEN THOUGH THEY SHOULD BE LOOKING FOR A GUY...
...THEY'RE CONCENTRATING ALL ATTENTION ON MAKOTO!
ITO-SAN! I FOUND SOME MORE!
GAK!
SO MANY OF 'EM?!
I KNOW THE PHOTO CLUB IS BEHIND IT...
...BUT THEY RUN SO FAST, I CAN'T CATCH THEM!
DO YOU MIND IF I BEAT THEM UP?
DO YOU THINK IT MAY BE THAT CLUB PRES-IDENT?
OH, THAT GUY?
BUT I DON'T KNOW WHAT HIS NAME IS!
DOOOOOM!!
NO! YOU MUSTN'T LOOK!
Tsuguni Love
AH HA HA HA HA!!

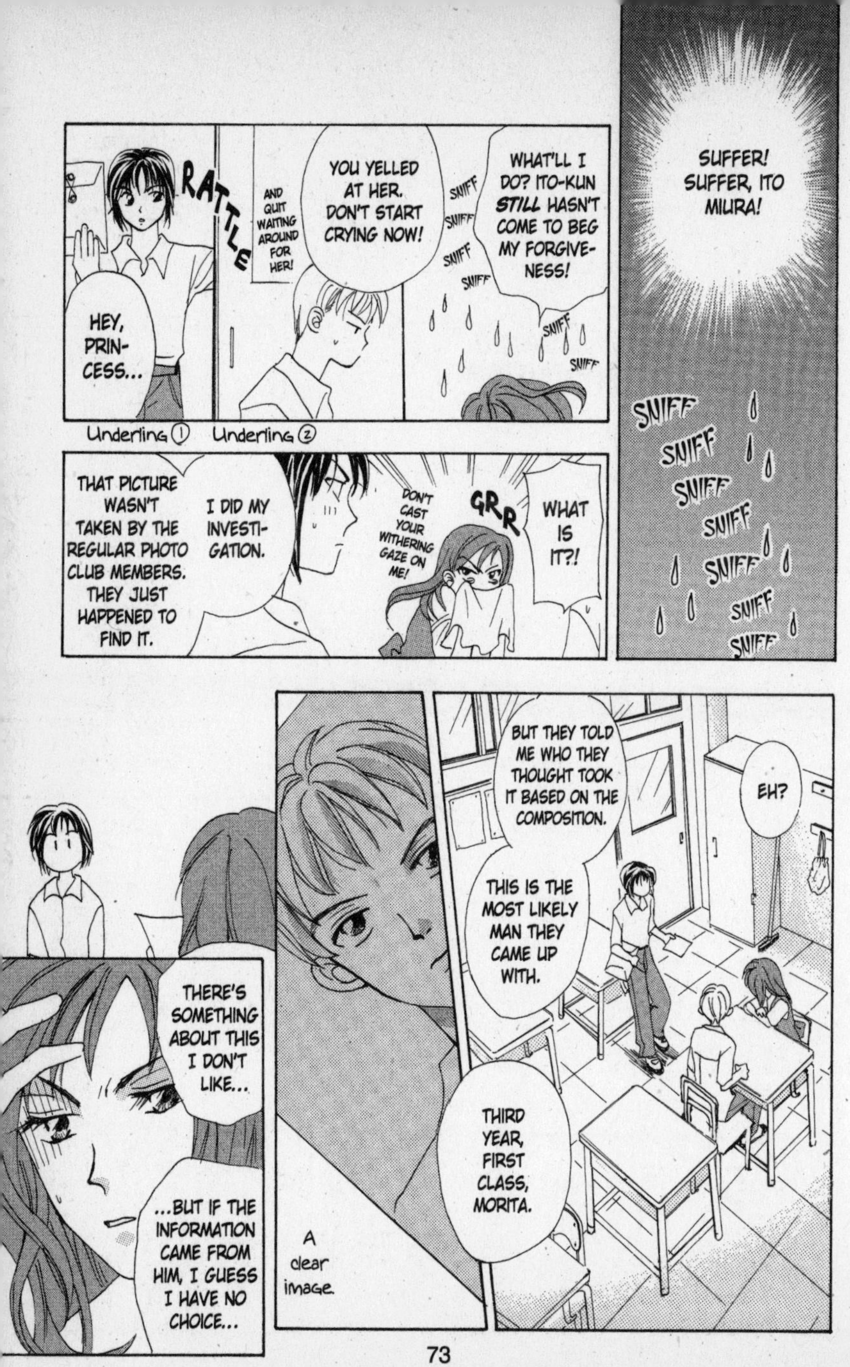
SUFFER! SUFFER, ITO MIURA!
SNIFF SNIFF SNIFF SNIFF SNIFF SNIFF SNIFF
WHAT'LL I DO? ITO-KUN *STILL* HASN'T COME TO BEG MY FORGIVENESS!
SNIFF SNIFF SNIFF SNIFF SNIFF SNIFF
YOU YELLED AT HER. DON'T START CRYING NOW!
AND QUIT WAITING AROUND FOR HER!
RATTLE
HEY, PRINCESS...
Underling ①
Underling ②
WHAT IS IT?!
GRR
DON'T CAST YOUR WITHERING GAZE ON ME!
I DID MY INVESTIGATION.
THAT PICTURE WASN'T TAKEN BY THE REGULAR PHOTO CLUB MEMBERS. THEY JUST HAPPENED TO FIND IT.
EH?
BUT THEY TOLD ME WHO THEY THOUGHT TOOK IT BASED ON THE COMPOSITION.
THIS IS THE MOST LIKELY MAN THEY CAME UP WITH.
THIRD YEAR, FIRST CLASS, MORITA.
A clear image.
THERE'S SOMETHING ABOUT THIS I DON'T LIKE...
...BUT IF THE INFORMATION CAME FROM HIM, I GUESS I HAVE NO CHOICE...

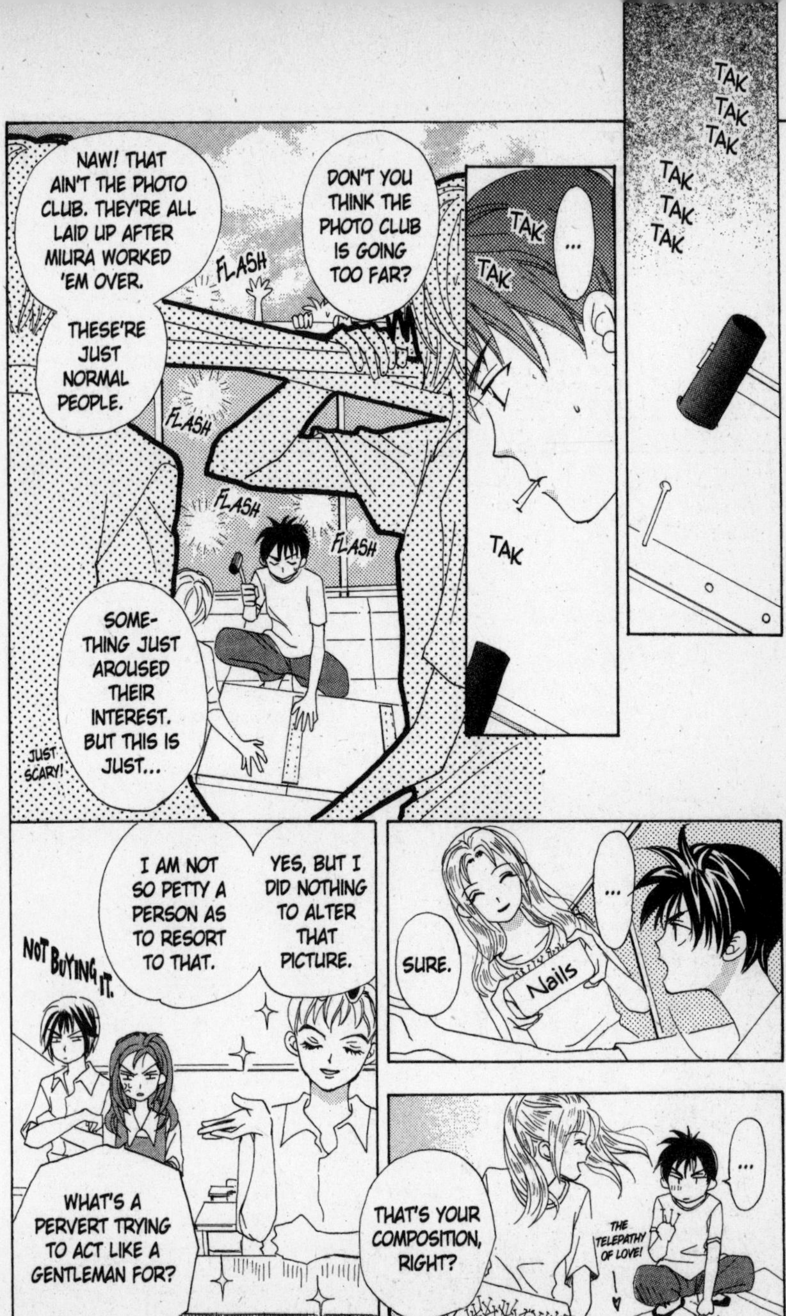
TAK
TAK
TAK
TAK
TAK
TAK
...
TAK
TAK
TAK
DON'T YOU THINK THE PHOTO CLUB IS GOING TOO FAR?
NAW! THAT AIN'T THE PHOTO CLUB. THEY'RE ALL LAID UP AFTER MIURA WORKED 'EM OVER.
FLASH
THESE'RE JUST NORMAL PEOPLE.
FLASH
FLASH
FLASH
SOME-THING JUST AROUSED THEIR INTEREST. BUT THIS IS JUST...
JUST SCARY!
...
SURE.
Nails
...
THAT'S YOUR COMPOSITION, RIGHT?
THE TELEPATHY OF LOVE!
YES, BUT I DID NOTHING TO ALTER THAT PICTURE.
I AM NOT SO PETTY A PERSON AS TO RESORT TO THAT.
NOT BUYING IT.
WHAT'S A PERVERT TRYING TO ACT LIKE A GENTLEMAN FOR?

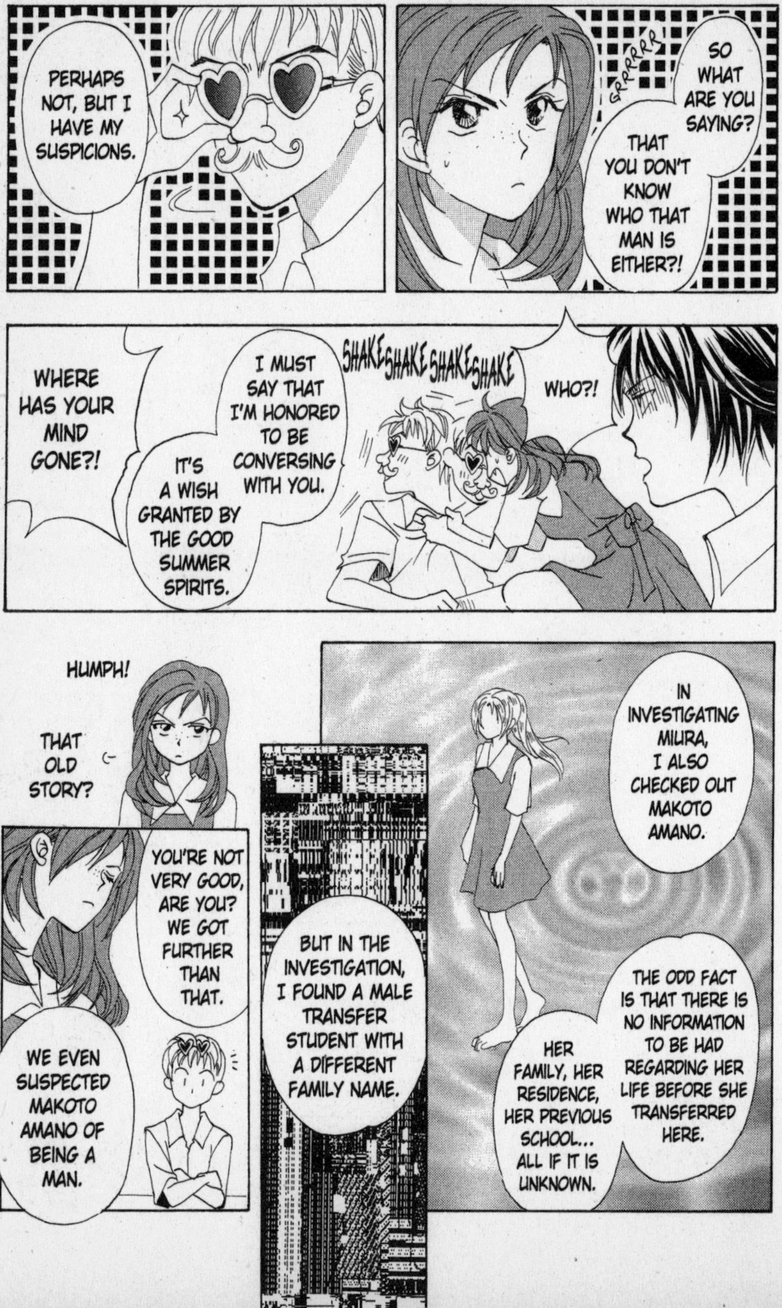
GRRRRRR
SO WHAT ARE YOU SAYING?
THAT YOU DON'T KNOW WHO THAT MAN IS EITHER?!
PERHAPS NOT, BUT I HAVE MY SUSPICIONS.
WHO?!
SHAKE SHAKE SHAKE SHAKE
I MUST SAY THAT I'M HONORED TO BE CONVERSING WITH YOU.
IT'S A WISH GRANTED BY THE GOOD SUMMER SPIRITS.
WHERE HAS YOUR MIND GONE?!
IN INVESTIGATING MIURA, I ALSO CHECKED OUT MAKOTO AMANO.
THE ODD FACT IS THAT THERE IS NO INFORMATION TO BE HAD REGARDING HER LIFE BEFORE SHE TRANSFERRED HERE.
HER FAMILY, HER RESIDENCE, HER PREVIOUS SCHOOL... ALL IF IT IS UNKNOWN.
BUT IN THE INVESTIGATION, I FOUND A MALE TRANSFER STUDENT WITH A DIFFERENT FAMILY NAME.
HUMPH!
THAT OLD STORY?
YOU'RE NOT VERY GOOD, ARE YOU? WE GOT FURTHER THAN THAT.
WE EVEN SUSPECTED MAKOTO AMANO OF BEING A MAN.

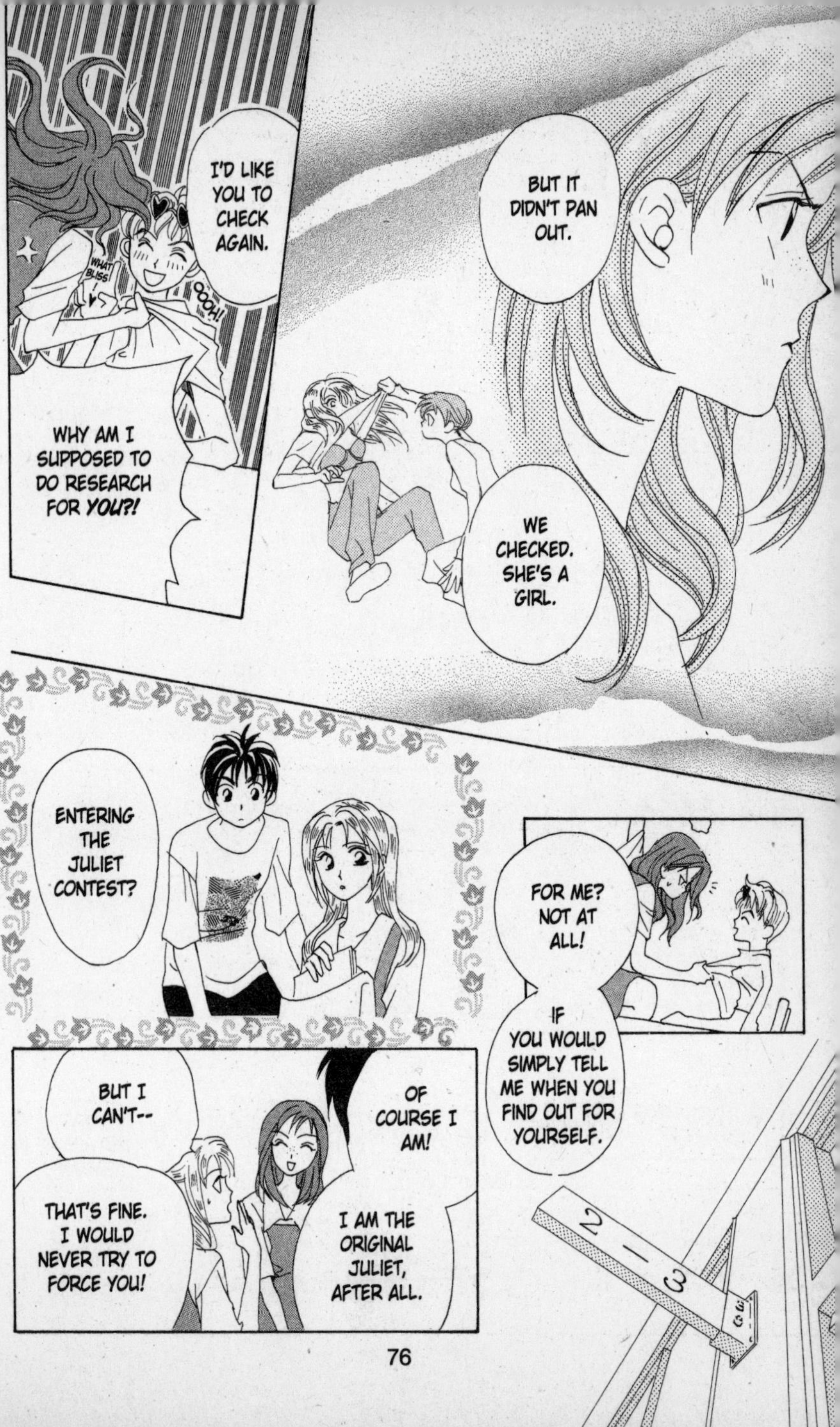
BUT IT DIDN'T PAN OUT.
WE CHECKED. SHE'S A GIRL.
I'D LIKE YOU TO CHECK AGAIN.
WHAT BLISS!
OOOH!
WHY AM I SUPPOSED TO DO RESEARCH FOR *YOU?!*
FOR ME? NOT AT ALL!
IF YOU WOULD SIMPLY TELL ME WHEN YOU FIND OUT FOR YOURSELF.
ENTERING THE JULIET CONTEST?
2-3
OF COURSE I AM!
I AM THE ORIGINAL JULIET, AFTER ALL.
BUT I CAN'T--
THAT'S FINE. I WOULD NEVER TRY TO FORCE YOU!

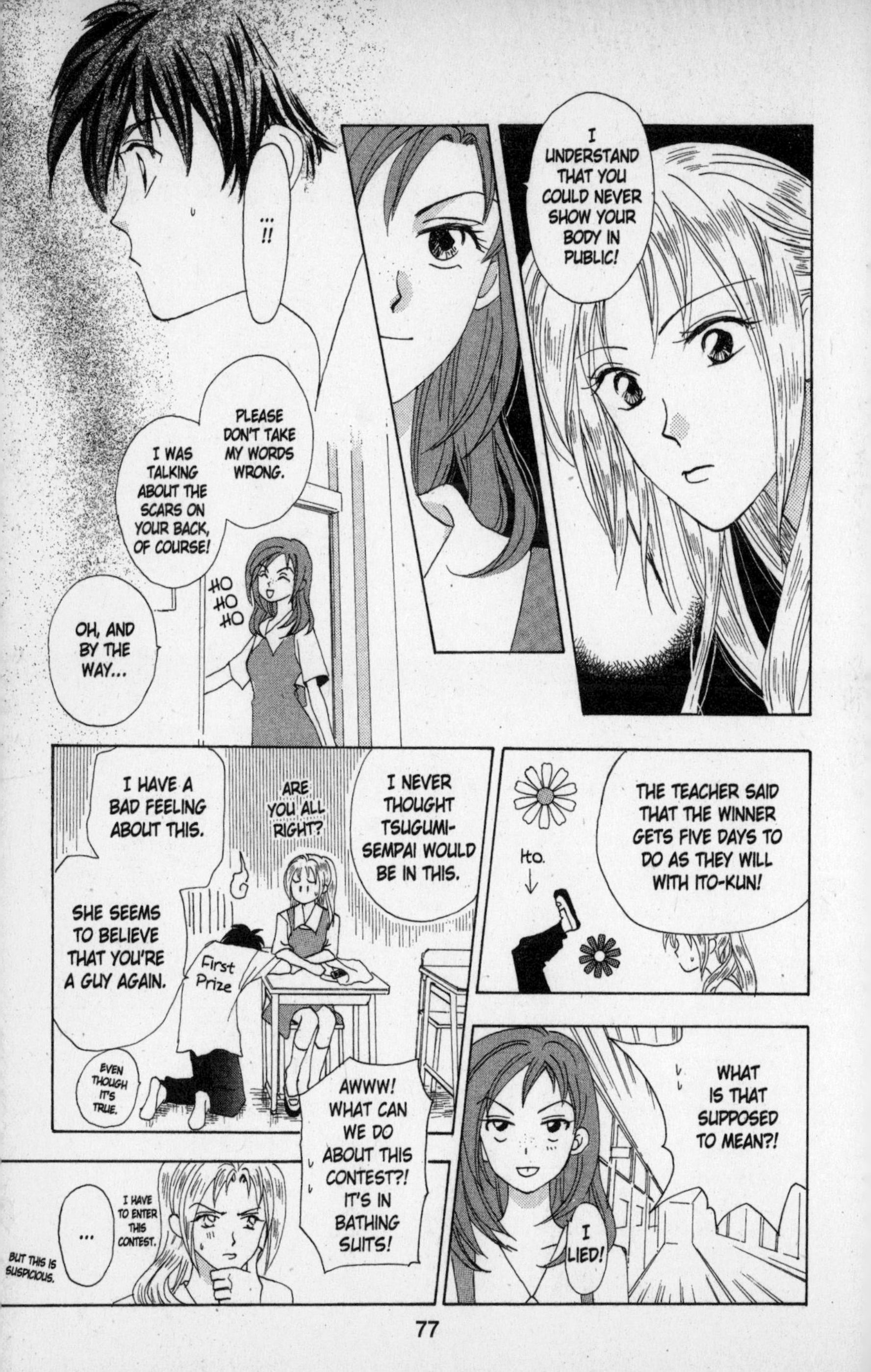
I UNDERSTAND THAT YOU COULD NEVER SHOW YOUR BODY IN PUBLIC!
...!!
PLEASE DON'T TAKE MY WORDS WRONG.
I WAS TALKING ABOUT THE SCARS ON YOUR BACK, OF COURSE!
HO HO HO
OH, AND BY THE WAY...
THE TEACHER SAID THAT THE WINNER GETS FIVE DAYS TO DO AS THEY WILL WITH ITO-KUN!
Ito.
I NEVER THOUGHT TSUGUMI-SEMPAI WOULD BE IN THIS.
ARE YOU ALL RIGHT?
I HAVE A BAD FEELING ABOUT THIS.
SHE SEEMS TO BELIEVE THAT YOU'RE A GUY AGAIN.
First Prize
EVEN THOUGH IT'S TRUE.
WHAT IS THAT SUPPOSED TO MEAN?!
I LIED!
AWWW! WHAT CAN WE DO ABOUT THIS CONTEST?! IT'S IN BATHING SUITS!
I HAVE TO ENTER THIS CONTEST.
...
BUT THIS IS SUSPICIOUS.

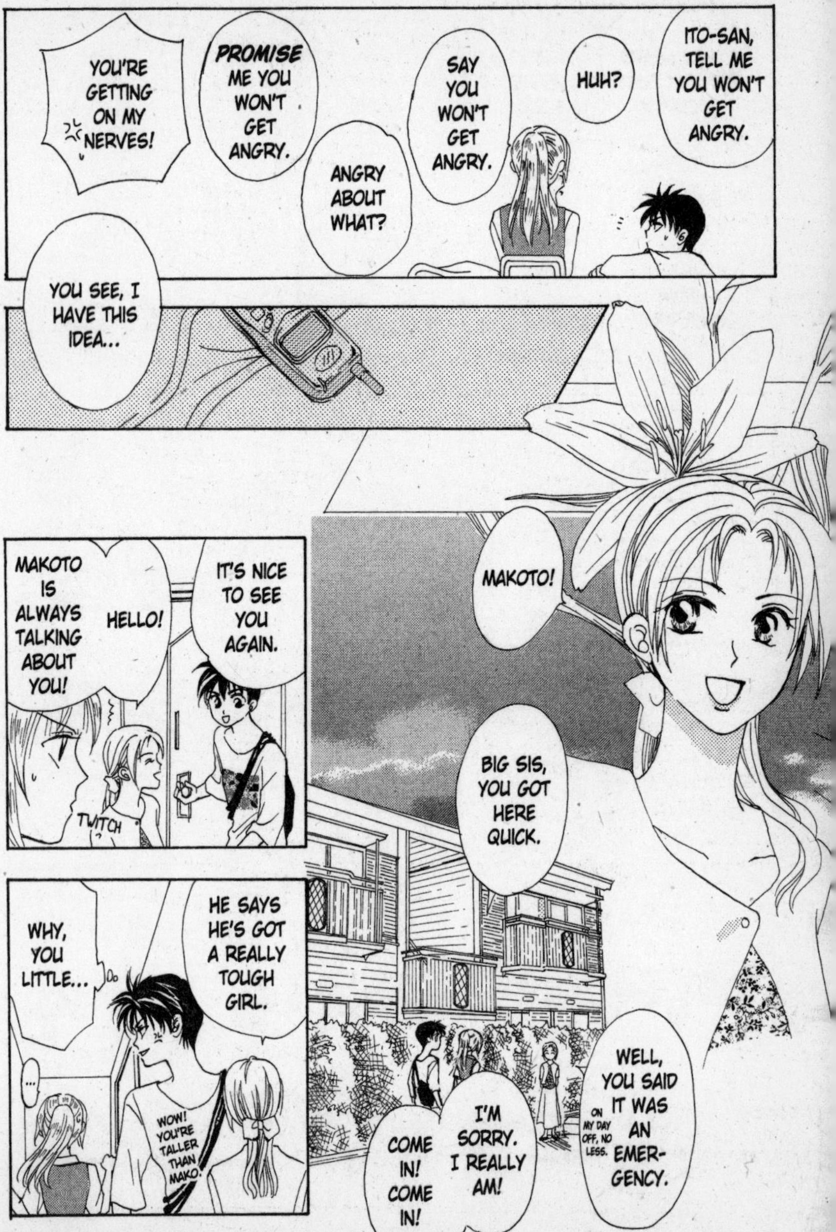
ITO-SAN, TELL ME YOU WON'T GET ANGRY.
HUH?
SAY YOU WON'T GET ANGRY.
ANGRY ABOUT WHAT?
PROMISE ME YOU WON'T GET ANGRY.
YOU'RE GETTING ON MY NERVES!
YOU SEE, I HAVE THIS IDEA...
MAKOTO!
BIG SIS, YOU GOT HERE QUICK.
WELL, YOU SAID IT WAS AN EMERGENCY.
ON MY DAY OFF, NO LESS.
I'M SORRY. I REALLY AM!
COME IN! COME IN!
IT'S NICE TO SEE YOU AGAIN.
HELLO!
MAKOTO IS ALWAYS TALKING ABOUT YOU!
TWITCH
HE SAYS HE'S GOT A REALLY TOUGH GIRL.
WHY, YOU LITTLE...
WOW! YOU'RE TALLER THAN MAKO.
...

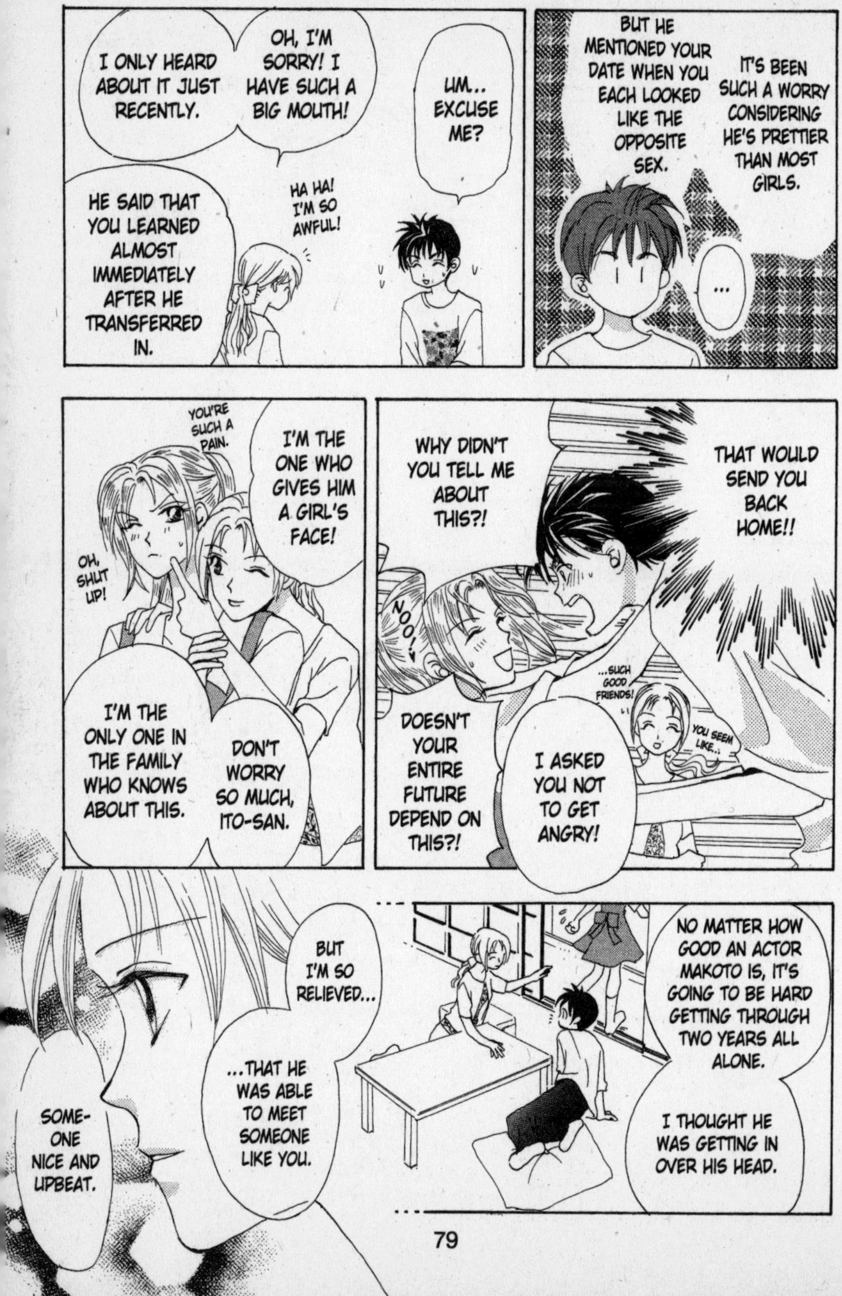
IT'S BEEN SUCH A WORRY CONSIDERING HE'S PRETTIER THAN MOST GIRLS.
BUT HE MENTIONED YOUR DATE WHEN YOU EACH LOOKED LIKE THE OPPOSITE SEX.
...
UM... EXCUSE ME?
OH, I'M SORRY! I HAVE SUCH A BIG MOUTH!
I ONLY HEARD ABOUT IT JUST RECENTLY.
HA HA! I'M SO AWFUL!
HE SAID THAT YOU LEARNED ALMOST IMMEDIATELY AFTER HE TRANSFERRED IN.
THAT WOULD SEND YOU BACK HOME!!
WHY DIDN'T YOU TELL ME ABOUT THIS?!
NOO!
YOU SEEM LIKE...
...SUCH GOOD FRIENDS!
I ASKED YOU NOT TO GET ANGRY!
DOESN'T YOUR ENTIRE FUTURE DEPEND ON THIS?!
I'M THE ONE WHO GIVES HIM A GIRL'S FACE!
YOU'RE SUCH A PAIN.
OH, SHUT UP!
DON'T WORRY SO MUCH, ITO-SAN.
I'M THE ONLY ONE IN THE FAMILY WHO KNOWS ABOUT THIS.
NO MATTER HOW GOOD AN ACTOR MAKOTO IS, IT'S GOING TO BE HARD GETTING THROUGH TWO YEARS ALL ALONE.
I THOUGHT HE WAS GETTING IN OVER HIS HEAD.
BUT I'M SO RELIEVED...
...THAT HE WAS ABLE TO MEET SOMEONE LIKE YOU.
SOME-ONE NICE AND UPBEAT.

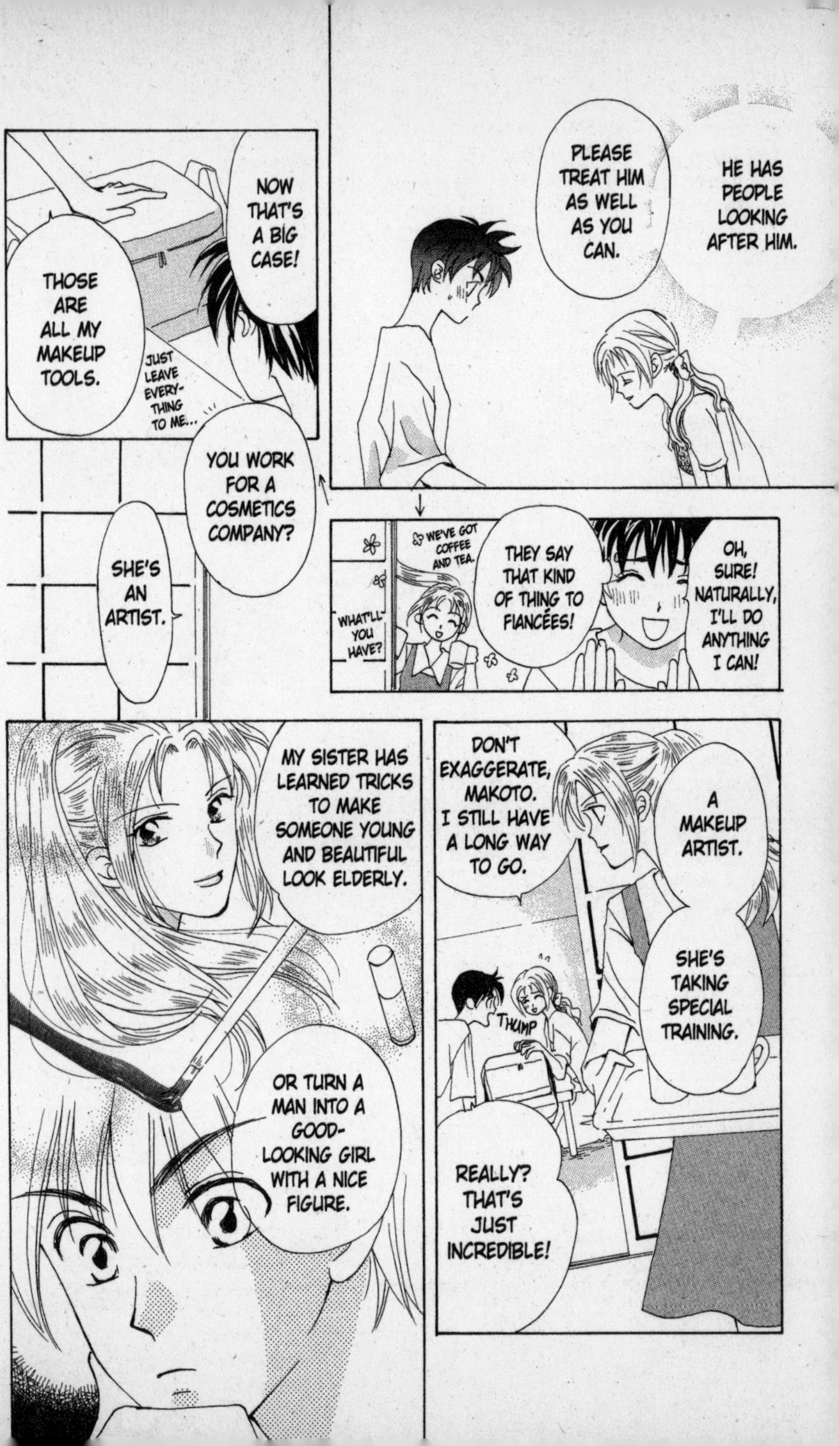
HE HAS PEOPLE LOOKING AFTER HIM.
PLEASE TREAT HIM AS WELL AS YOU CAN.
OH, SURE! NATURALLY, I'LL DO ANYTHING I CAN!
THEY SAY THAT KIND OF THING TO FIANCÉES!
WE'VE GOT COFFEE AND TEA.
WHAT'LL YOU HAVE?
NOW THAT'S A BIG CASE!
THOSE ARE ALL MY MAKEUP TOOLS.
JUST LEAVE EVERY-THING TO ME...
YOU WORK FOR A COSMETICS COMPANY?
SHE'S AN ARTIST.
A MAKEUP ARTIST.
DON'T EXAGGERATE, MAKOTO. I STILL HAVE A LONG WAY TO GO.
SHE'S TAKING SPECIAL TRAINING.
THUMP
REALLY? THAT'S JUST INCREDIBLE!
MY SISTER HAS LEARNED TRICKS TO MAKE SOMEONE YOUNG AND BEAUTIFUL LOOK ELDERLY.
OR TURN A MAN INTO A GOOD-LOOKING GIRL WITH A NICE FIGURE.

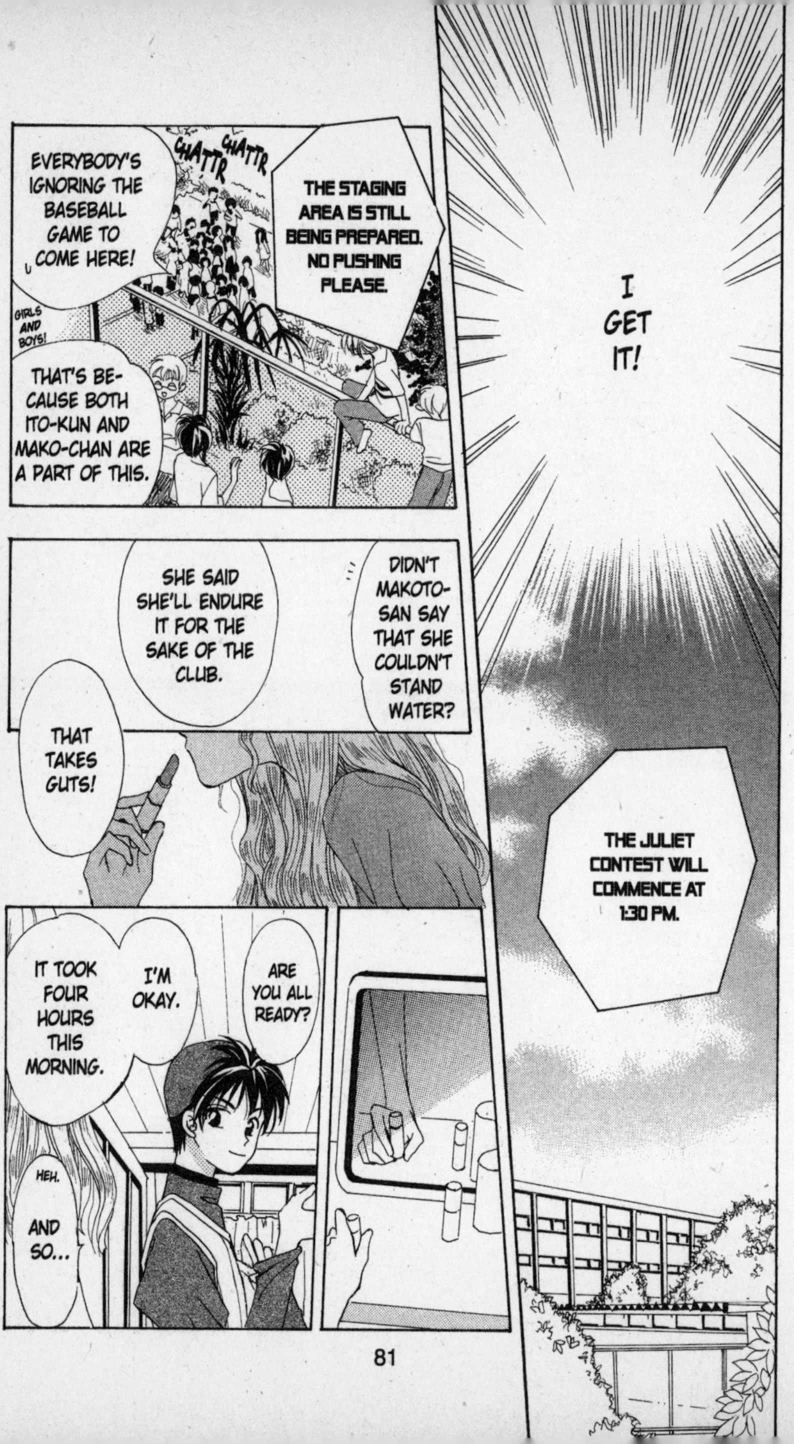
I GET IT!
THE JULIET CONTEST WILL COMMENCE AT 1:30 PM.
CHATTR CHATTR
THE STAGING AREA IS STILL BEING PREPARED. NO PUSHING PLEASE.
EVERYBODY'S IGNORING THE BASEBALL GAME TO COME HERE!
GIRLS AND BOYS!
THAT'S BE-CAUSE BOTH ITO-KUN AND MAKO-CHAN ARE A PART OF THIS.
DIDN'T MAKOTO-SAN SAY THAT SHE COULDN'T STAND WATER?
SHE SAID SHE'LL ENDURE IT FOR THE SAKE OF THE CLUB.
THAT TAKES GUTS!
ARE YOU ALL READY?
I'M OKAY.
IT TOOK FOUR HOURS THIS MORNING.
HEH.
AND SO...

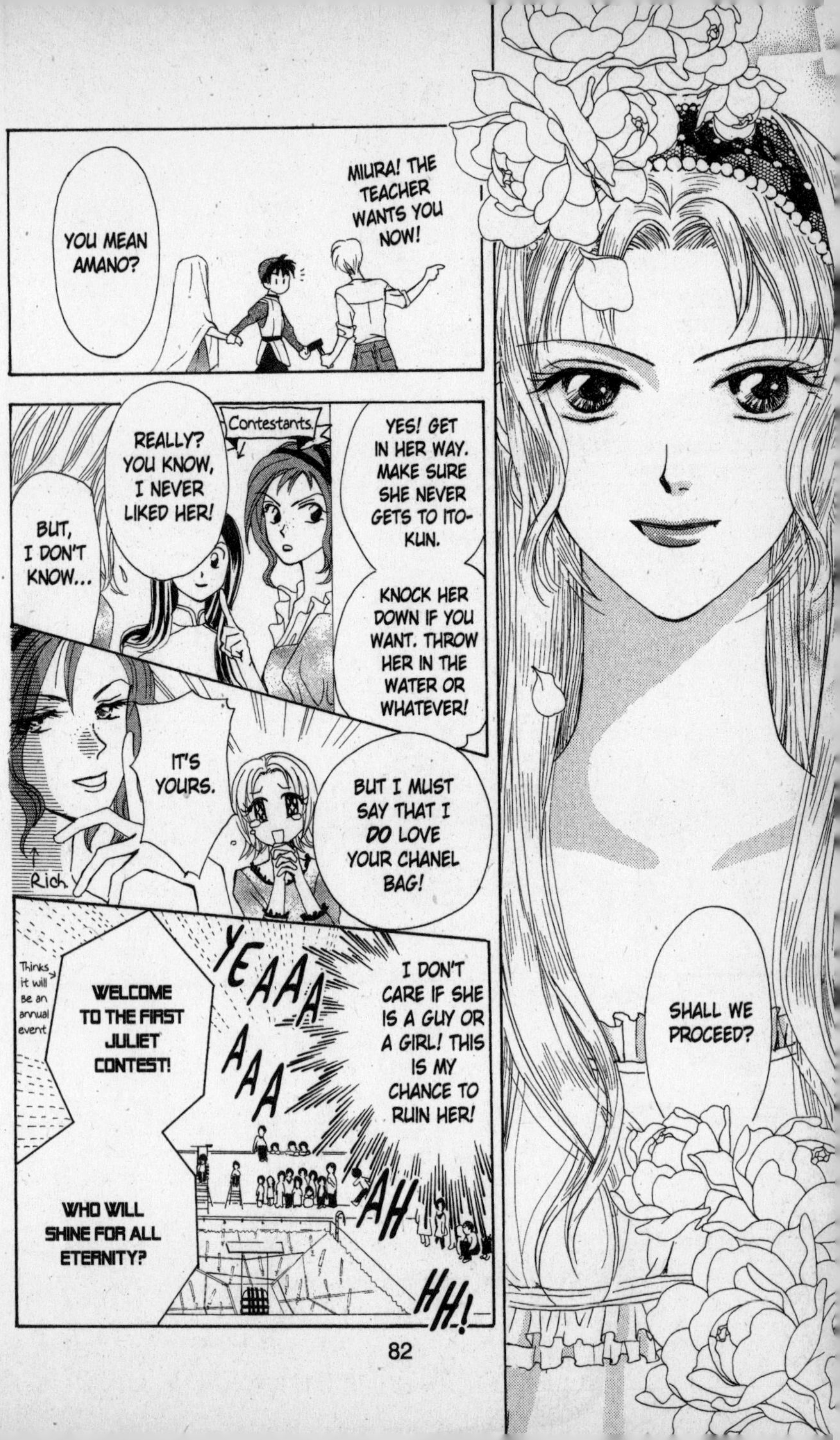
SHALL WE PROCEED?
MIURA! THE TEACHER WANTS YOU NOW!
YOU MEAN AMANO?
YES! GET IN HER WAY. MAKE SURE SHE NEVER GETS TO ITO-KUN.
KNOCK HER DOWN IF YOU WANT. THROW HER IN THE WATER OR WHATEVER!
Contestants.
REALLY? YOU KNOW, I NEVER LIKED HER!
BUT, I DON'T KNOW...
BUT I MUST SAY THAT I DO LOVE YOUR CHANEL BAG!
IT'S YOURS.
Rich.
I DON'T CARE IF SHE IS A GUY OR A GIRL! THIS IS MY CHANCE TO RUIN HER!
YEAAAAAAAHH!
WELCOME TO THE FIRST JULIET CONTEST!
Thinks it will be an annual event
WHO WILL SHINE FOR ALL ETERNITY?

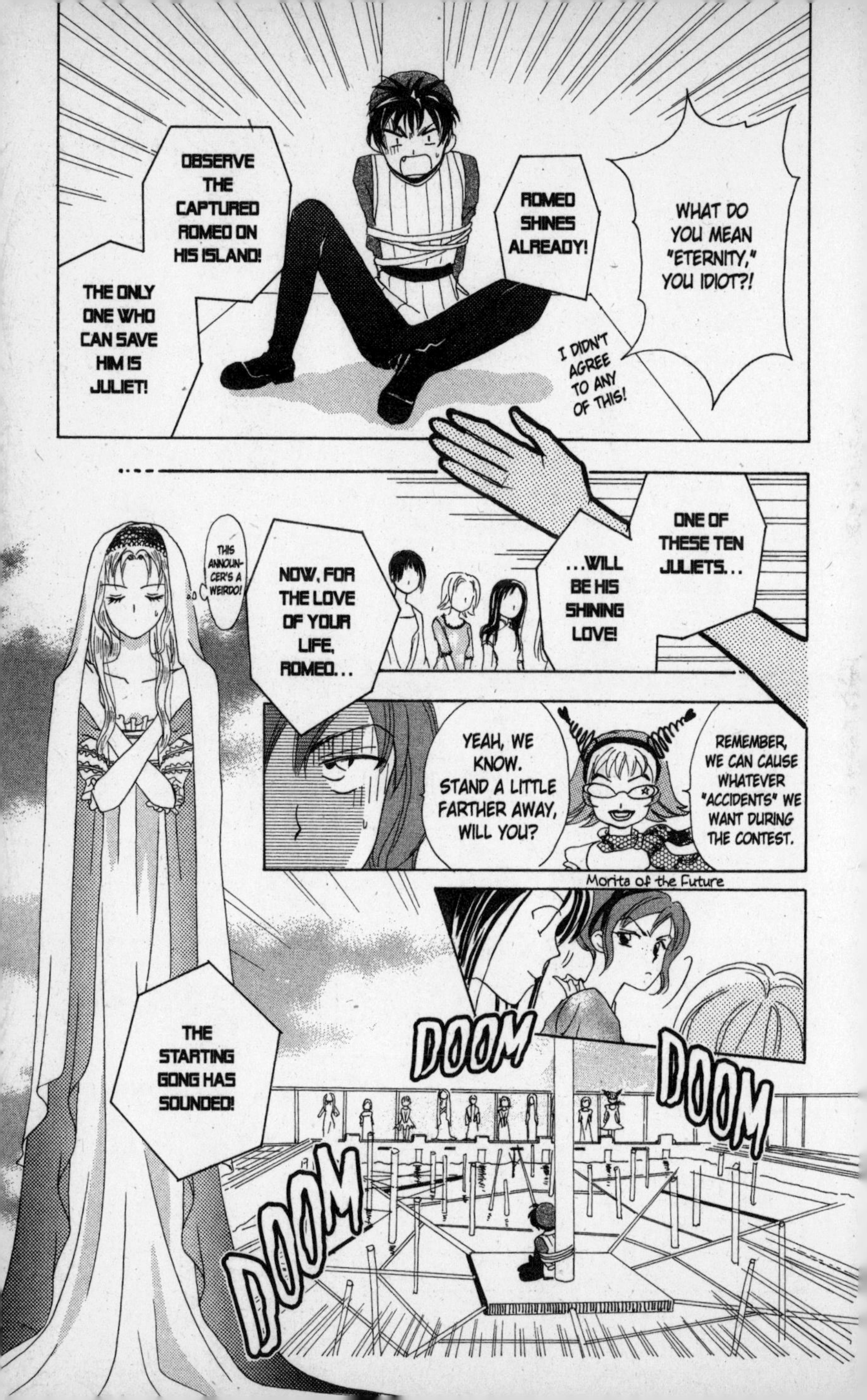
WHAT DO YOU MEAN "ETERNITY," YOU IDIOT?!
ROMEO SHINES ALREADY!
I DIDN'T AGREE TO ANY OF THIS!
OBSERVE THE CAPTURED ROMEO ON HIS ISLAND!
THE ONLY ONE WHO CAN SAVE HIM IS JULIET!
ONE OF THESE TEN JULIETS...
...WILL BE HIS SHINING LOVE!
NOW, FOR THE LOVE OF YOUR LIFE, ROMEO...
THIS ANNOUNCER'S A WEIRDO!
REMEMBER, WE CAN CAUSE WHATEVER "ACCIDENTS" WE WANT DURING THE CONTEST.
YEAH, WE KNOW. STAND A LITTLE FARTHER AWAY, WILL YOU?
Morita of the Future
DOOM
DOOM
DOOM
THE STARTING GONG HAS SOUNDED!

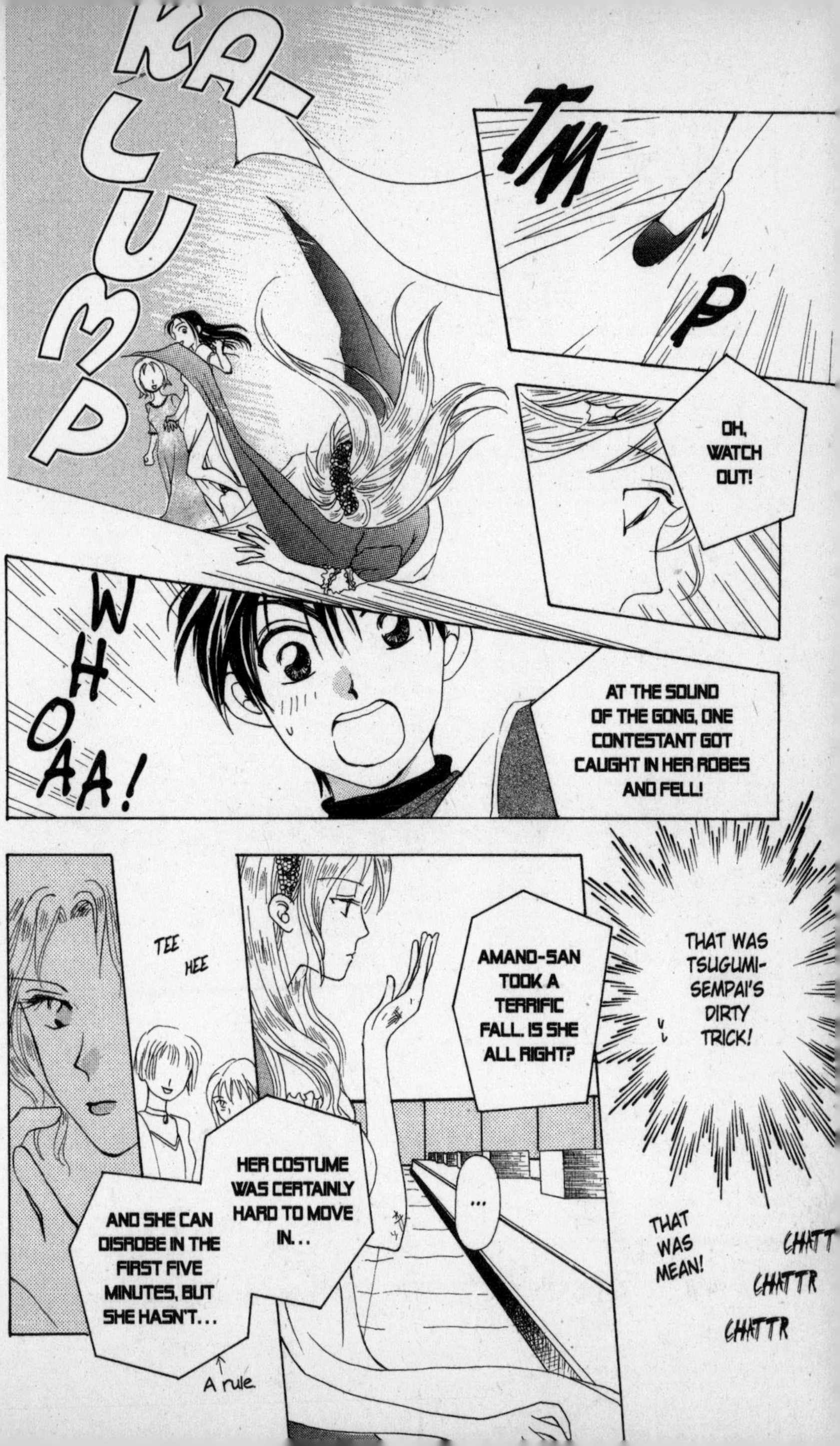
TMP
KA-LUMP
OH, WATCH OUT!
WHOAA!
AT THE SOUND OF THE GONG, ONE CONTESTANT GOT CAUGHT IN HER ROBES AND FELL!
THAT WAS TSUGUMI-SEMPAI'S DIRTY TRICK!
AMANO-SAN TOOK A TERRIFIC FALL. IS SHE ALL RIGHT?
TEE HEE
...
HER COSTUME WAS CERTAINLY HARD TO MOVE IN...
AND SHE CAN DISROBE IN THE FIRST FIVE MINUTES, BUT SHE HASN'T...
A rule
THAT WAS MEAN!
CHATT
CHATTR
CHATTR

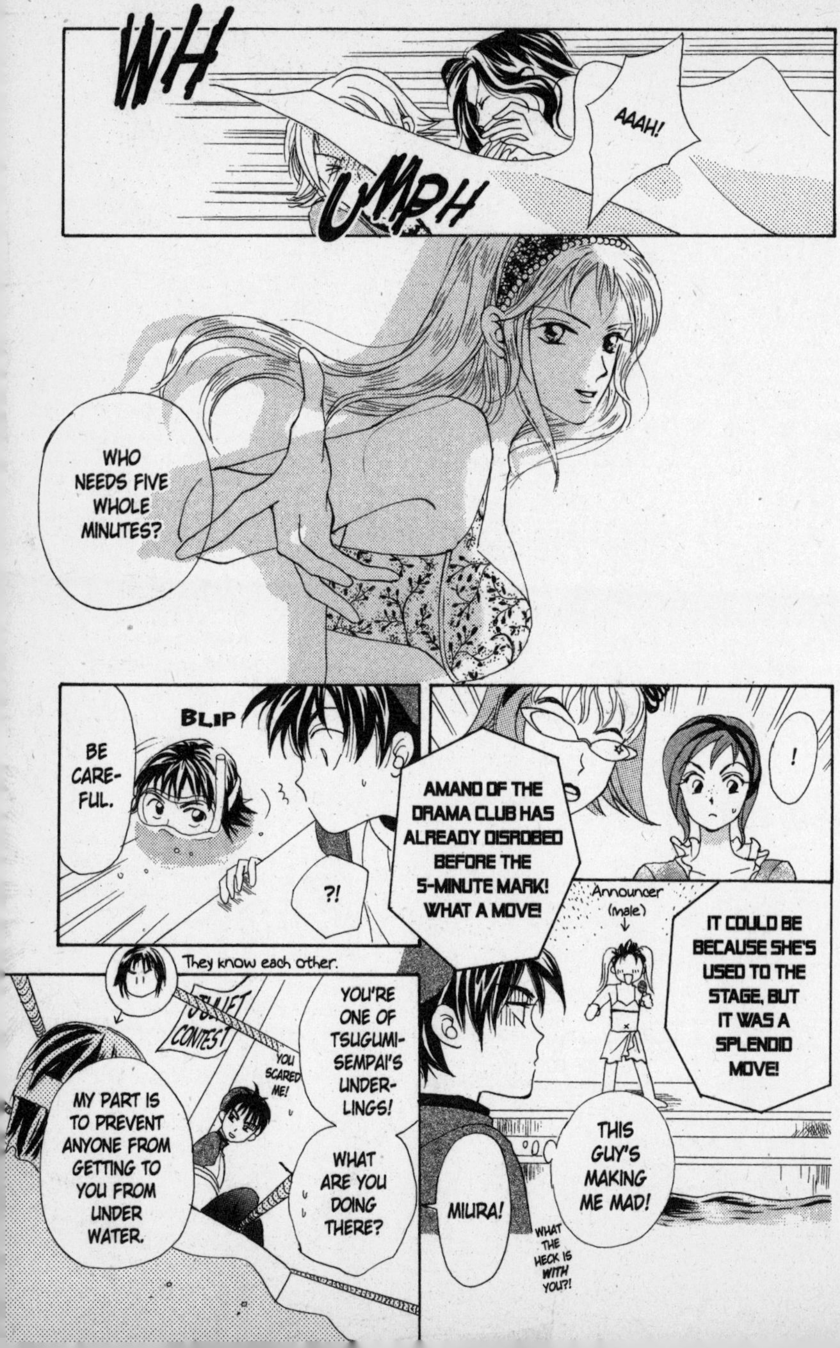
AAAH!
WH
UMPH
WHO NEEDS FIVE WHOLE MINUTES?
!
AMANO OF THE DRAMA CLUB HAS ALREADY DISROBED BEFORE THE 5-MINUTE MARK! WHAT A MOVE!
BLIP
BE CARE-FUL.
?!
Announcer (male)
IT COULD BE BECAUSE SHE'S USED TO THE STAGE, BUT IT WAS A SPLENDID MOVE!
THIS GUY'S MAKING ME MAD!
MIURA!
WHAT THE HECK IS WITH YOU?!
They know each other.
YOU'RE ONE OF TSUGUMI-SEMPAI'S UNDER-LINGS!
YOU SCARED ME!
WHAT ARE YOU DOING THERE?
MY PART IS TO PREVENT ANYONE FROM GETTING TO YOU FROM UNDER WATER.

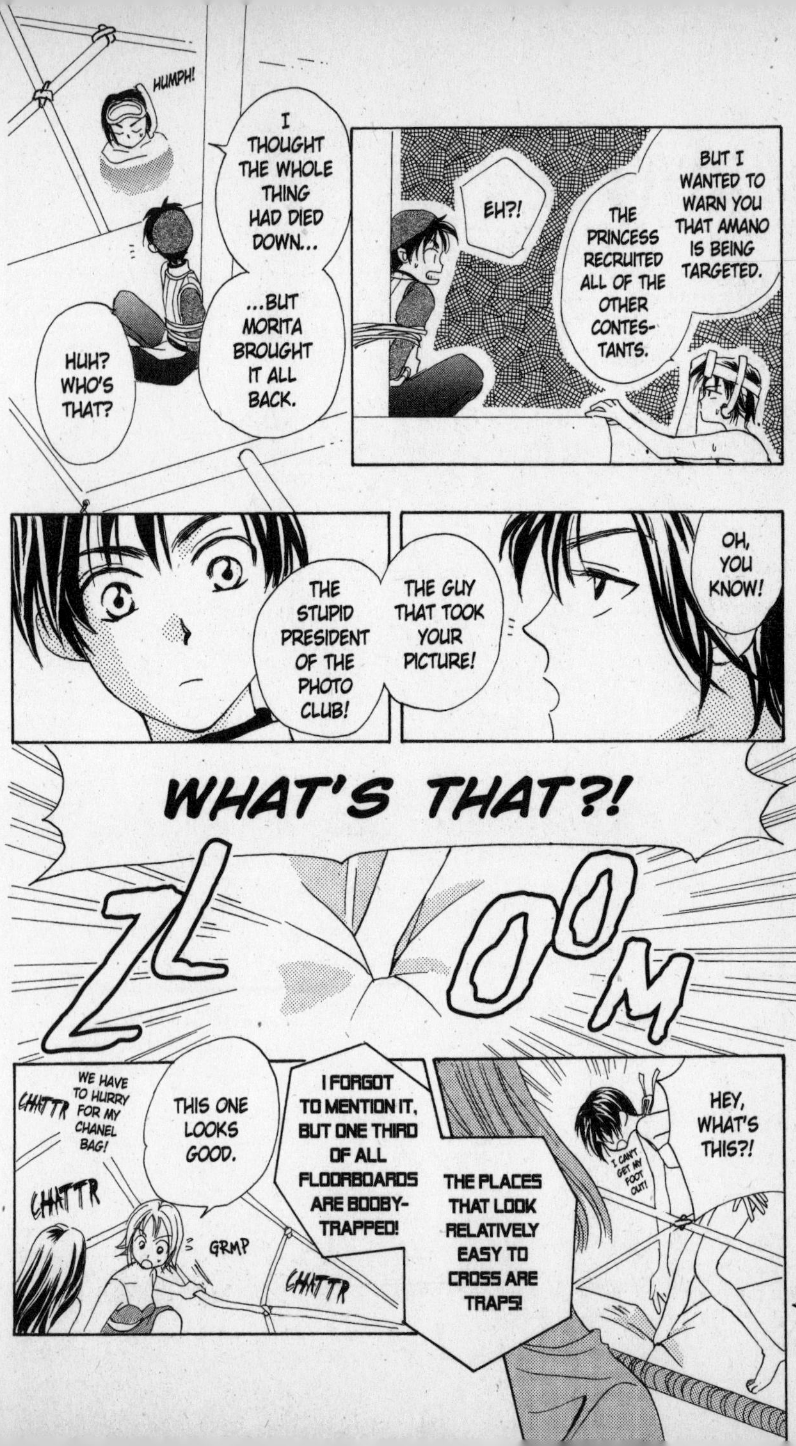
BUT I WANTED TO WARN YOU THAT AMANO IS BEING TARGETED.
THE PRINCESS RECRUITED ALL OF THE OTHER CONTES-TANTS.
EH?!
HUMPH!
I THOUGHT THE WHOLE THING HAD DIED DOWN...
...BUT MORITA BROUGHT IT ALL BACK.
HUH? WHO'S THAT?
OH, YOU KNOW!
THE GUY THAT TOOK YOUR PICTURE!
THE STUPID PRESIDENT OF THE PHOTO CLUB!
WHAT'S THAT?!
ZOOOM
HEY, WHAT'S THIS?!
I CAN'T GET MY FOOT OUT!
THE PLACES THAT LOOK RELATIVELY EASY TO CROSS ARE TRAPS!
I FORGOT TO MENTION IT, BUT ONE THIRD OF ALL FLOORBOARDS ARE BOOBY-TRAPPED!
THIS ONE LOOKS GOOD.
WE HAVE TO HURRY FOR MY CHANEL BAG!
CHATTR
CHATTR
GRMP
CHATTR

On stage ←

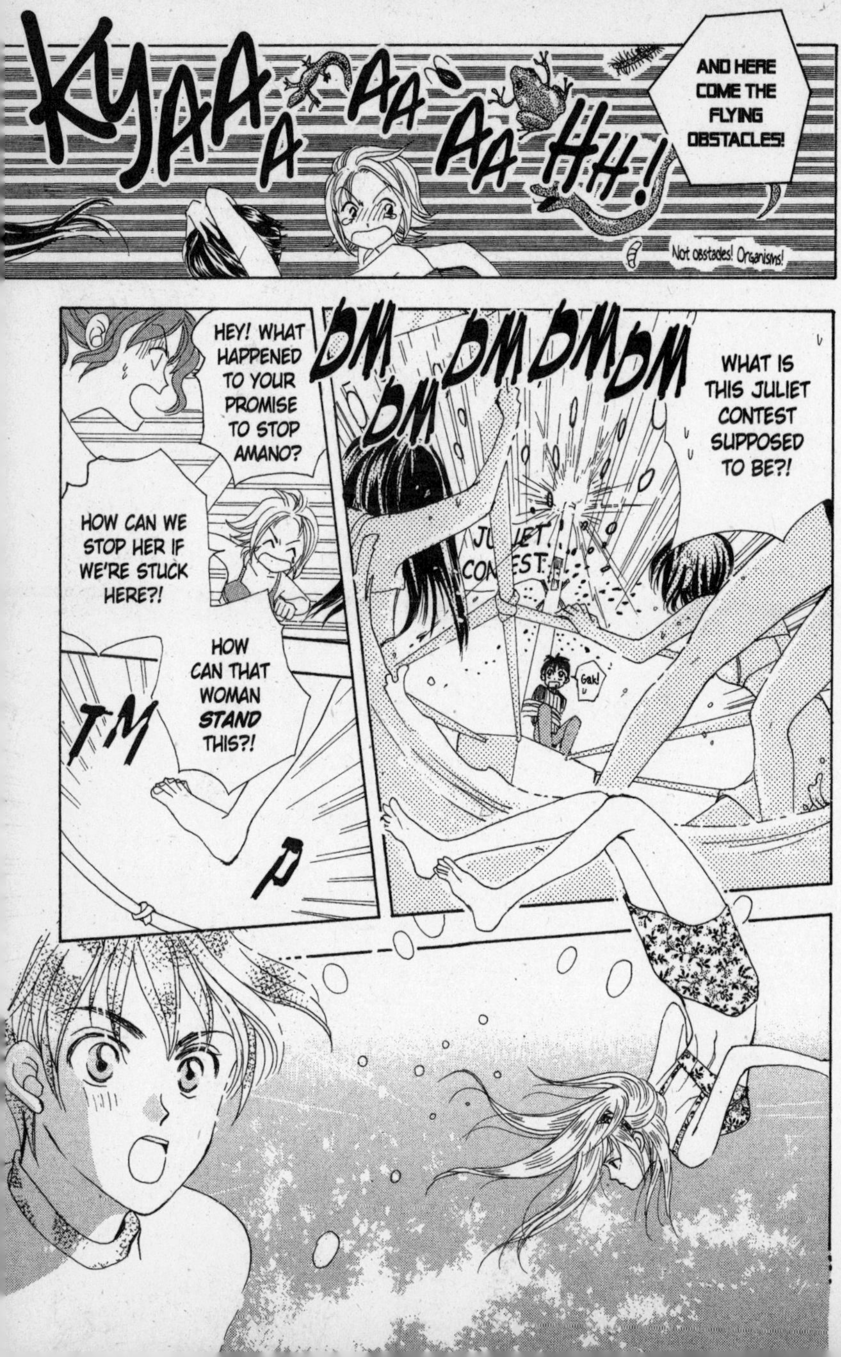
AND HERE COME THE FLYING OBSTACLES!
KYAAAAAAAAHH!
Not obstacles! Organisms!
WHAT IS THIS JULIET CONTEST SUPPOSED TO BE?!
DM DM DM DM DM DM
JULIET CONTEST
Gak!
HEY! WHAT HAPPENED TO YOUR PROMISE TO STOP AMANO?
HOW CAN WE STOP HER IF WE'RE STUCK HERE?!
HOW CAN THAT WOMAN STAND THIS?!
TM
P

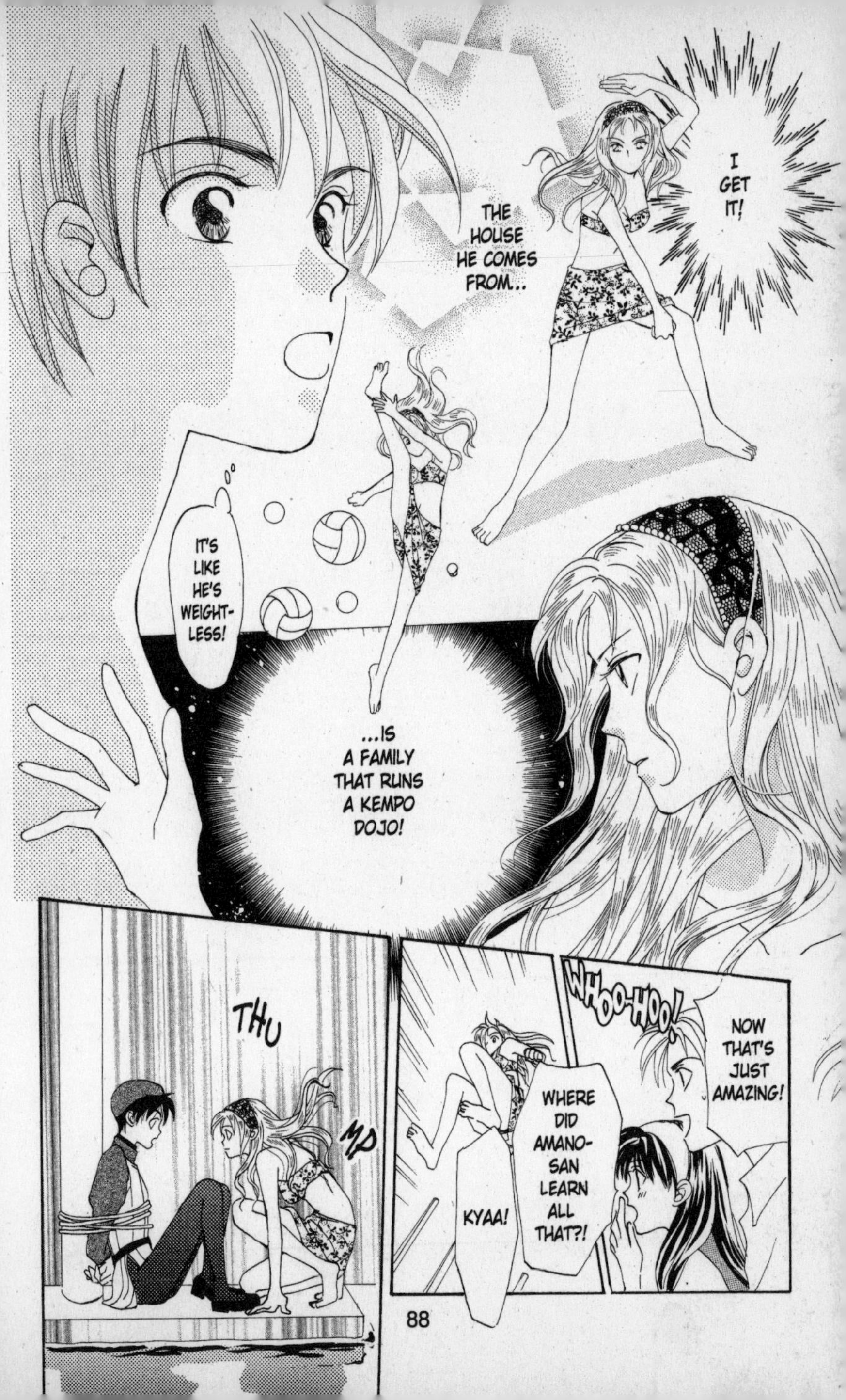

I GET IT!
THE HOUSE HE COMES FROM...
IT'S LIKE HE'S WEIGHT-LESS!
...IS A FAMILY THAT RUNS A KEMPO DOJO!
WHOO-HOO!
NOW THAT'S JUST AMAZING!
WHERE DID AMANO-SAN LEARN ALL THAT?!
KYAA!
THUMP

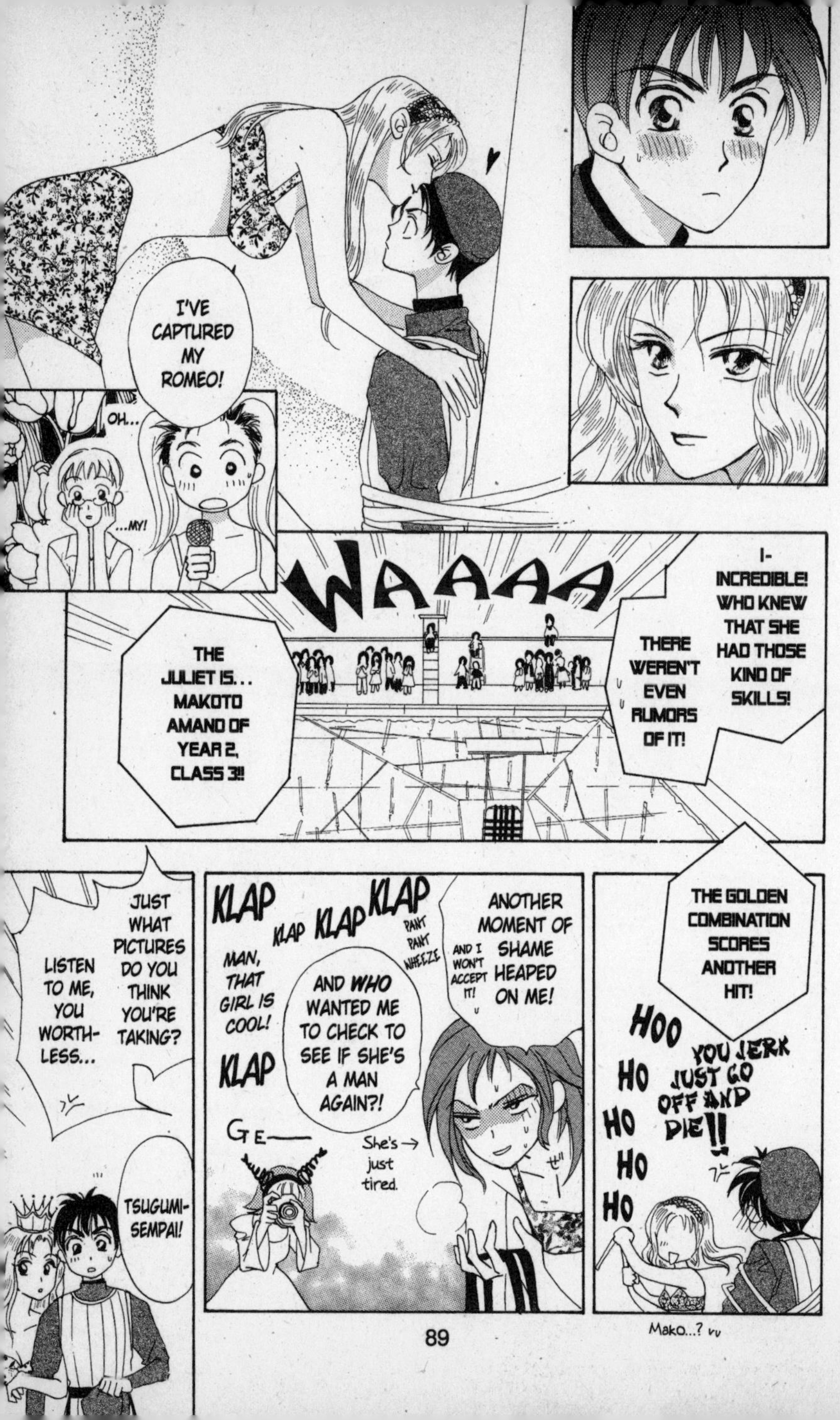
I'VE CAPTURED MY ROMEO!
OH...
...MY!
WAAAA
I- INCREDIBLE! WHO KNEW THAT SHE HAD THOSE KIND OF SKILLS!
THERE WEREN'T EVEN RUMORS OF IT!
THE JULIET IS... MAKOTO AMANO OF YEAR 2, CLASS 3!!
THE GOLDEN COMBINATION SCORES ANOTHER HIT!
HOO HO HO HO HO
YOU JERK JUST GO OFF AND DIE!!
Mako...?
ANOTHER MOMENT OF SHAME HEAPED ON ME!
AND I WON'T ACCEPT IT!
PANT PANT WHEEZE
KLAP KLAP KLAP KLAP
AND WHO WANTED ME TO CHECK TO SEE IF SHE'S A MAN AGAIN?!
MAN, THAT GIRL IS COOL!
KLAP
She's just tired.
GE——
JUST WHAT PICTURES DO YOU THINK YOU'RE TAKING?
LISTEN TO ME, YOU WORTHLESS...
TSUGUMI-SEMPAI!

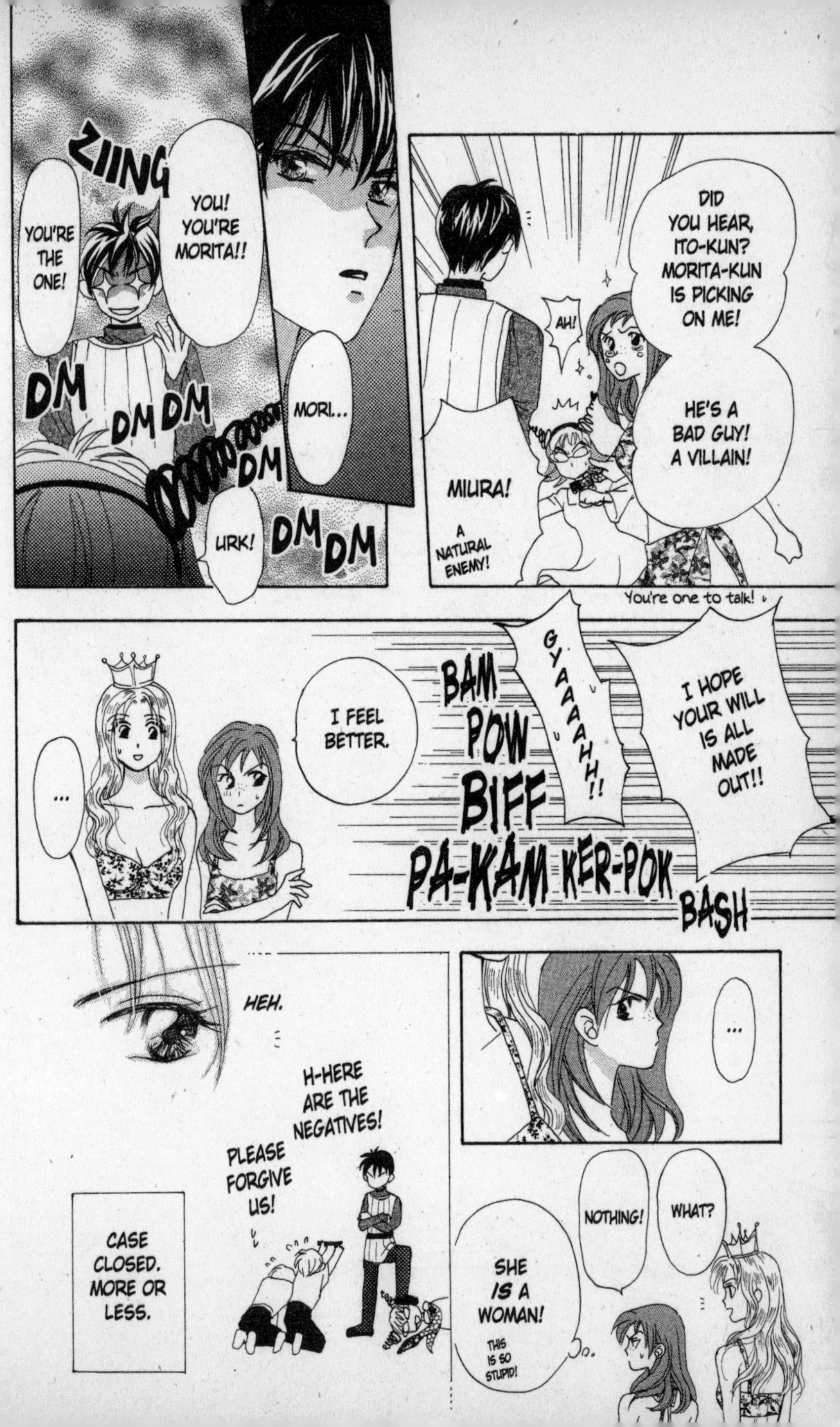
DID YOU HEAR, ITO-KUN? MORITA-KUN IS PICKING ON ME!
HE'S A BAD GUY! A VILLAIN!
AH!
MIURA!
A NATURAL ENEMY!
MORI...
ZIING
YOU! YOU'RE MORITA!!
YOU'RE THE ONE!
DM
DM DM
DM
URK!
DM DM
You're one to talk!
I HOPE YOUR WILL IS ALL MADE OUT!!
GYAAAAHH!!
BAM
POW
BIFF
PA-KAM KER-POK
BASH
I FEEL BETTER.
...
...
WHAT?
NOTHING!
SHE IS A WOMAN!
THIS IS SO STUPID!
HEH.
H-HERE ARE THE NEGATIVES!
PLEASE FORGIVE US!
CASE CLOSED. MORE OR LESS.

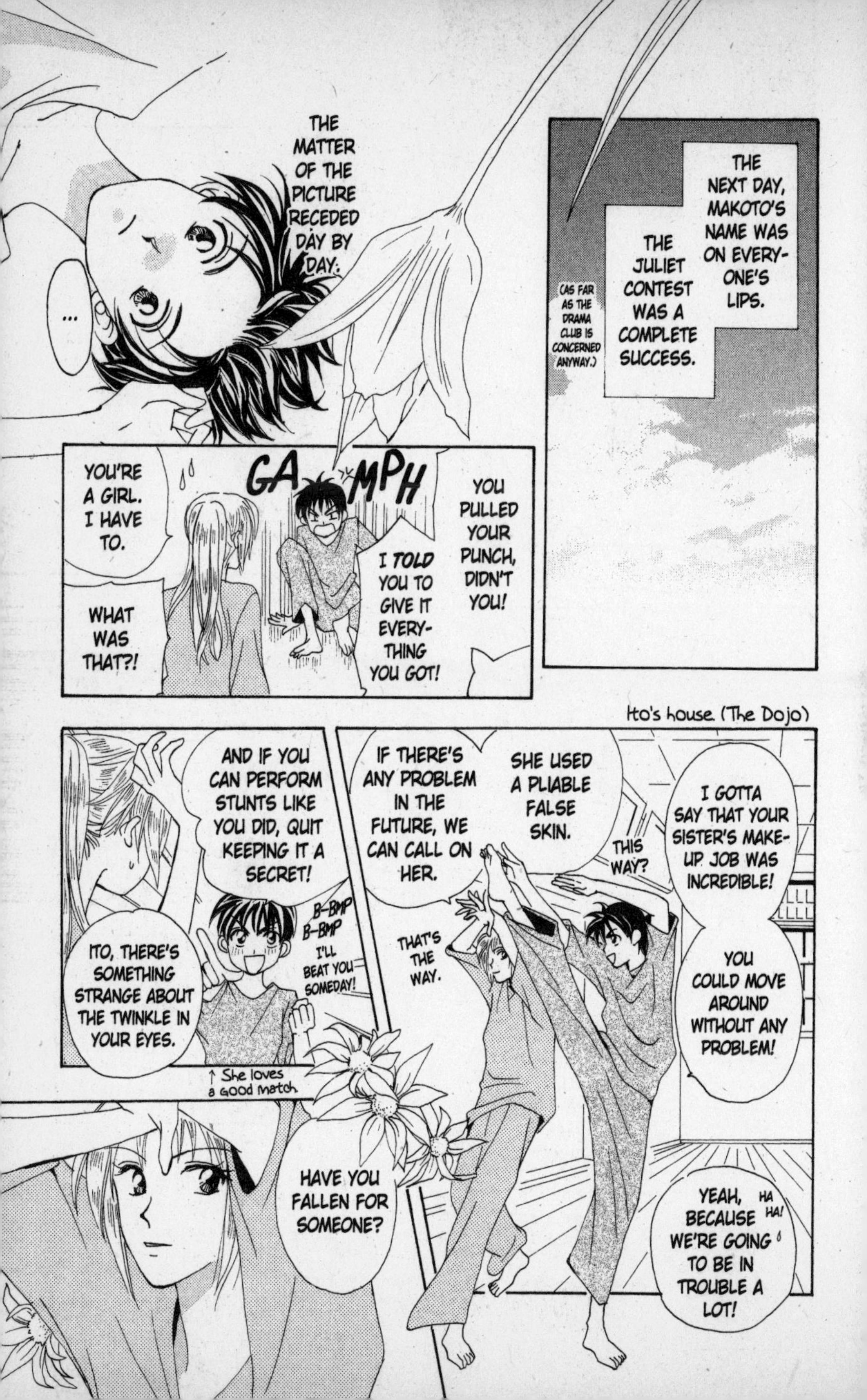
THE NEXT DAY, MAKOTO'S NAME WAS ON EVERYONE'S LIPS.
THE JULIET CONTEST WAS A COMPLETE SUCCESS.
(AS FAR AS THE DRAMA CLUB IS CONCERNED ANYWAY.)
THE MATTER OF THE PICTURE RECEDED DAY BY DAY.
...
YOU PULLED YOUR PUNCH, DIDN'T YOU!
I *TOLD* YOU TO GIVE IT EVERYTHING YOU GOT!
GAMPH
YOU'RE A GIRL. I HAVE TO.
WHAT WAS THAT?!
Ito's house. (The Dojo)
I GOTTA SAY THAT YOUR SISTER'S MAKE-UP JOB WAS INCREDIBLE!
THIS WAY?
SHE USED A PLIABLE FALSE SKIN.
IF THERE'S ANY PROBLEM IN THE FUTURE, WE CAN CALL ON HER.
YOU COULD MOVE AROUND WITHOUT ANY PROBLEM!
THAT'S THE WAY.
YEAH, BECAUSE WE'RE GOING TO BE IN TROUBLE A LOT!
HA HA!
AND IF YOU CAN PERFORM STUNTS LIKE YOU DID, QUIT KEEPING IT A SECRET!
B-BMP B-BMP
I'LL BEAT YOU SOMEDAY!
ITO, THERE'S SOMETHING STRANGE ABOUT THE TWINKLE IN YOUR EYES.
↑ She loves a good match.
HAVE YOU FALLEN FOR SOMEONE?

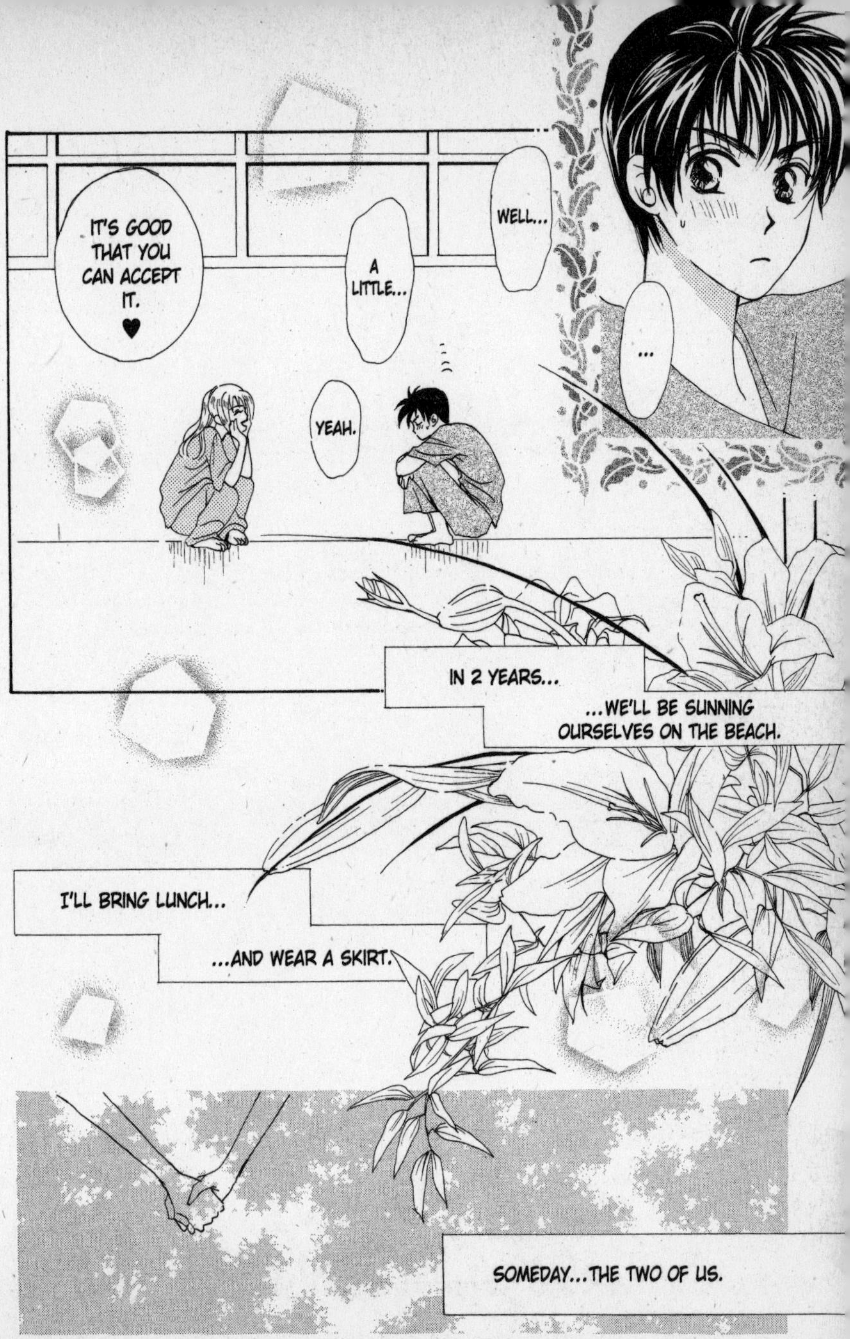
...
WELL...
A LITTLE...
IT'S GOOD THAT YOU CAN ACCEPT IT. ♥
YEAH.
IN 2 YEARS...
...WE'LL BE SUNNING OURSELVES ON THE BEACH.
I'LL BRING LUNCH...
...AND WEAR A SKIRT.
SOMEDAY...THE TWO OF US.

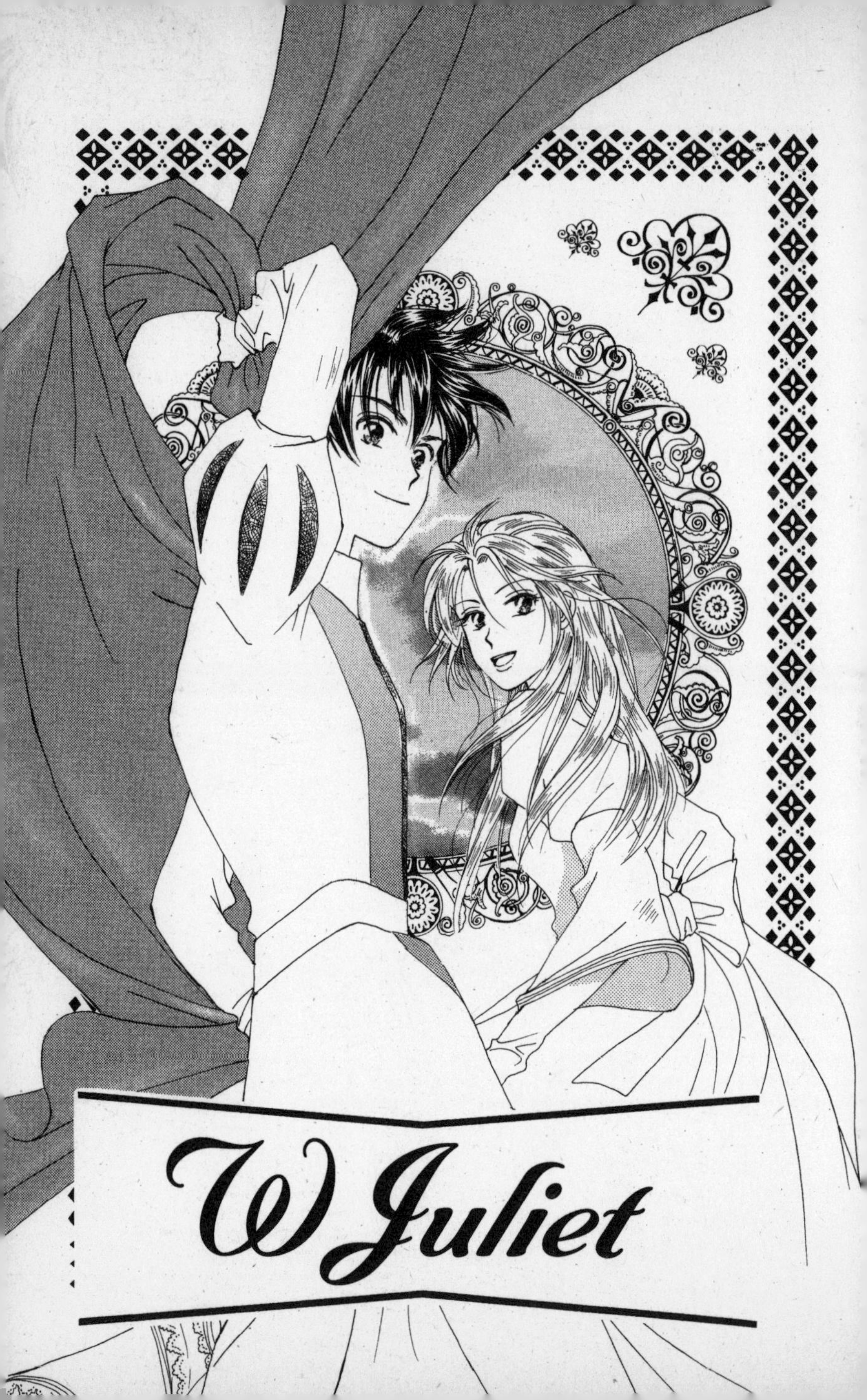
W Juliet

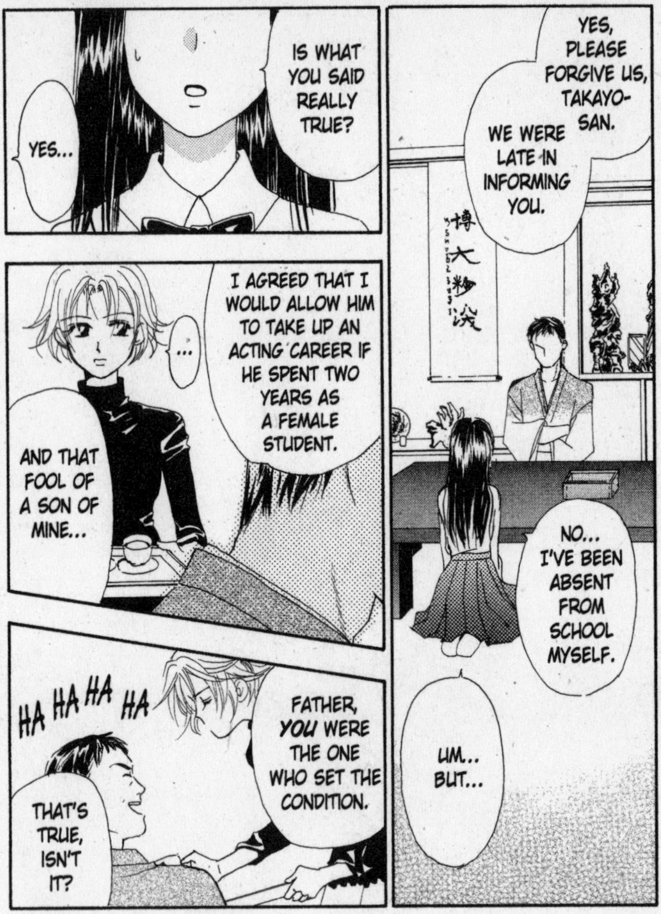
MAKOTO-KUN TRANSFERRED INTO SAKARA-GA-OKA HIGH SCHOOL?
YES, PLEASE FORGIVE US, TAKAYO-SAN.
WE WERE LATE IN INFORMING YOU.
NO... I'VE BEEN ABSENT FROM SCHOOL MYSELF.
UM... BUT...
IS WHAT YOU SAID REALLY TRUE?
YES...
I AGREED THAT I WOULD ALLOW HIM TO TAKE UP AN ACTING CAREER IF HE SPENT TWO YEARS AS A FEMALE STUDENT.
...
AND THAT FOOL OF A SON OF MINE...
FATHER, *YOU* WERE THE ONE WHO SET THE CONDITION.
HA HA HA HA
THAT'S TRUE, ISN'T IT?

Here's why the characters are this way! ①

I always draw her with one thought in mind, "Wouldn't it be fun to have a friend like her!"

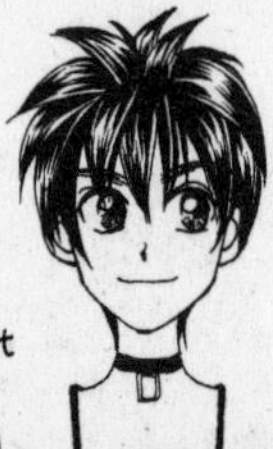

Ito Miura (17) ♀
177 cm (5' 10"), 54 kg (119 lbs),
Blood Type B, Star Sign: Leo.

- Father, Twin older brothers, and a younger brother. A family of five (A very male household.) More or less a good cook, but cannot make desserts.
- An easy character to write and draw. In fact, since she tends to write her own scenes, she saves me a lot of work! Her character has to be the easiest personality I've ever drawn, and there are a lot of readers who have just fallen for her!

It's all about her!

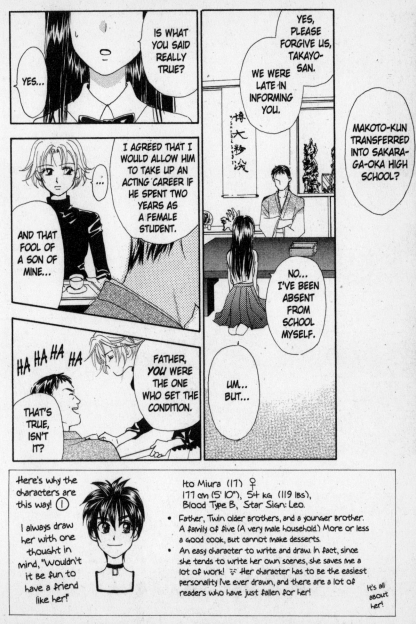

WOBBLE

RATTL

MR. NARITA...

I...

I DO NOT APPROVE OF THIS.

THE ONE WHO WILL INHERIT THE NARITA DOJO WILL BE MAKOTO.

IN ANY CASE, IT IS ALL OVER WHEN THE SCHOOL FINDS OUT THAT HE'S A MAN.

SO IT'S SIMPLY A MATTER OF TIME.

Report

SINCE IT'S YOU...

I WILL BRING HIM BACK MYSELF.

...

Veronica Cast...
to once go, and the
otographed during school hours
known to have made one close friend.

November 17 (Sat.)
9:30 - 3:00
Sakura-ga-Oka Full
School Performance

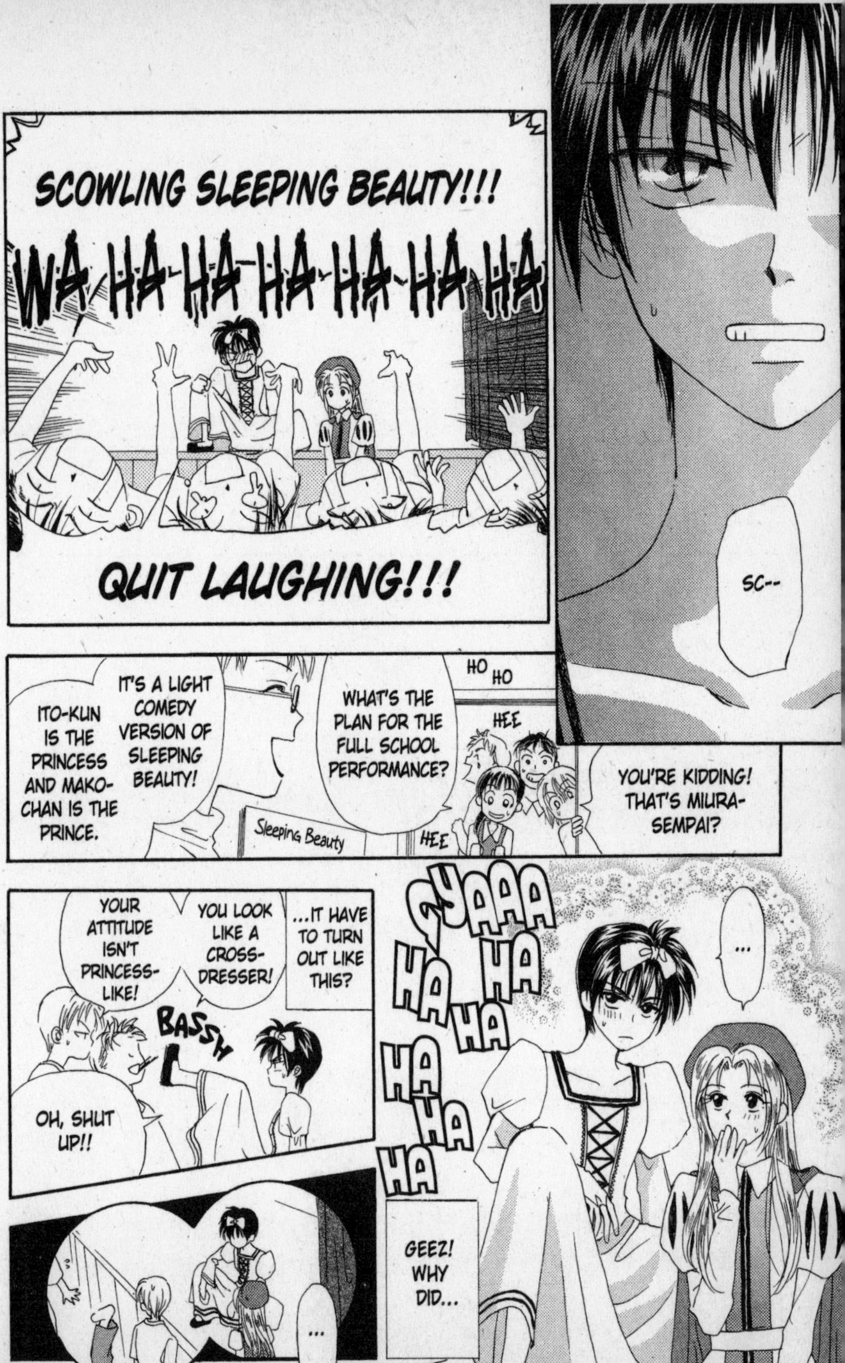
SC--
SCOWLING SLEEPING BEAUTY!!!
WA HA HA HA HA HA HA
QUIT LAUGHING!!!
YOU'RE KIDDING! THAT'S MIURA-SEMPAI?
HO HO
HEE
HEE
WHAT'S THE PLAN FOR THE FULL SCHOOL PERFORMANCE?
Sleeping Beauty
IT'S A LIGHT COMEDY VERSION OF SLEEPING BEAUTY!
ITO-KUN IS THE PRINCESS AND MAKO-CHAN IS THE PRINCE.
...
GYAAA HA HA HA HA HA HA HA
GEEZ! WHY DID...
...IT HAVE TO TURN OUT LIKE THIS?
YOU LOOK LIKE A CROSS-DRESSER!
YOUR ATTITUDE ISN'T PRINCESS-LIKE!
BASSH
OH, SHUT UP!!
...

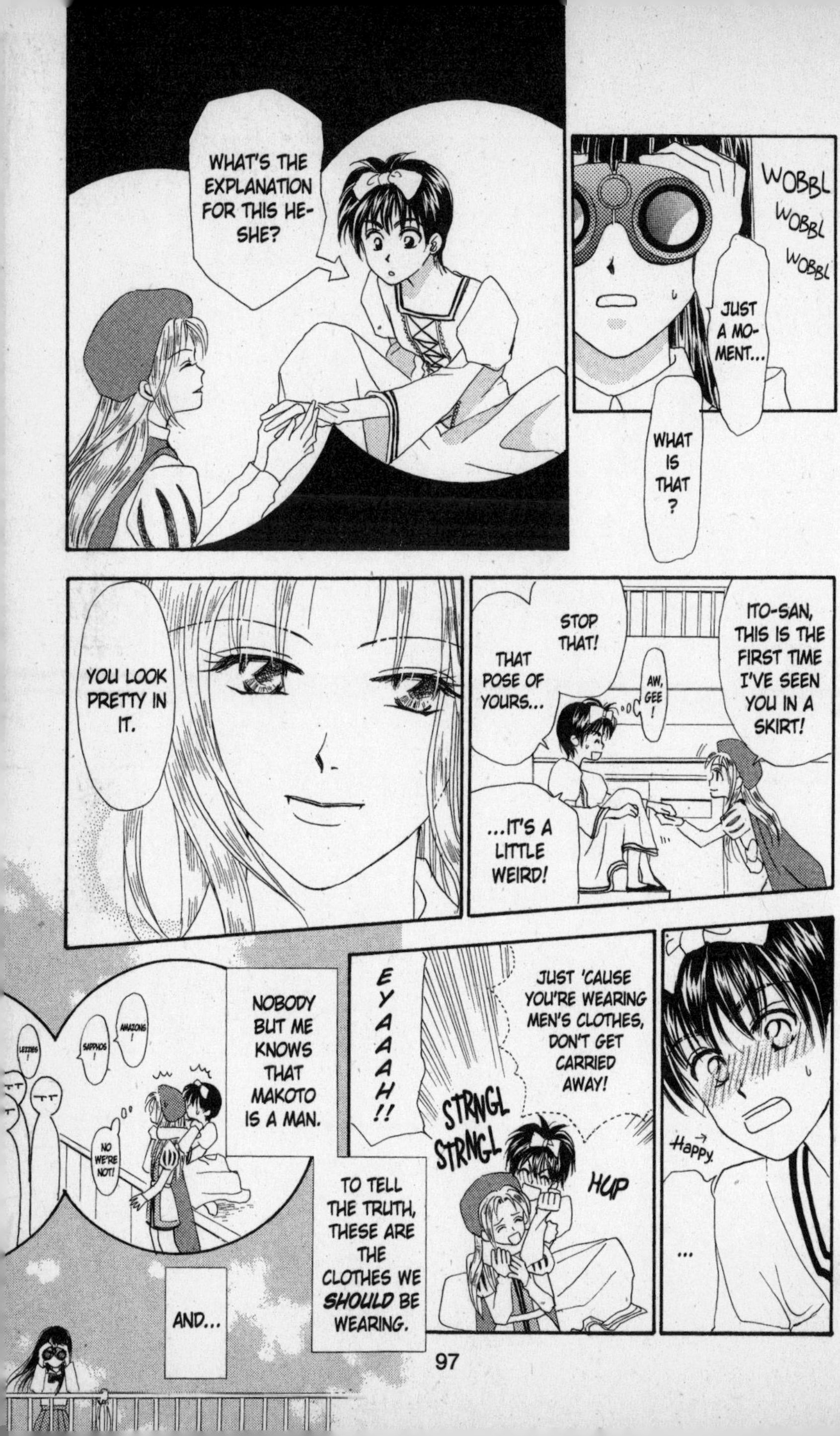
WOBBL
WOBBL
WOBBL
JUST A MO- MENT...
WHAT IS THAT ?
WHAT'S THE EXPLANATION FOR THIS HE- SHE?
ITO-SAN, THIS IS THE FIRST TIME I'VE SEEN YOU IN A SKIRT!
AW, GEE!
STOP THAT!
THAT POSE OF YOURS...
...IT'S A LITTLE WEIRD!
YOU LOOK PRETTY IN IT.
Happy.
...
JUST 'CAUSE YOU'RE WEARING MEN'S CLOTHES, DON'T GET CARRIED AWAY!
EYAAAAH!!
STRNGL
STRNGL
HUP
NOBODY BUT ME KNOWS THAT MAKOTO IS A MAN.
AMAZONS!
SAPPHOS!
LEZZIES!
NO WE'RE NOT!
TO TELL THE TRUTH, THESE ARE THE CLOTHES WE ***SHOULD*** BE WEARING.
AND...

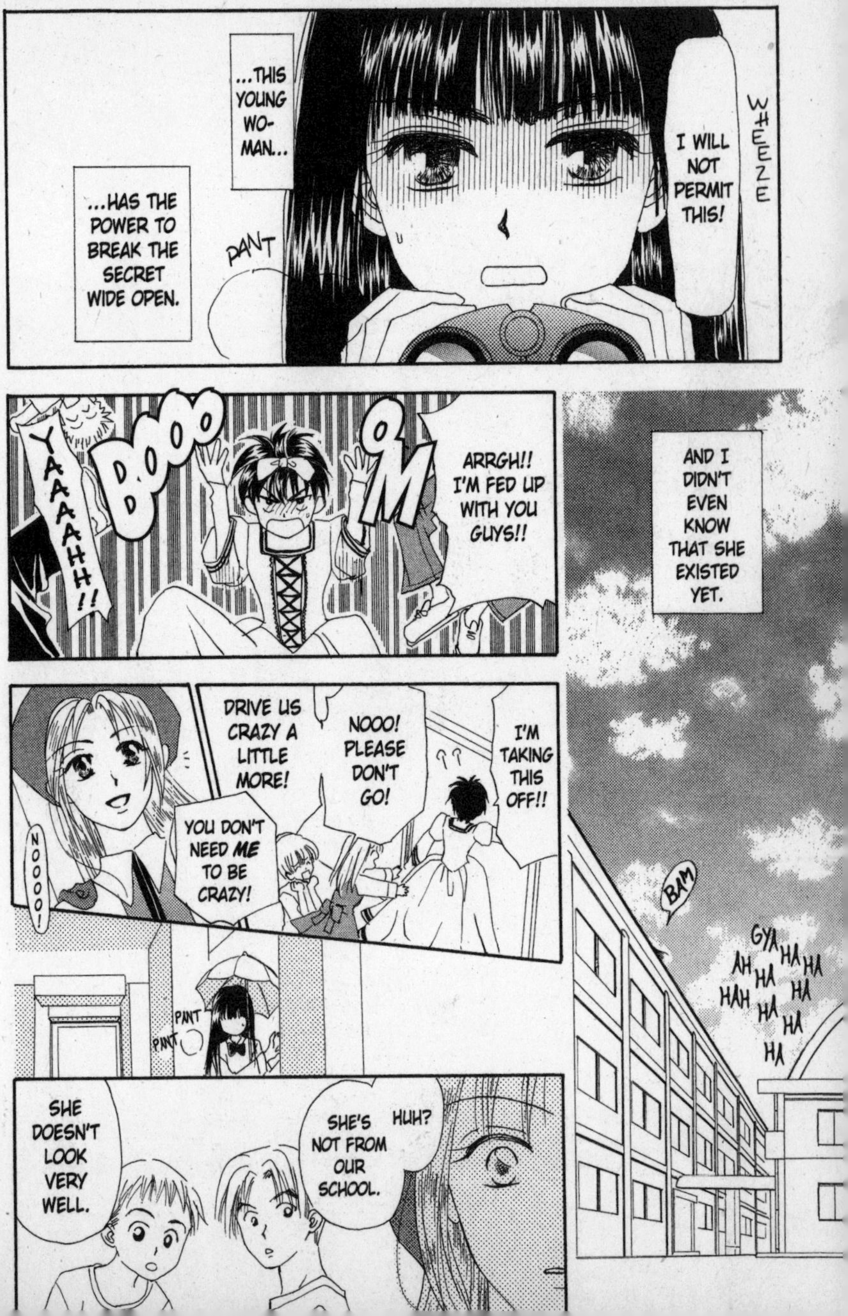
WHEEZE
I WILL NOT PERMIT THIS!
...THIS YOUNG WOMAN...
...HAS THE POWER TO BREAK THE SECRET WIDE OPEN.
PANT
AND I DIDN'T EVEN KNOW THAT SHE EXISTED YET.
BAM
GYA HA HA HA HA HA HA HA HA HA
AH HA HAH
ARRGH!! I'M FED UP WITH YOU GUYS!!
BOOOOM
YAAAAAHH!!
I'M TAKING THIS OFF!!
NOOO! PLEASE DON'T GO!
DRIVE US CRAZY A LITTLE MORE!
YOU DON'T NEED *ME* TO BE CRAZY!
NOOOOO!
PANT
PANT
HUH?
SHE'S NOT FROM OUR SCHOOL.
SHE DOESN'T LOOK VERY WELL.

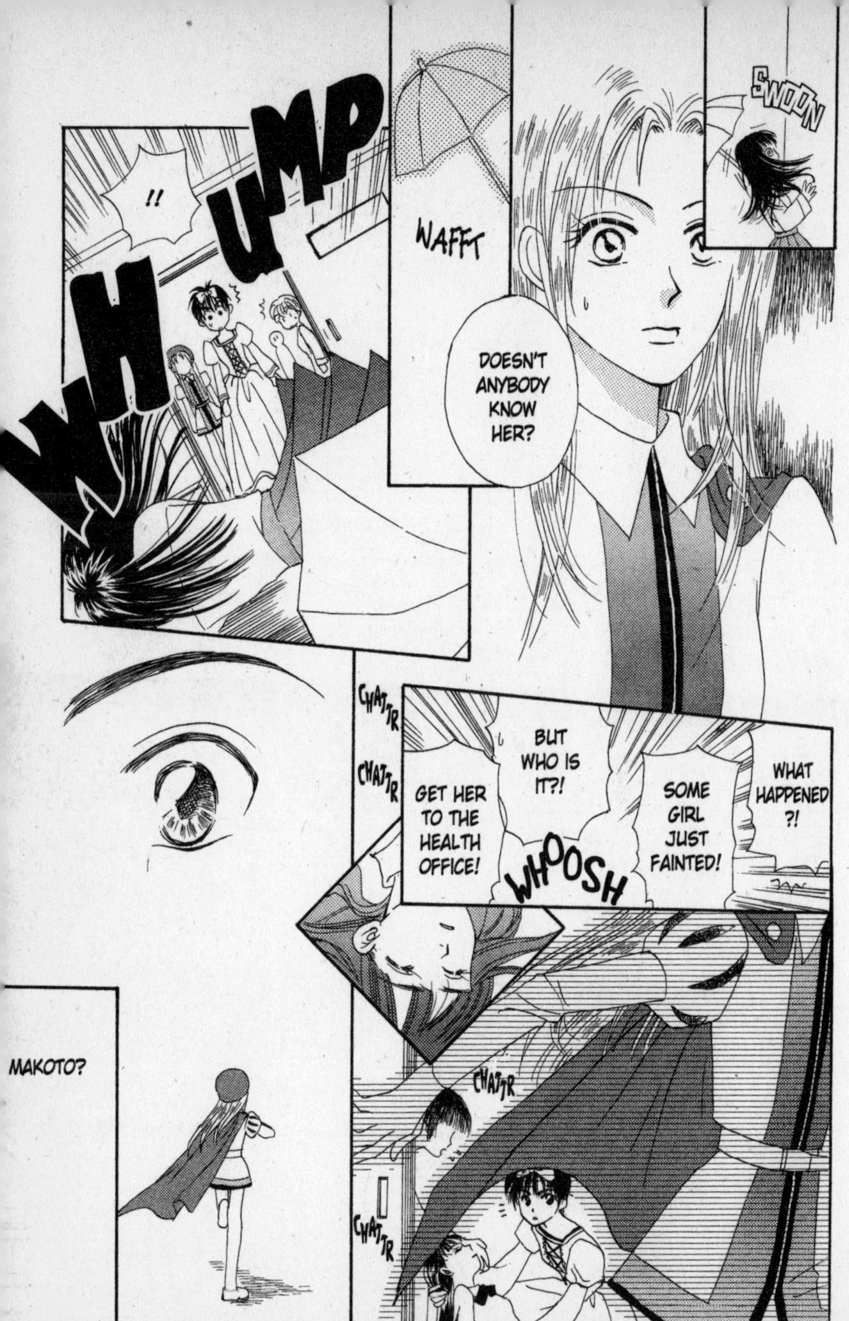
SWOON
WAFFT
DOESN'T ANYBODY KNOW HER?
!!
WHUMP
CHATTR
CHATTR
WHAT HAPPENED ?!
SOME GIRL JUST FAINTED!
BUT WHO IS IT?!
GET HER TO THE HEALTH OFFICE!
WHOOSH
CHATTR
CHATTR
MAKOTO?

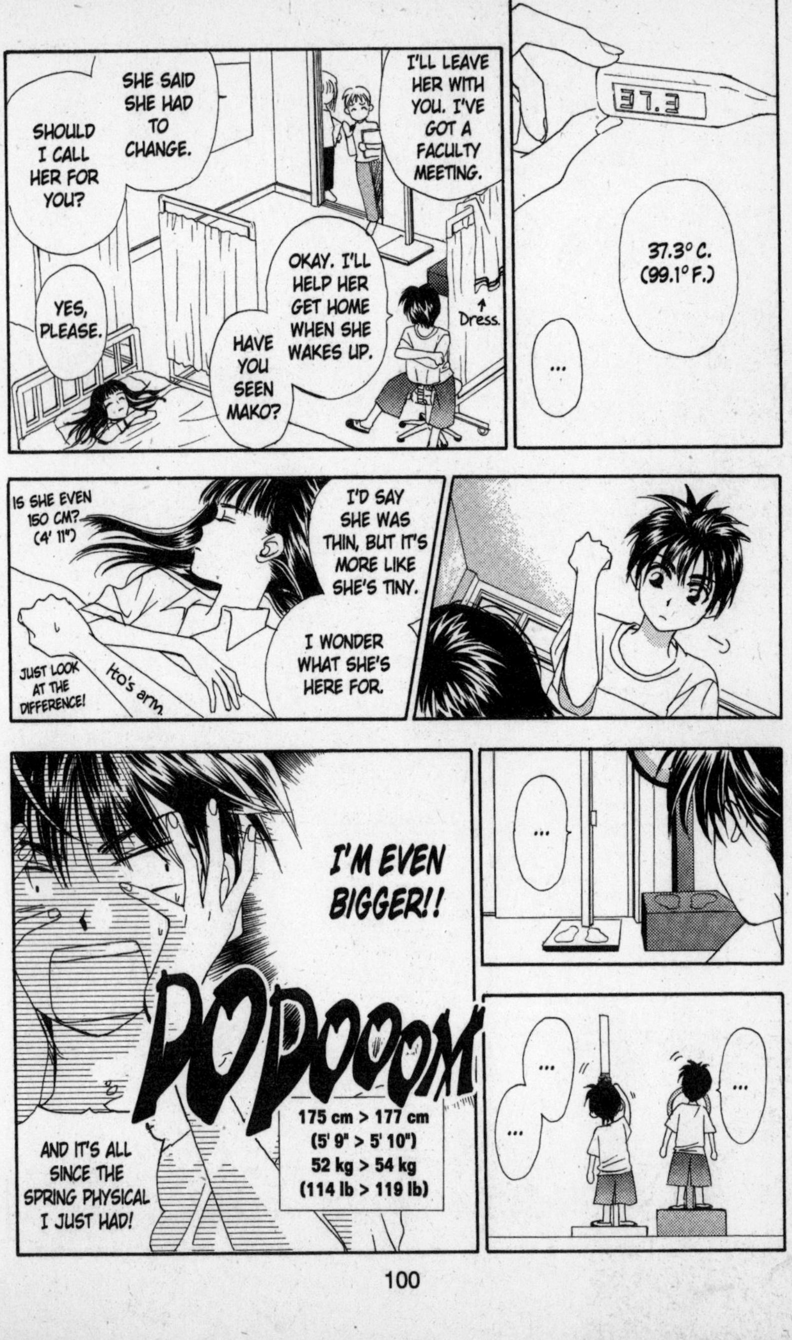
37.3
37.3° C. (99.1° F.)
...
I'LL LEAVE HER WITH YOU. I'VE GOT A FACULTY MEETING.
SHE SAID SHE HAD TO CHANGE.
SHOULD I CALL HER FOR YOU?
OKAY. I'LL HELP HER GET HOME WHEN SHE WAKES UP.
Dress.
HAVE YOU SEEN MAKO?
YES, PLEASE.
I'D SAY SHE WAS THIN, BUT IT'S MORE LIKE SHE'S TINY.
IS SHE EVEN 150 CM? (4' 11")
I WONDER WHAT SHE'S HERE FOR.
Ito's arm.
JUST LOOK AT THE DIFFERENCE!
...
...
...
...
I'M EVEN BIGGER!!
DODOOOM
175 cm > 177 cm (5' 9" > 5' 10") 52 kg > 54 kg (114 lb > 119 lb)
AND IT'S ALL SINCE THE SPRING PHYSICAL I JUST HAD!

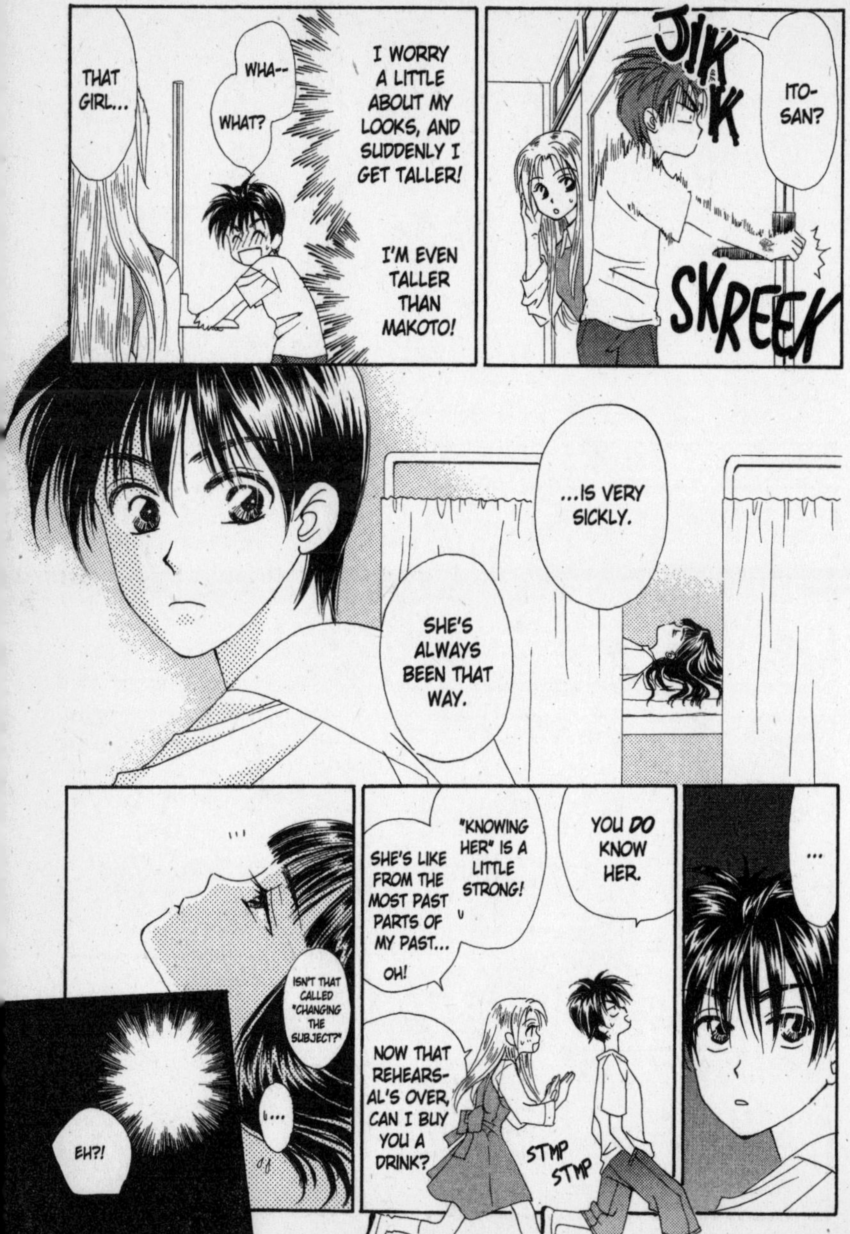
ITO-SAN?
JIKK
SKREEK
I WORRY A LITTLE ABOUT MY LOOKS, AND SUDDENLY I GET TALLER!
I'M EVEN TALLER THAN MAKOTO!
WHA--
WHAT?
THAT GIRL...
...IS VERY SICKLY.
SHE'S ALWAYS BEEN THAT WAY.
...
YOU *DO* KNOW HER.
"KNOWING HER" IS A LITTLE STRONG!
SHE'S LIKE FROM THE MOST PAST PARTS OF MY PAST...
OH!
NOW THAT REHEARSAL'S OVER, CAN I BUY YOU A DRINK?
STMP STMP
...
ISN'T THAT CALLED "CHANGING THE SUBJECT?"
I...
EH?!

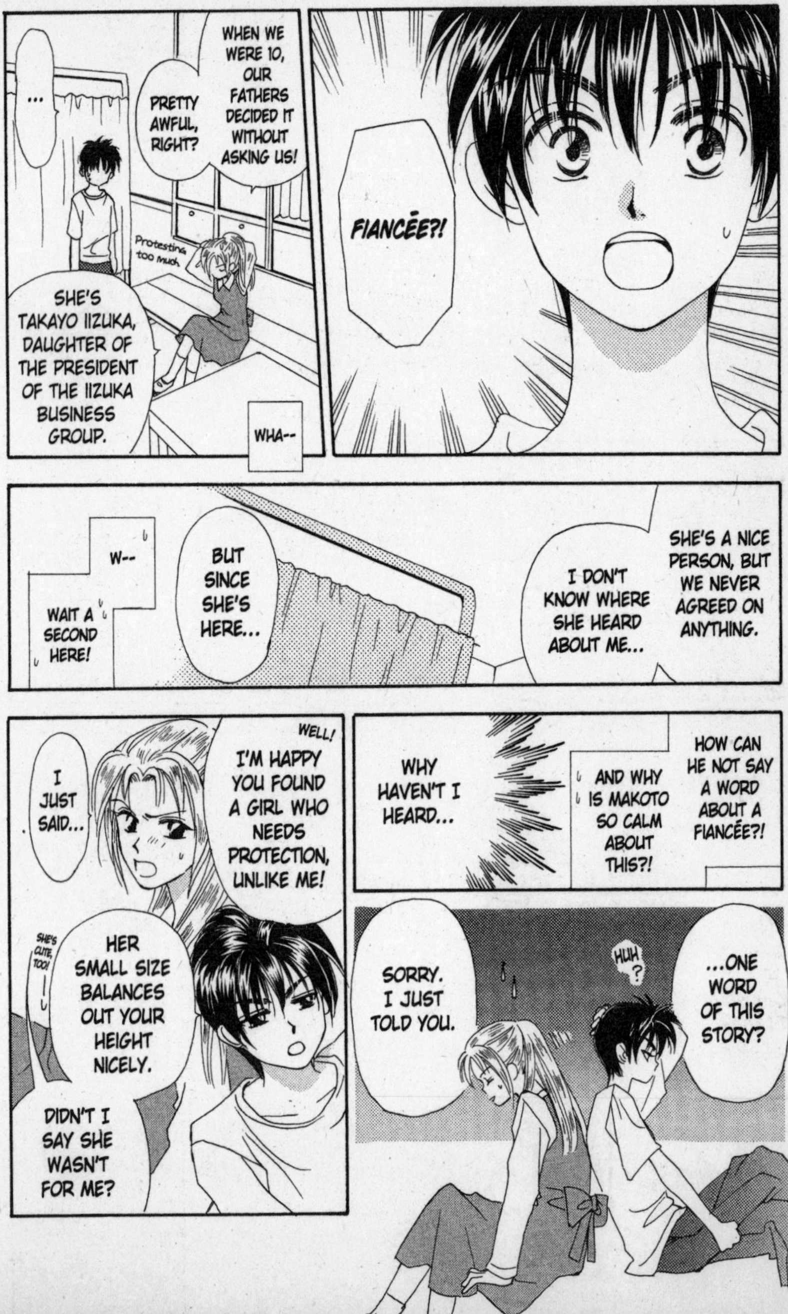
FIANCÉE?!
WHEN WE WERE 10, OUR FATHERS DECIDED IT WITHOUT ASKING US!
PRETTY AWFUL, RIGHT?
...
Protesting too much
SHE'S TAKAYO IIZUKA, DAUGHTER OF THE PRESIDENT OF THE IIZUKA BUSINESS GROUP.
WHA--
SHE'S A NICE PERSON, BUT WE NEVER AGREED ON ANYTHING.
I DON'T KNOW WHERE SHE HEARD ABOUT ME...
BUT SINCE SHE'S HERE...
W--
WAIT A SECOND HERE!
HOW CAN HE NOT SAY A WORD ABOUT A FIANCÉE?!
AND WHY IS MAKOTO SO CALM ABOUT THIS?!
WHY HAVEN'T I HEARD...
...ONE WORD OF THIS STORY?
HUH ?
SORRY. I JUST TOLD YOU.
WELL!
I'M HAPPY YOU FOUND A GIRL WHO NEEDS PROTECTION, UNLIKE ME!
I JUST SAID...
HER SMALL SIZE BALANCES OUT YOUR HEIGHT NICELY.
SHE'S CUTE, TOO!
DIDN'T I SAY SHE WASN'T FOR ME?

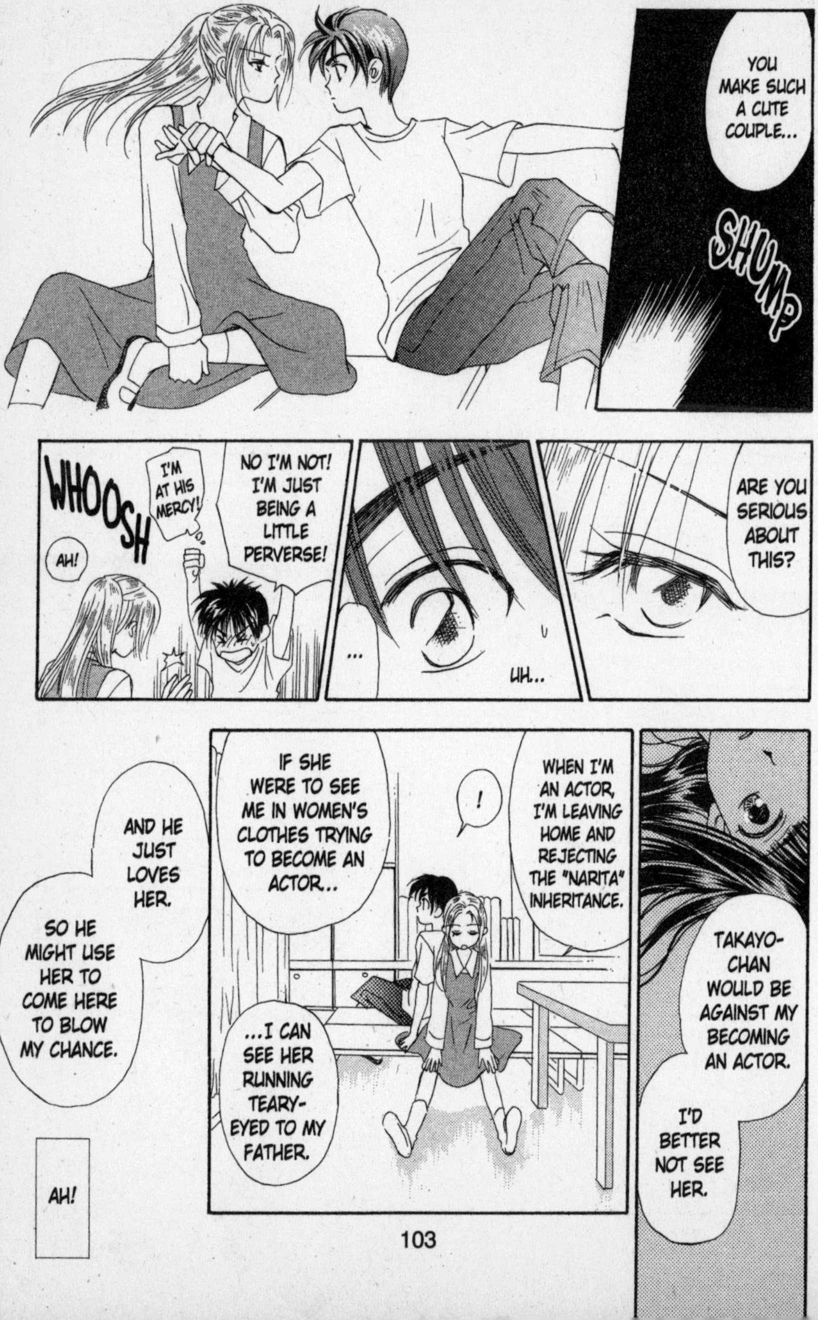
YOU MAKE SUCH A CUTE COUPLE...
SHUMP
ARE YOU SERIOUS ABOUT THIS?
UH...
...
NO I'M NOT! I'M JUST BEING A LITTLE PERVERSE!
I'M AT HIS MERCY!
WHOOSH
AH!
TAKAYO-CHAN WOULD BE AGAINST MY BECOMING AN ACTOR.
I'D BETTER NOT SEE HER.
WHEN I'M AN ACTOR, I'M LEAVING HOME AND REJECTING THE "NARITA" INHERITANCE.
!
IF SHE WERE TO SEE ME IN WOMEN'S CLOTHES TRYING TO BECOME AN ACTOR...
...I CAN SEE HER RUNNING TEARY-EYED TO MY FATHER.
AND HE JUST LOVES HER.
SO HE MIGHT USE HER TO COME HERE TO BLOW MY CHANCE.
AH!

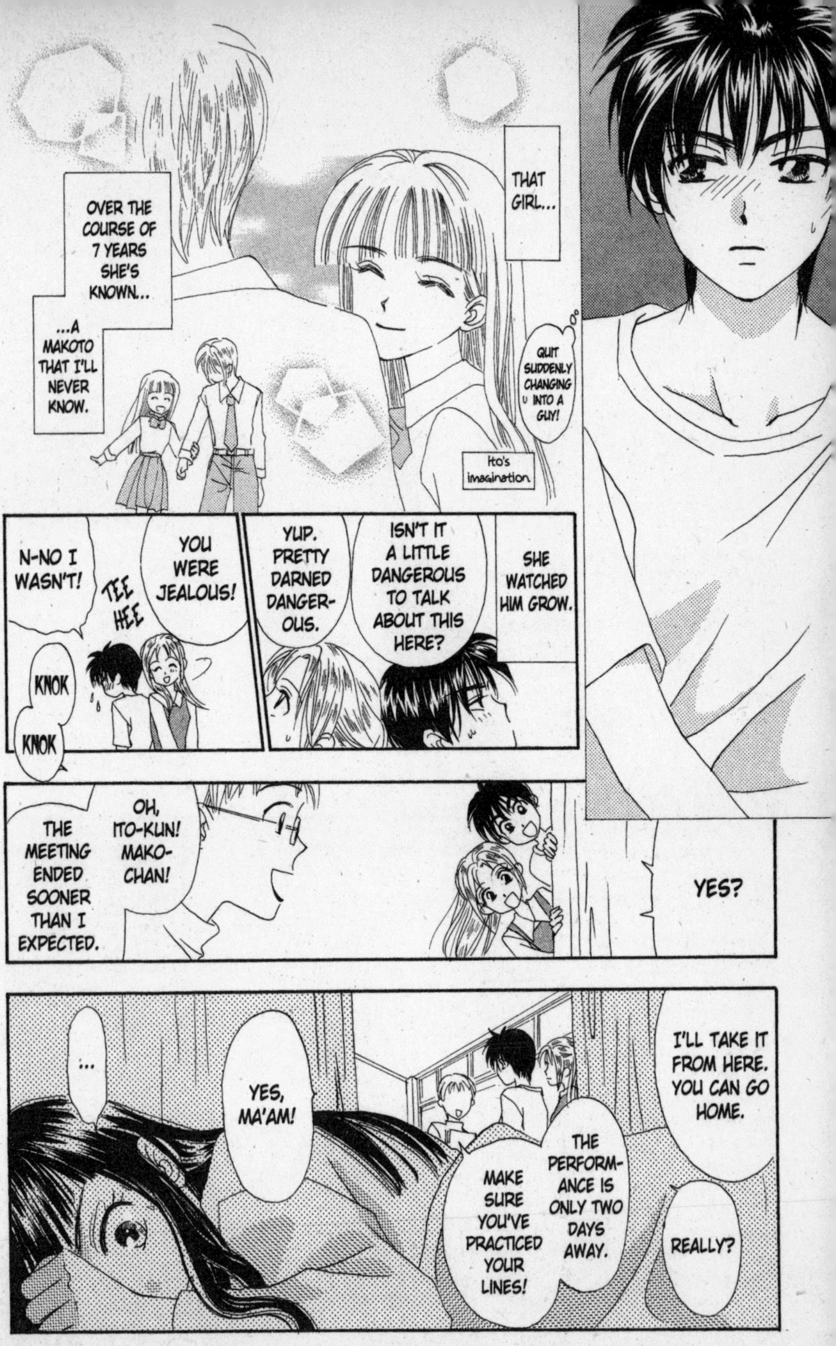
THAT GIRL...
OVER THE COURSE OF 7 YEARS SHE'S KNOWN...
...A MAKOTO THAT I'LL NEVER KNOW.
QUIT SUDDENLY CHANGING INTO A GUY!
Ito's imagination
SHE WATCHED HIM GROW.
ISN'T IT A LITTLE DANGEROUS TO TALK ABOUT THIS HERE?
YUP. PRETTY DARNED DANGER-OUS.
YOU WERE JEALOUS!
TEE HEE
N-NO I WASN'T!
KNOK
KNOK
YES?
OH, ITO-KUN! MAKO-CHAN!
THE MEETING ENDED SOONER THAN I EXPECTED.
I'LL TAKE IT FROM HERE. YOU CAN GO HOME.
REALLY?
THE PERFORM-ANCE IS ONLY TWO DAYS AWAY.
MAKE SURE YOU'VE PRACTICED YOUR LINES!
YES, MA'AM!
...

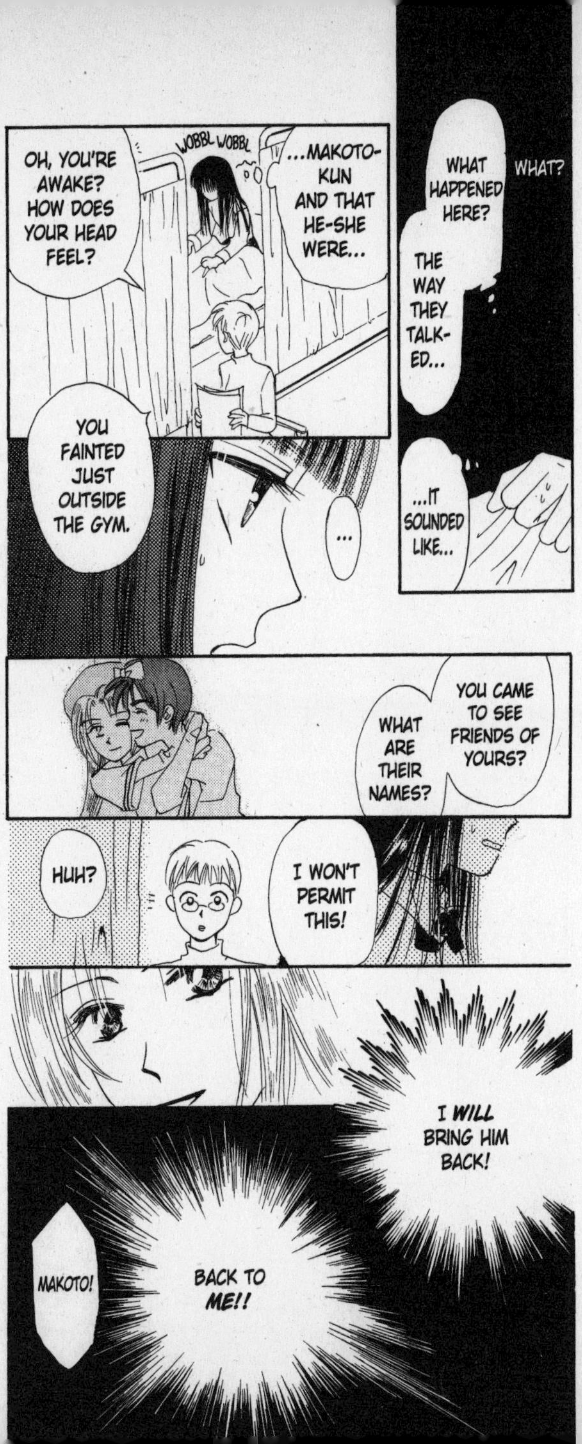
WHAT?
WHAT HAPPENED HERE?
THE WAY THEY TALKED...
...IT SOUNDED LIKE...
...MAKOTO-KUN AND THAT HE-SHE WERE...
WOBBL WOBBL
OH, YOU'RE AWAKE? HOW DOES YOUR HEAD FEEL?
...
YOU FAINTED JUST OUTSIDE THE GYM.
YOU CAME TO SEE FRIENDS OF YOURS?
WHAT ARE THEIR NAMES?
I WON'T PERMIT THIS!
HUH?
I *WILL* BRING HIM BACK!
BACK TO *ME!!*
MAKOTO!

PROFILE

As a "hello," I decided to go ahead and introduce myself.

Emura

Born March 19th. Pisces, blood type A, female. (But most people guess I'm type B or O.)

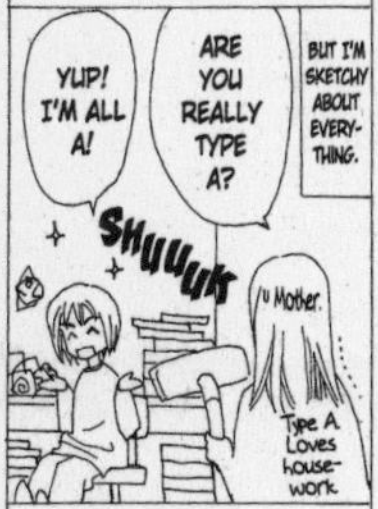
BUT I'M SKETCHY ABOUT EVERYTHING.
ARE YOU REALLY TYPE A?
YUP! I'M ALL A!
SHUUUK
Mother.
Type A. Loves house-work.

Height: 156 cm (5' 2"). Weight: 42-44 kg (92-97 lbs). Born and raised in Kanagawa Prefecture (just southeast of Tokyo).

I love sour stuff like umeboshi (pickled plums) and lemons. I eat lemons like they're going out of style! (It's true!) But I also like sweet stuff, but I can't take stuff made with sweet bean paste. I love the crunchy stuff. I'm a huge fan of sembei rice crackers! ♥ Even at my age, I've never had a cavity! (Never had a tooth pulled either!) I have my parents to thank for that! It looks like I can only talk about food!

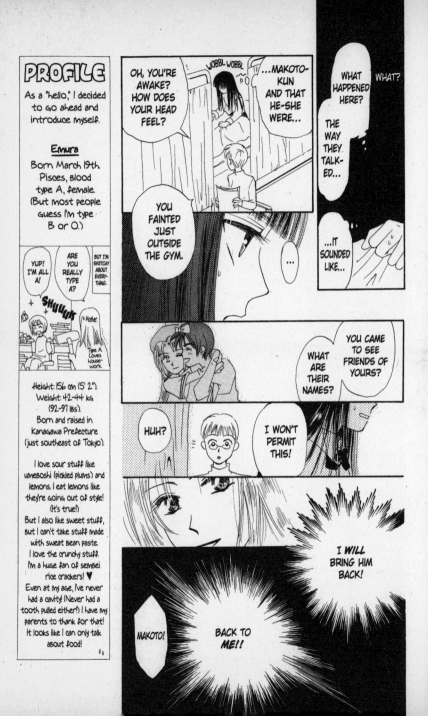

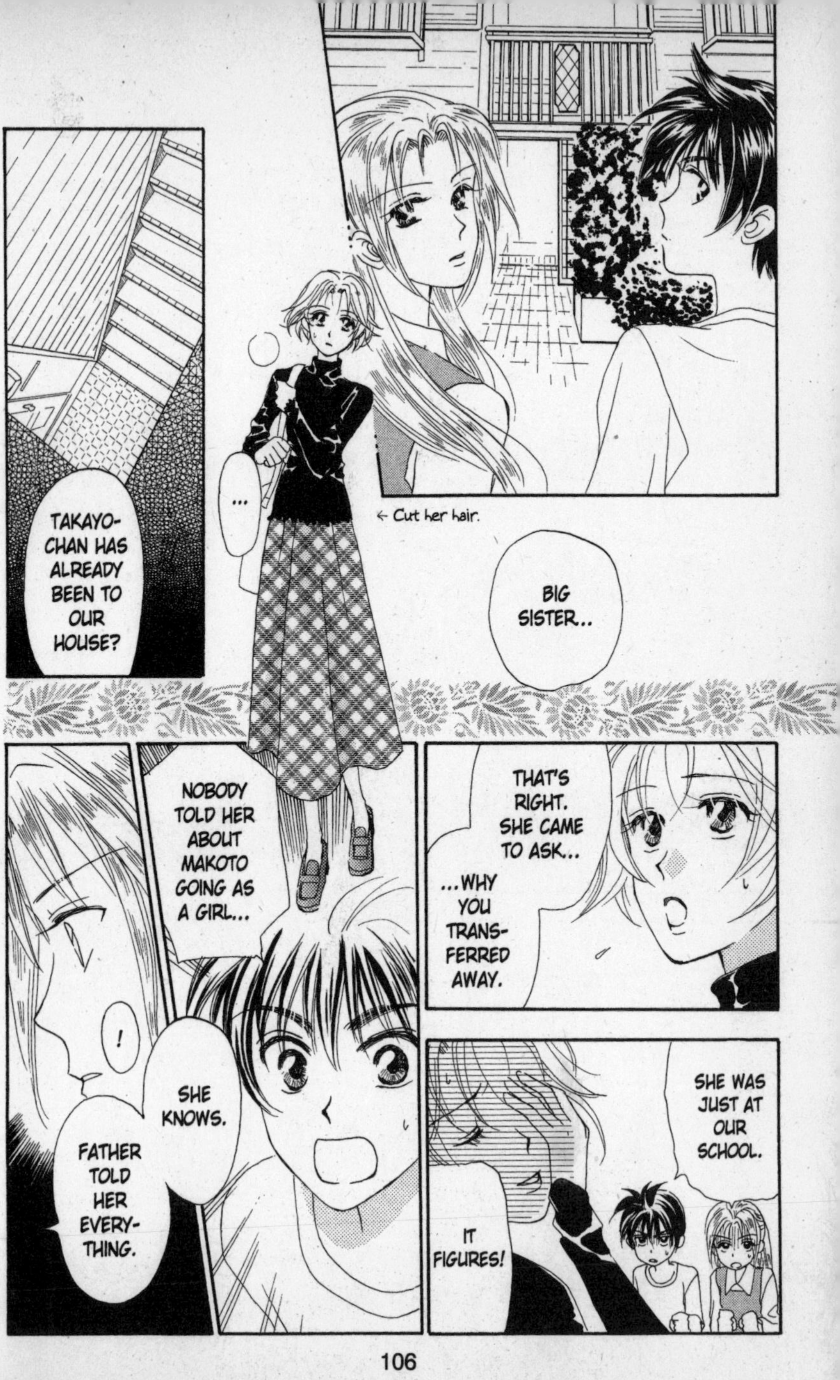
← Cut her hair.
BIG SISTER...
...
TAKAYO-CHAN HAS ALREADY BEEN TO OUR HOUSE?
THAT'S RIGHT. SHE CAME TO ASK...
...WHY YOU TRANS-FERRED AWAY.
SHE WAS JUST AT OUR SCHOOL.
IT FIGURES!
NOBODY TOLD HER ABOUT MAKOTO GOING AS A GIRL...
SHE KNOWS.
!
FATHER TOLD HER EVERY-THING.

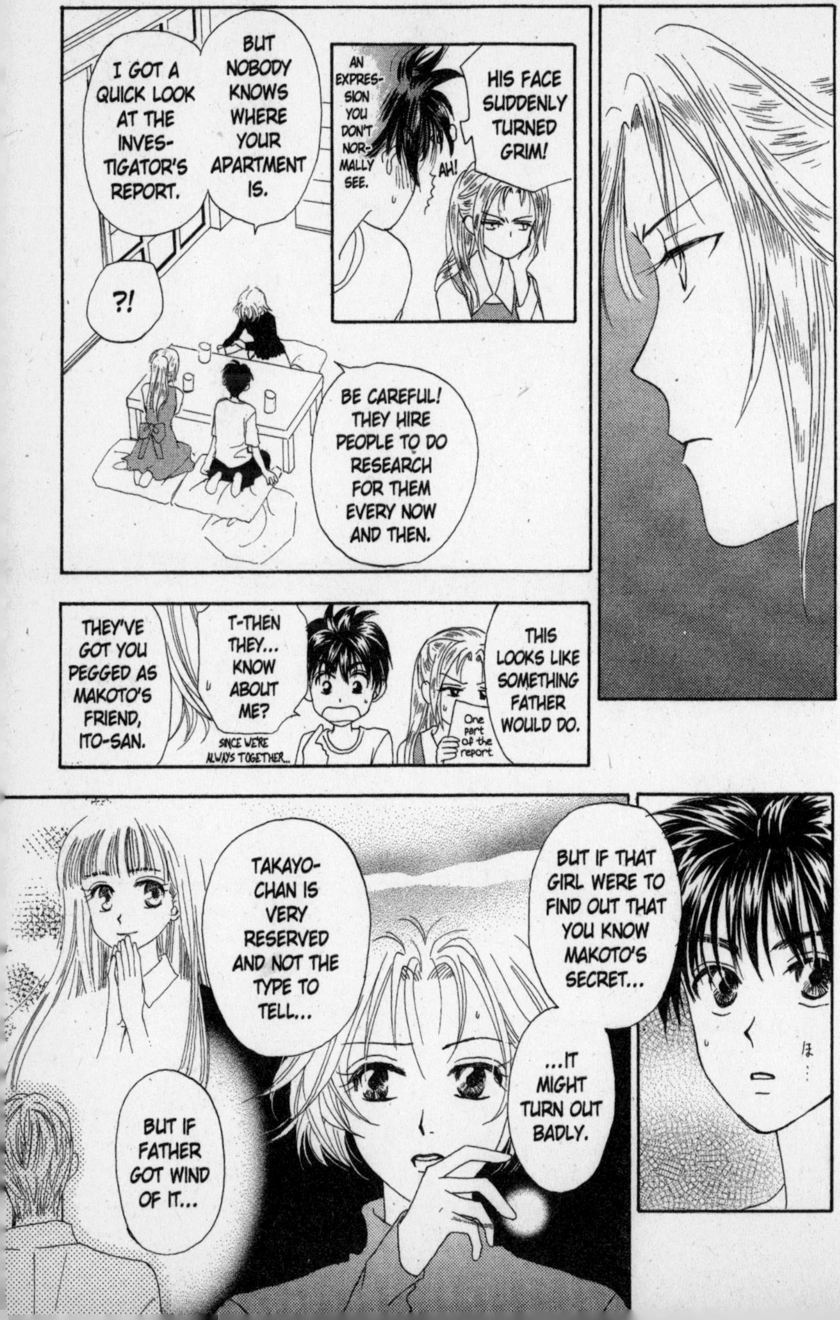
HIS FACE SUDDENLY TURNED GRIM!
AH!
AN EXPRESSION YOU DON'T NORMALLY SEE.
BUT NOBODY KNOWS WHERE YOUR APARTMENT IS.
I GOT A QUICK LOOK AT THE INVESTIGATOR'S REPORT.
?!
BE CAREFUL! THEY HIRE PEOPLE TO DO RESEARCH FOR THEM EVERY NOW AND THEN.
THIS LOOKS LIKE SOMETHING FATHER WOULD DO.
One part of the report
T-THEN THEY... KNOW ABOUT ME?
SINCE WE'RE ALWAYS TOGETHER...
THEY'VE GOT YOU PEGGED AS MAKOTO'S FRIEND, ITO-SAN.
BUT IF THAT GIRL WERE TO FIND OUT THAT YOU KNOW MAKOTO'S SECRET...
...IT MIGHT TURN OUT BADLY.
は…
TAKAYO-CHAN IS VERY RESERVED AND NOT THE TYPE TO TELL...
BUT IF FATHER GOT WIND OF IT...

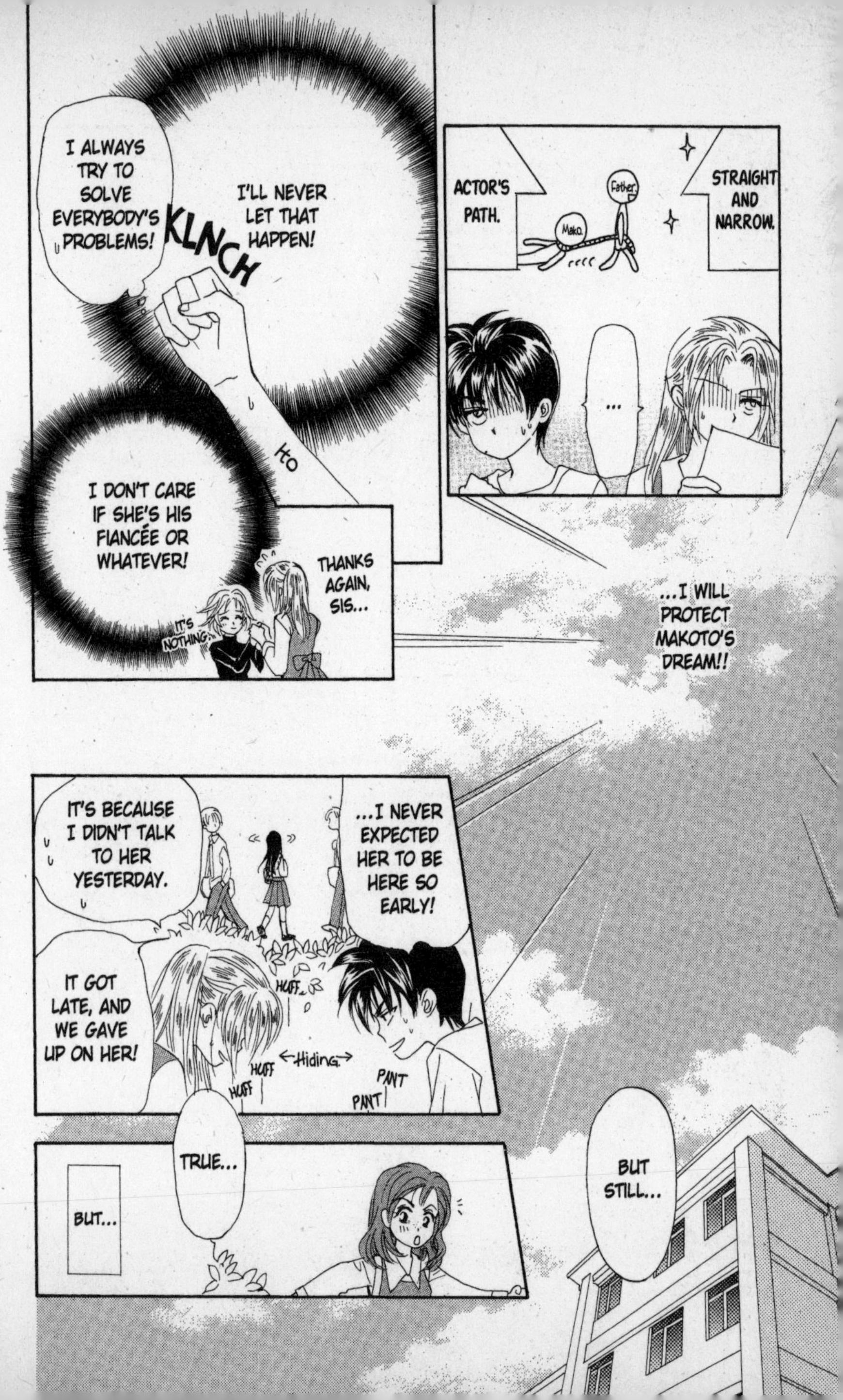
STRAIGHT AND NARROW.
Father
Mako.
ACTOR'S PATH.
...
I'LL NEVER LET THAT HAPPEN!
I ALWAYS TRY TO SOLVE EVERYBODY'S PROBLEMS!
KLNCH
Ho
I DON'T CARE IF SHE'S HIS FIANCÉE OR WHATEVER!
THANKS AGAIN, SIS...
IT'S NOTHING.
...I WILL PROTECT MAKOTO'S DREAM!!
...I NEVER EXPECTED HER TO BE HERE SO EARLY!
IT'S BECAUSE I DIDN'T TALK TO HER YESTERDAY.
IT GOT LATE, AND WE GAVE UP ON HER!
HUFF
←Hiding→
PANT
PANT
HUFF
HUFF
BUT STILL...
TRUE...
BUT...

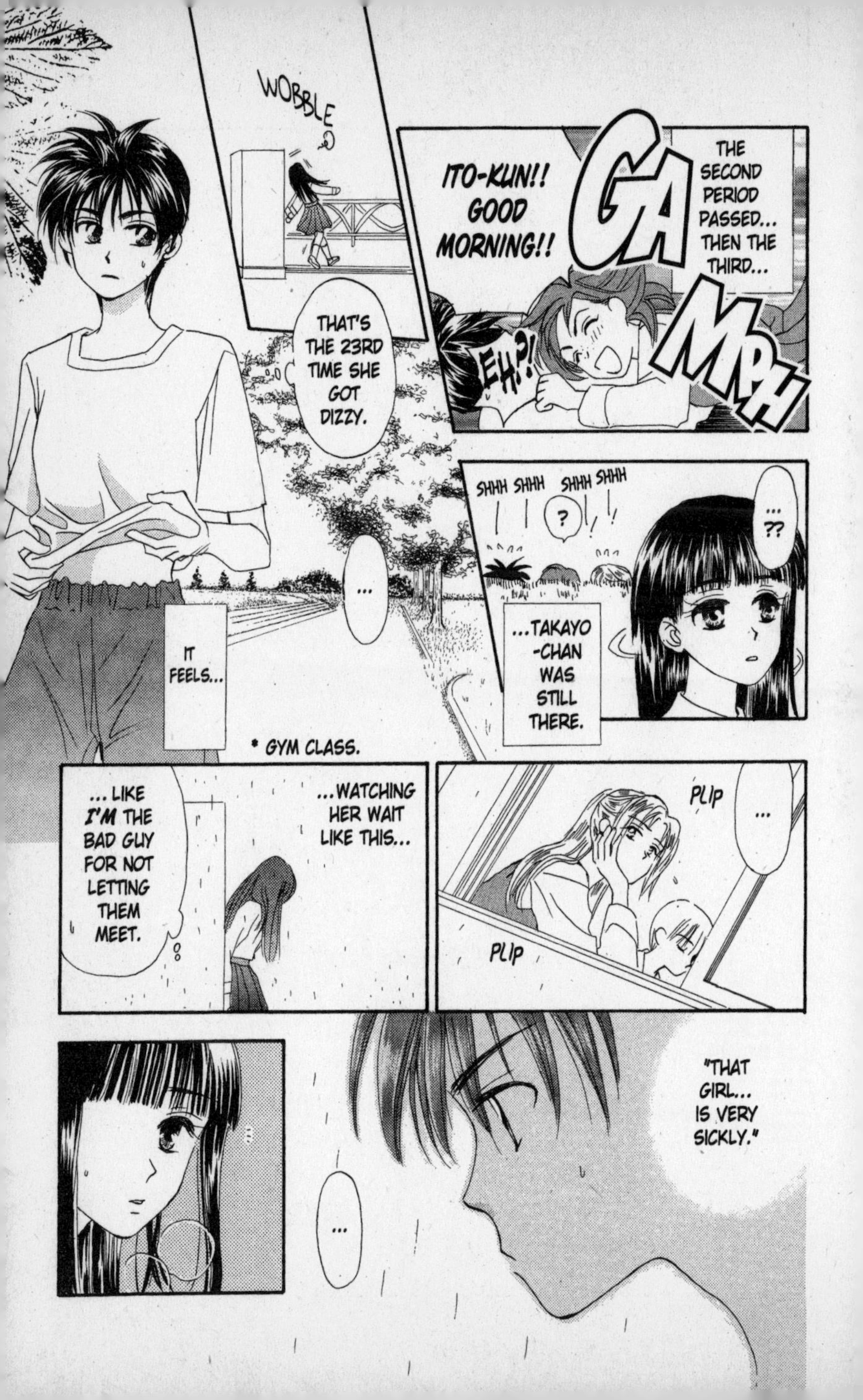
THE SECOND PERIOD PASSED... THEN THE THIRD...
GA
ITO-KUN!! GOOD MORNING!!
MPH
EH?!
WOBBLE
THAT'S THE 23RD TIME SHE GOT DIZZY.
...??
SHHH SHHH SHHH SHHH
?
...TAKAYO-CHAN WAS STILL THERE.
...
IT FEELS...
* GYM CLASS.
...
PLIP
PLIP
...WATCHING HER WAIT LIKE THIS...
... LIKE *I'M* THE BAD GUY FOR NOT LETTING THEM MEET.
"THAT GIRL... IS VERY SICKLY."
...

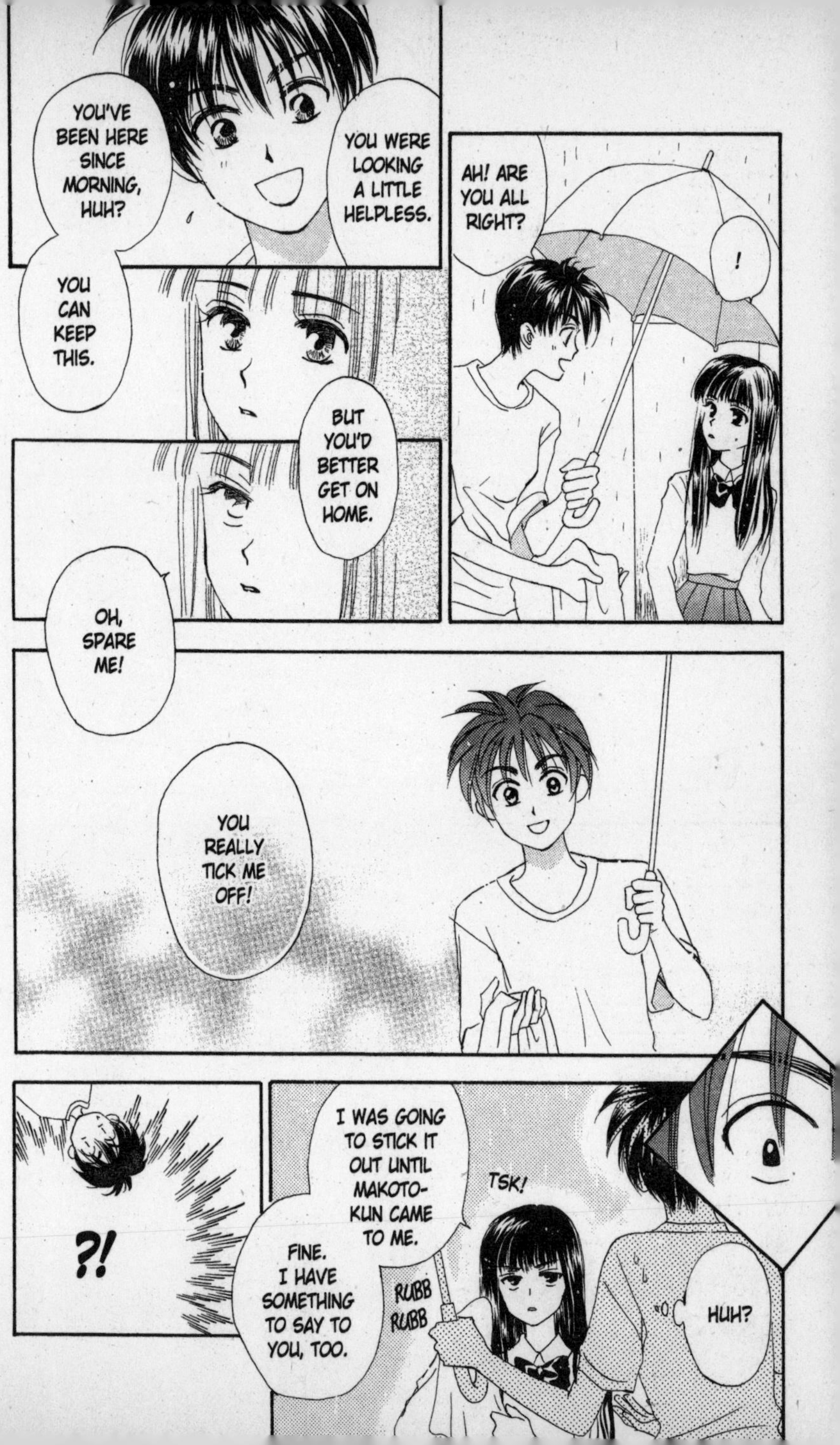
AH! ARE YOU ALL RIGHT?
!
YOU WERE LOOKING A LITTLE HELPLESS.
YOU'VE BEEN HERE SINCE MORNING, HUH?
YOU CAN KEEP THIS.
BUT YOU'D BETTER GET ON HOME.
OH, SPARE ME!
YOU REALLY TICK ME OFF!
I WAS GOING TO STICK IT OUT UNTIL MAKOTO-KUN CAME TO ME.
TSK!
FINE. I HAVE SOMETHING TO SAY TO YOU, TOO.
RUBB RUBB
HUH?
?!

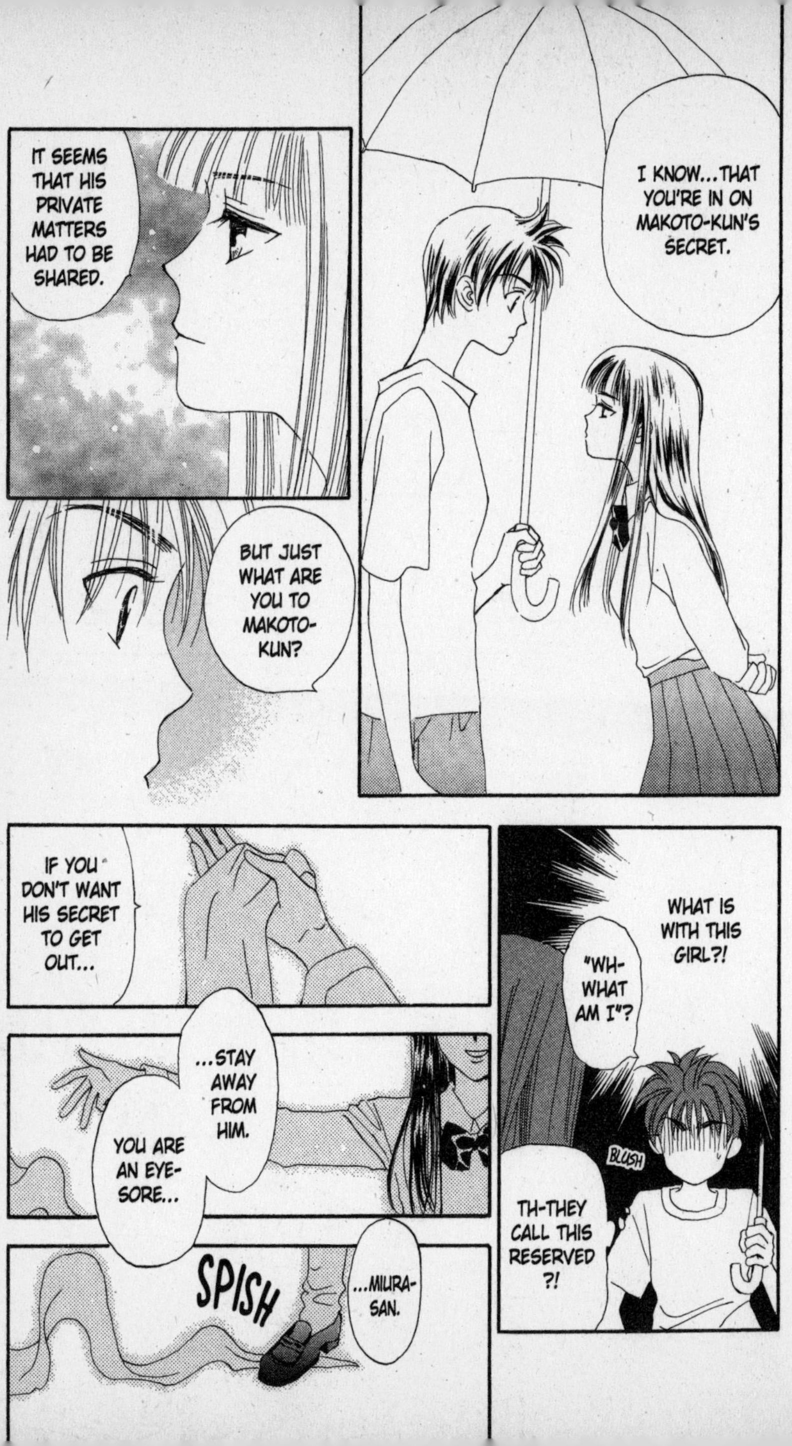
I KNOW...THAT YOU'RE IN ON MAKOTO-KUN'S SECRET.
IT SEEMS THAT HIS PRIVATE MATTERS HAD TO BE SHARED.
BUT JUST WHAT ARE YOU TO MAKOTO-KUN?
WHAT IS WITH THIS GIRL?!
"WH-WHAT AM I"?
BLUSH
TH-THEY CALL THIS RESERVED?!
IF YOU DON'T WANT HIS SECRET TO GET OUT...
...STAY AWAY FROM HIM.
YOU ARE AN EYE-SORE...
SPISH
...MIURA-SAN.

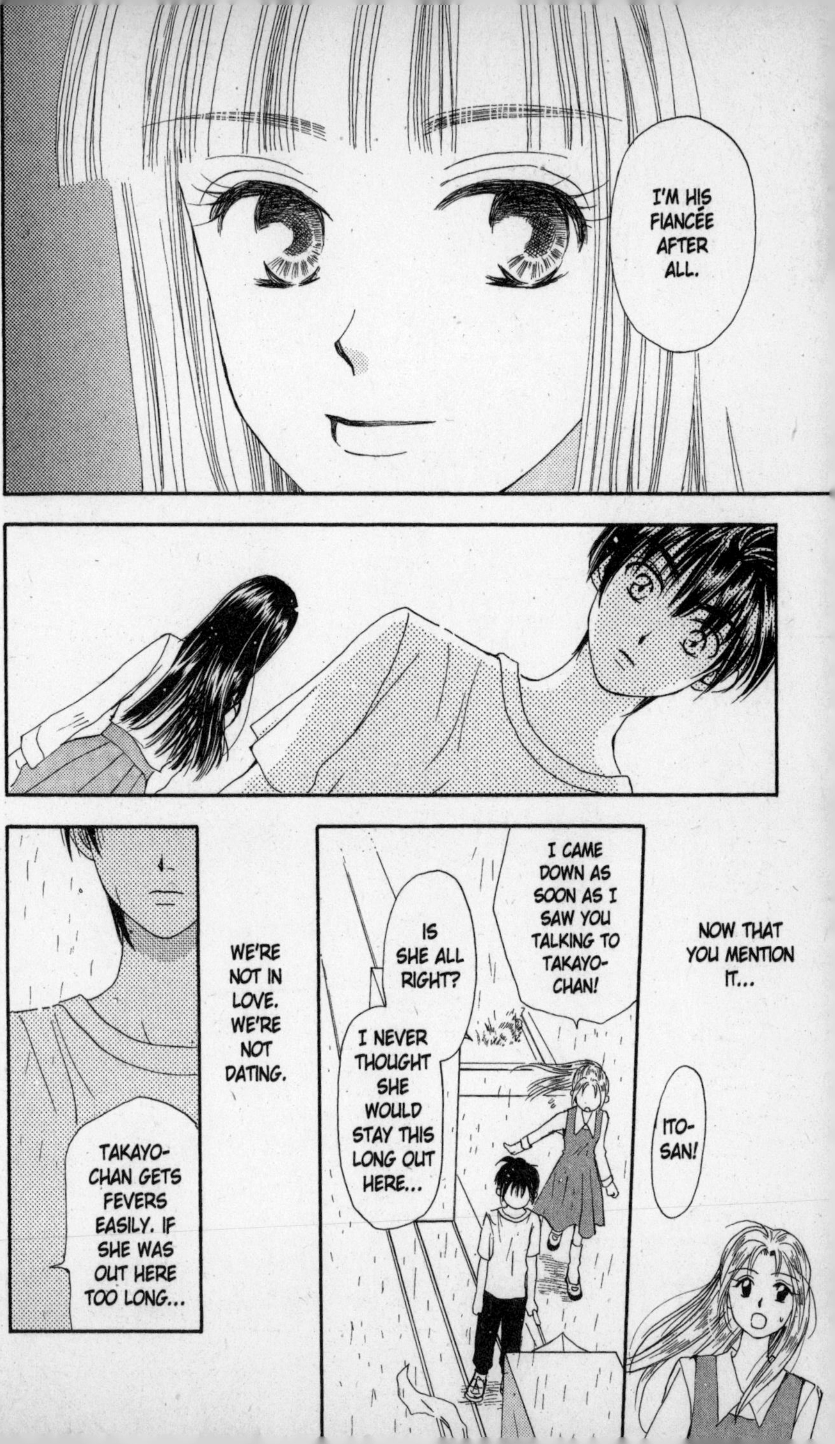
I'M HIS FIANCÉE AFTER ALL.
NOW THAT YOU MENTION IT...
ITO-SAN!
I CAME DOWN AS SOON AS I SAW YOU TALKING TO TAKAYO-CHAN!
IS SHE ALL RIGHT?
I NEVER THOUGHT SHE WOULD STAY THIS LONG OUT HERE...
WE'RE NOT IN LOVE. WE'RE NOT DATING.
TAKAYO-CHAN GETS FEVERS EASILY. IF SHE WAS OUT HERE TOO LONG...

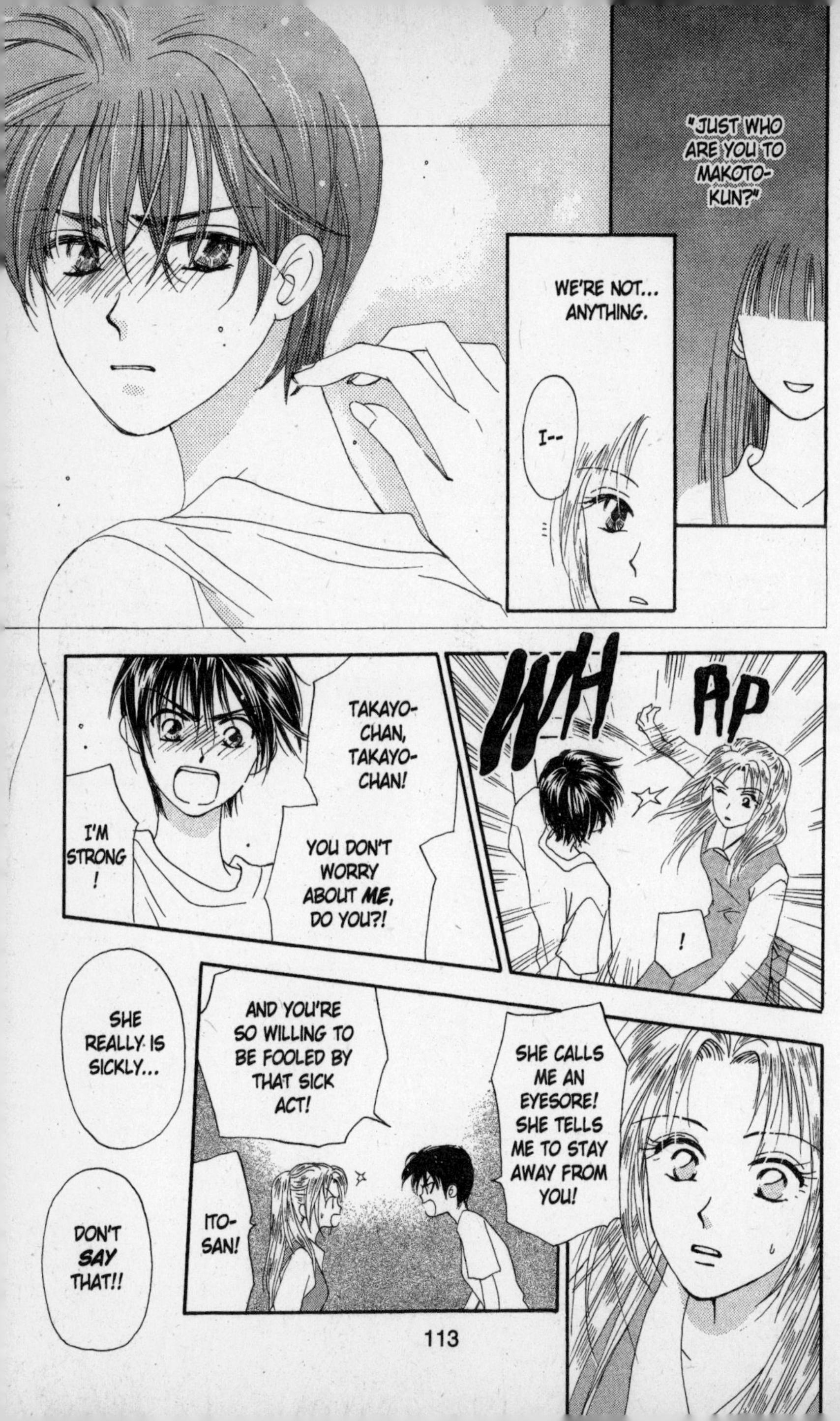
"JUST WHO ARE YOU TO MAKOTO-KUN?"
WE'RE NOT... ANYTHING.
I--
WHAP
!
TAKAYO-CHAN, TAKAYO-CHAN!
YOU DON'T WORRY ABOUT *ME*, DO YOU?!
I'M STRONG!
SHE CALLS ME AN EYESORE! SHE TELLS ME TO STAY AWAY FROM YOU!
AND YOU'RE SO WILLING TO BE FOOLED BY THAT SICK ACT!
ITO-SAN!
SHE REALLY IS SICKLY...
DON'T *SAY* THAT!!

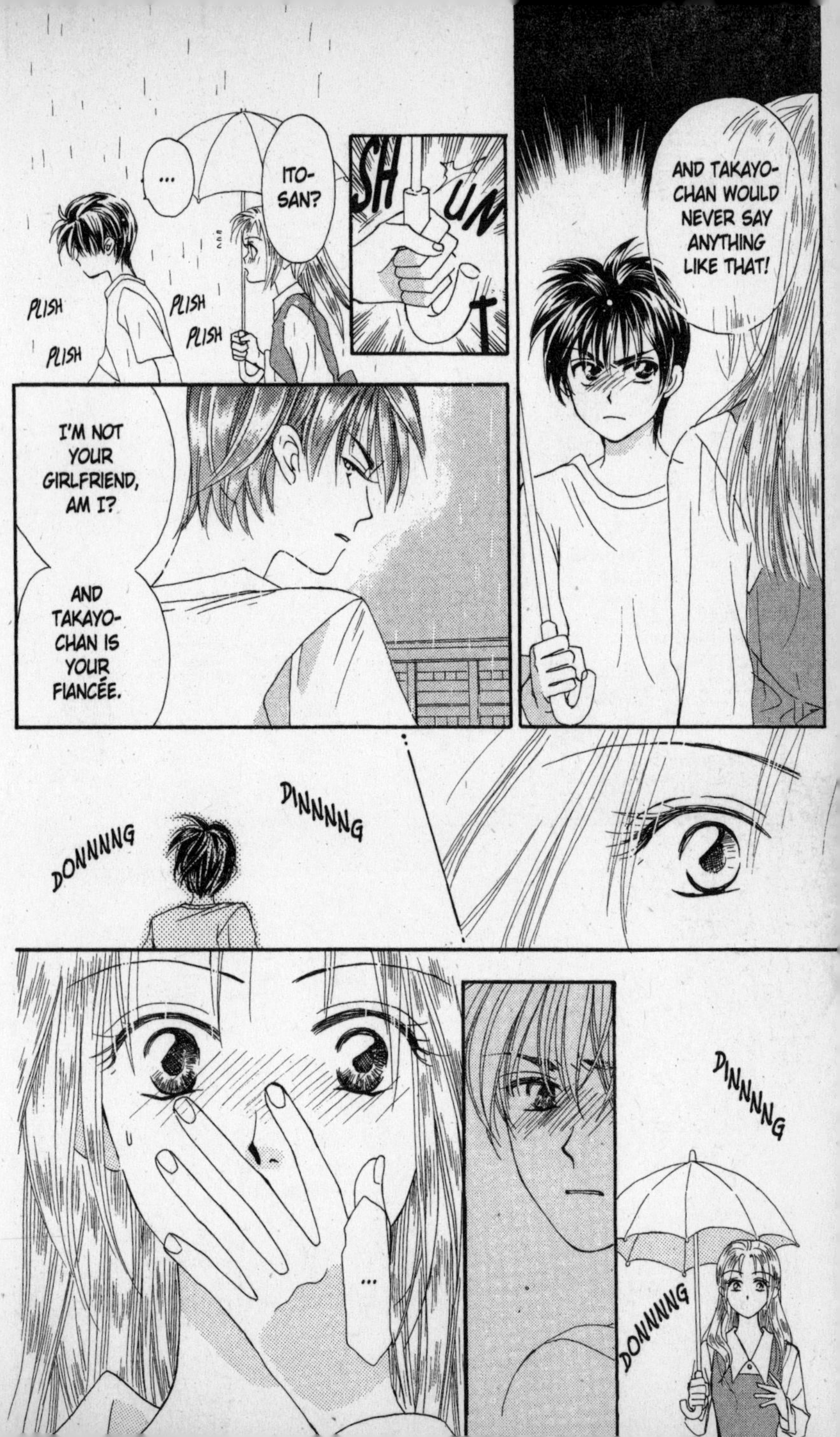
AND TAKAYO-CHAN WOULD NEVER SAY ANYTHING LIKE THAT!
SHUNT
ITO-SAN?
...
PLISH
PLISH
PLISH
PLISH
I'M NOT YOUR GIRLFRIEND, AM I?
AND TAKAYO-CHAN IS YOUR FIANCÉE.
DINNNNG
DONNNNG
DINNNNG
DONNNNG
...

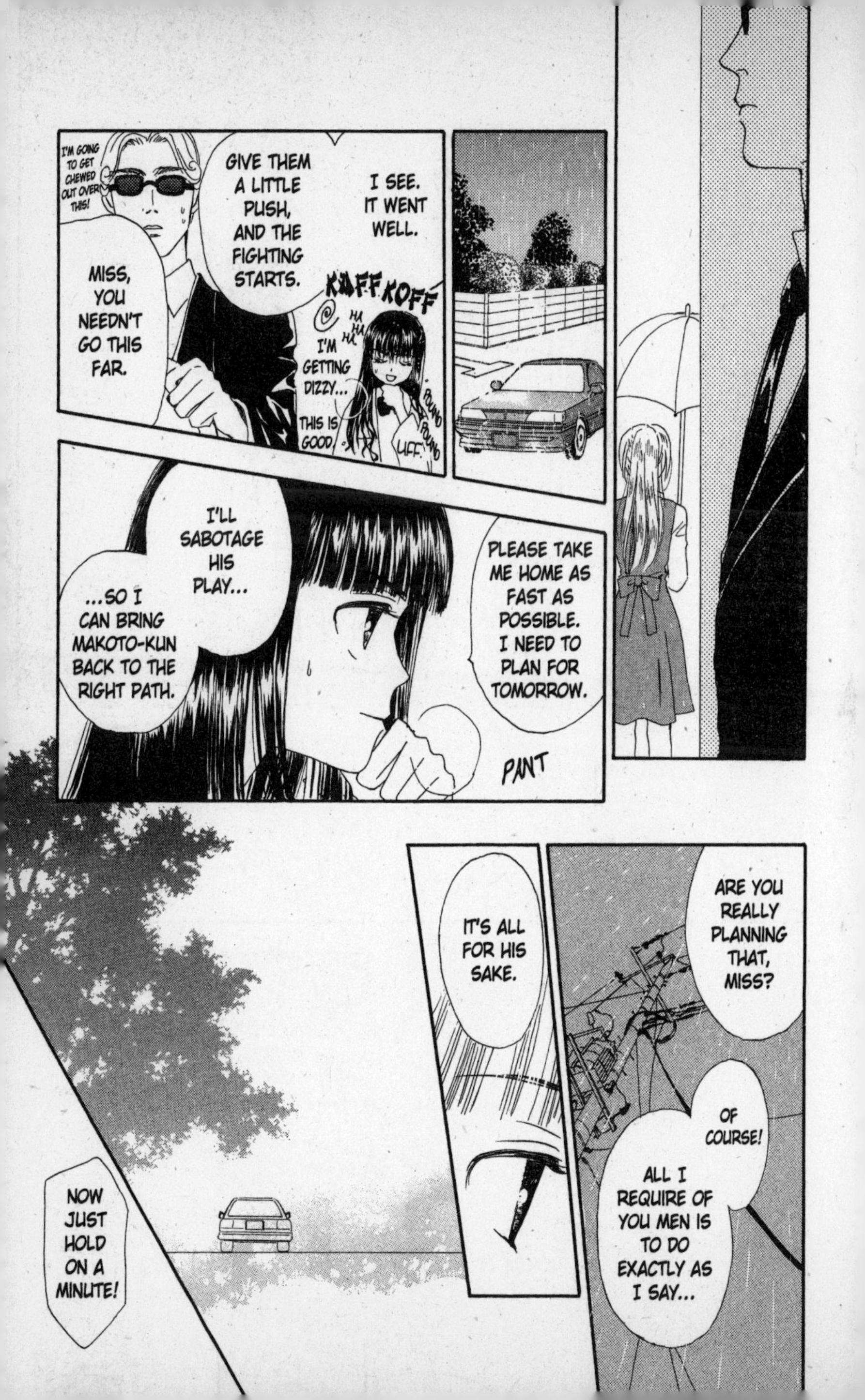
I SEE. IT WENT WELL.
GIVE THEM A LITTLE PUSH, AND THE FIGHTING STARTS.
KAFF KOFF
HA HA HA
I'M GETTING DIZZY...
THIS IS GOOD.
POUND POUND
UFF.
I'M GOING TO GET CHEWED OUT OVER THIS!
MISS, YOU NEEDN'T GO THIS FAR.
PLEASE TAKE ME HOME AS FAST AS POSSIBLE. I NEED TO PLAN FOR TOMORROW.
PANT
I'LL SABOTAGE HIS PLAY...
...SO I CAN BRING MAKOTO-KUN BACK TO THE RIGHT PATH.
ARE YOU REALLY PLANNING THAT, MISS?
OF COURSE!
ALL I REQUIRE OF YOU MEN IS TO DO EXACTLY AS I SAY...
IT'S ALL FOR HIS SAKE.
NOW JUST HOLD ON A MINUTE!

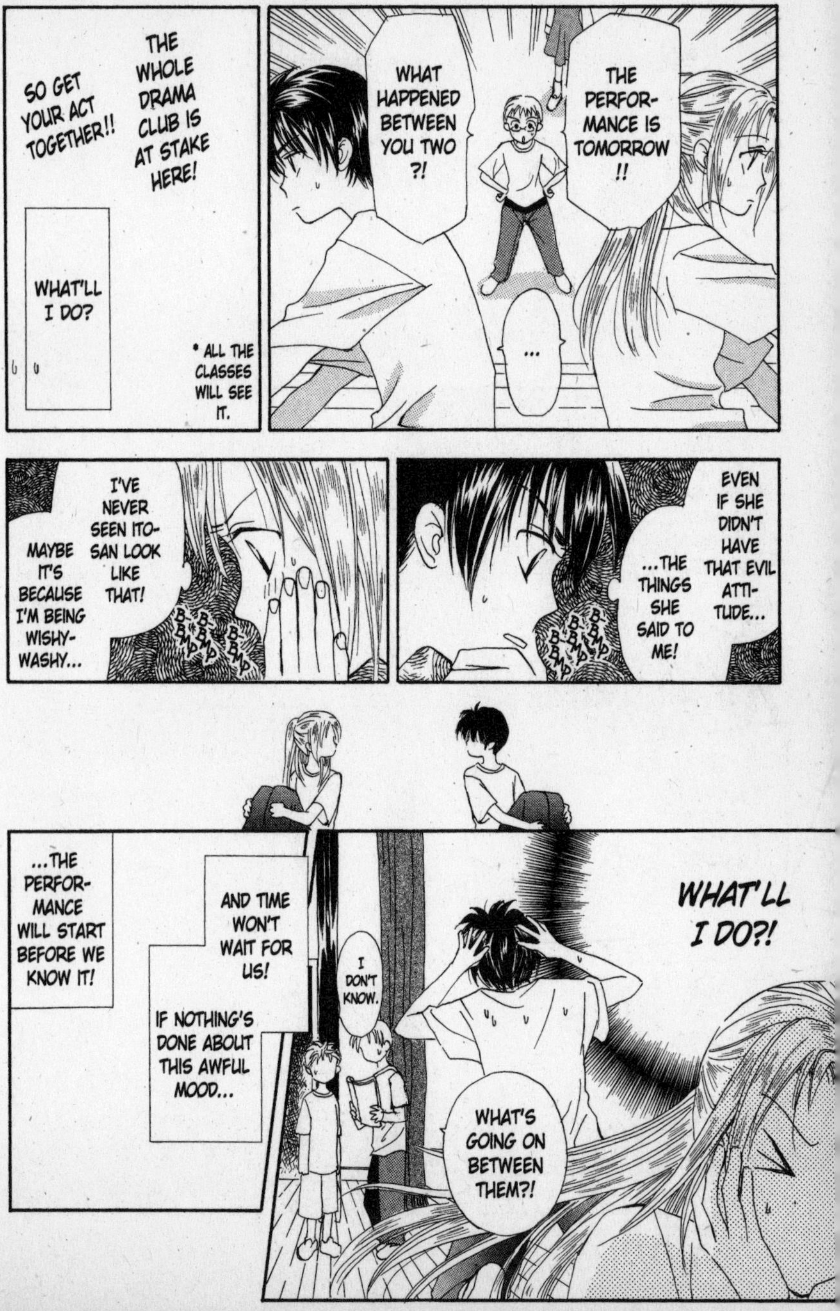
THE PERFORMANCE IS TOMORROW!!
WHAT HAPPENED BETWEEN YOU TWO?!
...
THE WHOLE DRAMA CLUB IS AT STAKE HERE!
SO GET YOUR ACT TOGETHER!!
* ALL THE CLASSES WILL SEE IT.
WHAT'LL I DO?
EVEN IF SHE DIDN'T HAVE THAT EVIL ATTITUDE...
...THE THINGS SHE SAID TO ME!
B-BMP B-BMP B-BMP
I'VE NEVER SEEN ITO-SAN LOOK LIKE THAT!
MAYBE IT'S BECAUSE I'M BEING WISHY-WASHY...
B-BMP B-BMP B-BMP
WHAT'LL I DO?!
WHAT'S GOING ON BETWEEN THEM?!
I DON'T KNOW.
AND TIME WON'T WAIT FOR US!
IF NOTHING'S DONE ABOUT THIS AWFUL MOOD...
...THE PERFORMANCE WILL START BEFORE WE KNOW IT!

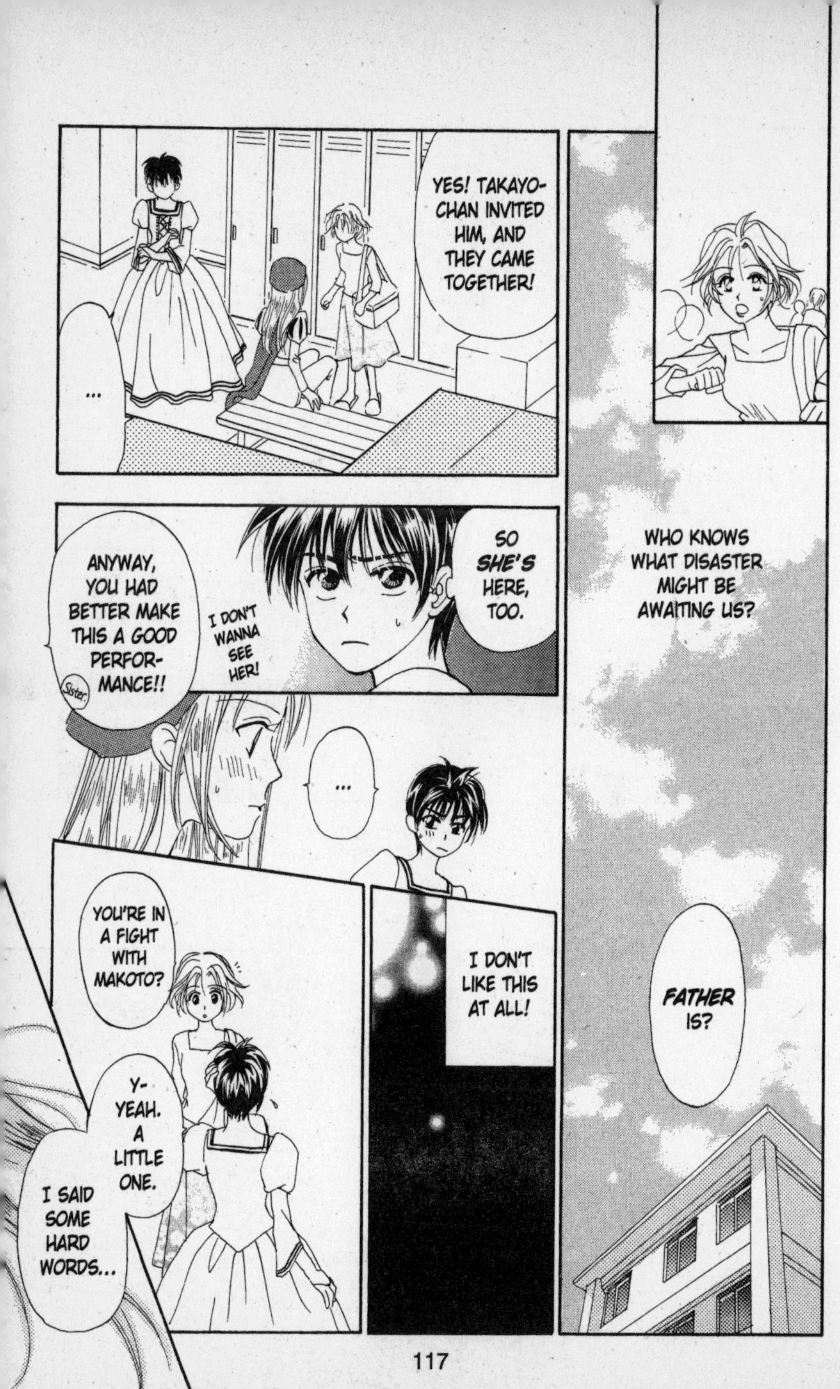
WHO KNOWS WHAT DISASTER MIGHT BE AWAITING US?
FATHER IS?
YES! TAKAYO-CHAN INVITED HIM, AND THEY CAME TOGETHER!
...
SO SHE'S HERE, TOO.
I DON'T WANNA SEE HER!
ANYWAY, YOU HAD BETTER MAKE THIS A GOOD PERFORMANCE!!
Sister.
...
I DON'T LIKE THIS AT ALL!
YOU'RE IN A FIGHT WITH MAKOTO?
Y-YEAH. A LITTLE ONE.
I SAID SOME HARD WORDS...

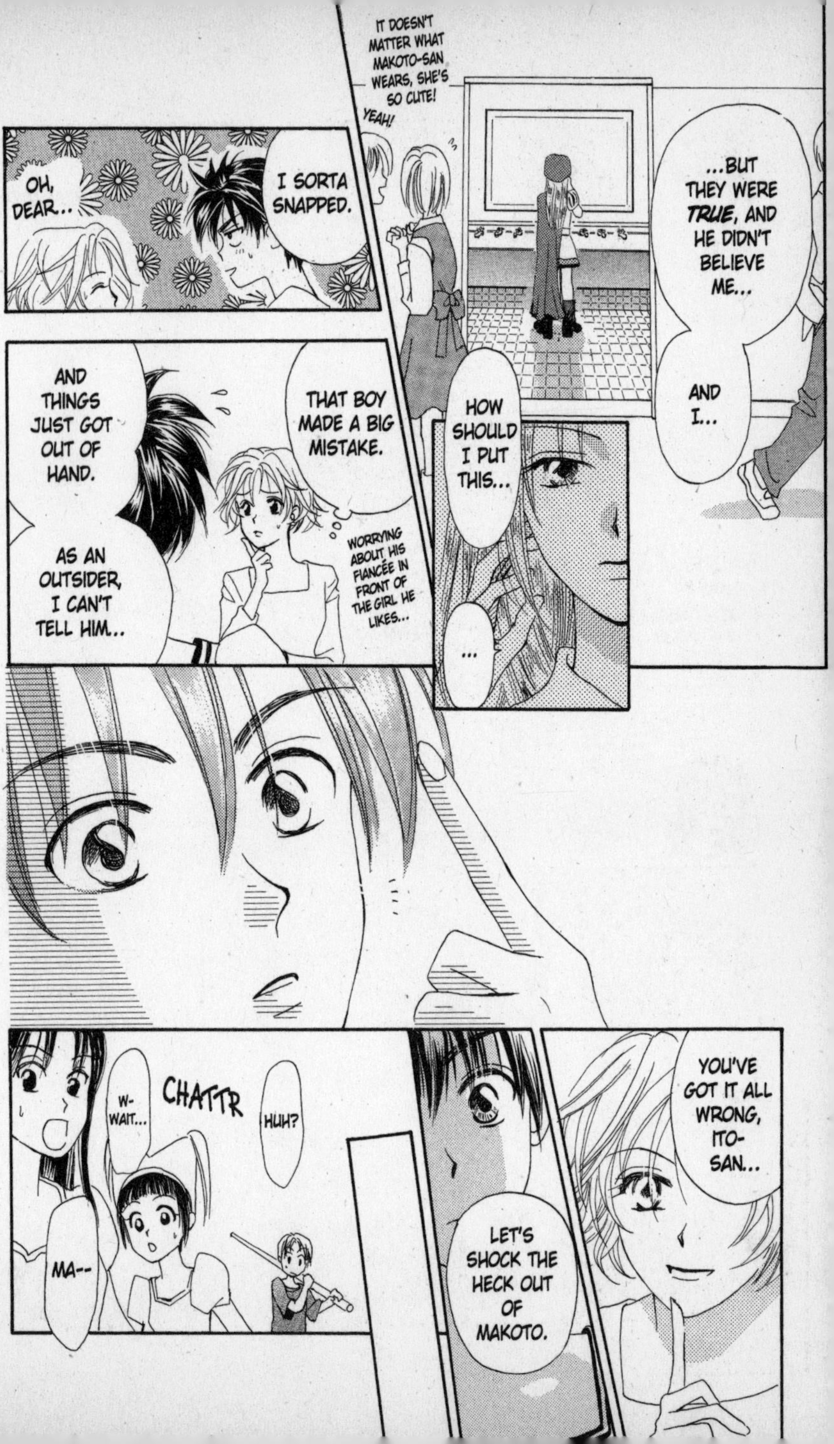
IT DOESN'T MATTER WHAT MAKOTO-SAN WEARS, SHE'S SO CUTE!
YEAH!
...BUT THEY WERE *TRUE*, AND HE DIDN'T BELIEVE ME...
AND I...
I SORTA SNAPPED.
OH, DEAR...
HOW SHOULD I PUT THIS...
...
THAT BOY MADE A BIG MISTAKE.
WORRYING ABOUT HIS FIANCÉE IN FRONT OF THE GIRL HE LIKES...
AND THINGS JUST GOT OUT OF HAND.
AS AN OUTSIDER, I CAN'T TELL HIM...
YOU'VE GOT IT ALL WRONG, ITO-SAN...
LET'S SHOCK THE HECK OUT OF MAKOTO.
HUH?
CHATTR
W-WAIT...
MA--

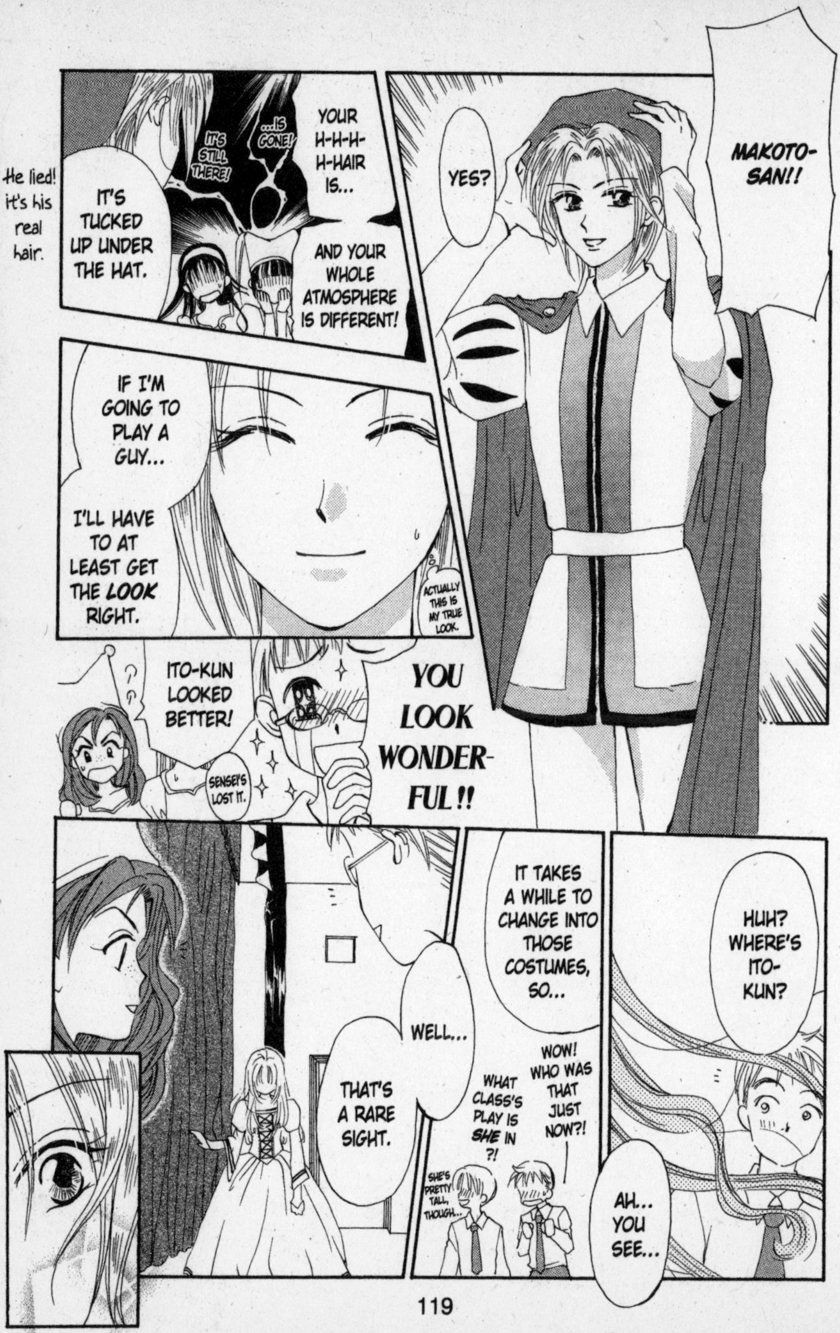
MAKOTO-SAN!!
YES?
YOUR H-H-H-H-HAIR IS...
...IS GONE!
AND YOUR WHOLE ATMOSPHERE IS DIFFERENT!
IT'S STILL THERE!
IT'S TUCKED UP UNDER THE HAT.
He lied! it's his real hair.
IF I'M GOING TO PLAY A GUY...
I'LL HAVE TO AT LEAST GET THE LOOK RIGHT.
ACTUALLY THIS IS MY TRUE LOOK.
YOU LOOK WONDERFUL!!
ITO-KUN LOOKED BETTER!
SENSEI'S LOST IT.
HUH? WHERE'S ITO-KUN?
AH... YOU SEE...
IT TAKES A WHILE TO CHANGE INTO THOSE COSTUMES, SO...
WOW! WHO WAS THAT JUST NOW?!
WHAT CLASS'S PLAY IS SHE IN ?!
SHE'S PRETTY TALL, THOUGH...
WELL...
THAT'S A RARE SIGHT.

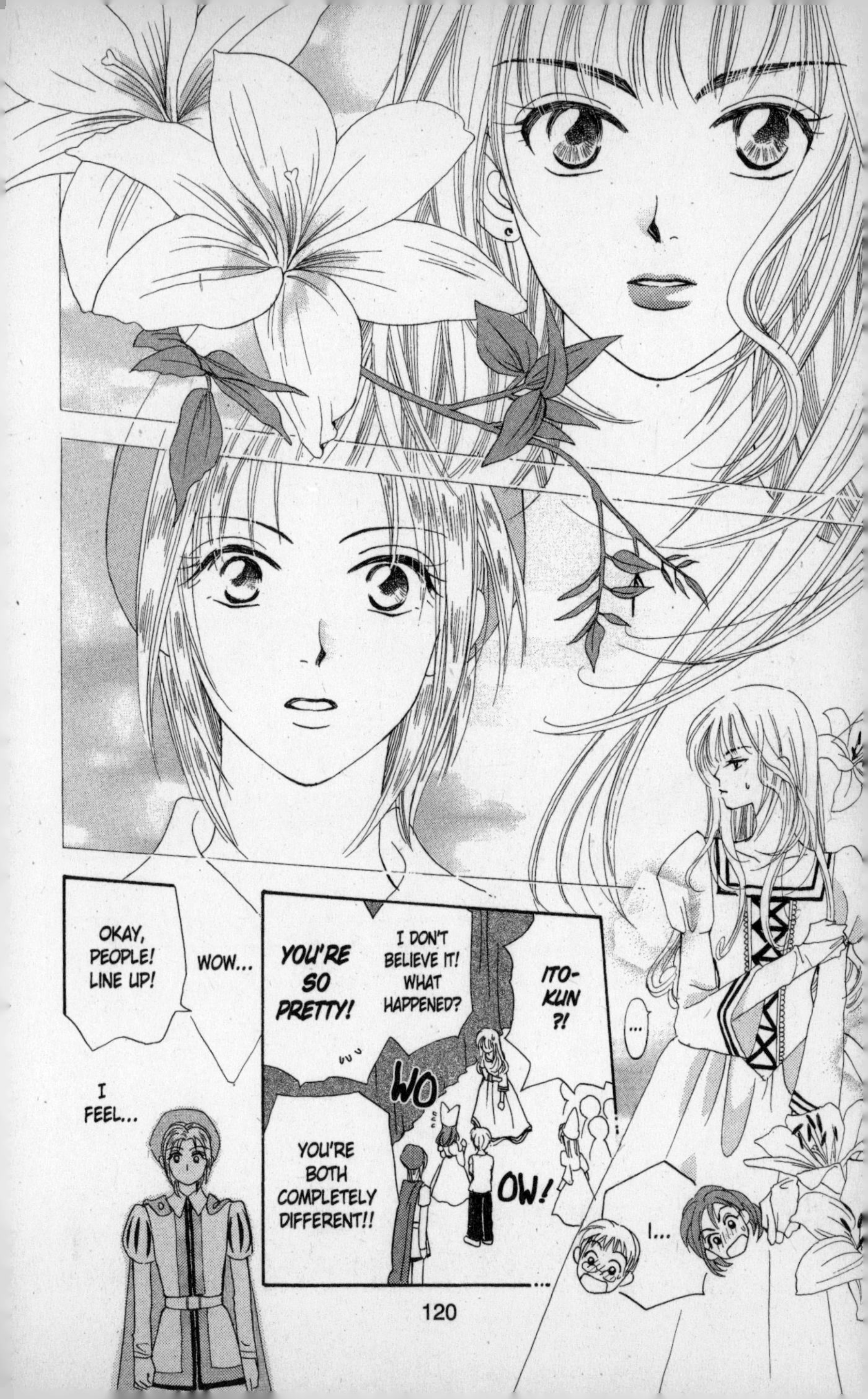
...
I...
ITO-KUN?!
I DON'T BELIEVE IT! WHAT HAPPENED?
YOU'RE SO PRETTY!
WO
OW!
YOU'RE BOTH COMPLETELY DIFFERENT!!
WOW...
OKAY, PEOPLE! LINE UP!
I FEEL...

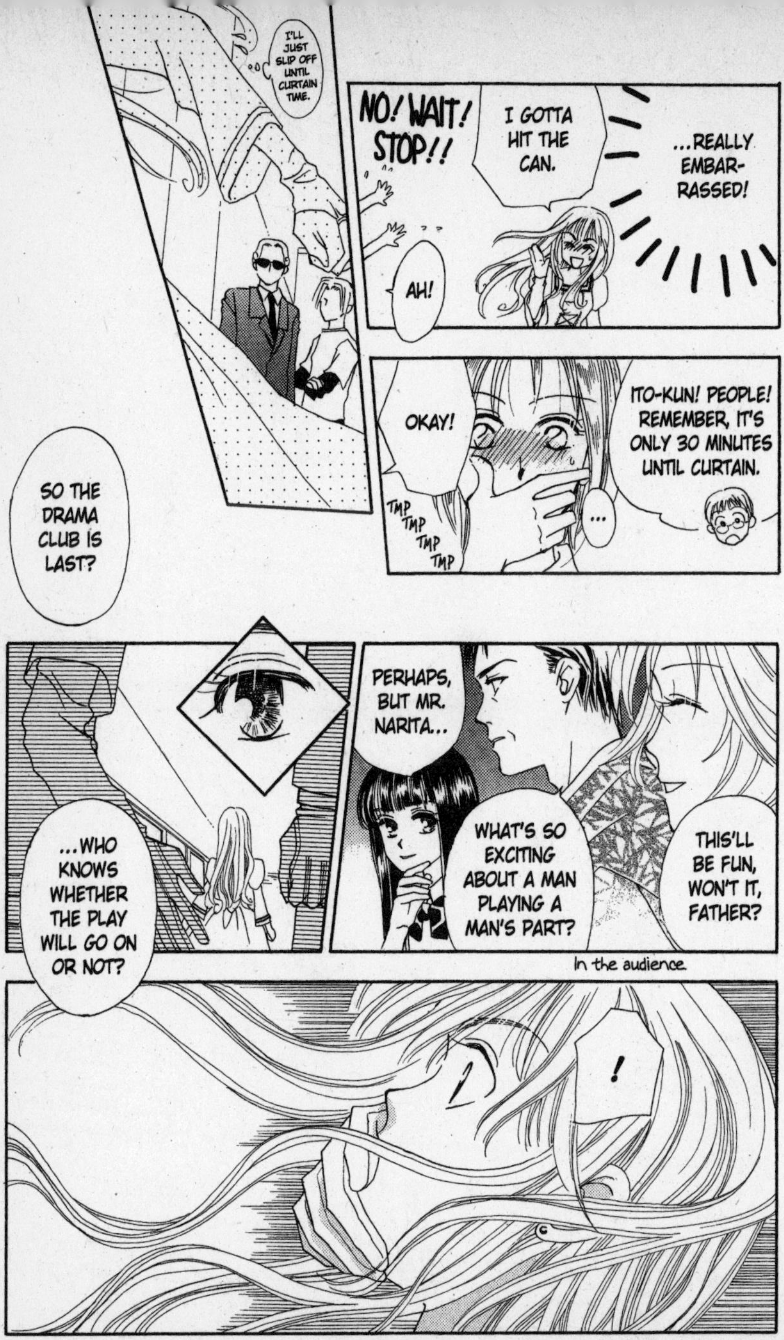
...REALLY EMBARRASSED!
I GOTTA HIT THE CAN.
NO! WAIT! STOP!!
AH!
ITO-KUN! PEOPLE! REMEMBER, IT'S ONLY 30 MINUTES UNTIL CURTAIN.
...
OKAY!
TMP TMP TMP TMP
I'LL JUST SLIP OFF UNTIL CURTAIN TIME.
SO THE DRAMA CLUB IS LAST?
THIS'LL BE FUN, WON'T IT, FATHER?
WHAT'S SO EXCITING ABOUT A MAN PLAYING A MAN'S PART?
PERHAPS, BUT MR. NARITA...
In the audience.
...WHO KNOWS WHETHER THE PLAY WILL GO ON OR NOT?
!

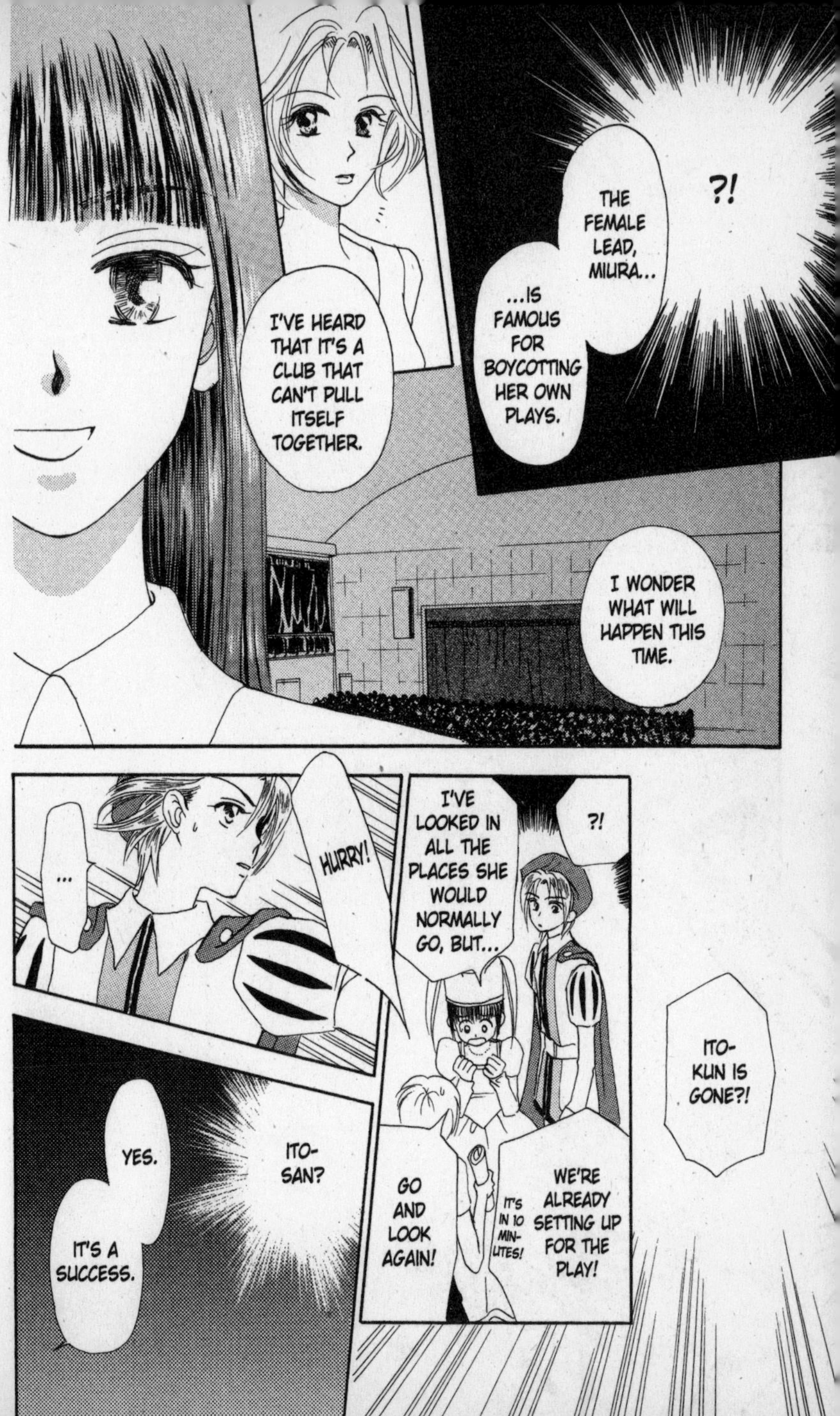
?!
THE FEMALE LEAD, MIURA...
...IS FAMOUS FOR BOYCOTTING HER OWN PLAYS.
I'VE HEARD THAT IT'S A CLUB THAT CAN'T PULL ITSELF TOGETHER.
I WONDER WHAT WILL HAPPEN THIS TIME.
?!
I'VE LOOKED IN ALL THE PLACES SHE WOULD NORMALLY GO, BUT...
ITO-KUN IS GONE?!
WE'RE ALREADY SETTING UP FOR THE PLAY!
IT'S IN 10 MINUTES!
GO AND LOOK AGAIN!
HURRY!
...
ITO-SAN?
YES.
IT'S A SUCCESS.

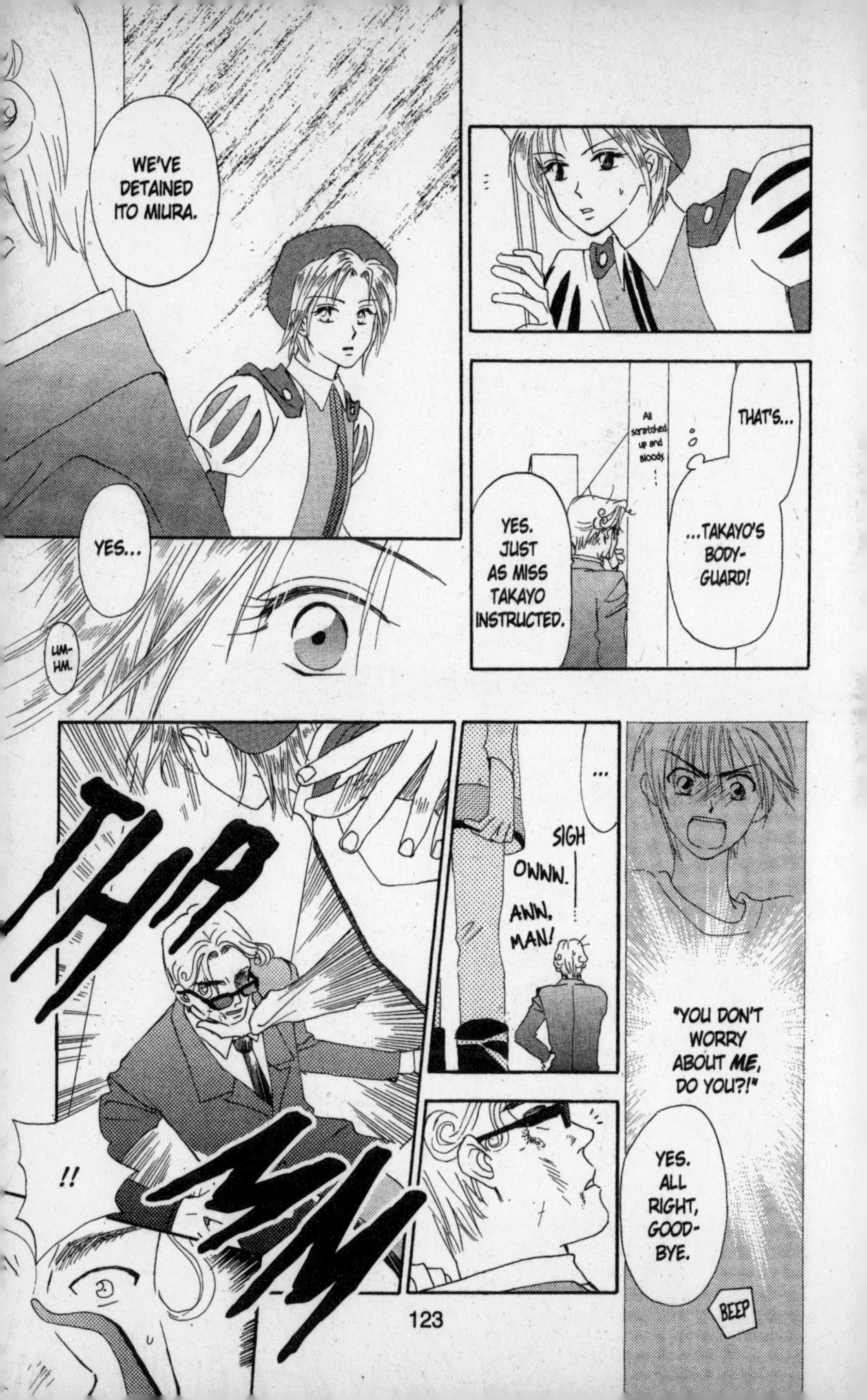
THAT'S...
...TAKAYO'S BODY-GUARD!
All scratched up and bloody...
YES. JUST AS MISS TAKAYO INSTRUCTED.
WE'VE DETAINED ITO MIURA.
YES...
UM-HM.
"YOU DON'T WORRY ABOUT *ME*, DO YOU?!"
YES. ALL RIGHT, GOOD-BYE.
BEEP
...
SIGH
OWWW.
AWW, MAN!
THAMM
!!

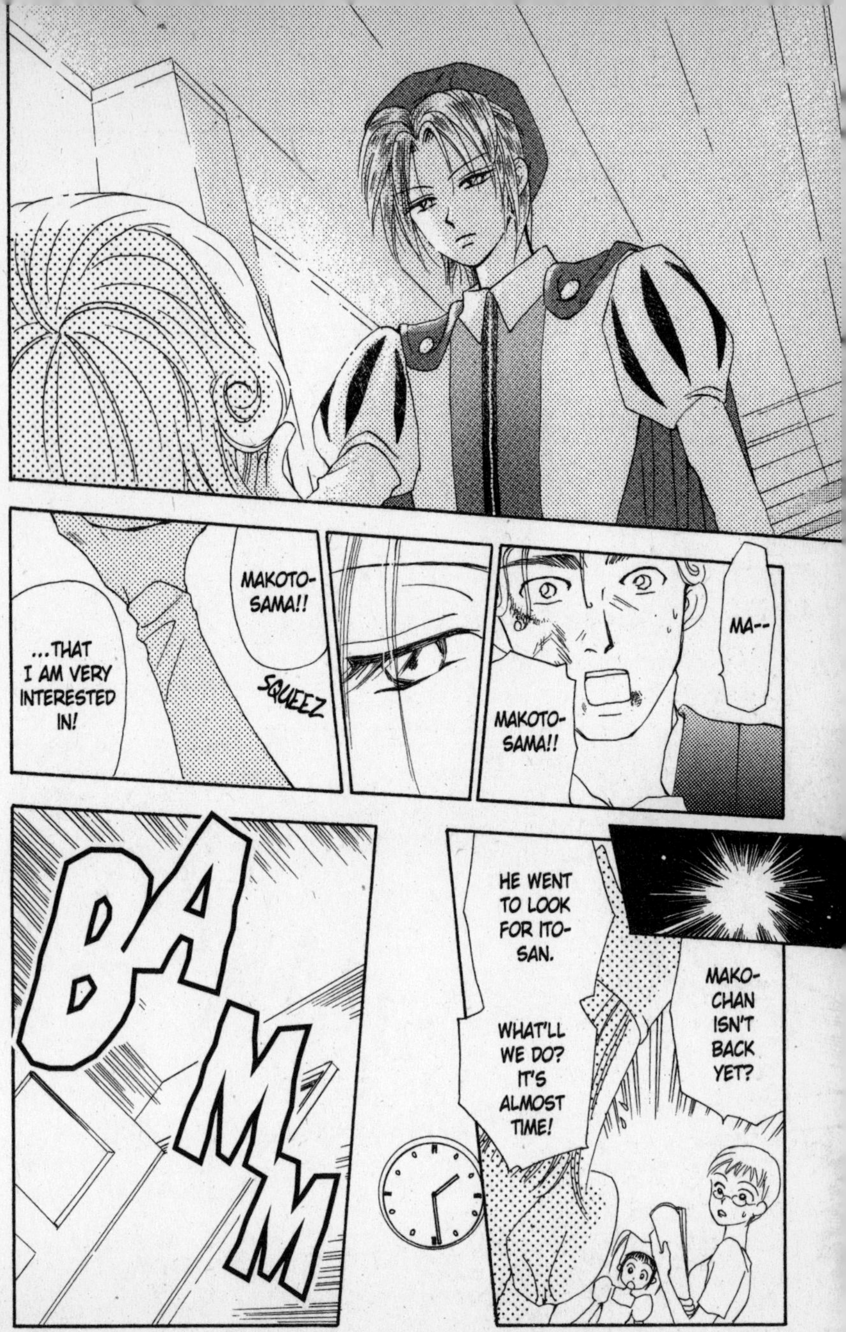
MA--
MAKOTO-SAMA!!
MAKOTO-SAMA!!
...THAT I AM VERY INTERESTED IN!
SQUEEZ
MAKO-CHAN ISN'T BACK YET?
HE WENT TO LOOK FOR ITO-SAN.
WHAT'LL WE DO? IT'S ALMOST TIME!
BAMM

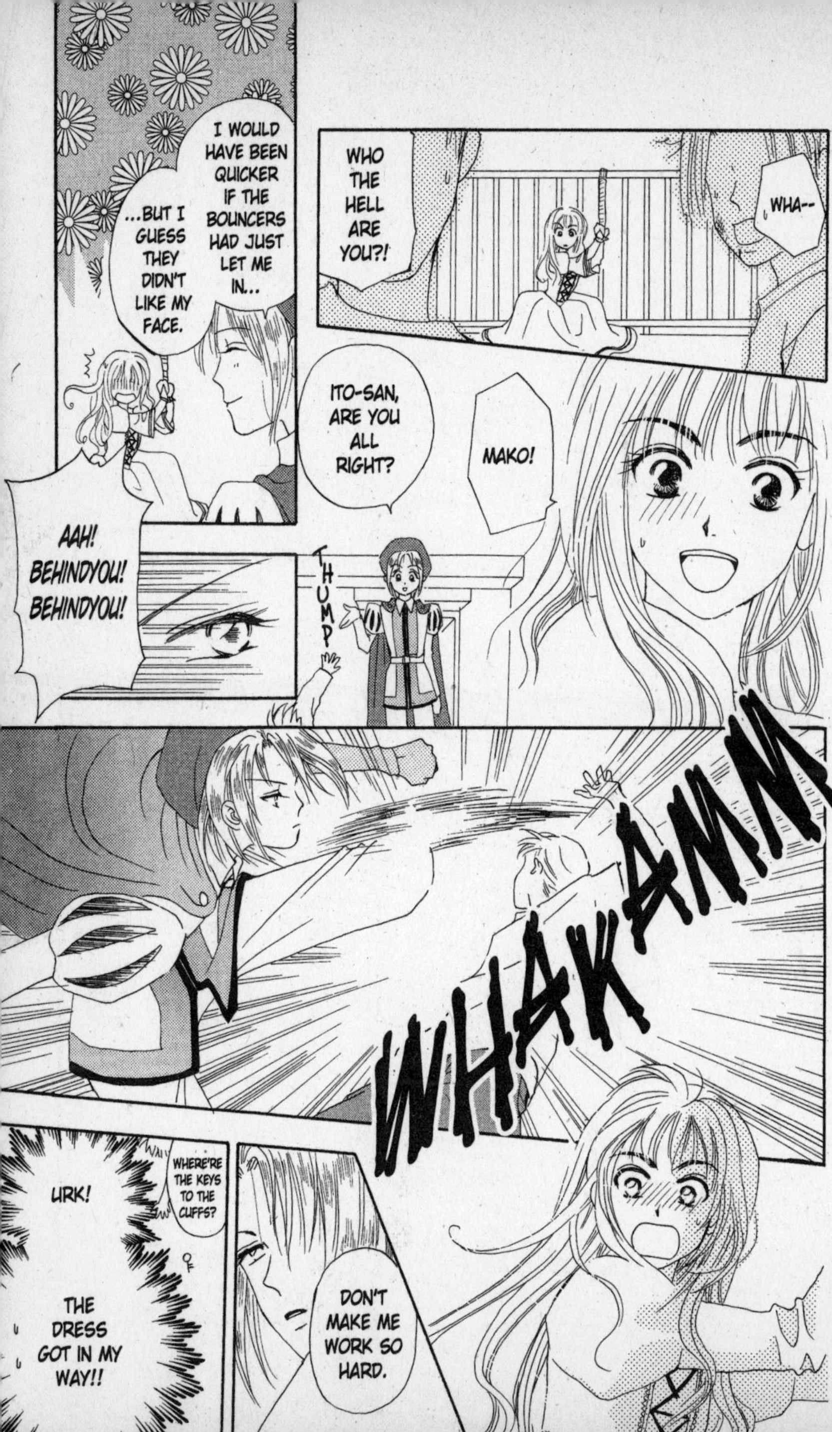
WHA--
WHO THE HELL ARE YOU?!
I WOULD HAVE BEEN QUICKER IF THE BOUNCERS HAD JUST LET ME IN...
...BUT I GUESS THEY DIDN'T LIKE MY FACE.
MAKO!
ITO-SAN, ARE YOU ALL RIGHT?
THUMP
AAH! BEHINDYOU! BEHINDYOU!
WHAKAMM
WHERE'RE THE KEYS TO THE CUFFS?
DON'T MAKE ME WORK SO HARD.
URK!
THE DRESS GOT IN MY WAY!!

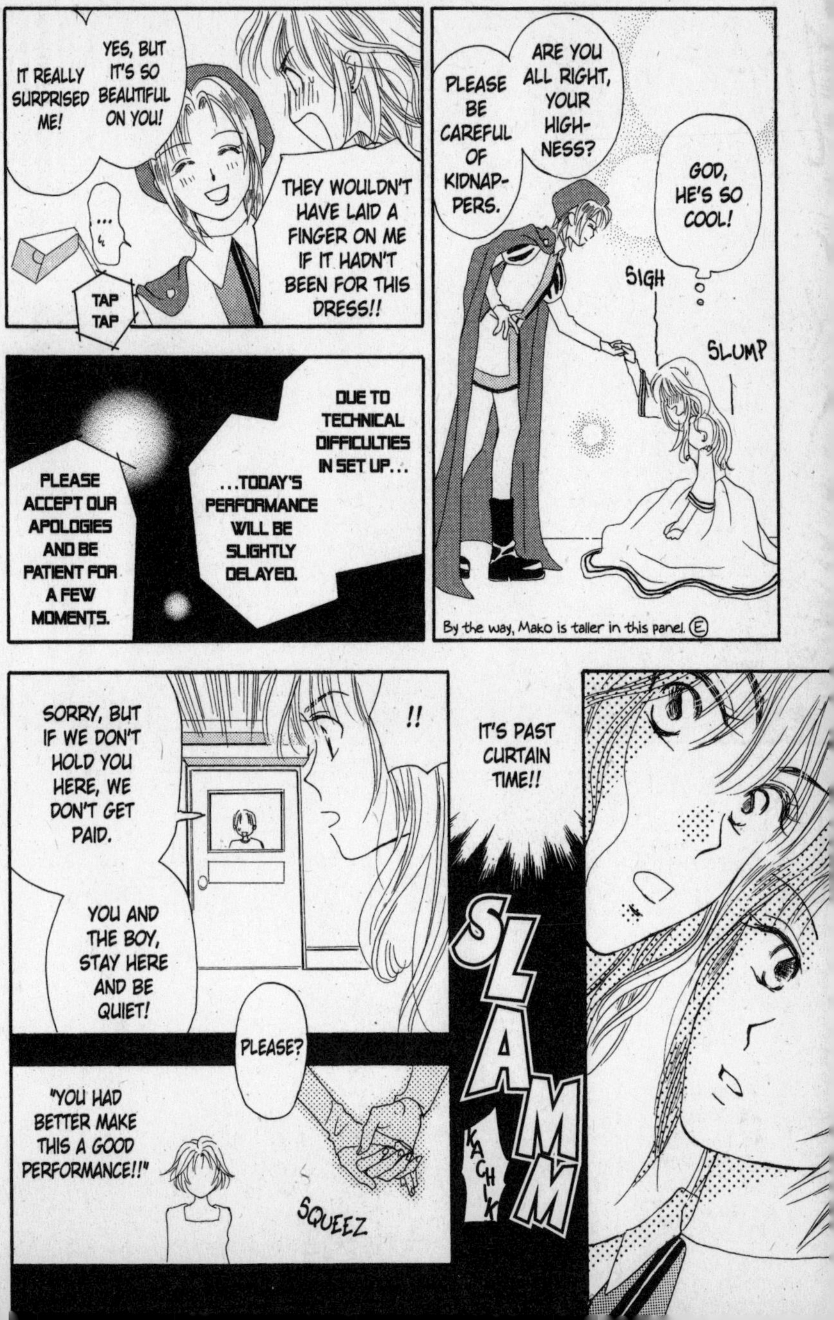
ARE YOU ALL RIGHT, YOUR HIGH-NESS?
PLEASE BE CAREFUL OF KIDNAP-PERS.
GOD, HE'S SO COOL!
SIGH
SLUMP
By the way, Mako is taller in this panel. Ⓔ
YES, BUT IT'S SO BEAUTIFUL ON YOU!
IT REALLY SURPRISED ME!
THEY WOULDN'T HAVE LAID A FINGER ON ME IF IT HADN'T BEEN FOR THIS DRESS!!
...
TAP TAP
DUE TO TECHNICAL DIFFICULTIES IN SET UP...
...TODAY'S PERFORMANCE WILL BE SLIGHTLY DELAYED.
PLEASE ACCEPT OUR APOLOGIES AND BE PATIENT FOR A FEW MOMENTS.
IT'S PAST CURTAIN TIME!!
SLAMM
KACHIK
!!
SORRY, BUT IF WE DON'T HOLD YOU HERE, WE DON'T GET PAID.
YOU AND THE BOY, STAY HERE AND BE QUIET!
PLEASE?
"YOU HAD BETTER MAKE THIS A GOOD PERFORMANCE!!"
SQUEEZ

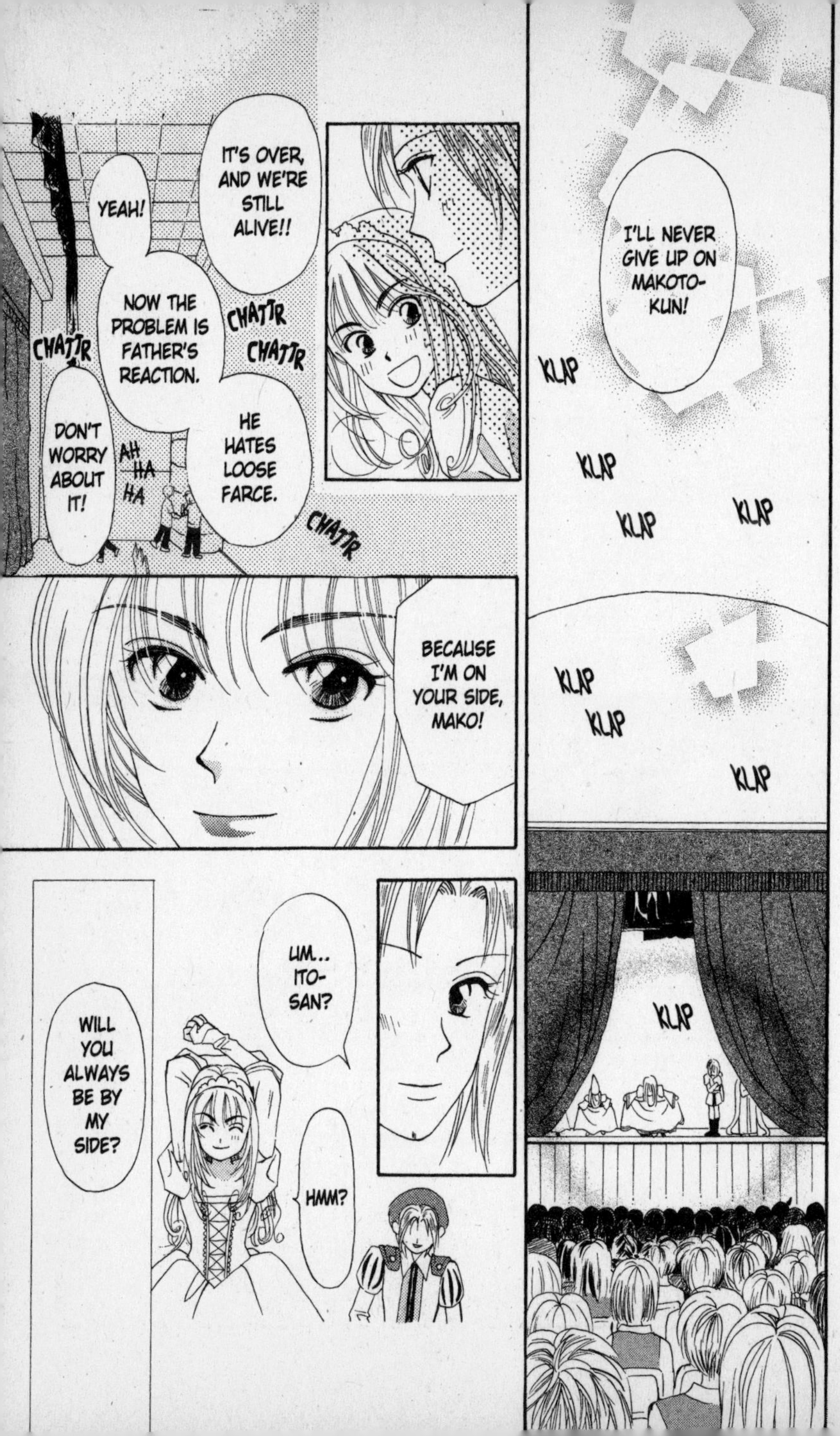
I'LL NEVER GIVE UP ON MAKOTO-KUN!
KLAP
KLAP
KLAP
KLAP
KLAP
KLAP
KLAP
KLAP
IT'S OVER, AND WE'RE STILL ALIVE!!
YEAH!
CHATTR
NOW THE PROBLEM IS FATHER'S REACTION.
CHATTR
CHATTR
HE HATES LOOSE FARCE.
CHATTR
DON'T WORRY ABOUT IT!
AH HA HA
BECAUSE I'M ON YOUR SIDE, MAKO!
UM... ITO-SAN?
HMM?
WILL YOU ALWAYS BE BY MY SIDE?

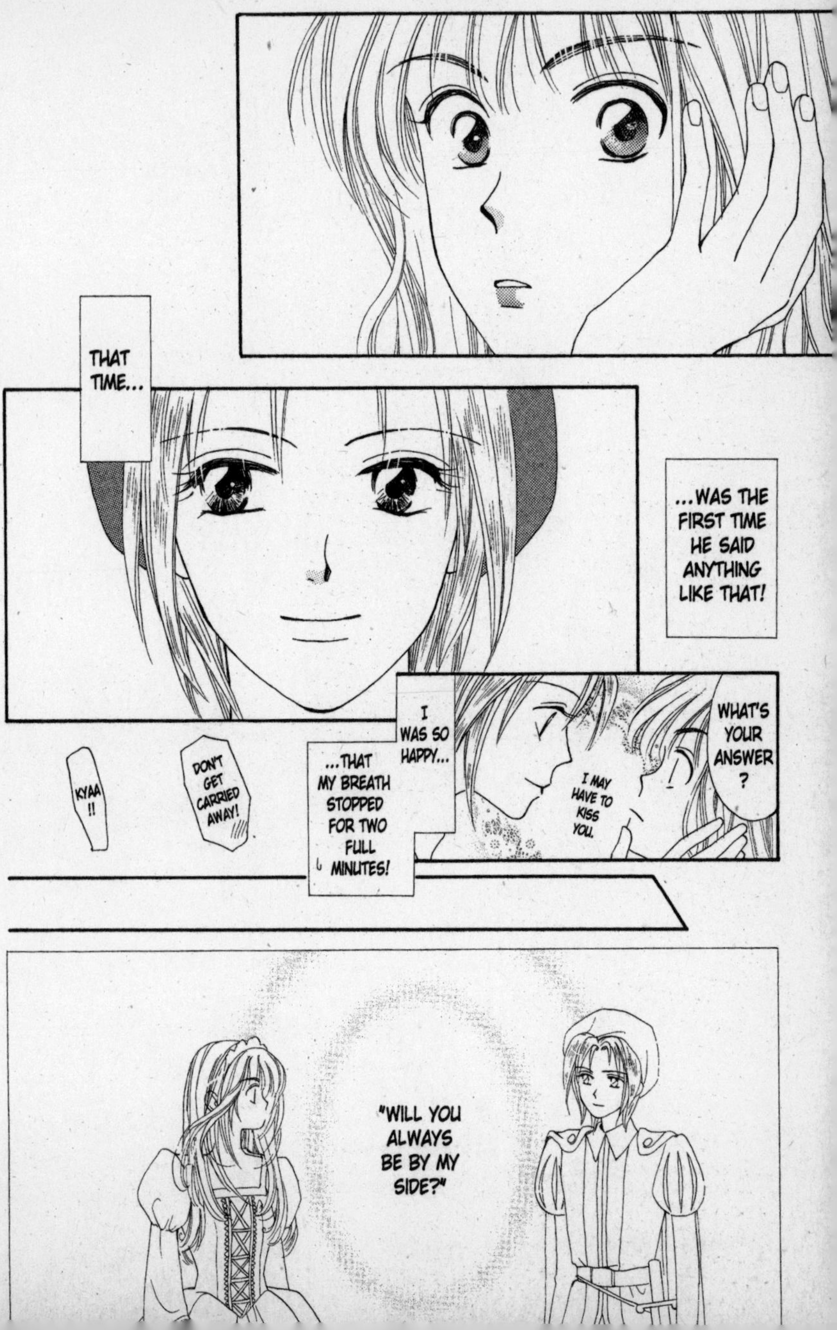
THAT TIME...
...WAS THE FIRST TIME HE SAID ANYTHING LIKE THAT!
WHAT'S YOUR ANSWER?
I MAY HAVE TO KISS YOU.
I WAS SO HAPPY...
...THAT MY BREATH STOPPED FOR TWO FULL MINUTES!
DON'T GET CARRIED AWAY!
KYAA!!
"WILL YOU ALWAYS BE BY MY SIDE?"

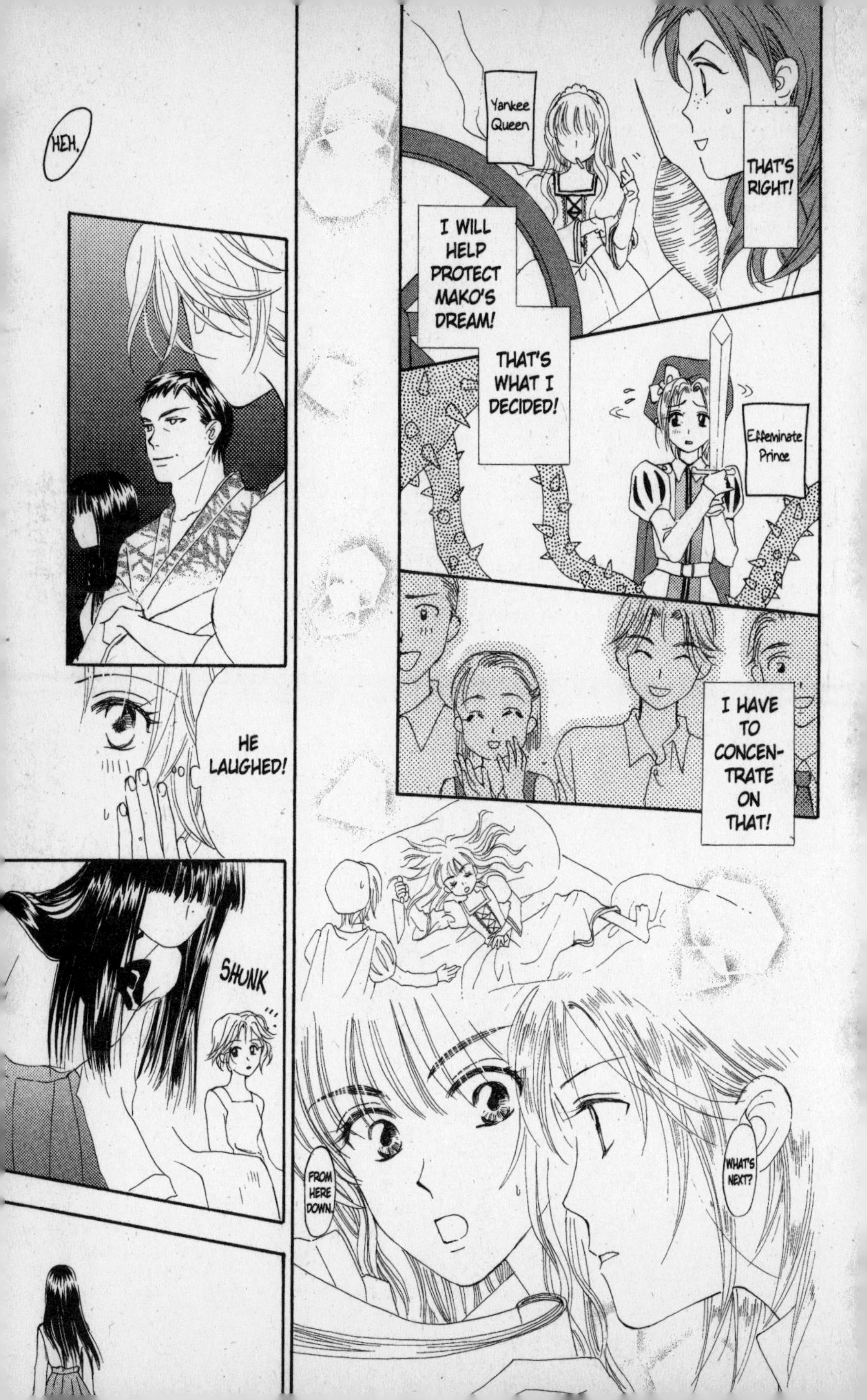
THAT'S RIGHT!
Yankee Queen
I WILL HELP PROTECT MAKO'S DREAM!
THAT'S WHAT I DECIDED!
Effeminate Prince
I HAVE TO CONCENTRATE ON THAT!
WHAT'S NEXT?
FROM HERE DOWN.
HEH.
HE LAUGHED!
SHUNK

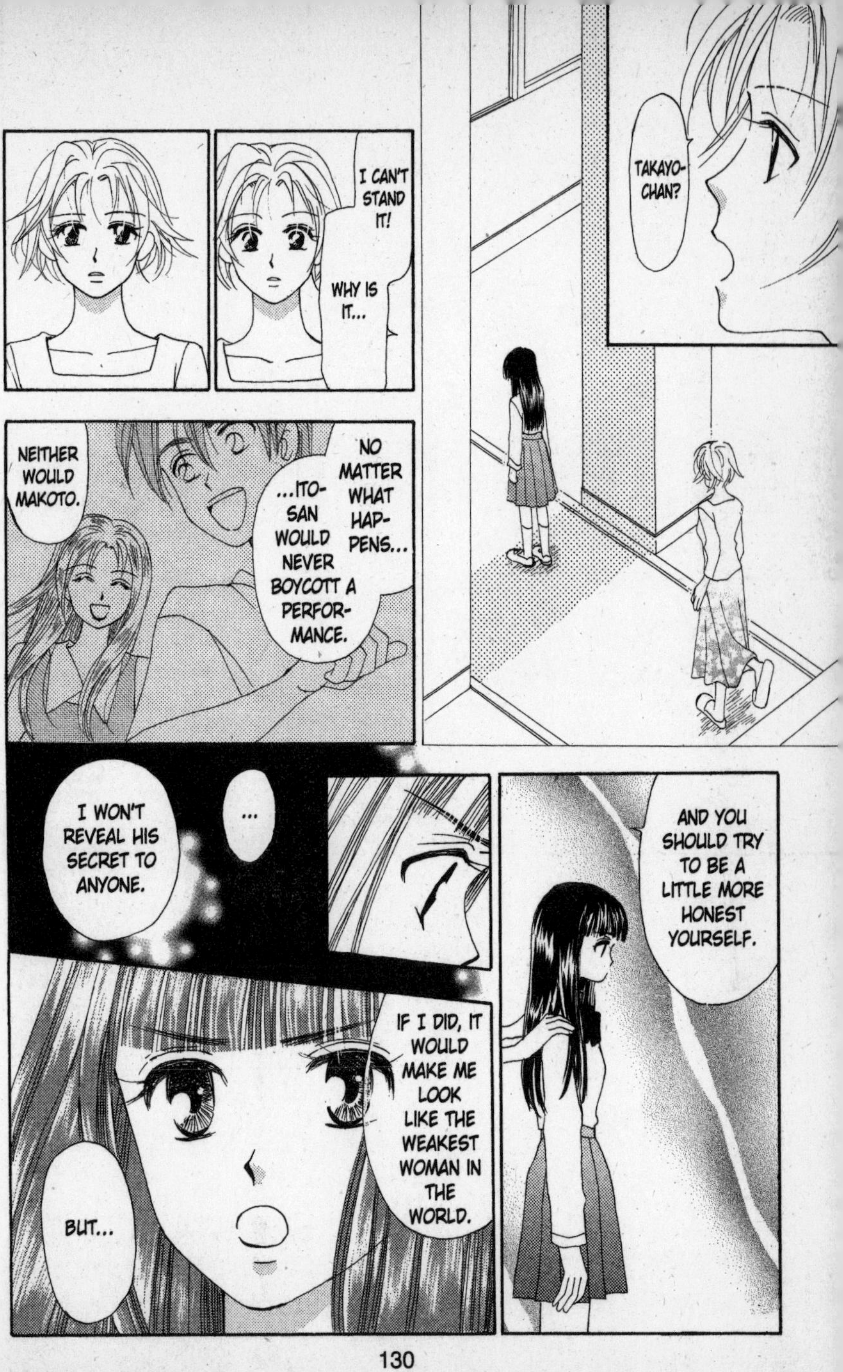
TAKAYO-CHAN?
I CAN'T STAND IT!
WHY IS IT...
NO MATTER WHAT HAPPENS...
...ITO-SAN WOULD NEVER BOYCOTT A PERFORMANCE.
NEITHER WOULD MAKOTO.
AND YOU SHOULD TRY TO BE A LITTLE MORE HONEST YOURSELF.
...
I WON'T REVEAL HIS SECRET TO ANYONE.
IF I DID, IT WOULD MAKE ME LOOK LIKE THE WEAKEST WOMAN IN THE WORLD.
BUT...

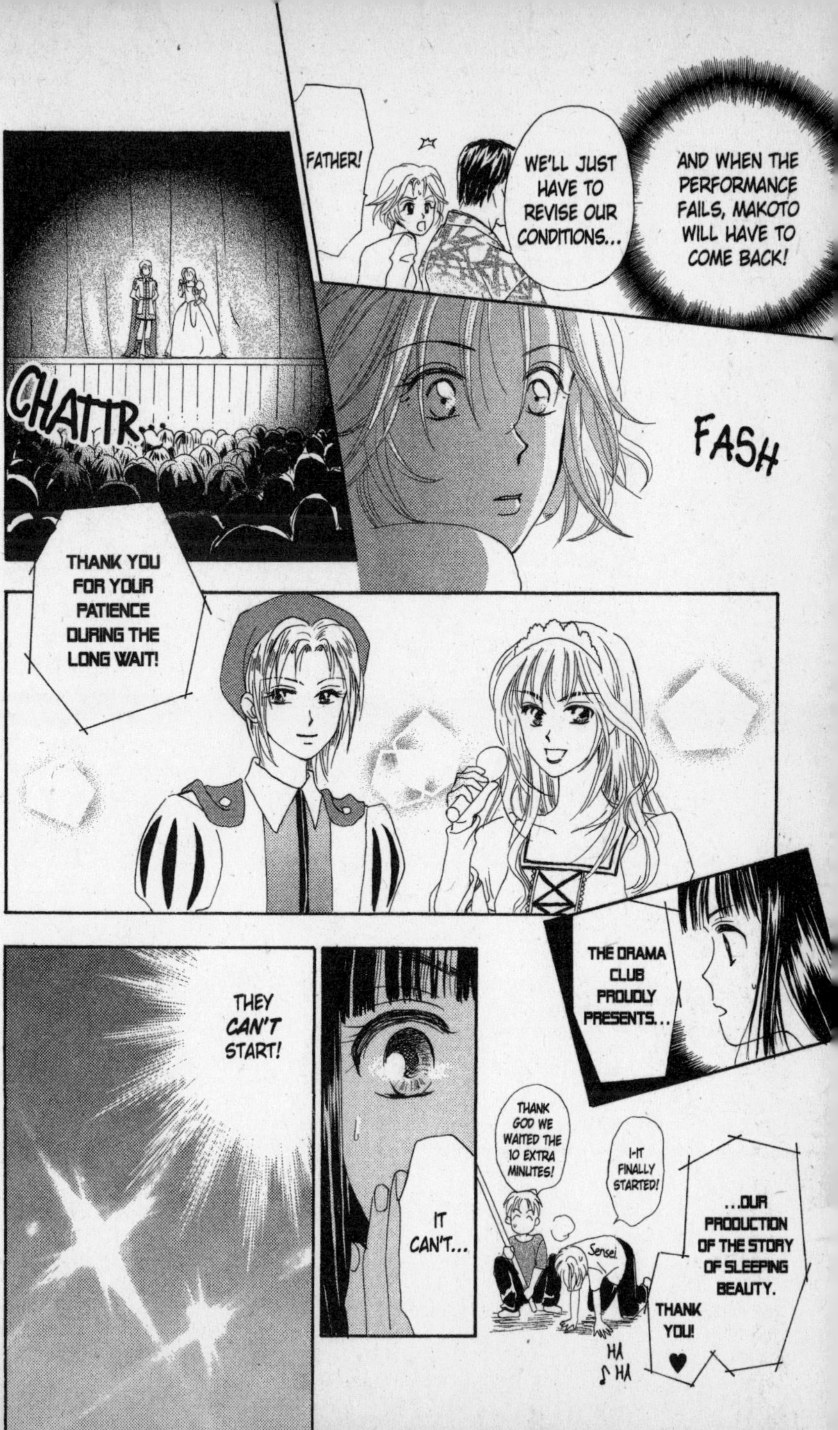
AND WHEN THE PERFORMANCE FAILS, MAKOTO WILL HAVE TO COME BACK!
WE'LL JUST HAVE TO REVISE OUR CONDITIONS...
FATHER!
FASH
CHATTR...
THANK YOU FOR YOUR PATIENCE DURING THE LONG WAIT!
THE DRAMA CLUB PROUDLY PRESENTS...
...OUR PRODUCTION OF THE STORY OF SLEEPING BEAUTY.
THANK YOU! ♥
I-IT FINALLY STARTED!
THANK GOD WE WAITED THE 10 EXTRA MINUTES!
Sensei
HA HA
IT CAN'T...
THEY *CAN'T* START!

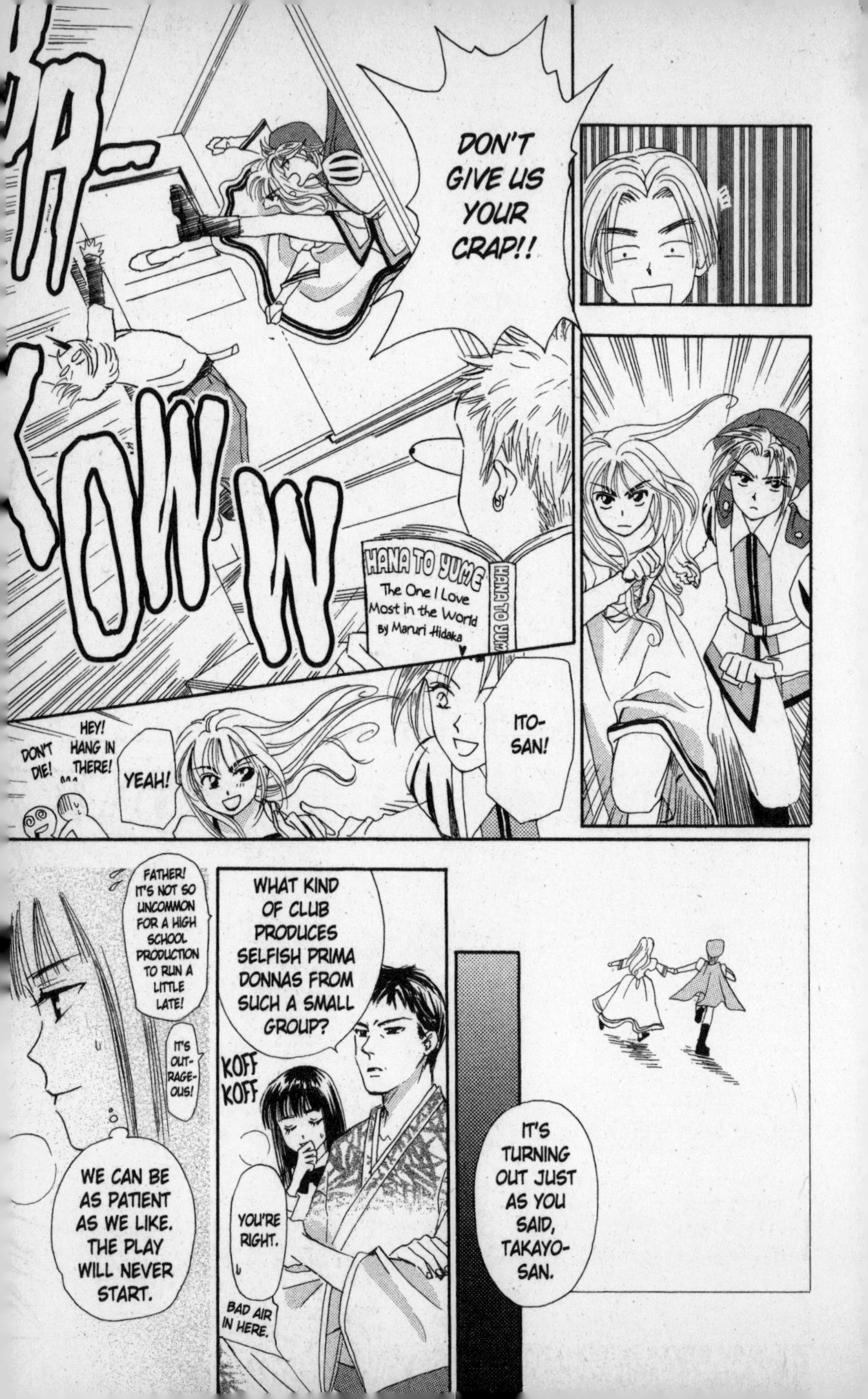
DON'T GIVE US YOUR CRAP!!
HANA TO YUME
The One I Love Most in the World
By Maruri Hidaka
HANA TO YUME
ITO-SAN!
YEAH!
HEY! HANG IN THERE!
DON'T DIE!
IT'S TURNING OUT JUST AS YOU SAID, TAKAYO-SAN.
WHAT KIND OF CLUB PRODUCES SELFISH PRIMA DONNAS FROM SUCH A SMALL GROUP?
KOFF KOFF
YOU'RE RIGHT.
BAD AIR IN HERE.
FATHER! IT'S NOT SO UNCOMMON FOR A HIGH SCHOOL PRODUCTION TO RUN A LITTLE LATE!
IT'S OUT-RAGE-OUS!
WE CAN BE AS PATIENT AS WE LIKE. THE PLAY WILL NEVER START.

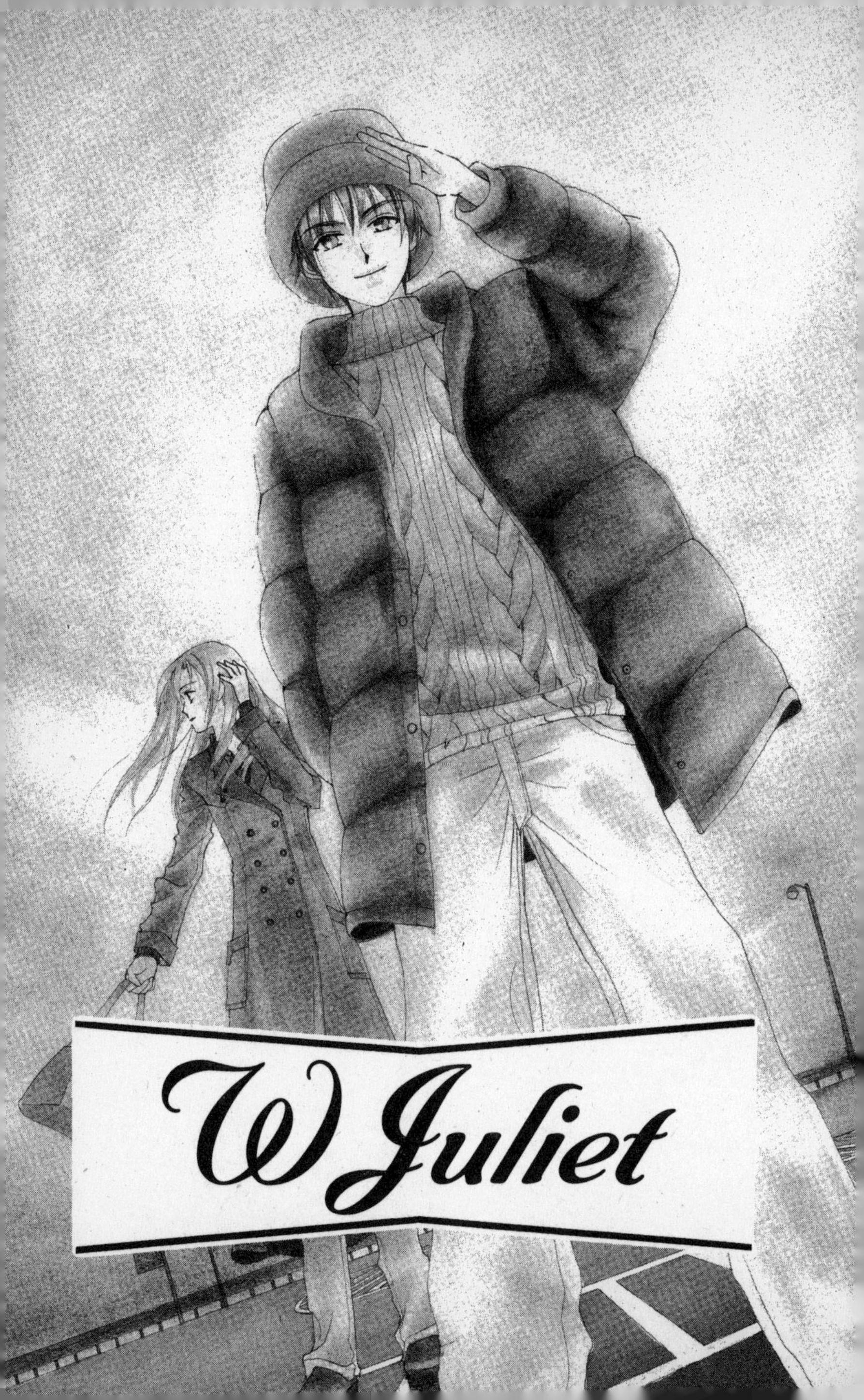
W Juliet

This is the first time my magazine has asked me to do work on a reader's prize. It's issue 1 of Hana to Yume (Flowers and Dreams), so the theme is a New Year's Card. This is the design I did for them.

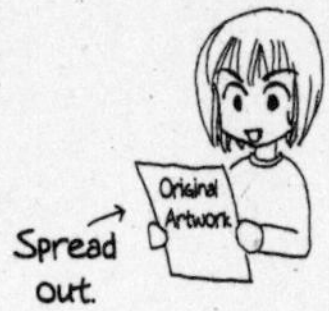
Original Artwork
Spread out.

The size of original artwork that I have now has gotten quite a bit smaller.

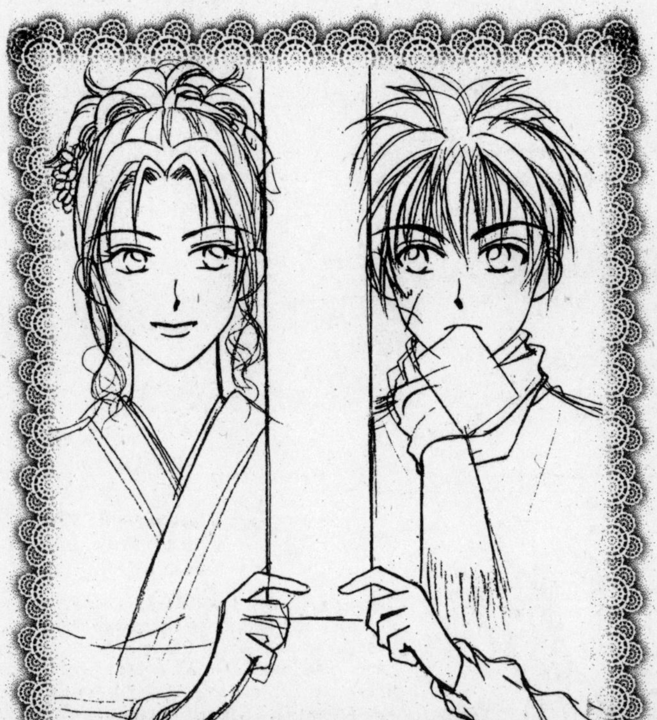

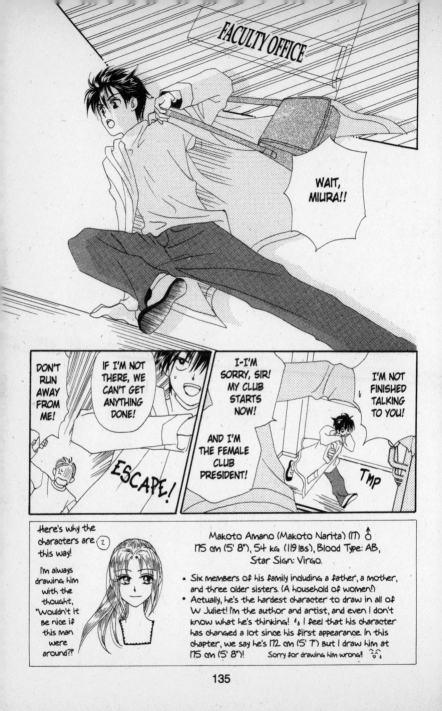

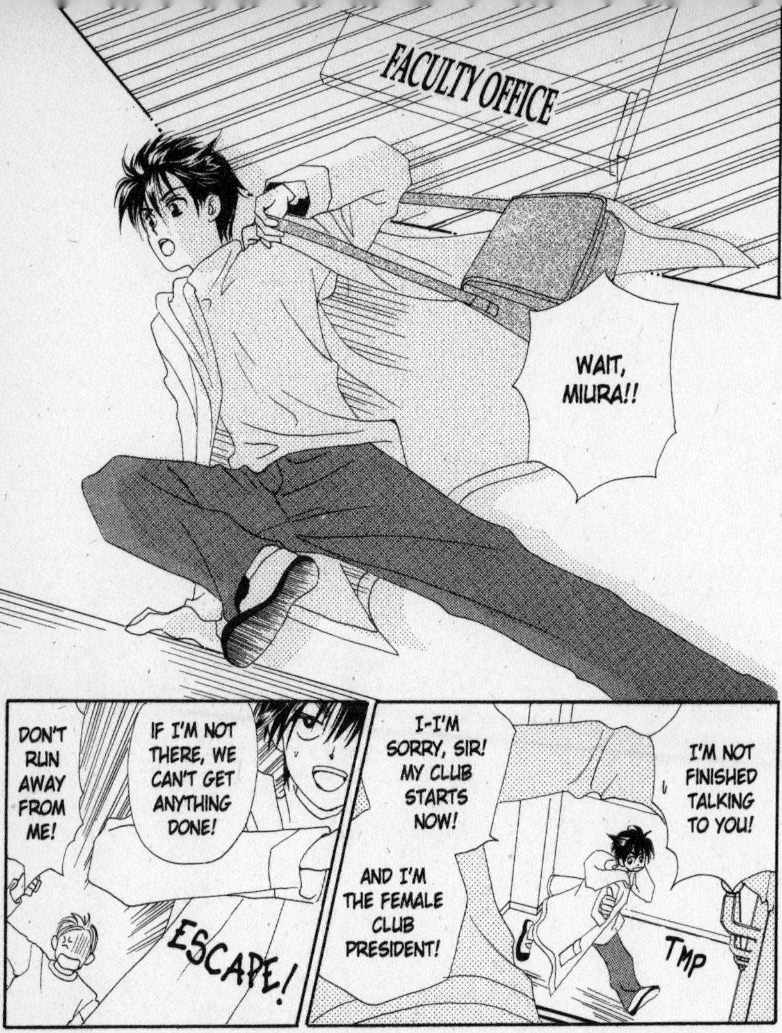
FACULTY OFFICE
WAIT, MIURA!!
I'M NOT FINISHED TALKING TO YOU!
I-I'M SORRY, SIR! MY CLUB STARTS NOW!
AND I'M THE FEMALE CLUB PRESIDENT!
TMP
IF I'M NOT THERE, WE CAN'T GET ANYTHING DONE!
DON'T RUN AWAY FROM ME!
ESCAPE!

Here's why the characters are this way! (2)

I'm always drawing him with the thought, "Wouldn't it be nice if this man were around?!"

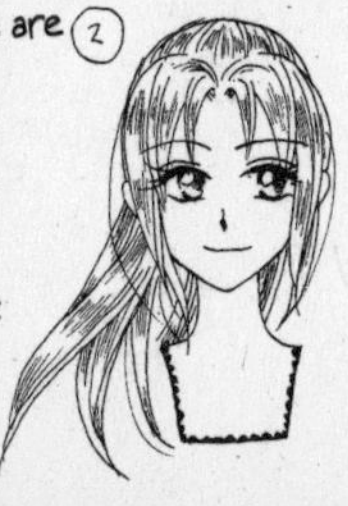

Makoto Amano (Makoto Narita) (17) ♂
175 cm (5' 8"), 54 kg (119 lbs), Blood Type: AB,
Star Sign: Virgo.

- Six members of his family including a father, a mother, and three older sisters. (A household of women!)
- Actually, he's the hardest character to draw in all of W Juliet! I'm the author and artist, and even I don't know what he's thinking! I feel that his character has changed a lot since his first appearance. In this chapter, we say he's 172 cm (5' 7") but I draw him at 175 cm (5' 8")! Sorry for drawing him wrong!!

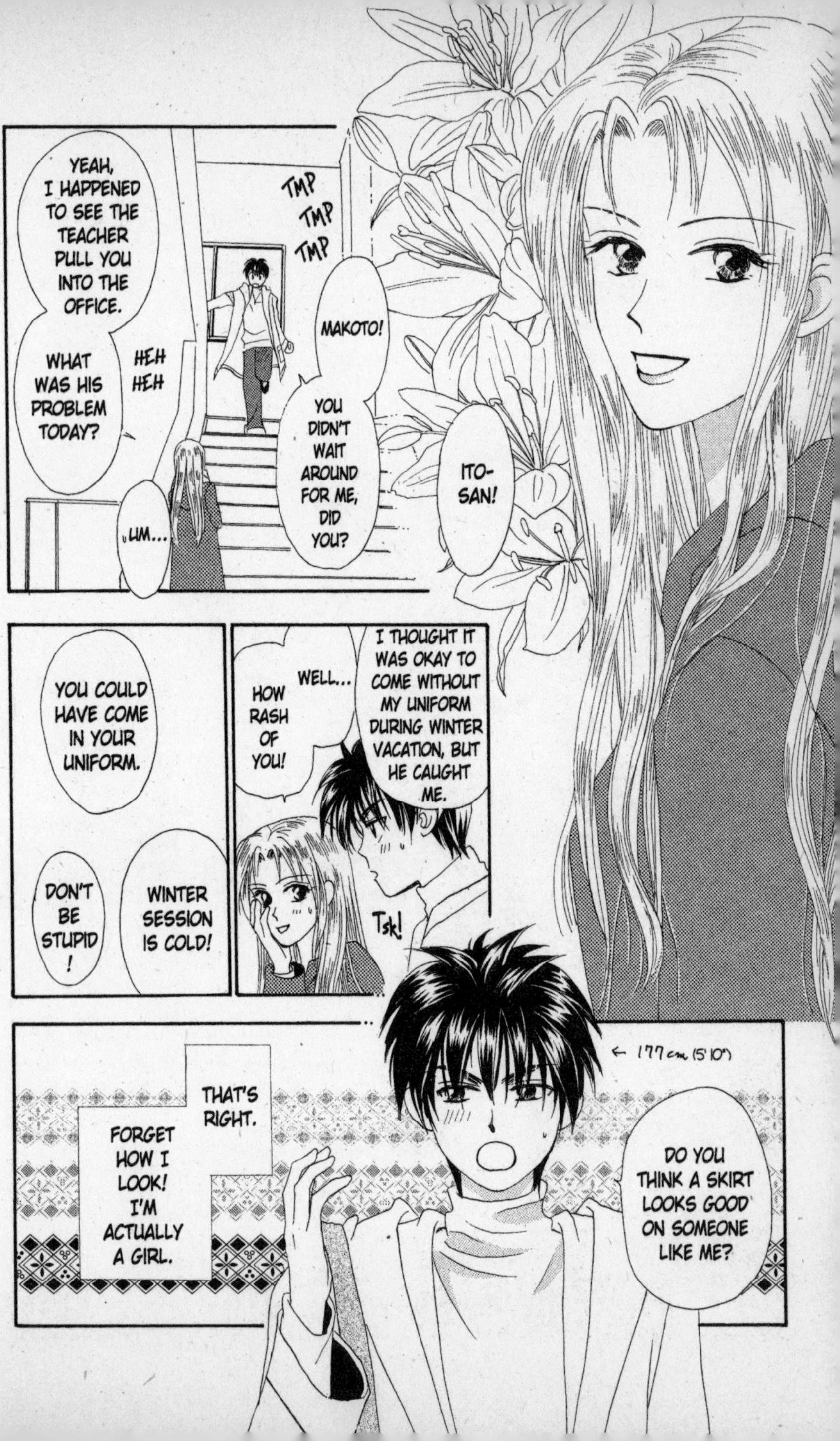
TMP TMP TMP
MAKOTO!
YOU DIDN'T WAIT AROUND FOR ME, DID YOU?
ITO-SAN!
YEAH, I HAPPENED TO SEE THE TEACHER PULL YOU INTO THE OFFICE.
WHAT WAS HIS PROBLEM TODAY?
HEH HEH
...UM...
I THOUGHT IT WAS OKAY TO COME WITHOUT MY UNIFORM DURING WINTER VACATION, BUT HE CAUGHT ME.
WELL...
HOW RASH OF YOU!
Tsk!
YOU COULD HAVE COME IN YOUR UNIFORM.
WINTER SESSION IS COLD!
DON'T BE STUPID!
← 177cm (5'10")
DO YOU THINK A SKIRT LOOKS GOOD ON SOMEONE LIKE ME?
THAT'S RIGHT.
FORGET HOW I LOOK! I'M ACTUALLY A GIRL.

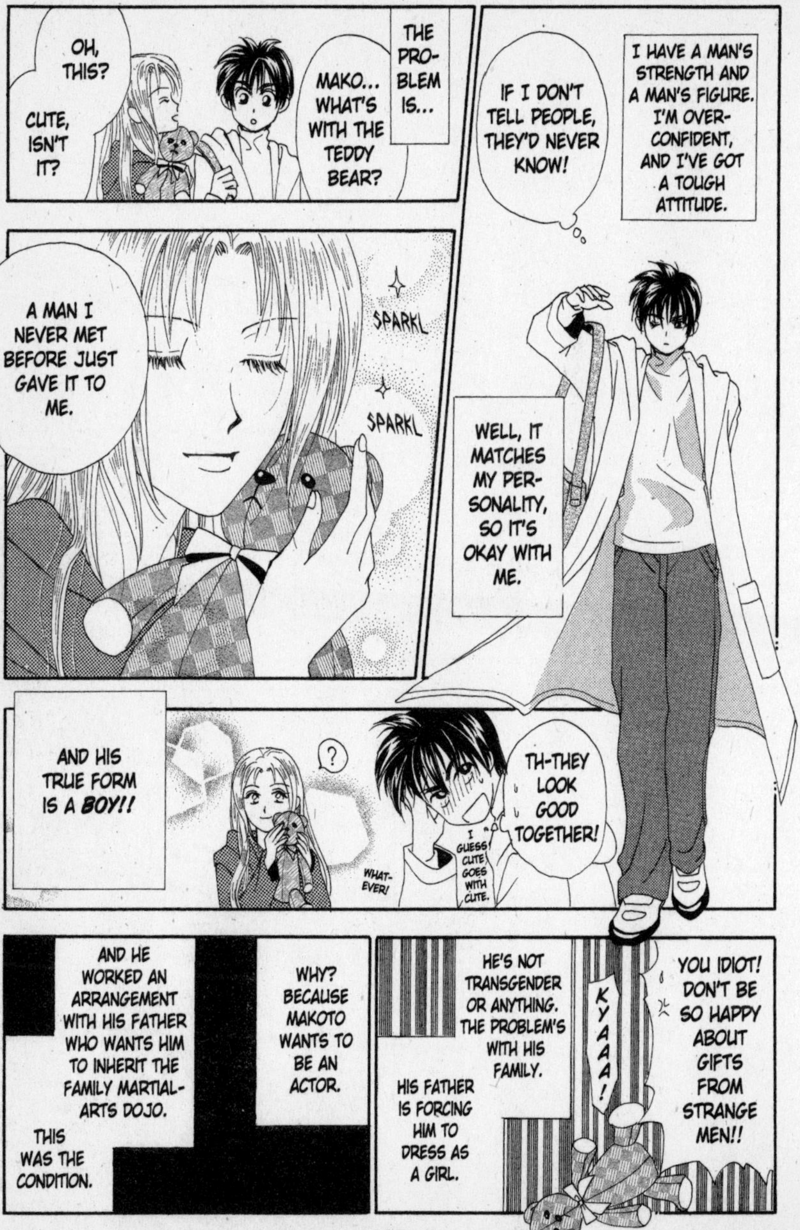
I HAVE A MAN'S STRENGTH AND A MAN'S FIGURE. I'M OVER-CONFIDENT, AND I'VE GOT A TOUGH ATTITUDE.
IF I DON'T TELL PEOPLE, THEY'D NEVER KNOW!
WELL, IT MATCHES MY PER-SONALITY, SO IT'S OKAY WITH ME.
THE PRO-BLEM IS...
MAKO... WHAT'S WITH THE TEDDY BEAR?
OH, THIS?
CUTE, ISN'T IT?
SPARKL
SPARKL
A MAN I NEVER MET BEFORE JUST GAVE IT TO ME.
TH-THEY LOOK GOOD TOGETHER!
I GUESS CUTE GOES WITH CUTE.
WHAT-EVER!
?
AND HIS TRUE FORM IS A *BOY!!*
YOU IDIOT! DON'T BE SO HAPPY ABOUT GIFTS FROM STRANGE MEN!!
KYAAA!
HE'S NOT TRANSGENDER OR ANYTHING. THE PROBLEM'S WITH HIS FAMILY.
HIS FATHER IS FORCING HIM TO DRESS AS A GIRL.
WHY? BECAUSE MAKOTO WANTS TO BE AN ACTOR.
AND HE WORKED AN ARRANGEMENT WITH HIS FATHER WHO WANTS HIM TO INHERIT THE FAMILY MARTIAL-ARTS DOJO.
THIS WAS THE CONDITION.

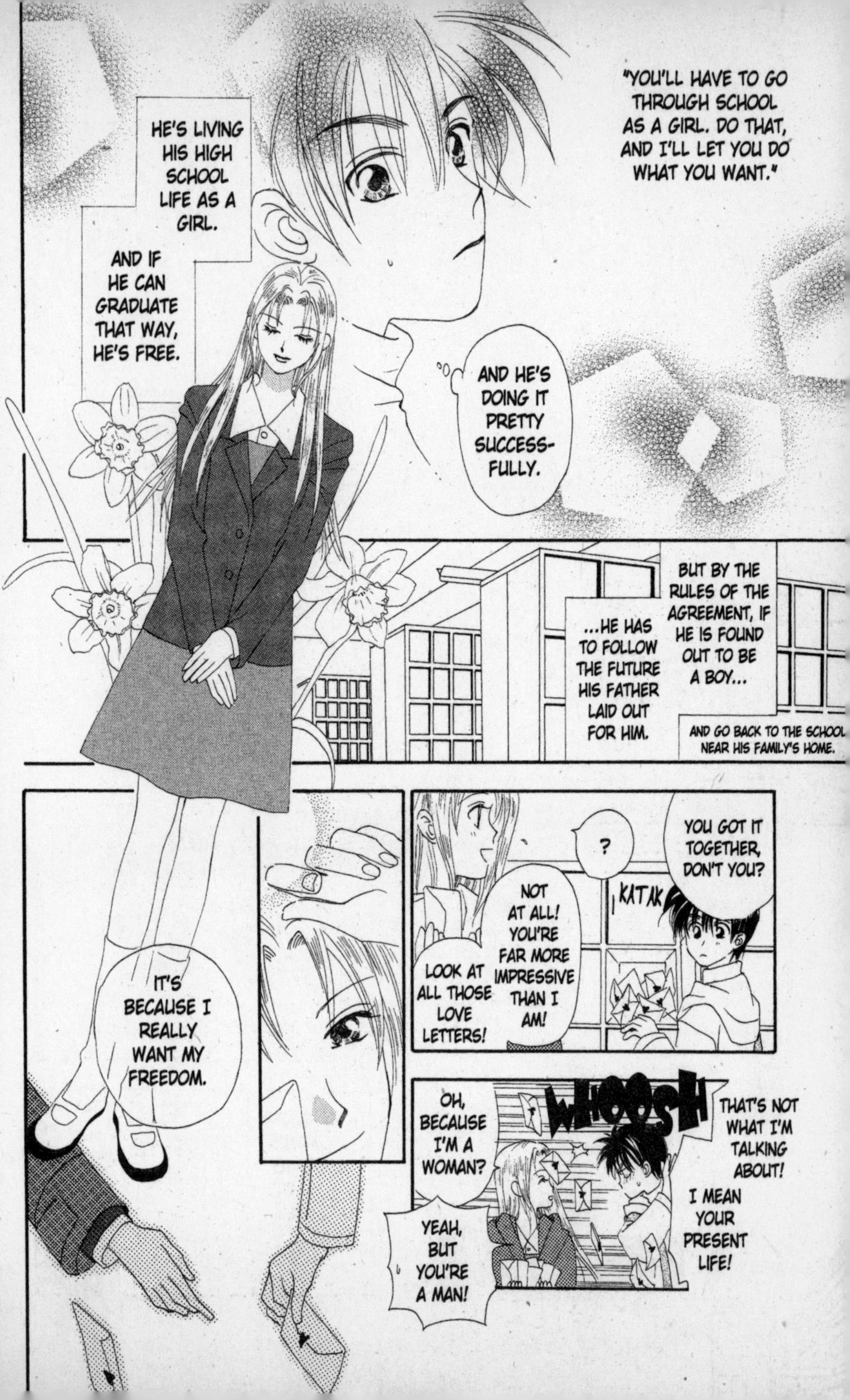
"YOU'LL HAVE TO GO THROUGH SCHOOL AS A GIRL. DO THAT, AND I'LL LET YOU DO WHAT YOU WANT."
HE'S LIVING HIS HIGH SCHOOL LIFE AS A GIRL.
AND IF HE CAN GRADUATE THAT WAY, HE'S FREE.
AND HE'S DOING IT PRETTY SUCCESS-FULLY.
BUT BY THE RULES OF THE AGREEMENT, IF HE IS FOUND OUT TO BE A BOY...
...HE HAS TO FOLLOW THE FUTURE HIS FATHER LAID OUT FOR HIM.
AND GO BACK TO THE SCHOOL NEAR HIS FAMILY'S HOME.
YOU GOT IT TOGETHER, DON'T YOU?
?
KATAK
NOT AT ALL! YOU'RE FAR MORE IMPRESSIVE THAN I AM!
LOOK AT ALL THOSE LOVE LETTERS!
WHOOSH
THAT'S NOT WHAT I'M TALKING ABOUT!
I MEAN YOUR PRESENT LIFE!
OH, BECAUSE I'M A WOMAN?
YEAH, BUT YOU'RE A MAN!
IT'S BECAUSE I REALLY WANT MY FREEDOM.

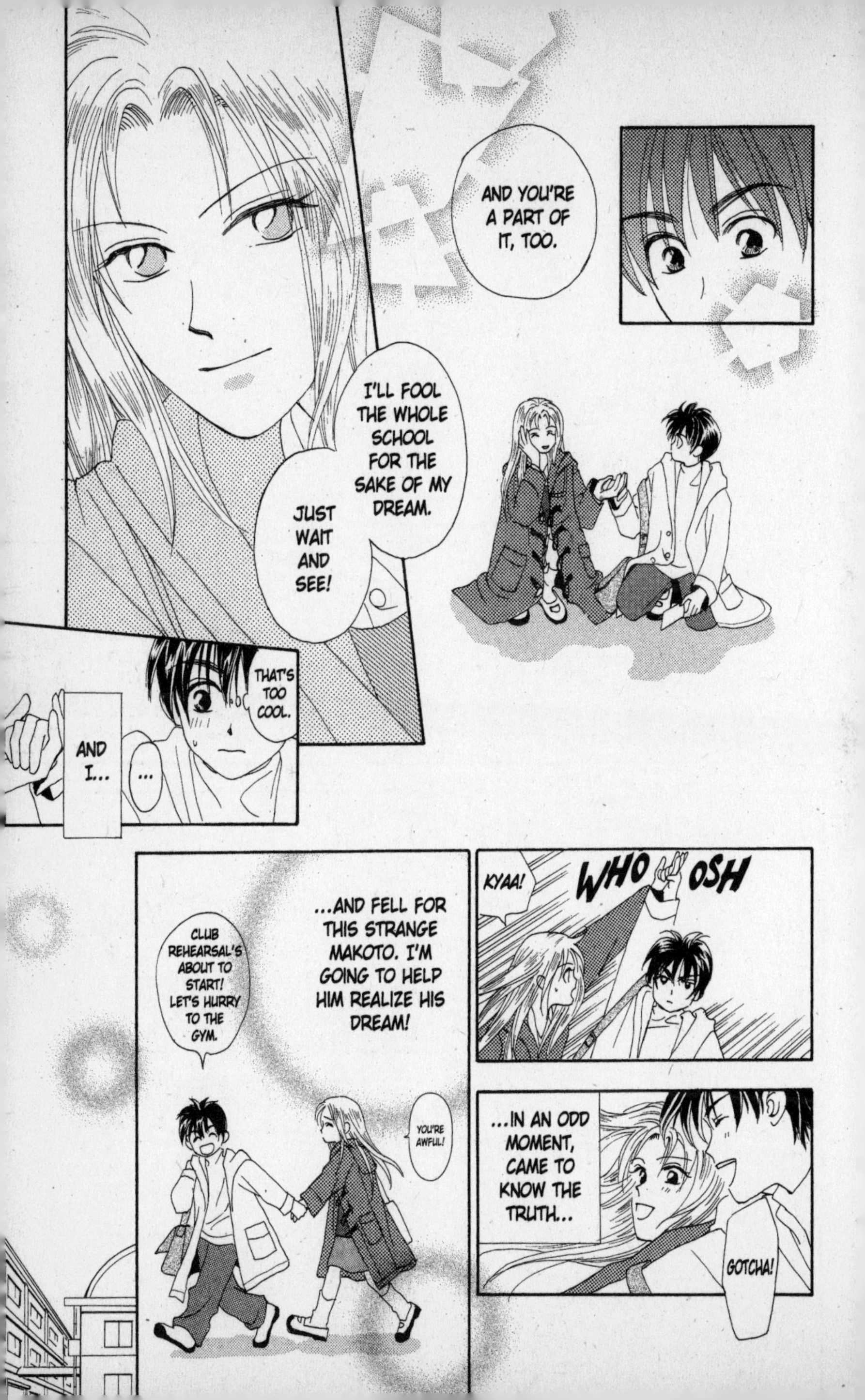
AND YOU'RE A PART OF IT, TOO.
I'LL FOOL THE WHOLE SCHOOL FOR THE SAKE OF MY DREAM.
JUST WAIT AND SEE!
THAT'S TOO COOL.
...
AND I...
KYAA!
WHOOSH
...IN AN ODD MOMENT, CAME TO KNOW THE TRUTH...
GOTCHA!
...AND FELL FOR THIS STRANGE MAKOTO. I'M GOING TO HELP HIM REALIZE HIS DREAM!
CLUB REHEARSAL'S ABOUT TO START! LET'S HURRY TO THE GYM.
YOU'RE AWFUL!

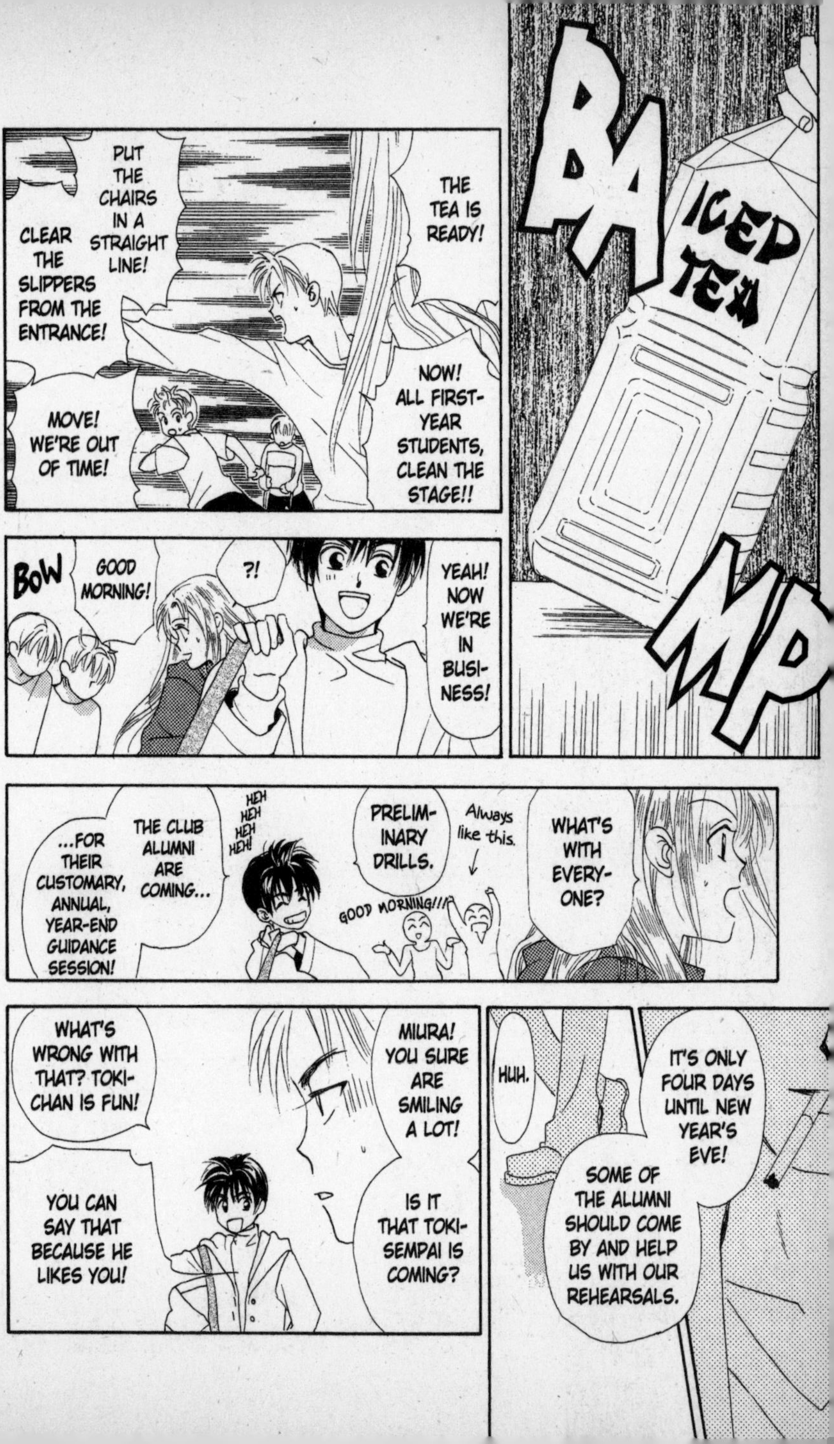
BAMP
ICED TEA
THE TEA IS READY!
NOW! ALL FIRST-YEAR STUDENTS, CLEAN THE STAGE!!
PUT THE CHAIRS IN A STRAIGHT LINE!
CLEAR THE SLIPPERS FROM THE ENTRANCE!
MOVE! WE'RE OUT OF TIME!
YEAH! NOW WE'RE IN BUSINESS!
?!
GOOD MORNING!
BOW
WHAT'S WITH EVERYONE?
Always like this.
GOOD MORNING!!!
PRELIMINARY DRILLS.
HEH HEH HEH HEH!
THE CLUB ALUMNI ARE COMING...
...FOR THEIR CUSTOMARY, ANNUAL, YEAR-END GUIDANCE SESSION!
IT'S ONLY FOUR DAYS UNTIL NEW YEAR'S EVE!
HUH.
SOME OF THE ALUMNI SHOULD COME BY AND HELP US WITH OUR REHEARSALS.
MIURA! YOU SURE ARE SMILING A LOT!
WHAT'S WRONG WITH THAT? TOKI-CHAN IS FUN!
IS IT THAT TOKI-SEMPAI IS COMING?
YOU CAN SAY THAT BECAUSE HE LIKES YOU!

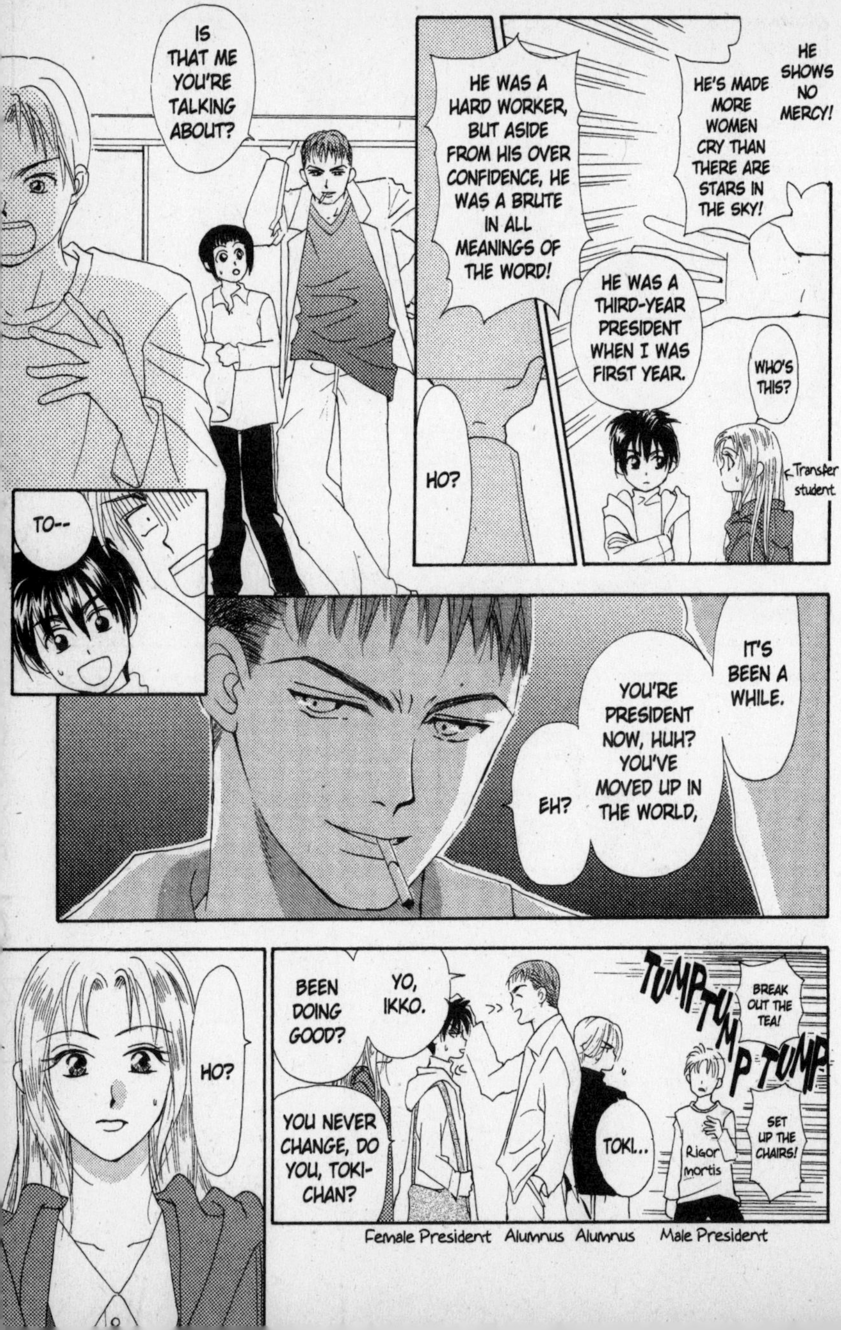
HE SHOWS NO MERCY!
HE'S MADE MORE WOMEN CRY THAN THERE ARE STARS IN THE SKY!
HE WAS A HARD WORKER, BUT ASIDE FROM HIS OVER CONFIDENCE, HE WAS A BRUTE IN ALL MEANINGS OF THE WORD!
WHO'S THIS?
Transfer student
HE WAS A THIRD-YEAR PRESIDENT WHEN I WAS FIRST YEAR.
HO?
IS THAT ME YOU'RE TALKING ABOUT?
TO--
IT'S BEEN A WHILE.
YOU'RE PRESIDENT NOW, HUH? YOU'VE MOVED UP IN THE WORLD,
EH?
BREAK OUT THE TEA!
TUMP TUMP TUMP
SET UP THE CHAIRS!
Rigor mortis
TOKI...
YO, IKKO.
BEEN DOING GOOD?
YOU NEVER CHANGE, DO YOU, TOKI-CHAN?
Female President
Alumnus
Alumnus
Male President
HO?

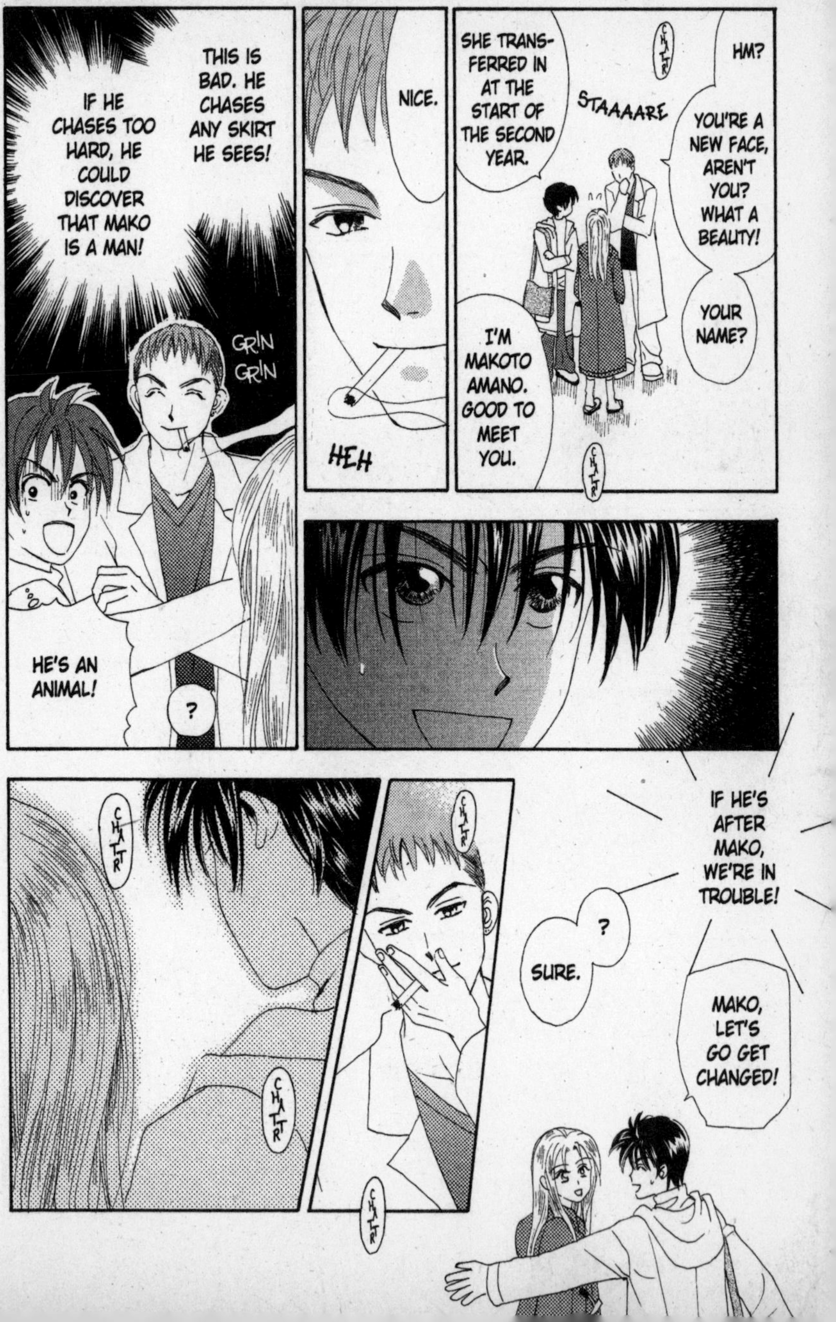
HM?
YOU'RE A NEW FACE, AREN'T YOU? WHAT A BEAUTY!
YOUR NAME?
STAAAARE
CHATTER
SHE TRANSFERRED IN AT THE START OF THE SECOND YEAR.
I'M MAKOTO AMANO. GOOD TO MEET YOU.
CHATTER
NICE.
HEH
THIS IS BAD. HE CHASES ANY SKIRT HE SEES!
IF HE CHASES TOO HARD, HE COULD DISCOVER THAT MAKO IS A MAN!
GRIN GRIN
HE'S AN ANIMAL!
?
IF HE'S AFTER MAKO, WE'RE IN TROUBLE!
?
SURE.
MAKO, LET'S GO GET CHANGED!
CHATTER
CHATTER
CHATTER
CHATTER

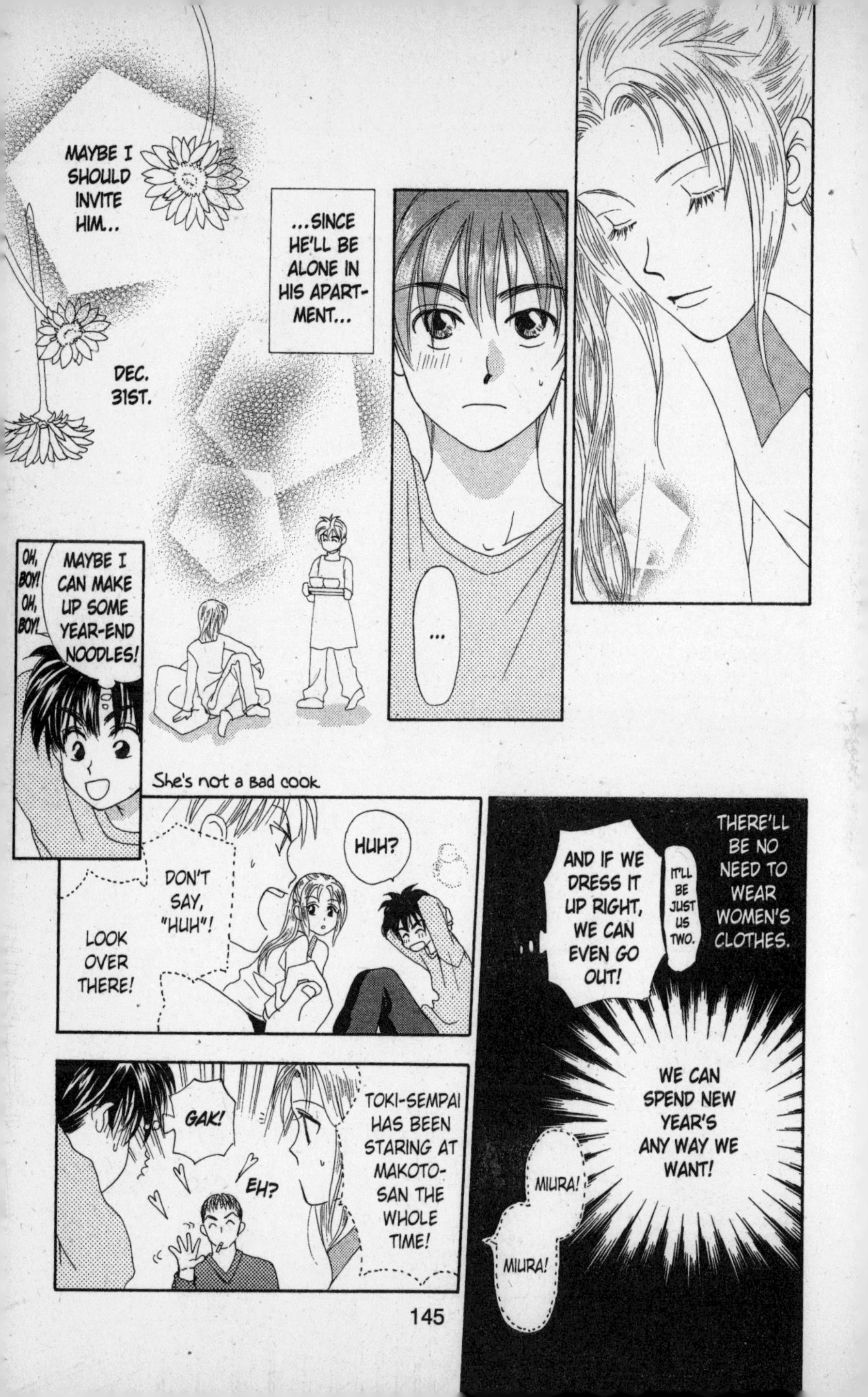

...
MAYBE I SHOULD INVITE HIM...
...SINCE HE'LL BE ALONE IN HIS APARTMENT...
DEC. 31ST.
MAYBE I CAN MAKE UP SOME YEAR-END NOODLES!
OH, BOY! OH, BOY!
She's not a bad cook.
THERE'LL BE NO NEED TO WEAR WOMEN'S CLOTHES.
IT'LL BE JUST US TWO.
AND IF WE DRESS IT UP RIGHT, WE CAN EVEN GO OUT!
WE CAN SPEND NEW YEAR'S ANY WAY WE WANT!
MIURA!
MIURA!
HUH?
DON'T SAY, "HUH"!
LOOK OVER THERE!
TOKI-SEMPAI HAS BEEN STARING AT MAKOTO-SAN THE WHOLE TIME!
GAK!
EH?

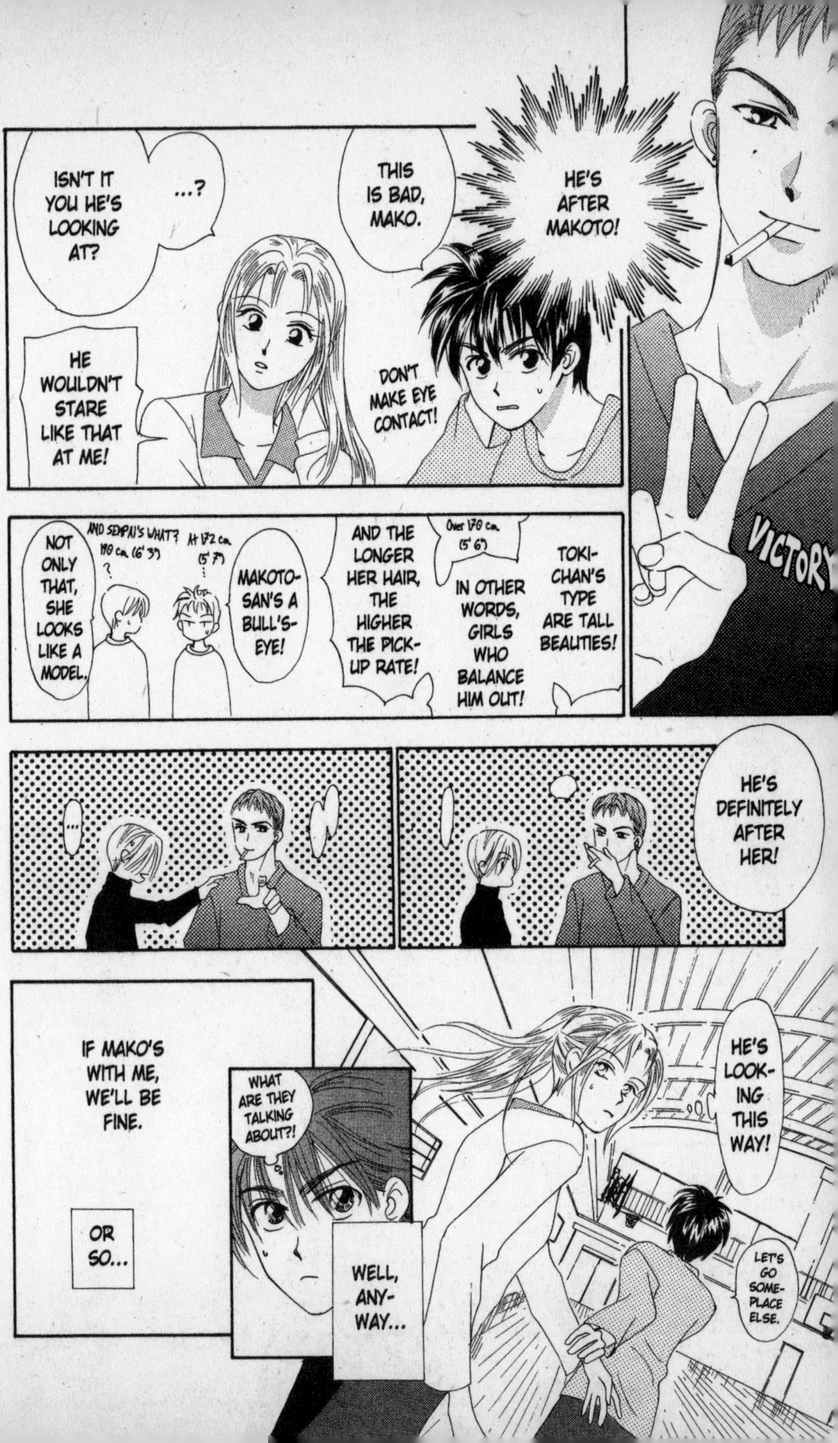
VICTORY
HE'S AFTER MAKOTO!
THIS IS BAD, MAKO.
...?
ISN'T IT YOU HE'S LOOKING AT?
DON'T MAKE EYE CONTACT!
HE WOULDN'T STARE LIKE THAT AT ME!
TOKI-CHAN'S TYPE ARE TALL BEAUTIES!
IN OTHER WORDS, GIRLS WHO BALANCE HIM OUT!
Over 170 cm. (5'6")
AND THE LONGER HER HAIR, THE HIGHER THE PICK-UP RATE!
MAKOTO-SAN'S A BULL'S-EYE!
At 172 cm. (5'7")
AND SEMPAI'S WHAT? 190 cm. (6'3")
NOT ONLY THAT, SHE LOOKS LIKE A MODEL.
HE'S DEFINITELY AFTER HER!
...
HE'S LOOK-ING THIS WAY!
LET'S GO SOME-PLACE ELSE.
WHAT ARE THEY TALKING ABOUT?!
WELL, ANY-WAY...
IF MAKO'S WITH ME, WE'LL BE FINE.
OR SO...

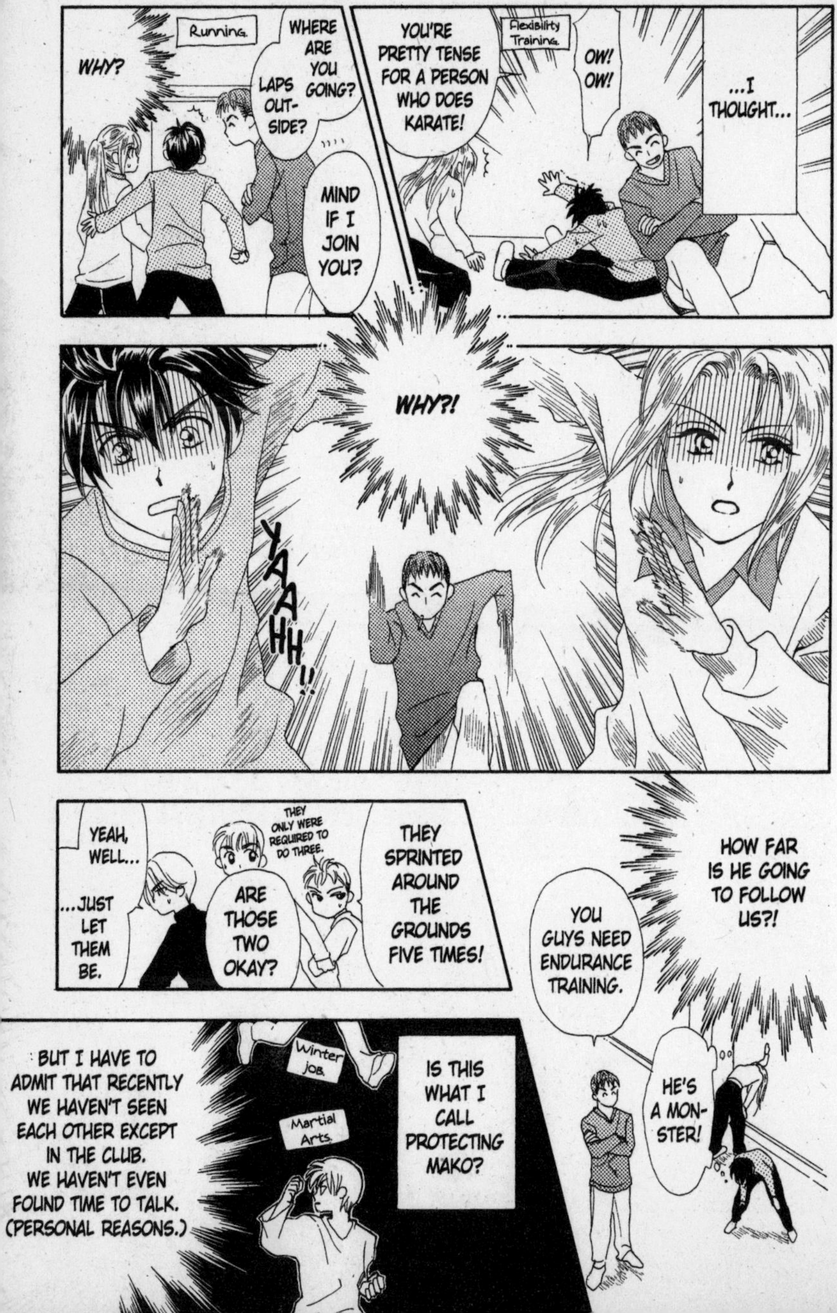
...I THOUGHT...
OW! OW!
Flexibility Training.
YOU'RE PRETTY TENSE FOR A PERSON WHO DOES KARATE!
WHERE ARE YOU GOING?
LAPS OUTSIDE?
Running.
MIND IF I JOIN YOU?
WHY?
WHY?!
YAAAHH!!
HOW FAR IS HE GOING TO FOLLOW US?!
YOU GUYS NEED ENDURANCE TRAINING.
THEY SPRINTED AROUND THE GROUNDS FIVE TIMES!
THEY ONLY WERE REQUIRED TO DO THREE.
ARE THOSE TWO OKAY?
YEAH, WELL...
...JUST LET THEM BE.
HE'S A MONSTER!
IS THIS WHAT I CALL PROTECTING MAKO?
Winter job.
Martial Arts.
BUT I HAVE TO ADMIT THAT RECENTLY WE HAVEN'T SEEN EACH OTHER EXCEPT IN THE CLUB. WE HAVEN'T EVEN FOUND TIME TO TALK. (PERSONAL REASONS.)

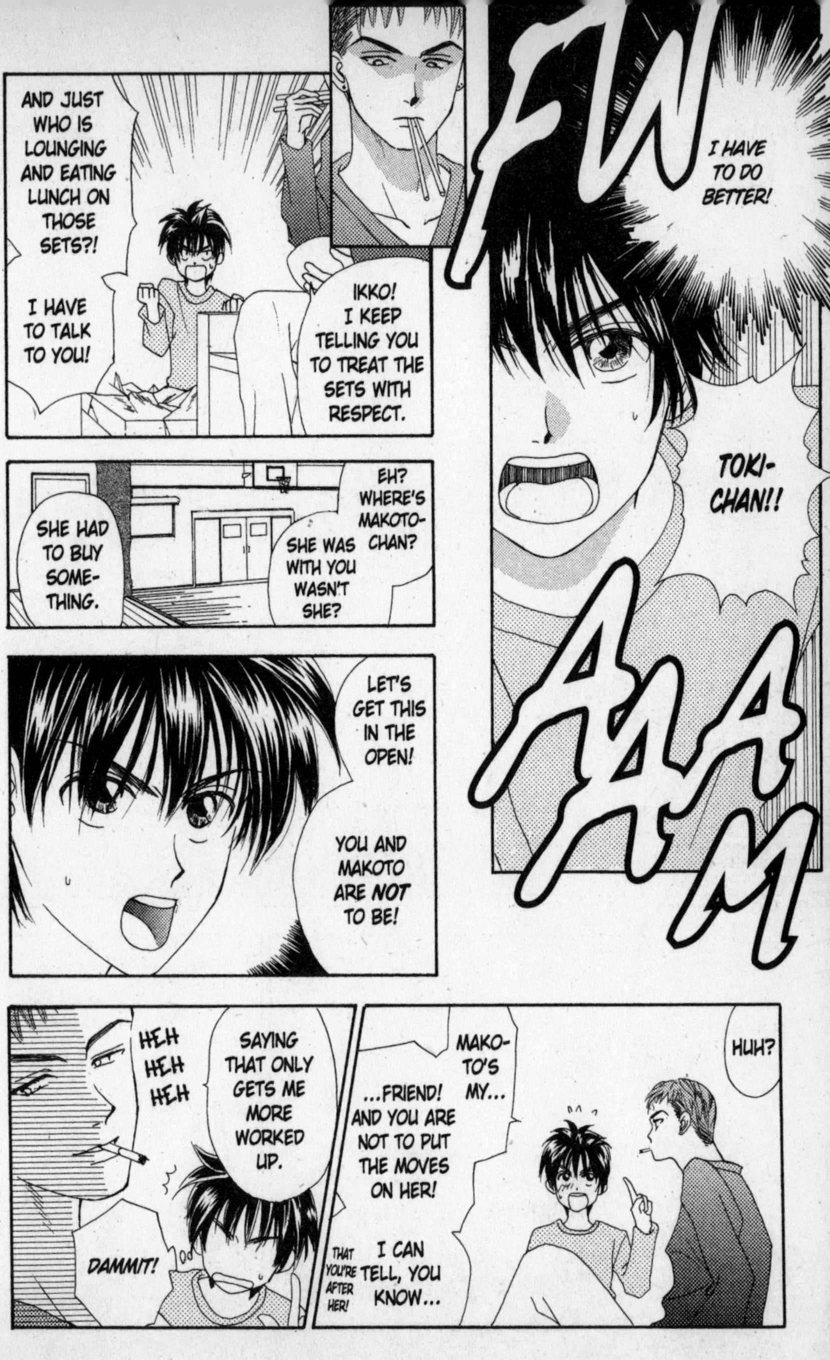
FW
I HAVE TO DO BETTER!
TOKI-CHAN!!
AAAM
IKKO! I KEEP TELLING YOU TO TREAT THE SETS WITH RESPECT.
AND JUST WHO IS LOUNGING AND EATING LUNCH ON THOSE SETS?!
I HAVE TO TALK TO YOU!
EH? WHERE'S MAKOTO-CHAN?
SHE WAS WITH YOU WASN'T SHE?
SHE HAD TO BUY SOMETHING.
LET'S GET THIS IN THE OPEN!
YOU AND MAKOTO ARE *NOT* TO BE!
HUH?
MAKO-TO'S MY...
...FRIEND! AND YOU ARE NOT TO PUT THE MOVES ON HER!
I CAN TELL, YOU KNOW...
THAT YOU'RE AFTER HER!
SAYING THAT ONLY GETS ME MORE WORKED UP.
HEH HEH HEH
DAMMIT!

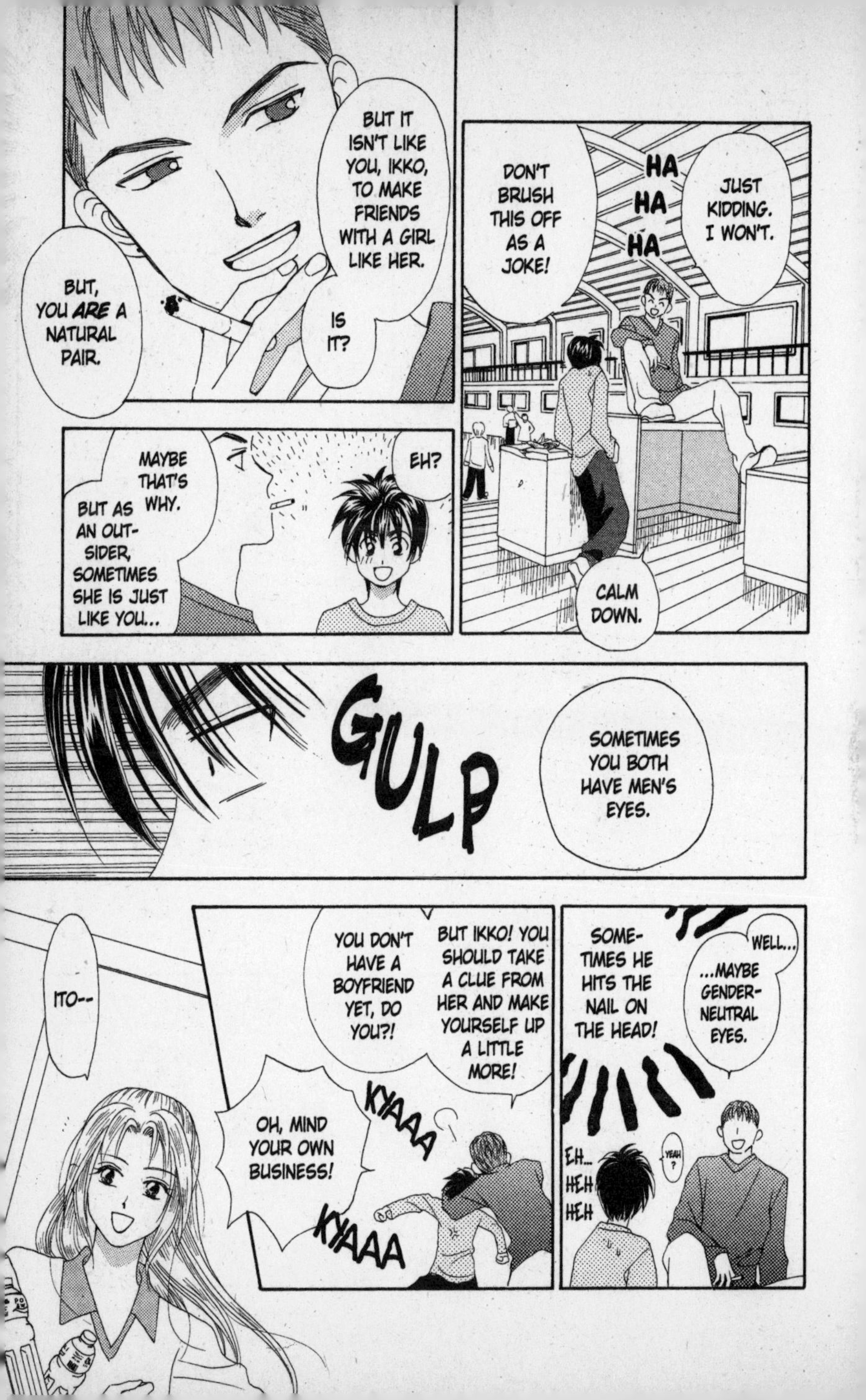

HA HA HA
JUST KIDDING. I WON'T.
DON'T BRUSH THIS OFF AS A JOKE!
CALM DOWN.
BUT IT ISN'T LIKE YOU, IKKO, TO MAKE FRIENDS WITH A GIRL LIKE HER.
IS IT?
BUT, YOU ***ARE*** A NATURAL PAIR.
EH?
MAYBE THAT'S WHY.
BUT AS AN OUT-SIDER, SOMETIMES SHE IS JUST LIKE YOU...
SOMETIMES YOU BOTH HAVE MEN'S EYES.
GULP
WELL...
...MAYBE GENDER-NEUTRAL EYES.
SOME-TIMES HE HITS THE NAIL ON THE HEAD!
YEAH?
EH... HEH HEH
BUT IKKO! YOU SHOULD TAKE A CLUE FROM HER AND MAKE YOURSELF UP A LITTLE MORE!
YOU DON'T HAVE A BOYFRIEND YET, DO YOU?!
KYAAA
KYAAA
OH, MIND YOUR OWN BUSINESS!
ITO--

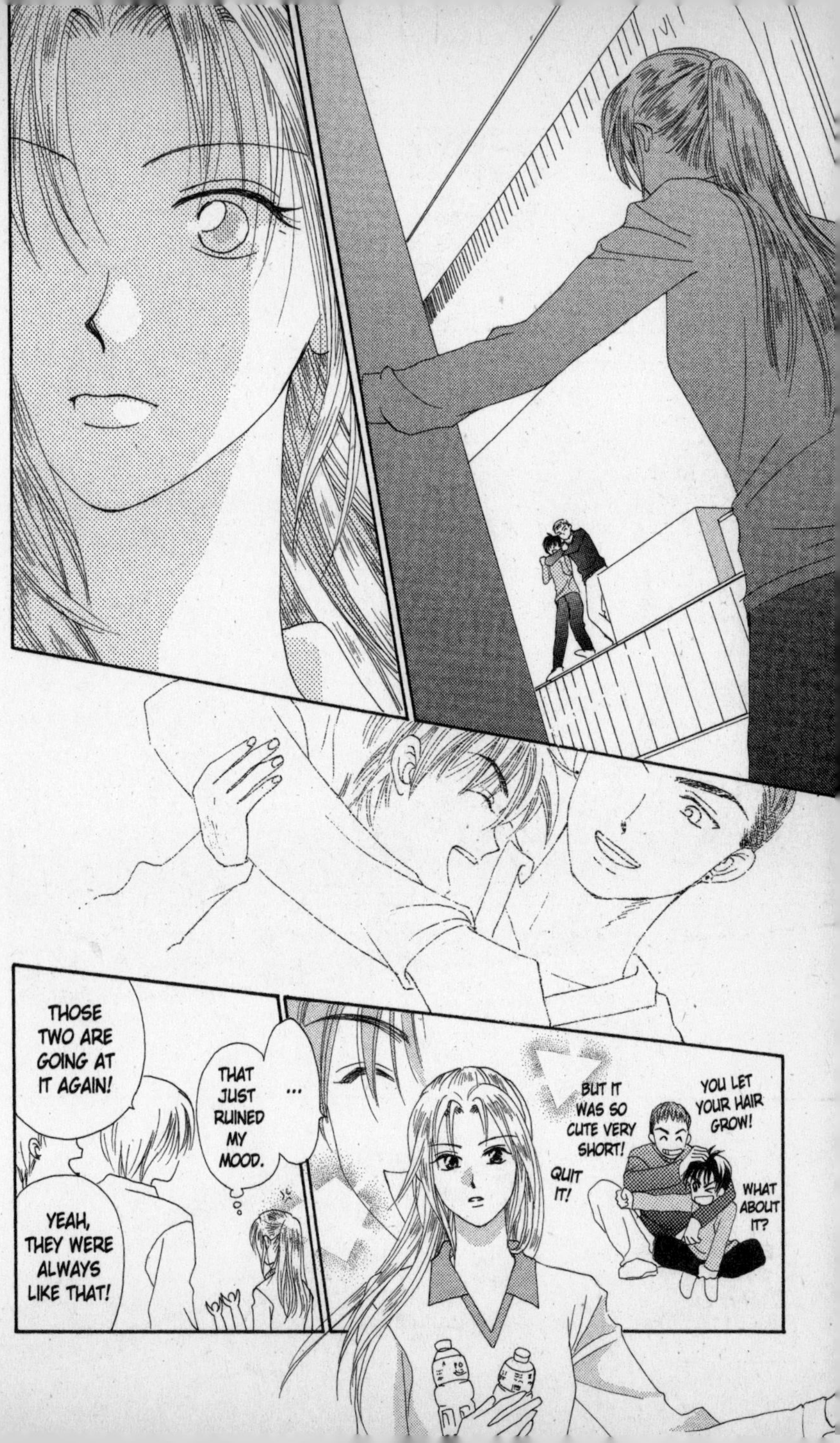
YOU LET YOUR HAIR GROW!
WHAT ABOUT IT?
BUT IT WAS SO CUTE VERY SHORT!
QUIT IT!
...
THOSE TWO ARE GOING AT IT AGAIN!
THAT JUST RUINED MY MOOD.
YEAH, THEY WERE ALWAYS LIKE THAT!

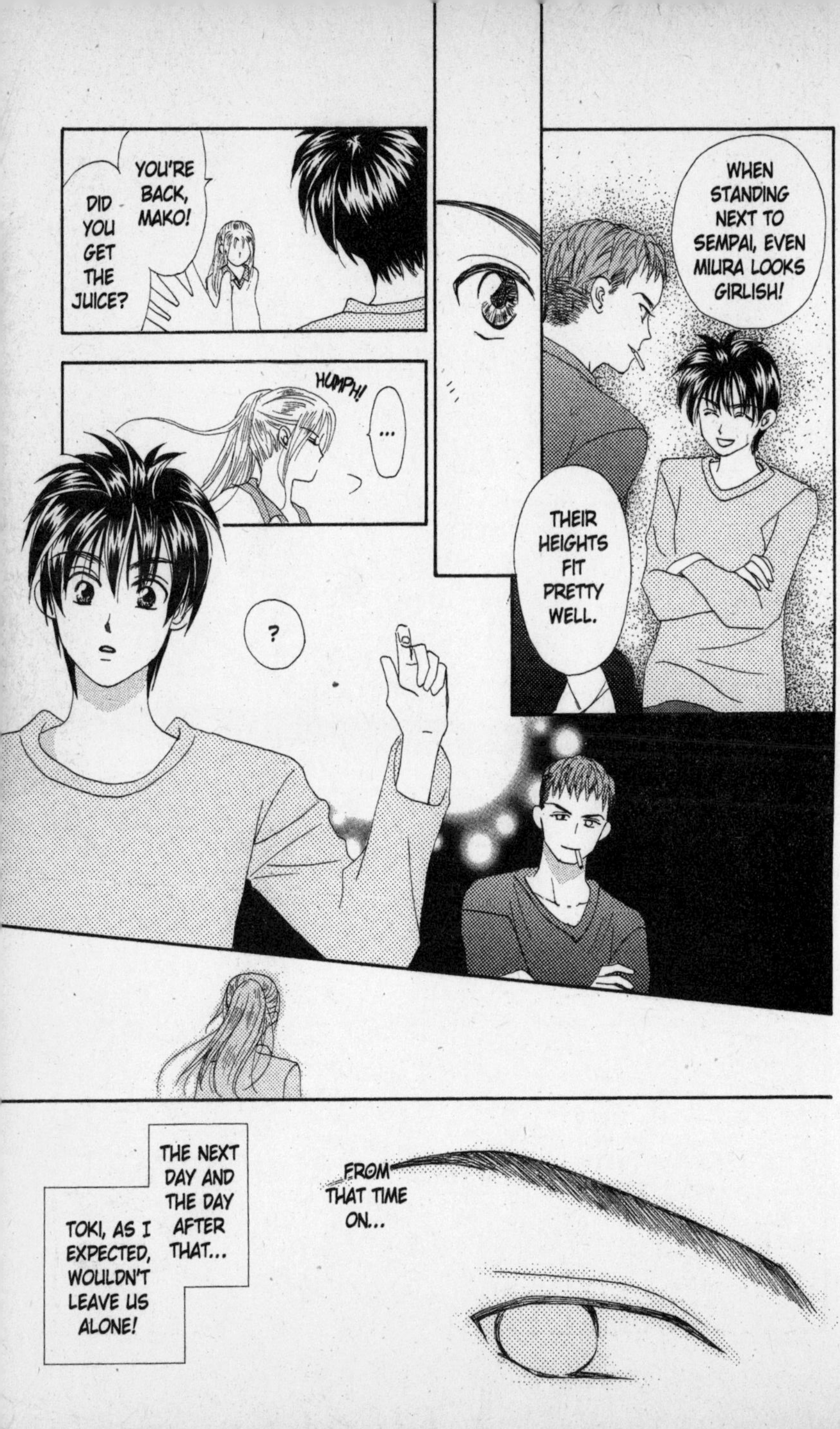
WHEN STANDING NEXT TO SEMPAI, EVEN MIURA LOOKS GIRLISH!
THEIR HEIGHTS FIT PRETTY WELL.
YOU'RE BACK, MAKO!
DID YOU GET THE JUICE?
HUMPH!
...
?
FROM THAT TIME ON...
THE NEXT DAY AND THE DAY AFTER THAT...
TOKI, AS I EXPECTED, WOULDN'T LEAVE US ALONE!

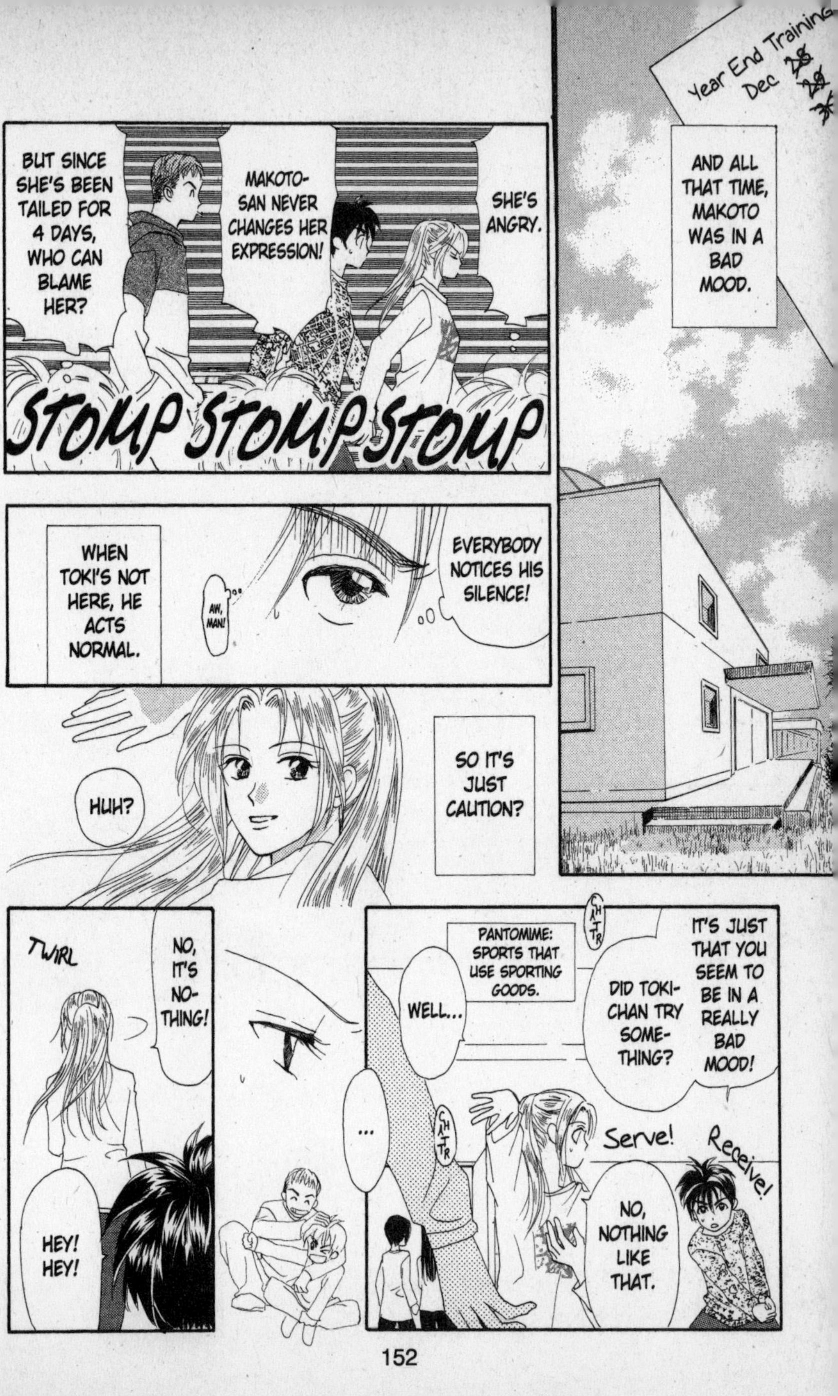
Year End Training
Dec 28 29 30
AND ALL THAT TIME, MAKOTO WAS IN A BAD MOOD.
SHE'S ANGRY.
MAKOTO-SAN NEVER CHANGES HER EXPRESSION!
BUT SINCE SHE'S BEEN TAILED FOR 4 DAYS, WHO CAN BLAME HER?
STOMP STOMP STOMP
EVERYBODY NOTICES HIS SILENCE!
AW, MAN!
WHEN TOKI'S NOT HERE, HE ACTS NORMAL.
SO IT'S JUST CAUTION?
HUH?
IT'S JUST THAT YOU SEEM TO BE IN A REALLY BAD MOOD!
DID TOKI-CHAN TRY SOMETHING?
PANTOMIME: SPORTS THAT USE SPORTING GOODS.
CHATTR
WELL...
Serve!
Receive!
NO, NOTHING LIKE THAT.
CHATTR
NO, IT'S NOTHING!
TWIRL
...
HEY! HEY!

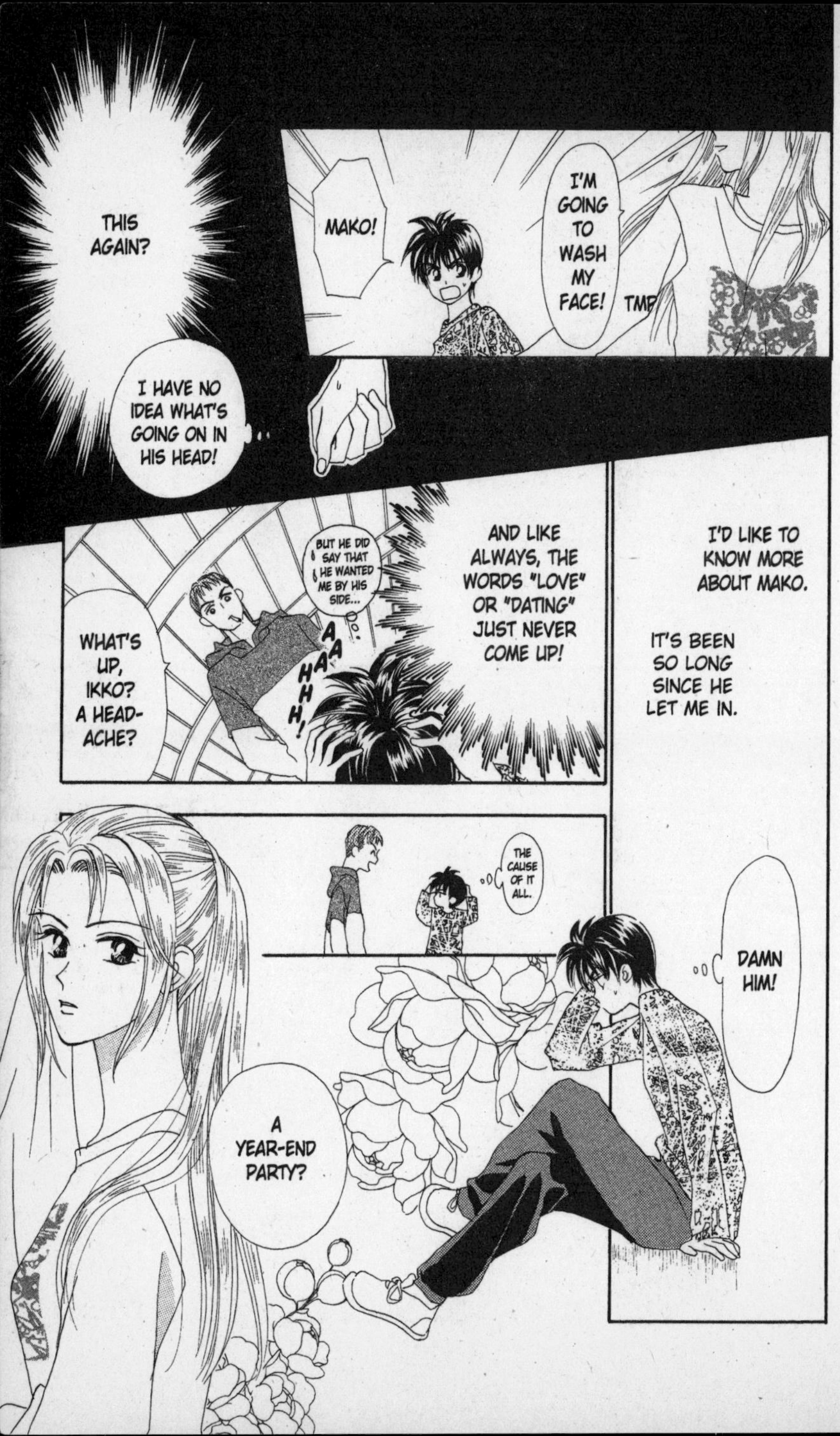
I'M GOING TO WASH MY FACE!
TMP
MAKO!
THIS AGAIN?
I HAVE NO IDEA WHAT'S GOING ON IN HIS HEAD!
I'D LIKE TO KNOW MORE ABOUT MAKO.
IT'S BEEN SO LONG SINCE HE LET ME IN.
AND LIKE ALWAYS, THE WORDS "LOVE" OR "DATING" JUST NEVER COME UP!
BUT HE DID SAY THAT HE WANTED ME BY HIS SIDE...
AAAHHH!
WHAT'S UP, IKKO? A HEAD-ACHE?
DAMN HIM!
THE CAUSE OF IT ALL.
A YEAR-END PARTY?

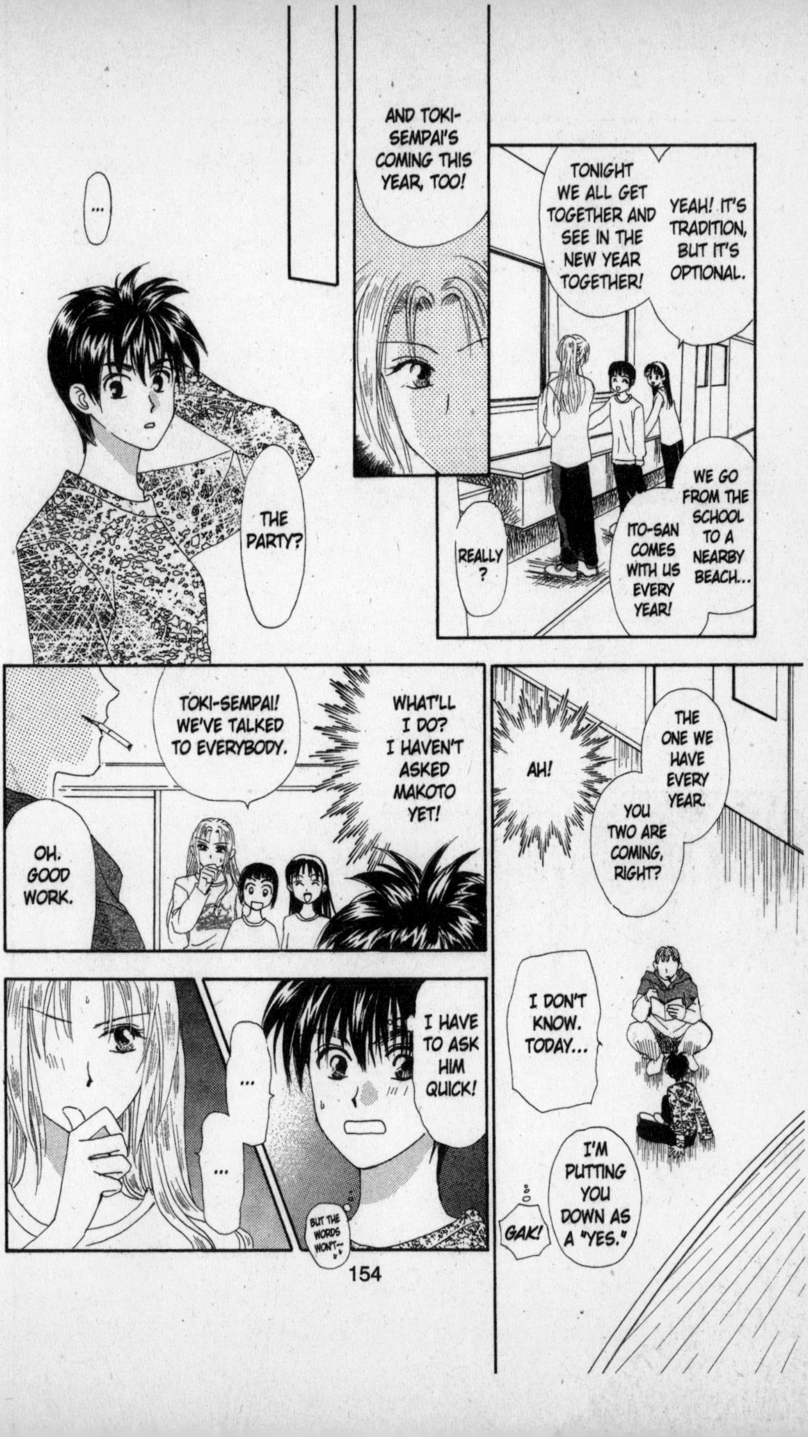
TONIGHT WE ALL GET TOGETHER AND SEE IN THE NEW YEAR TOGETHER!
YEAH! IT'S TRADITION, BUT IT'S OPTIONAL.
WE GO FROM THE SCHOOL TO A NEARBY BEACH...
ITO-SAN COMES WITH US EVERY YEAR!
REALLY?
AND TOKI-SEMPAI'S COMING THIS YEAR, TOO!
...
THE PARTY?
THE ONE WE HAVE EVERY YEAR.
YOU TWO ARE COMING, RIGHT?
AH!
WHAT'LL I DO? I HAVEN'T ASKED MAKOTO YET!
TOKI-SEMPAI! WE'VE TALKED TO EVERYBODY.
OH. GOOD WORK.
I DON'T KNOW. TODAY...
I'M PUTTING YOU DOWN AS A "YES."
GAK!
I HAVE TO ASK HIM QUICK!
...
...
BUT THE WORDS WON'T...

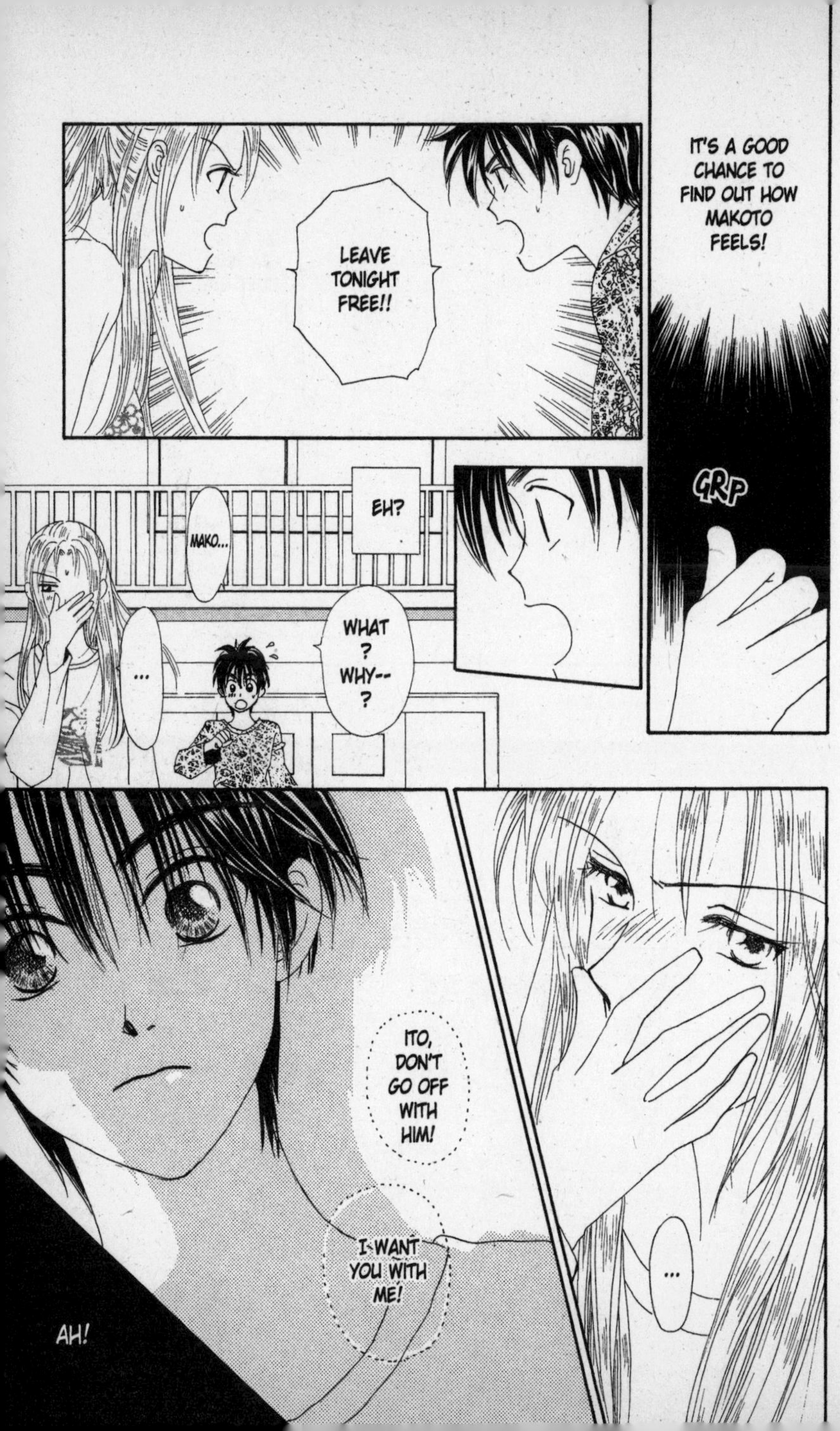
IT'S A GOOD CHANCE TO FIND OUT HOW MAKOTO FEELS!
GRP
LEAVE TONIGHT FREE!!
EH?
MAKO...
WHAT? WHY--?
...
...
ITO, DON'T GO OFF WITH HIM!
I WANT YOU WITH ME!
AH!

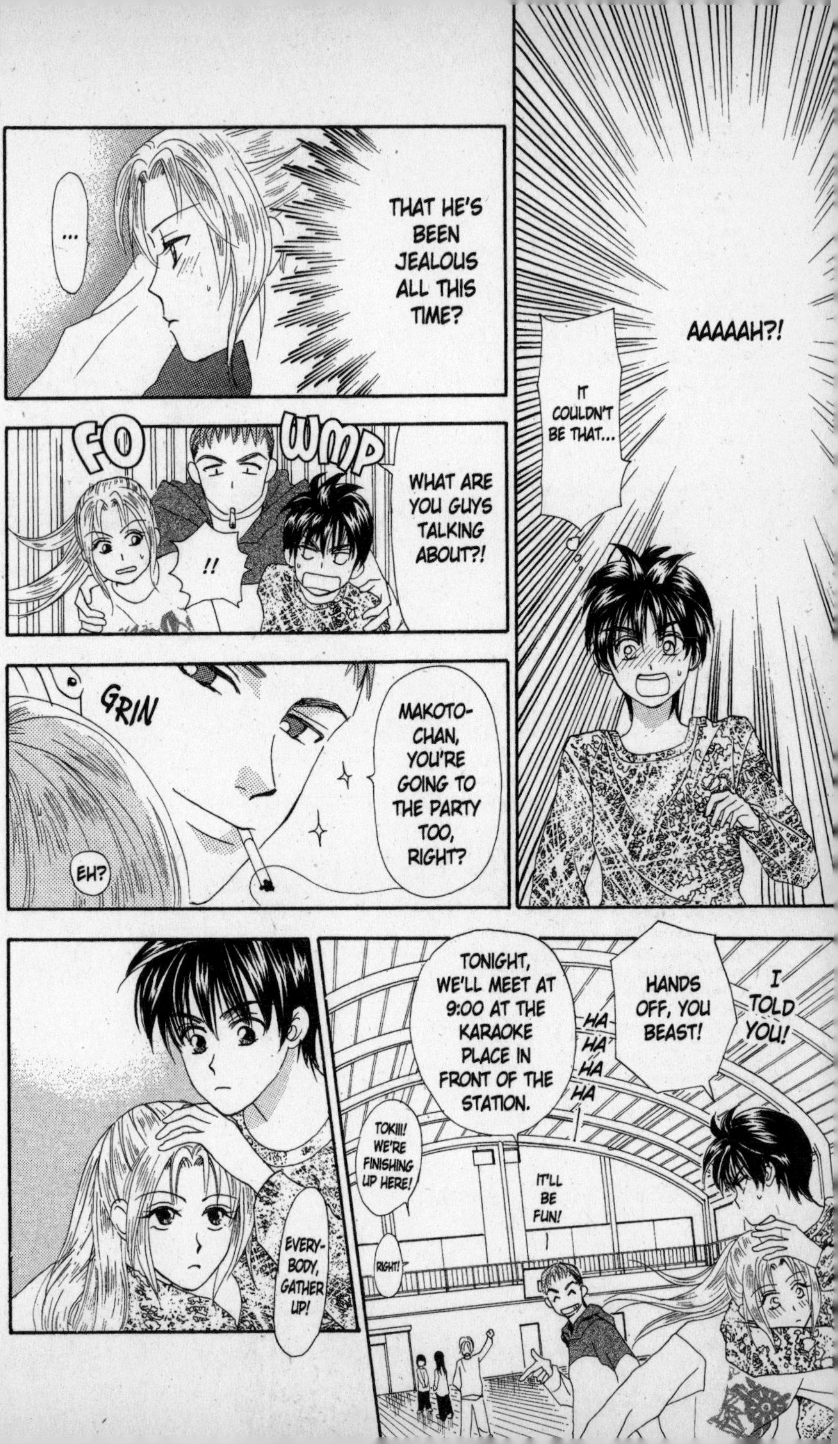
AAAAAH?!
IT COULDN'T BE THAT...
THAT HE'S BEEN JEALOUS ALL THIS TIME?
...
FO
WMP
WHAT ARE YOU GUYS TALKING ABOUT?!
!!
GRIN
MAKOTO-CHAN, YOU'RE GOING TO THE PARTY TOO, RIGHT?
EH?
I TOLD YOU!
HANDS OFF, YOU BEAST!
HA HA HA HA
TONIGHT, WE'LL MEET AT 9:00 AT THE KARAOKE PLACE IN FRONT OF THE STATION.
IT'LL BE FUN!
TOKIII! WE'RE FINISHING UP HERE!
RIGHT!
EVERY-BODY, GATHER UP!

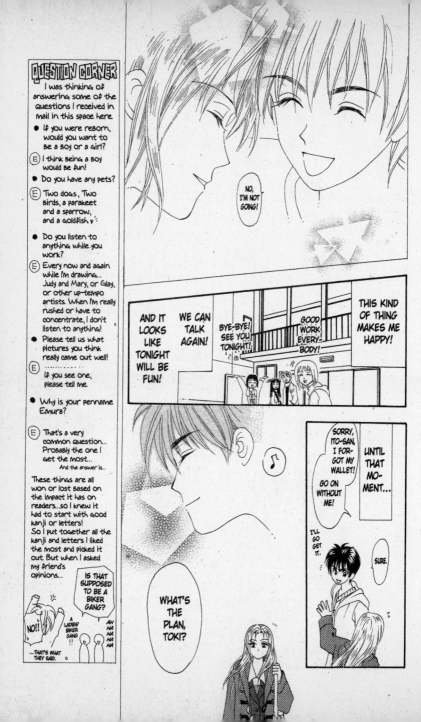

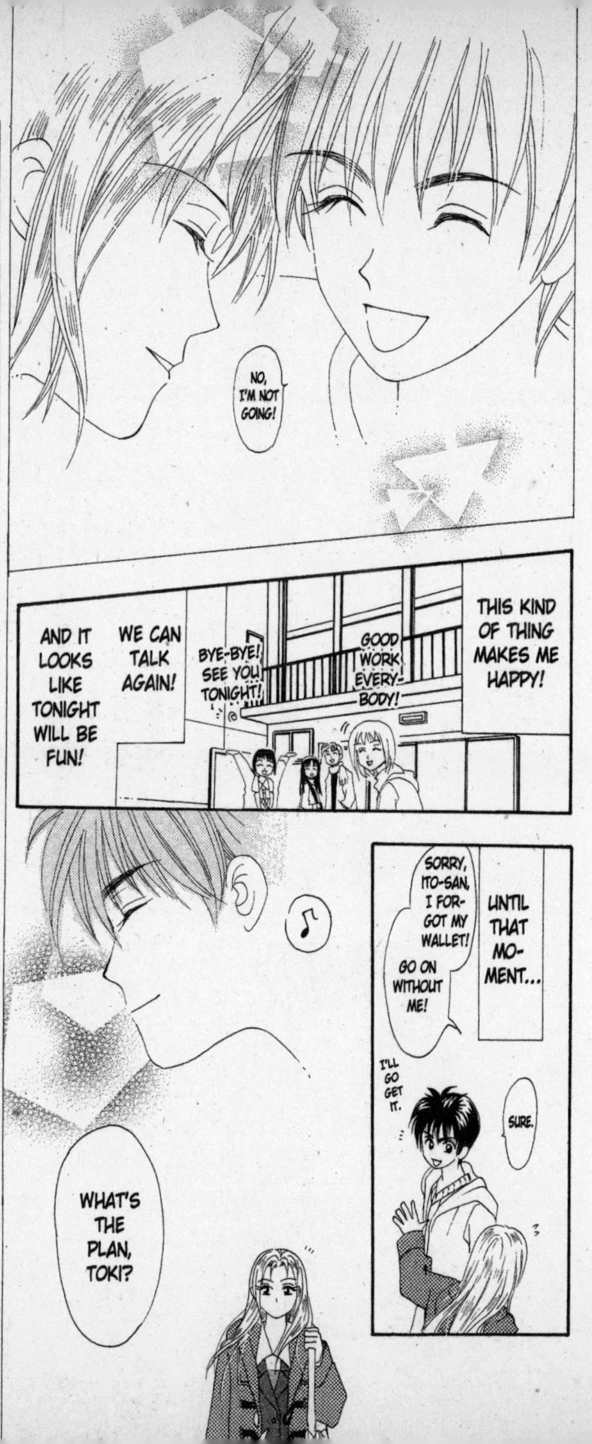
NO, I'M NOT GOING!
THIS KIND OF THING MAKES ME HAPPY!
GOOD WORK EVERY-BODY!
BYE-BYE! SEE YOU TONIGHT!
WE CAN TALK AGAIN!
AND IT LOOKS LIKE TONIGHT WILL BE FUN!
UNTIL THAT MO-MENT...
SORRY, ITO-SAN, I FOR-GOT MY WALLET!
GO ON WITHOUT ME!
SURE.
I'LL GO GET IT.
WHAT'S THE PLAN, TOKI?

QUESTION CORNER

I was thinking of answering some of the questions I received in mail in this space here.

- If you were reborn, would you want to be a boy or a girl?

(E) I think being a boy would be fun!

- Do you have any pets?

(E) Two dogs, two birds, a parakeet and a sparrow, and a goldfish. ♥

- Do you listen to anything while you work?

(E) Every now and again while I'm drawing... Judy and Mary, or Glay, or other up-tempo artists. When I'm really rushed or have to concentrate, I don't listen to anything!

- Please tell us what pictures you think really came out well!

(E) ....

If you see one, please tell me.

- Why is your penname Emura?

(E) That's a very common question.. Probably the one I get the most...

And the answer is...

These things are all won or lost based on the impact it has on readers...so I knew it had to start with good kanji or letters! So I put together all the kanji and letters I liked the most and picked it out. But when I asked my friend's opinions...

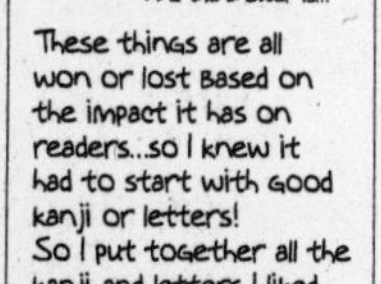
IS THAT SUPPOSED TO BE A BIKER GANG?
NO!!
A LADIES' BIKER GANG!!
AH HA HA HA HA HA
...THAT'S WHAT THEY SAID.

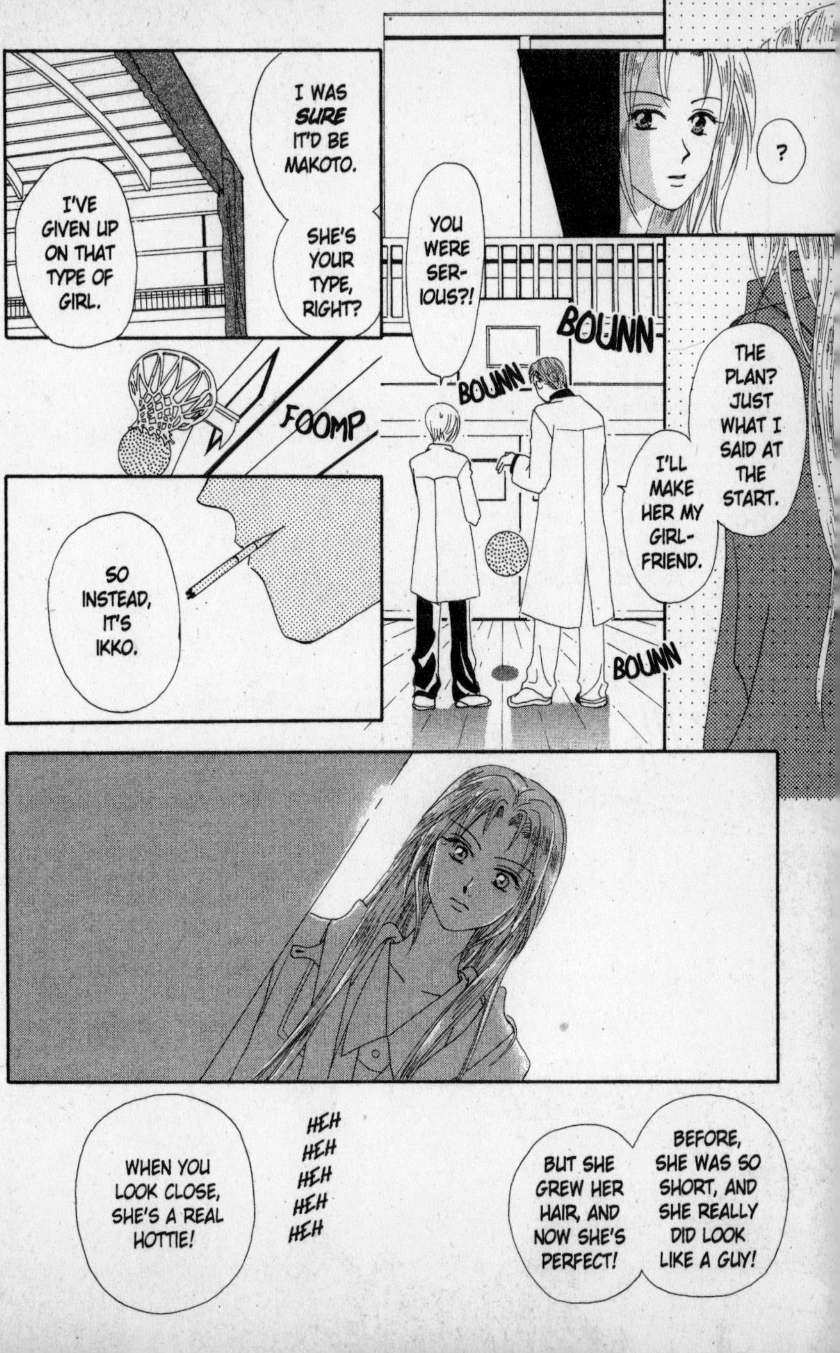
?
THE PLAN? JUST WHAT I SAID AT THE START.
I'LL MAKE HER MY GIRL-FRIEND.
BOUNN
BOUNN
YOU WERE SER-IOUS?!
BOUNN
I WAS SURE IT'D BE MAKOTO.
SHE'S YOUR TYPE, RIGHT?
I'VE GIVEN UP ON THAT TYPE OF GIRL.
FOOMP
SO INSTEAD, IT'S IKKO.
BEFORE, SHE WAS SO SHORT, AND SHE REALLY DID LOOK LIKE A GUY!
BUT SHE GREW HER HAIR, AND NOW SHE'S PERFECT!
HEH HEH HEH HEH HEH
WHEN YOU LOOK CLOSE, SHE'S A REAL HOTTIE!

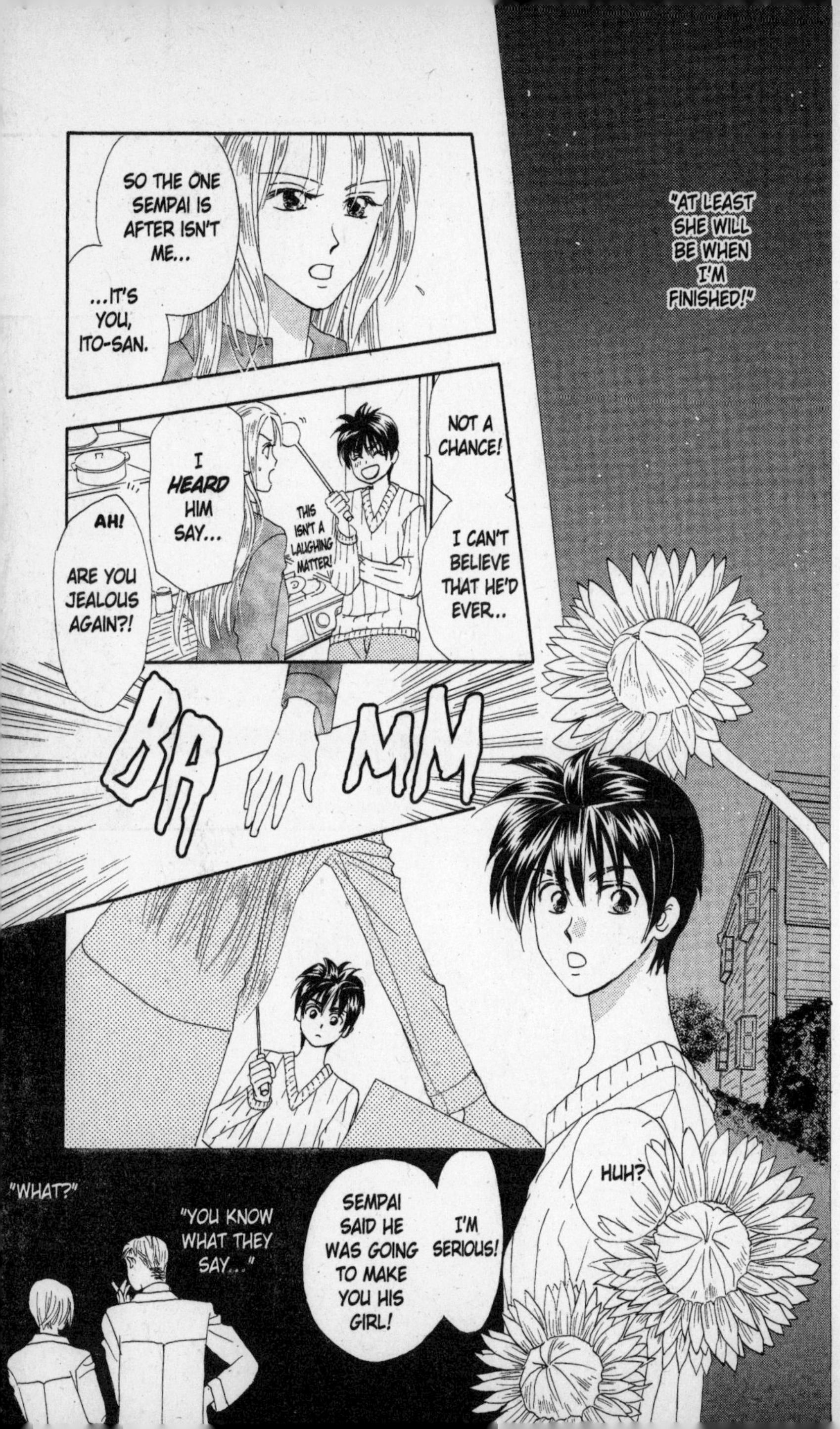
"AT LEAST SHE WILL BE WHEN I'M FINISHED!"
SO THE ONE SEMPAI IS AFTER ISN'T ME...
...IT'S YOU, ITO-SAN.
NOT A CHANCE!
I CAN'T BELIEVE THAT HE'D EVER...
I *HEARD* HIM SAY...
THIS ISN'T A LAUGHING MATTER!
AH!
ARE YOU JEALOUS AGAIN?!
BAMM
HUH?
I'M SERIOUS!
SEMPAI SAID HE WAS GOING TO MAKE YOU HIS GIRL!
"YOU KNOW WHAT THEY SAY..."
"WHAT?"

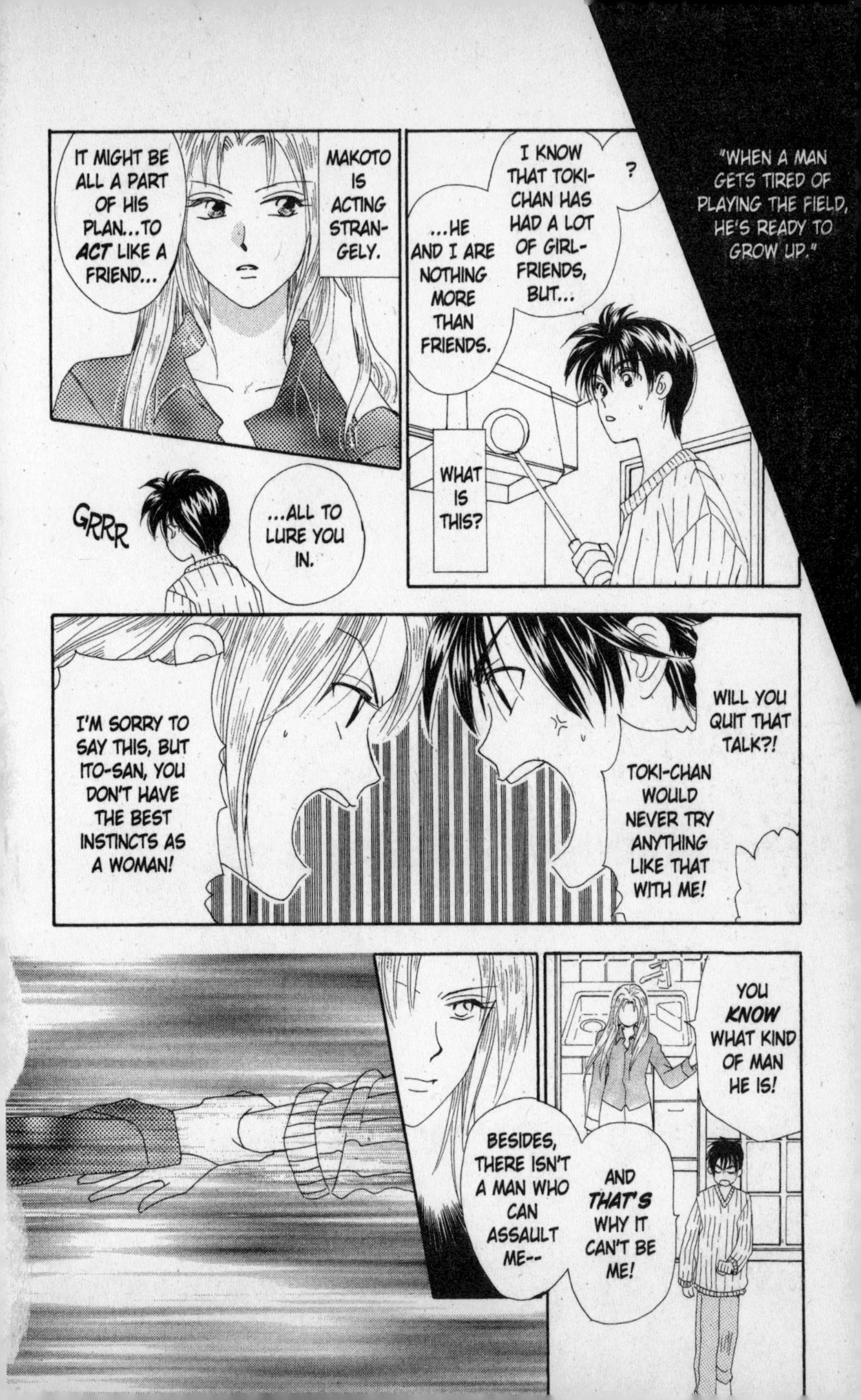
"WHEN A MAN GETS TIRED OF PLAYING THE FIELD, HE'S READY TO GROW UP."
I KNOW THAT TOKI-CHAN HAS HAD A LOT OF GIRL-FRIENDS, BUT...
?
...HE AND I ARE NOTHING MORE THAN FRIENDS.
WHAT IS THIS?
MAKOTO IS ACTING STRAN-GELY.
IT MIGHT BE ALL A PART OF HIS PLAN...TO *ACT* LIKE A FRIEND...
...ALL TO LURE YOU IN.
GRRR
WILL YOU QUIT THAT TALK?!
TOKI-CHAN WOULD NEVER TRY ANYTHING LIKE THAT WITH ME!
I'M SORRY TO SAY THIS, BUT ITO-SAN, YOU DON'T HAVE THE BEST INSTINCTS AS A WOMAN!
YOU *KNOW* WHAT KIND OF MAN HE IS!
AND *THAT'S* WHY IT CAN'T BE ME!
BESIDES, THERE ISN'T A MAN WHO CAN ASSAULT ME--

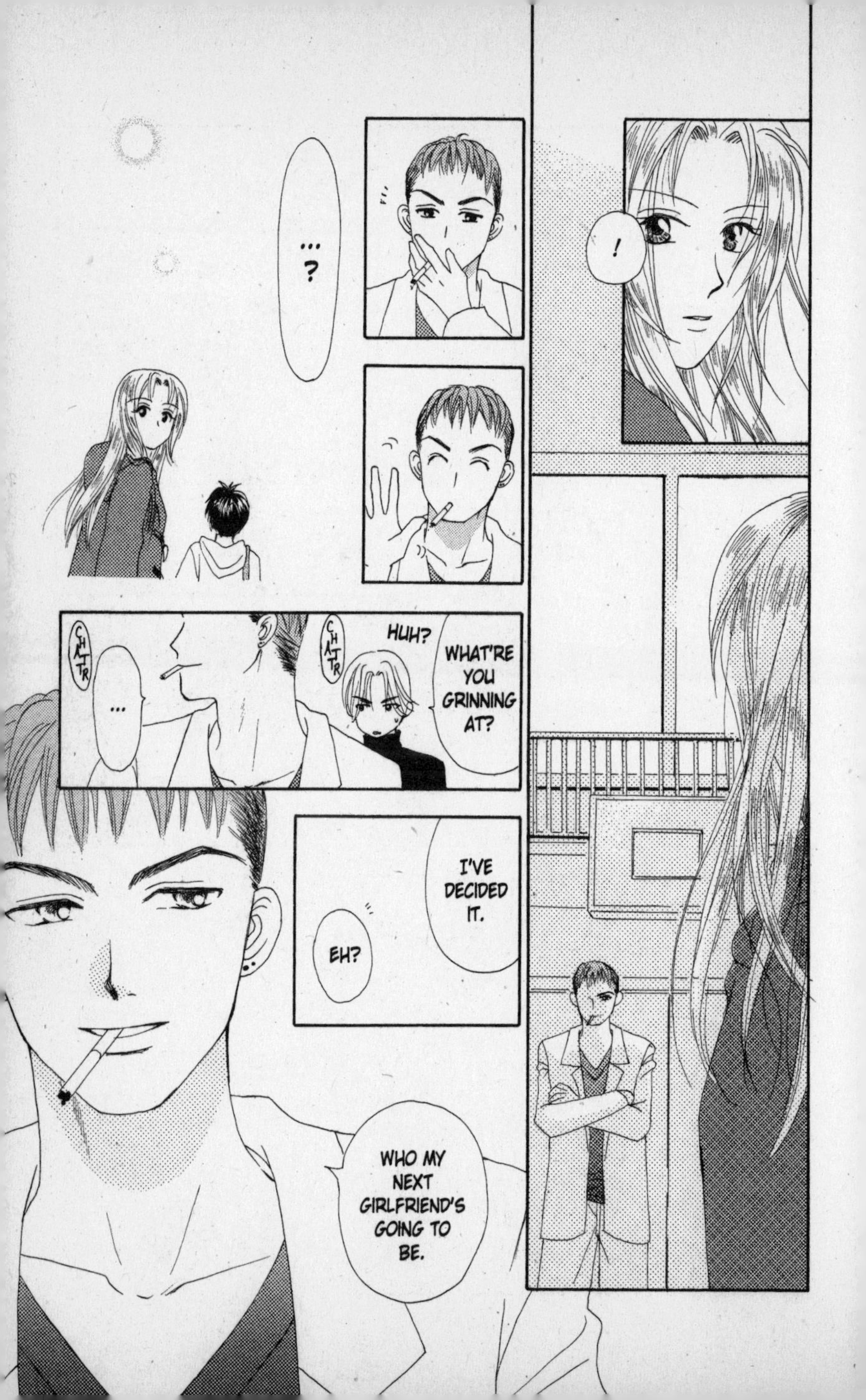
!
...?
WHAT'RE YOU GRINNING AT?
HUH?
CHATR
...
CHATR
I'VE DECIDED IT.
EH?
WHO MY NEXT GIRLFRIEND'S GOING TO BE.

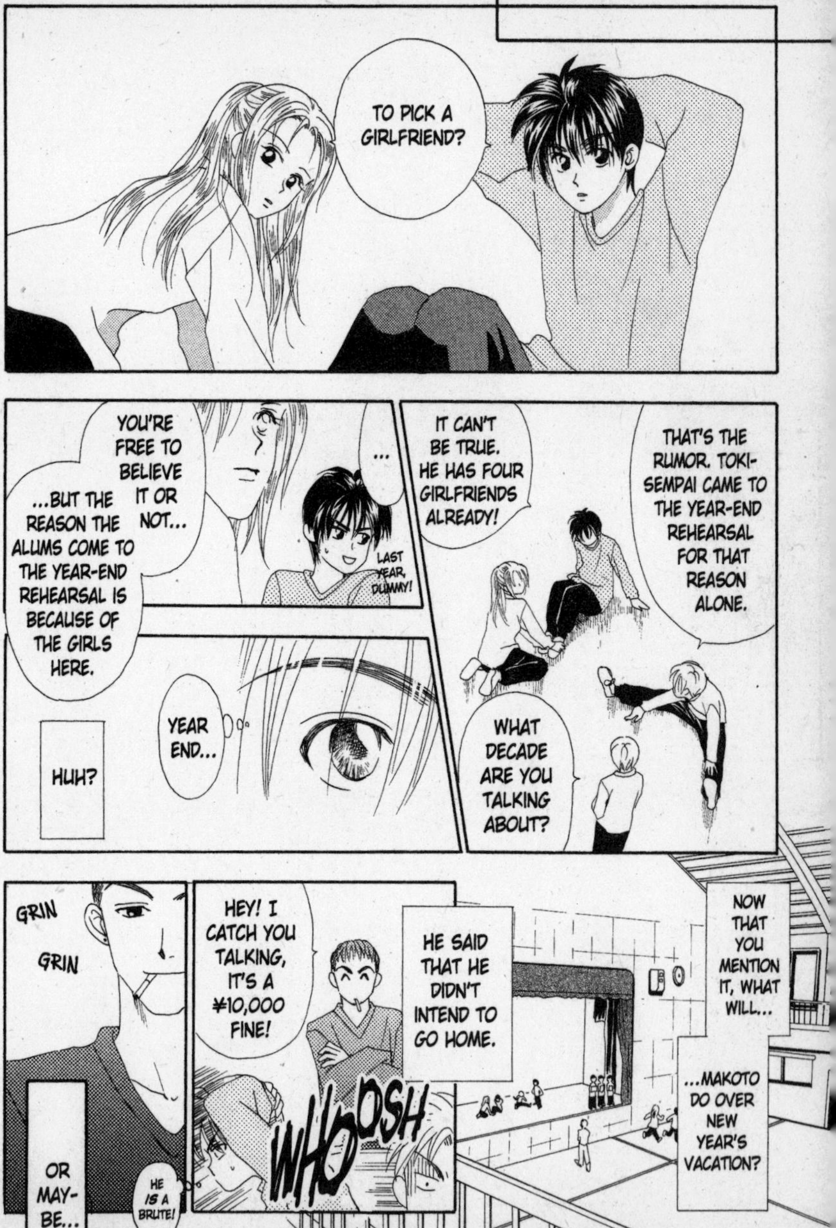
TO PICK A GIRLFRIEND?
THAT'S THE RUMOR. TOKI-SEMPAI CAME TO THE YEAR-END REHEARSAL FOR THAT REASON ALONE.
IT CAN'T BE TRUE. HE HAS FOUR GIRLFRIENDS ALREADY!
LAST YEAR, DUMMY!
...
YOU'RE FREE TO BELIEVE IT OR NOT...
...BUT THE REASON THE ALUMS COME TO THE YEAR-END REHEARSAL IS BECAUSE OF THE GIRLS HERE.
WHAT DECADE ARE YOU TALKING ABOUT?
YEAR END...
HUH?
NOW THAT YOU MENTION IT, WHAT WILL...
...MAKOTO DO OVER NEW YEAR'S VACATION?
HE SAID THAT HE DIDN'T INTEND TO GO HOME.
HEY! I CATCH YOU TALKING, IT'S A ¥10,000 FINE!
WHOOSH
HE IS A BRUTE!
GRIN
GRIN
OR MAY-BE...

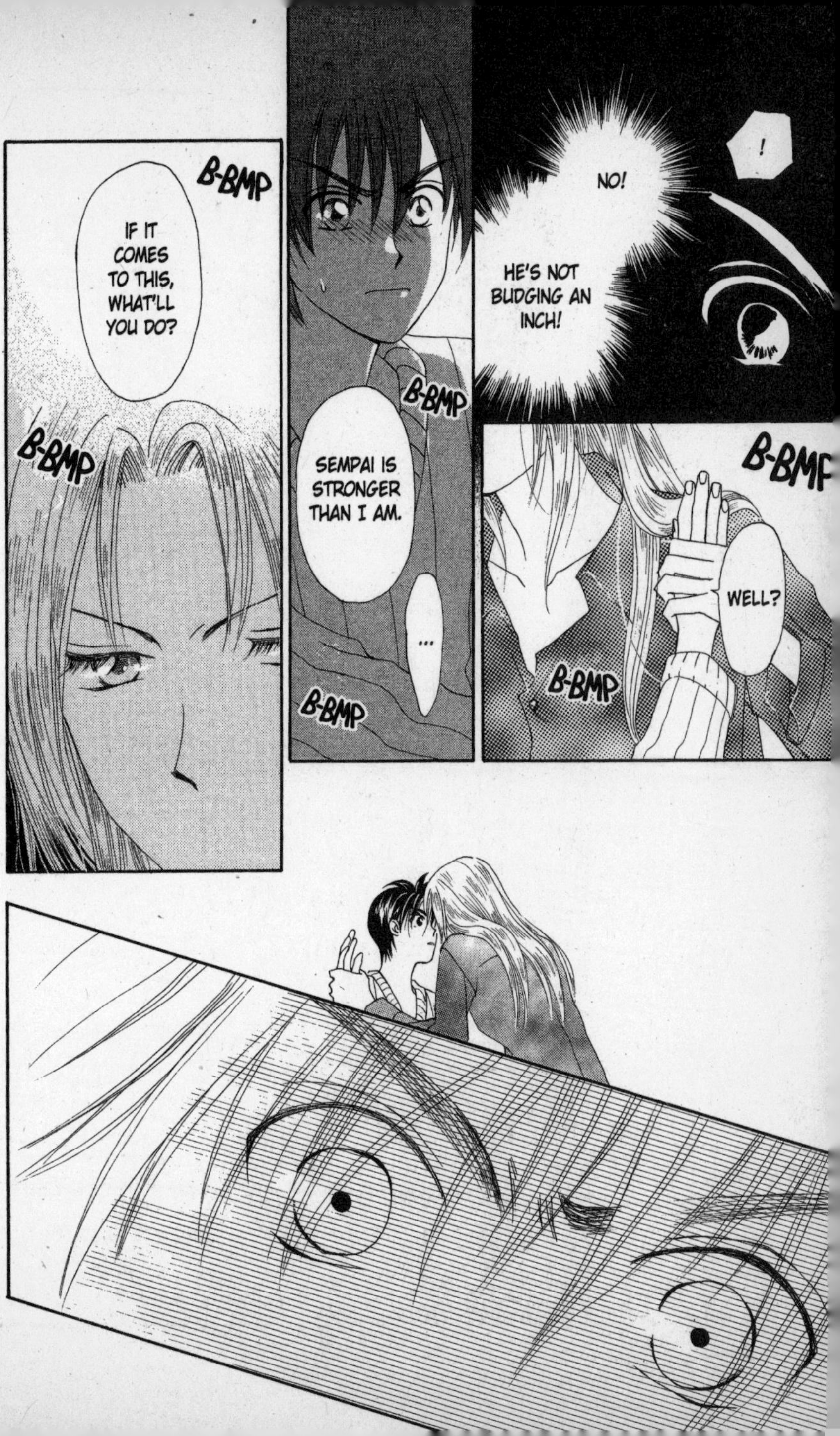
!
NO!
HE'S NOT BUDGING AN INCH!
B-BM
WELL?
B-BMP
B-BMP
SEMPAI IS STRONGER THAN I AM.
...
B-BMP
B-BMP
IF IT COMES TO THIS, WHAT'LL YOU DO?
B-BMP

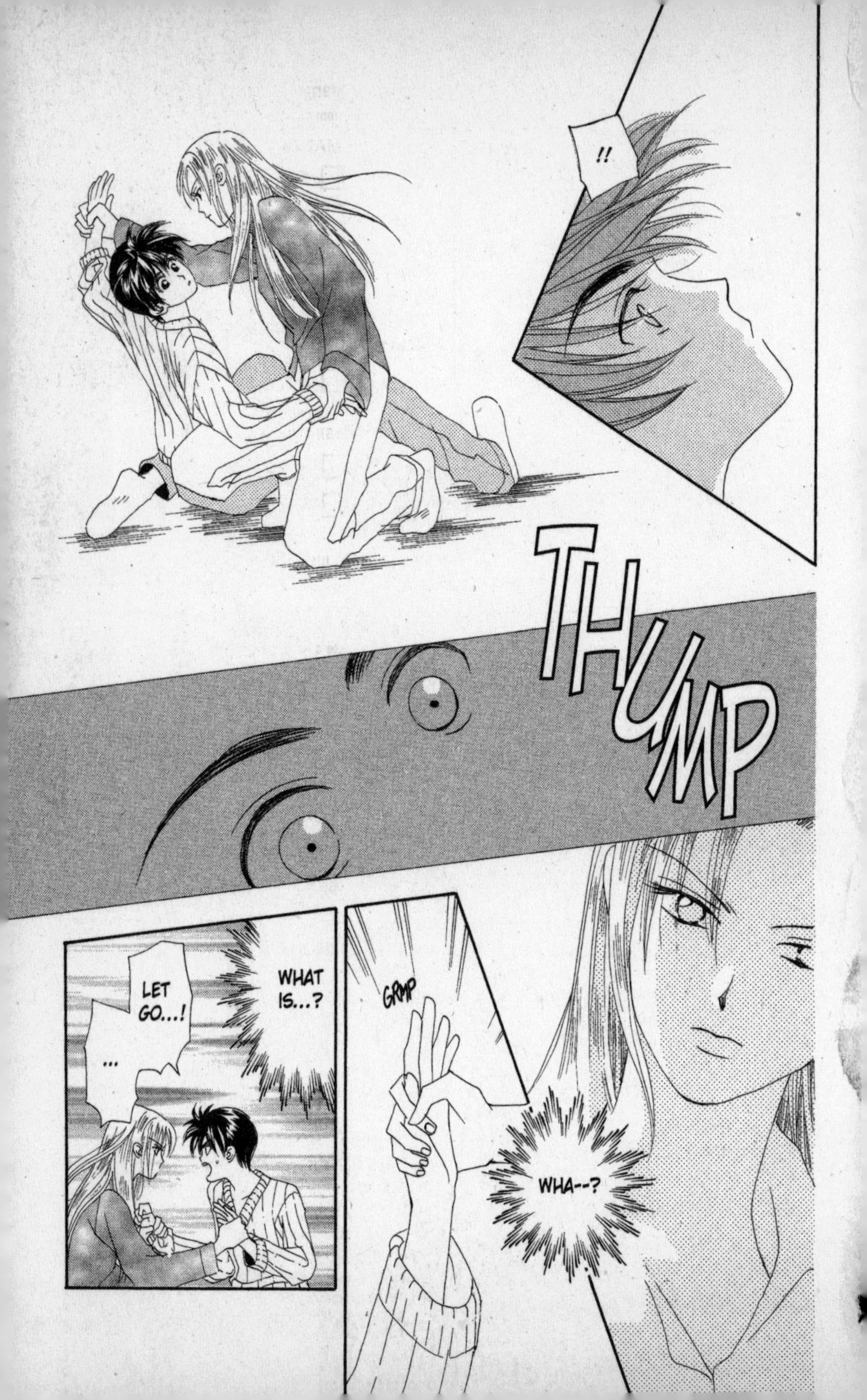
!!
THUMP
WHA--?
GRMP
WHAT IS...?
LET GO...!
...

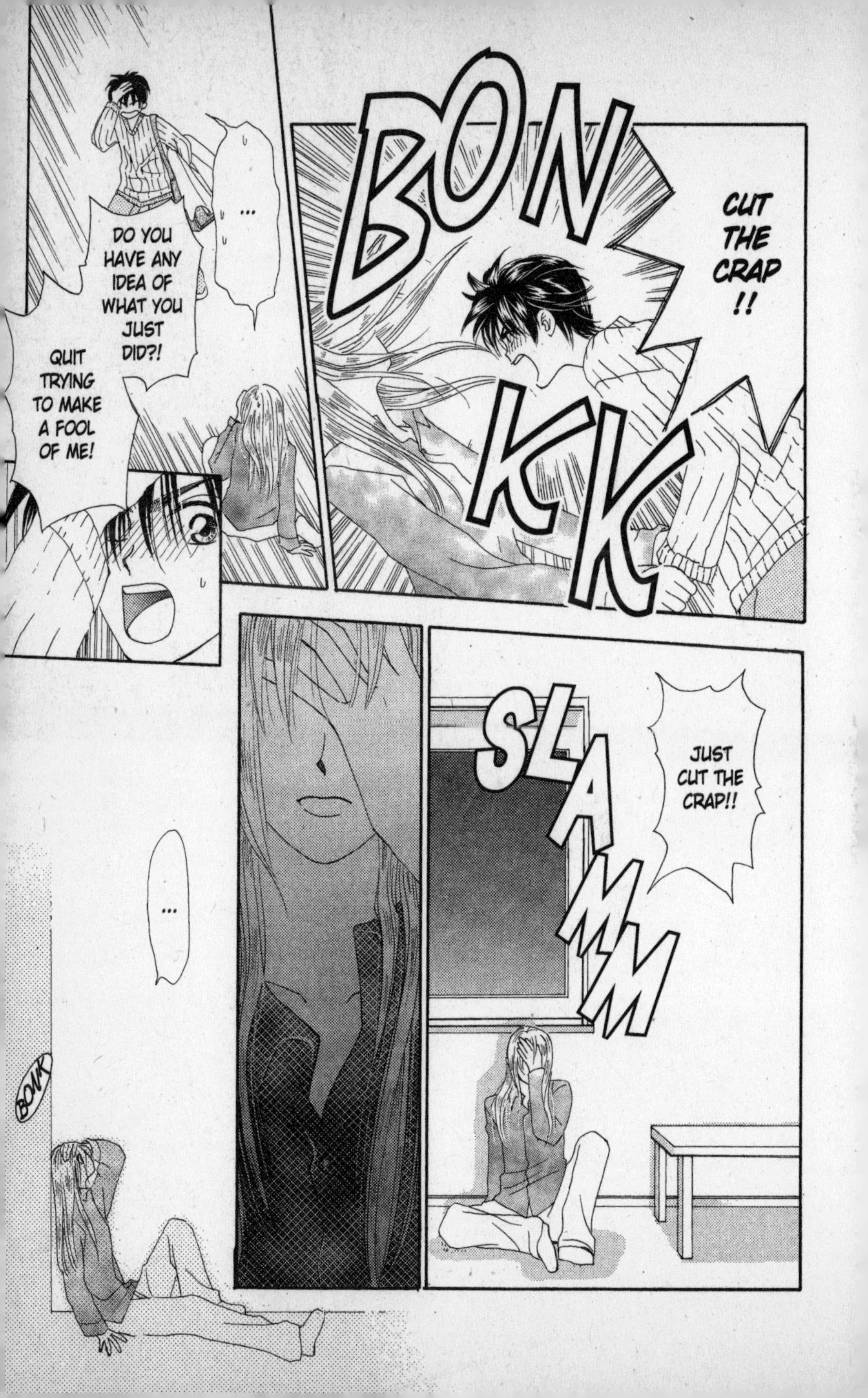
CUT THE CRAP!!
BONKK
...
DO YOU HAVE ANY IDEA OF WHAT YOU JUST DID?!
QUIT TRYING TO MAKE A FOOL OF ME!
JUST CUT THE CRAP!!
SLAMMM
...
BONK

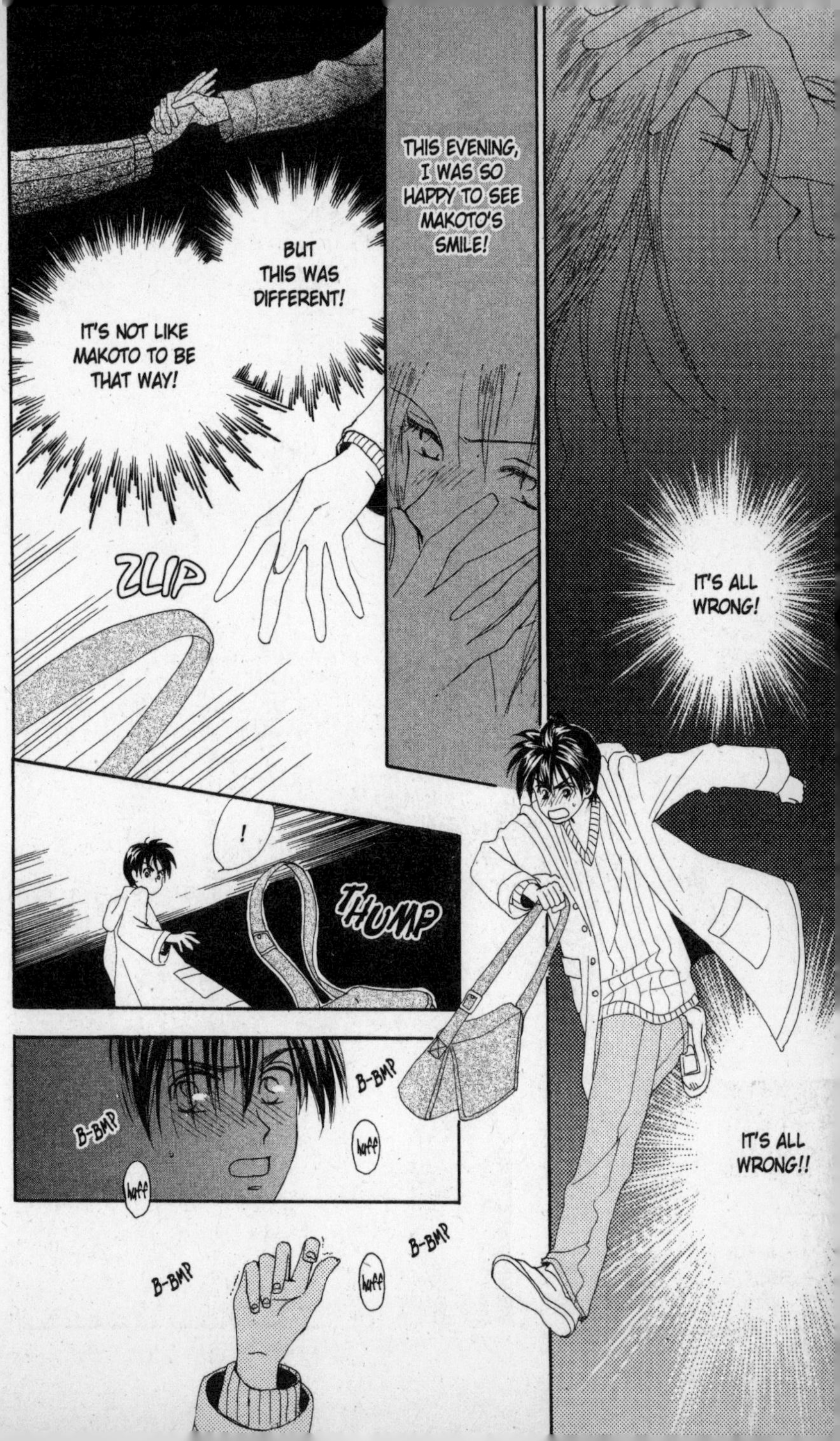
IT'S ALL WRONG!
IT'S ALL WRONG!!
THIS EVENING, I WAS SO HAPPY TO SEE MAKOTO'S SMILE!
BUT THIS WAS DIFFERENT!
IT'S NOT LIKE MAKOTO TO BE THAT WAY!
ZLIP
!
THUMP
B-BMP
huff
B-BMP
huff
B-BMP
huff
B-BMP

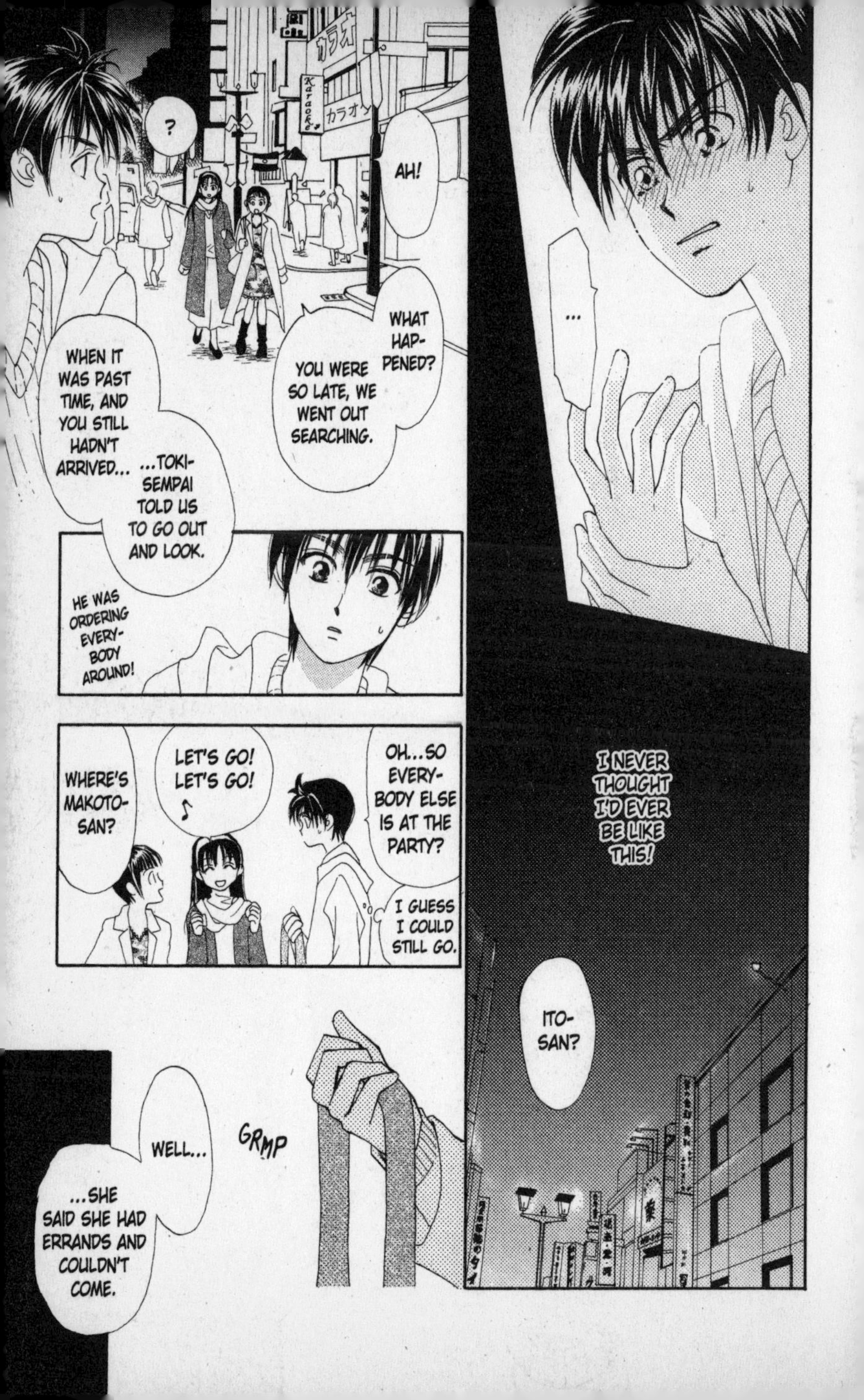
...
I NEVER THOUGHT I'D EVER BE LIKE THIS!
ITO-SAN?
?
AH!
WHAT HAPPENED?
YOU WERE SO LATE, WE WENT OUT SEARCHING.
WHEN IT WAS PAST TIME, AND YOU STILL HADN'T ARRIVED...
...TOKI-SEMPAI TOLD US TO GO OUT AND LOOK.
HE WAS ORDERING EVERYBODY AROUND!
OH...SO EVERYBODY ELSE IS AT THE PARTY?
I GUESS I COULD STILL GO.
LET'S GO! LET'S GO! ♪
WHERE'S MAKOTO-SAN?
GRMP
WELL...
...SHE SAID SHE HAD ERRANDS AND COULDN'T COME.

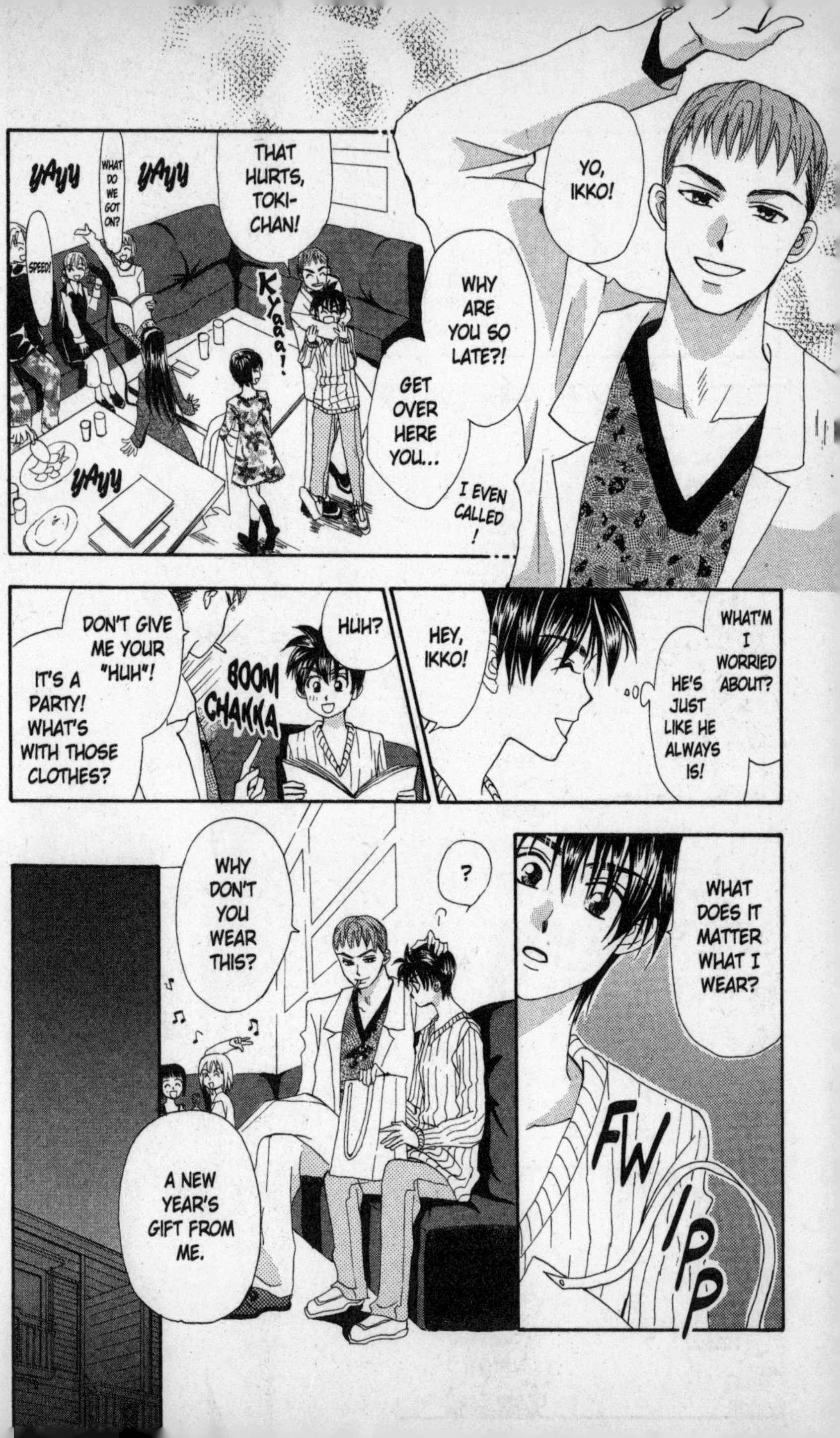
YO, IKKO!
WHY ARE YOU SO LATE?!
GET OVER HERE YOU...
I EVEN CALLED!
THAT HURTS, TOKI-CHAN!
KYAAA!
WHAT DO WE GOT ON?
YAYY
YAYY
SPEED!
YAYY
WHAT'M I WORRIED ABOUT?
HE'S JUST LIKE HE ALWAYS IS!
HEY, IKKO!
HUH?
BOOM CHAKKA
DON'T GIVE ME YOUR "HUH"!
IT'S A PARTY! WHAT'S WITH THOSE CLOTHES?
WHAT DOES IT MATTER WHAT I WEAR?
FWIPP
?
WHY DON'T YOU WEAR THIS?
A NEW YEAR'S GIFT FROM ME.

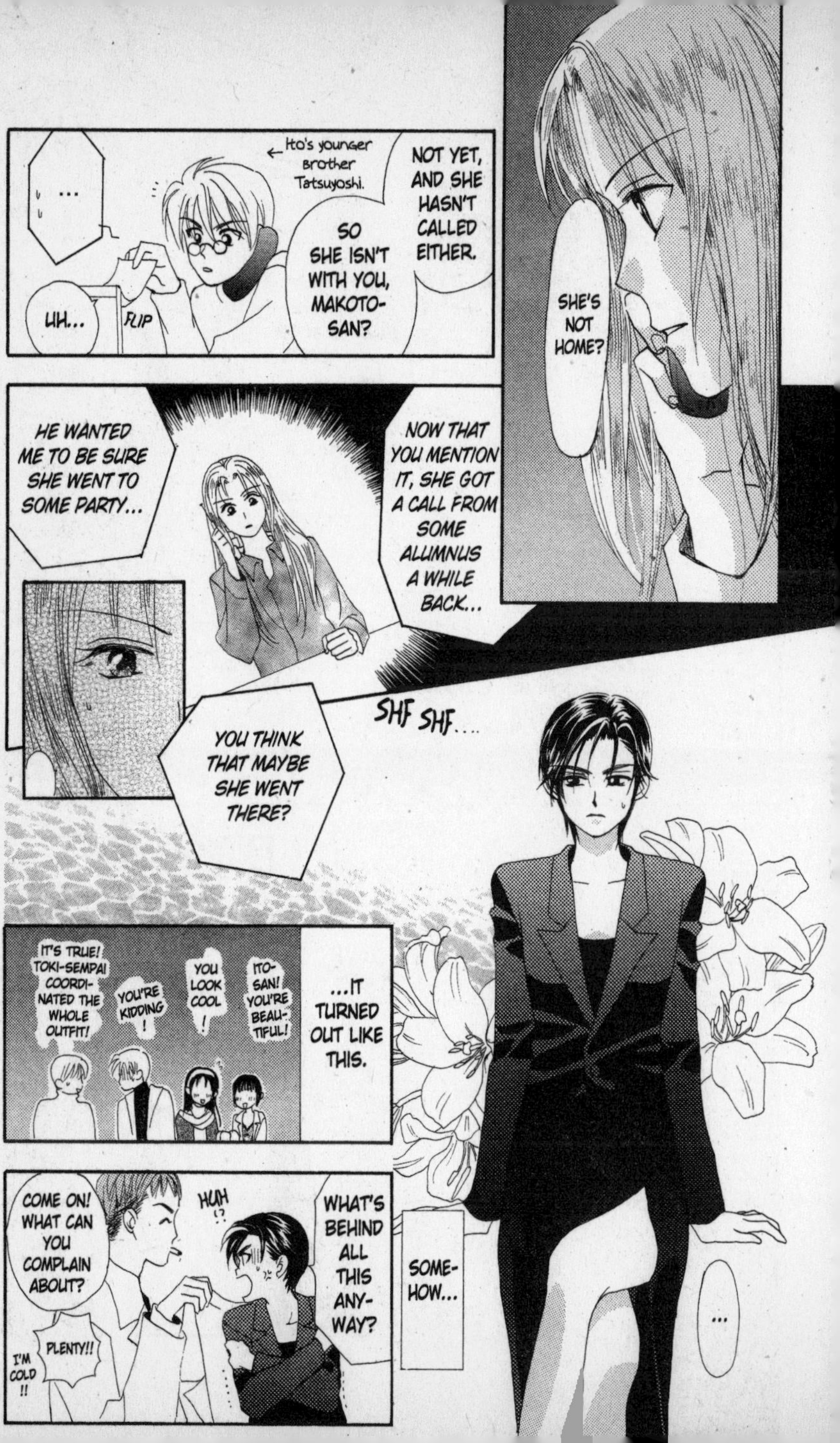
SHE'S NOT HOME?
NOT YET, AND SHE HASN'T CALLED EITHER.
← Ito's younger brother Tatsuyoshi.
SO SHE ISN'T WITH YOU, MAKOTO-SAN?
...
UH...
FLIP
NOW THAT YOU MENTION IT, SHE GOT A CALL FROM SOME ALUMNUS A WHILE BACK...
HE WANTED ME TO BE SURE SHE WENT TO SOME PARTY...
YOU THINK THAT MAYBE SHE WENT THERE?
SHF SHF....
...
...IT TURNED OUT LIKE THIS.
ITO-SAN! YOU'RE BEAUTIFUL!
YOU LOOK COOL!
YOU'RE KIDDING!
IT'S TRUE! TOKI-SEMPAI COORDINATED THE WHOLE OUTFIT!
SOMEHOW...
WHAT'S BEHIND ALL THIS ANYWAY?
HUH!?
COME ON! WHAT CAN YOU COMPLAIN ABOUT?
PLENTY!!
I'M COLD!!

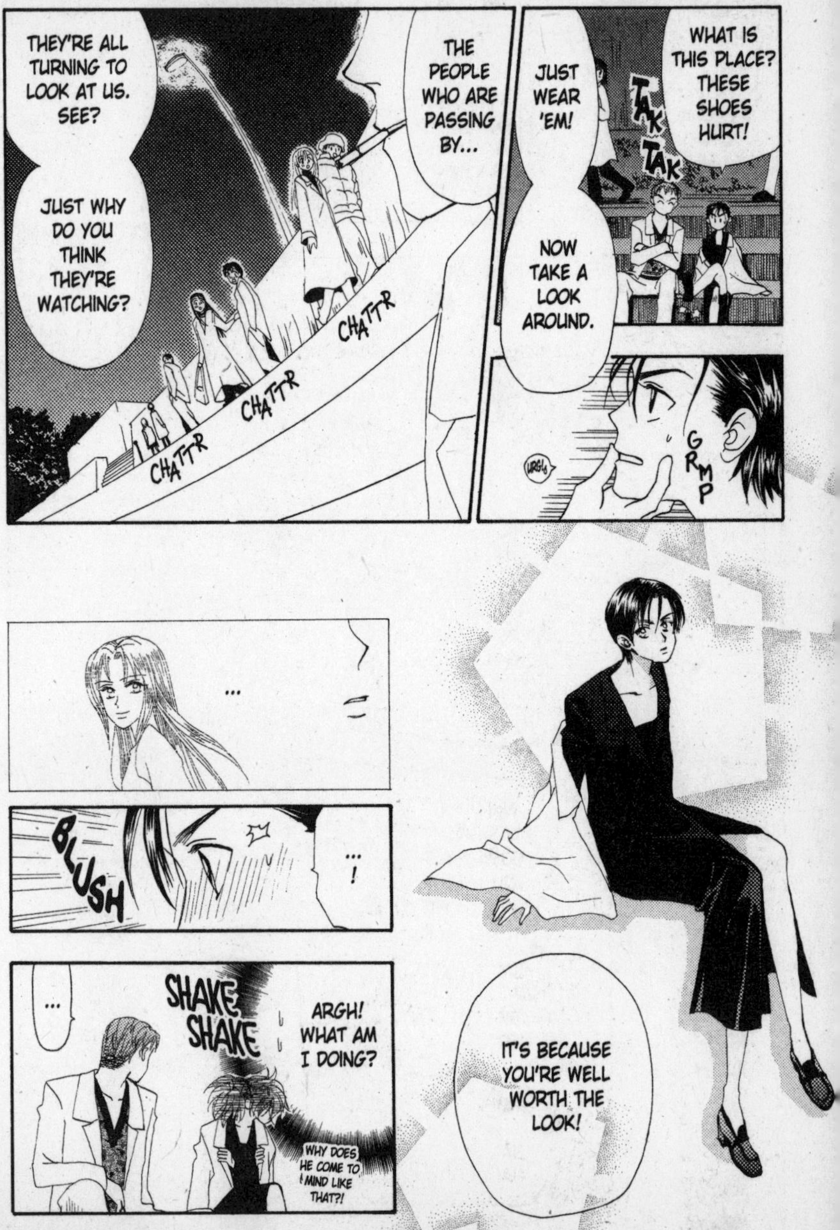
WHAT IS THIS PLACE? THESE SHOES HURT!
TAK TAK
JUST WEAR 'EM!
NOW TAKE A LOOK AROUND.
URGH
GRMP
THE PEOPLE WHO ARE PASSING BY...
THEY'RE ALL TURNING TO LOOK AT US. SEE?
JUST WHY DO YOU THINK THEY'RE WATCHING?
CHATTR
CHATTR
CHATTR
IT'S BECAUSE YOU'RE WELL WORTH THE LOOK!
...
BLUSH
...!
...
SHAKE SHAKE
ARGH! WHAT AM I DOING?
WHY DOES HE COME TO MIND LIKE THAT?!

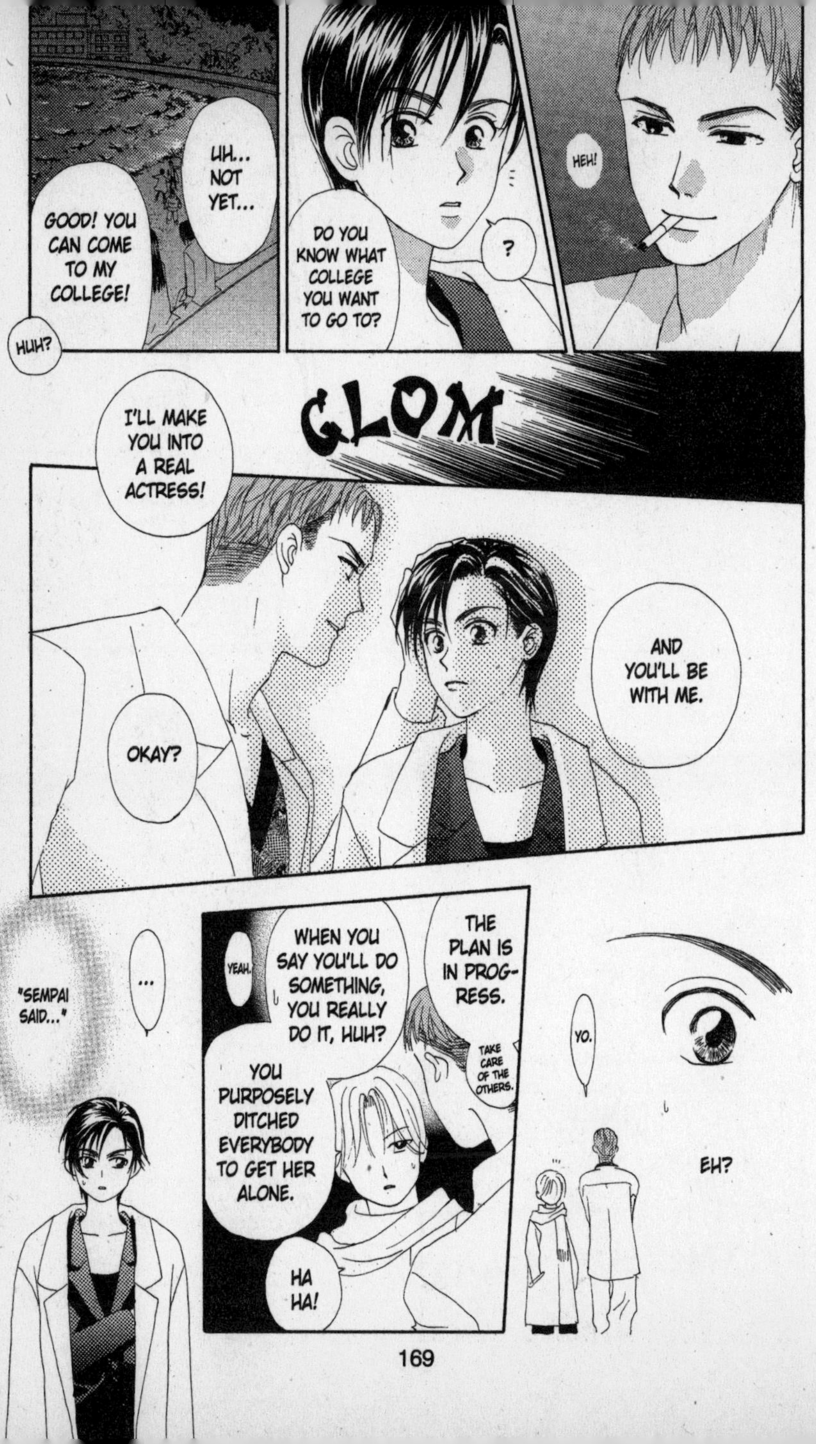
HEH!
?
DO YOU KNOW WHAT COLLEGE YOU WANT TO GO TO?
UH... NOT YET...
GOOD! YOU CAN COME TO MY COLLEGE!
HUH?
GLOM
I'LL MAKE YOU INTO A REAL ACTRESS!
AND YOU'LL BE WITH ME.
OKAY?
YO.
EH?
THE PLAN IS IN PROGRESS.
TAKE CARE OF THE OTHERS.
WHEN YOU SAY YOU'LL DO SOMETHING, YOU REALLY DO IT, HUH?
YEAH.
YOU PURPOSELY DITCHED EVERYBODY TO GET HER ALONE.
HA HA!
...
"SEMPAI SAID..."

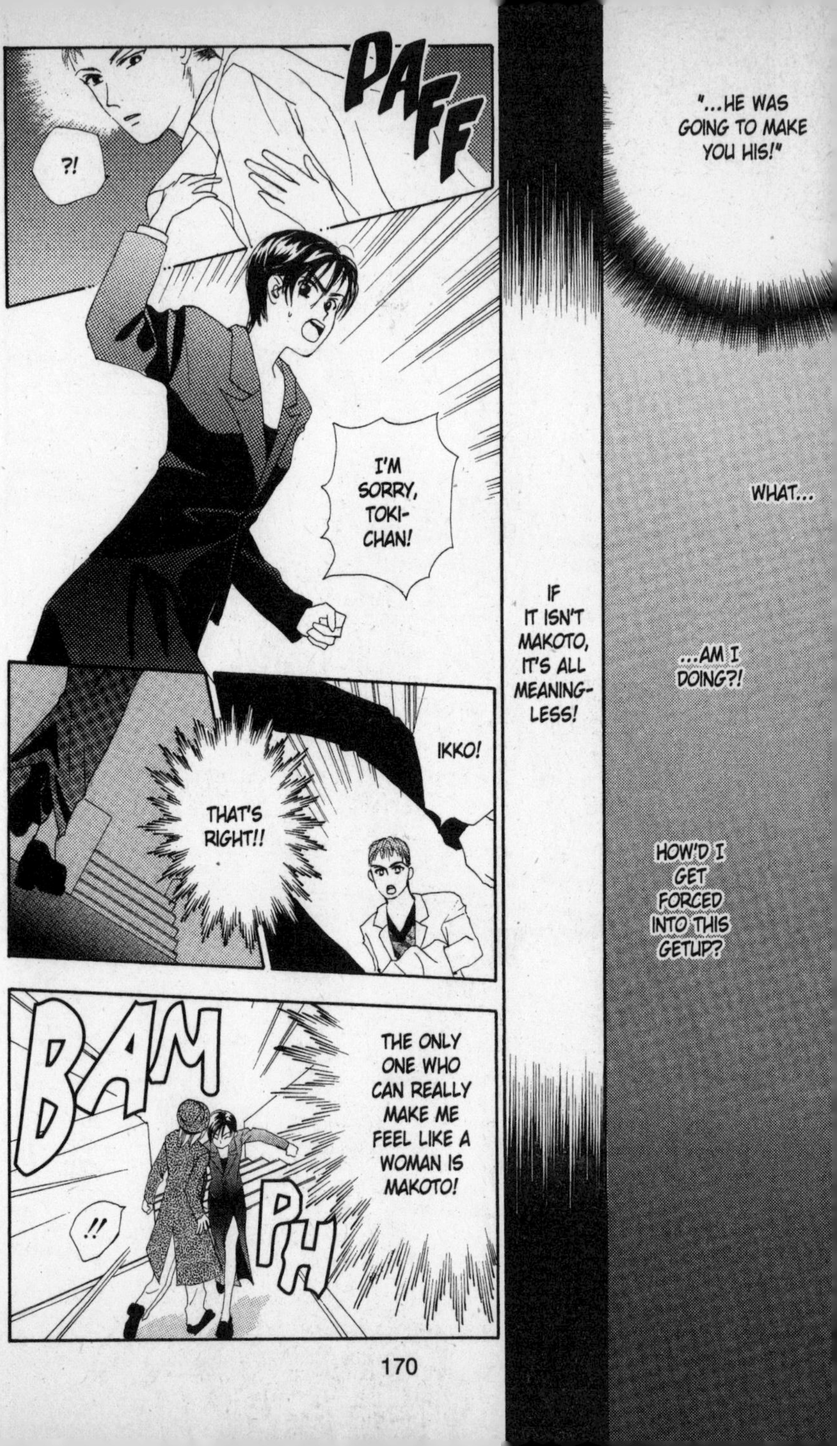
"...HE WAS GOING TO MAKE YOU HIS!"
WHAT...
...AM I DOING?!
HOW'D I GET FORCED INTO THIS GETUP?
IF IT ISN'T MAKOTO, IT'S ALL MEANING-LESS!
PAFF
?!
I'M SORRY, TOKI-CHAN!
IKKO!
THAT'S RIGHT!!
THE ONLY ONE WHO CAN REALLY MAKE ME FEEL LIKE A WOMAN IS MAKOTO!
BAM
PH
!!

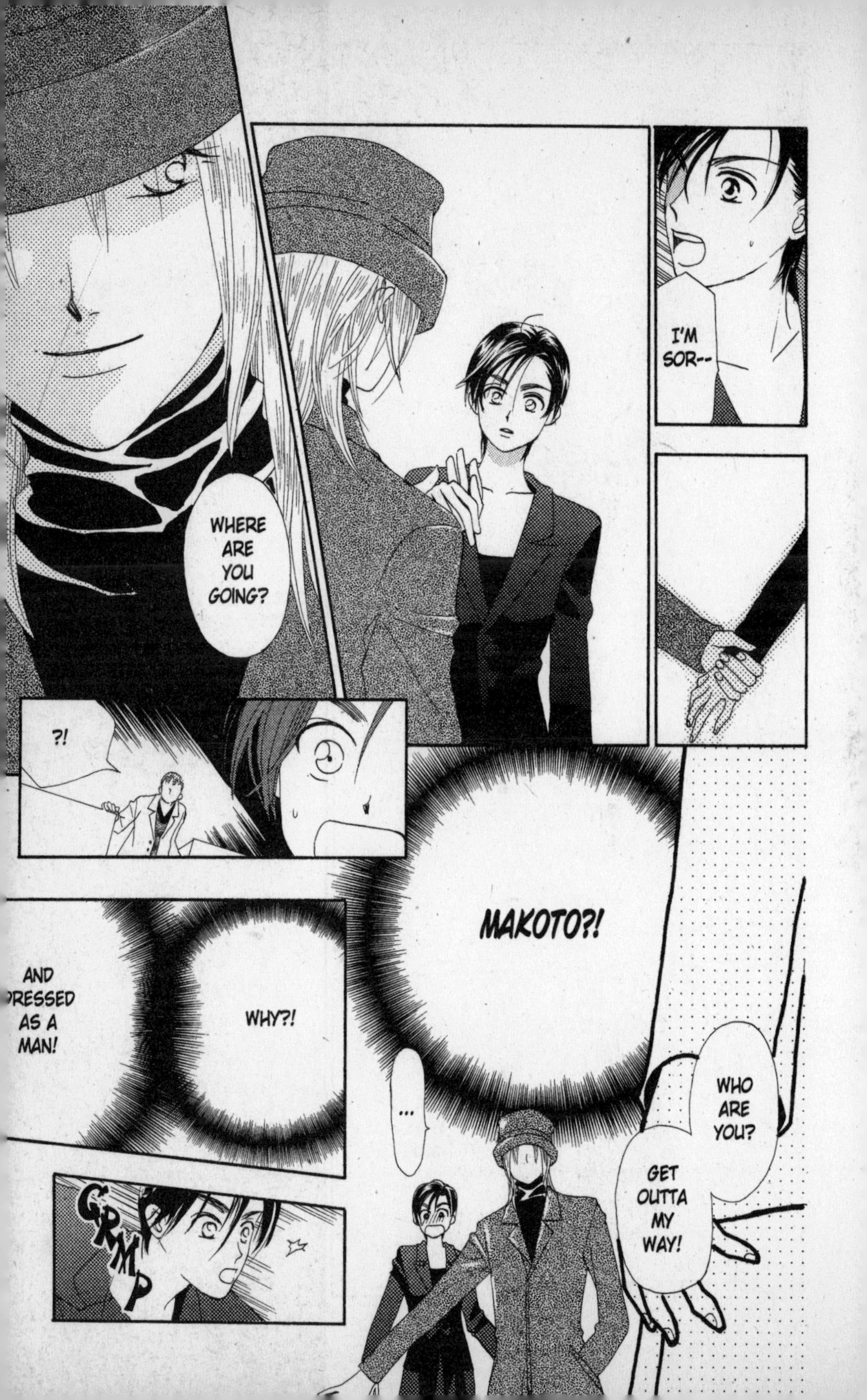
I'M SOR--
WHERE ARE YOU GOING?
?!
MAKOTO?!
WHY?!
AND DRESSED AS A MAN!
WHO ARE YOU?
GET OUTTA MY WAY!
...
GRMP

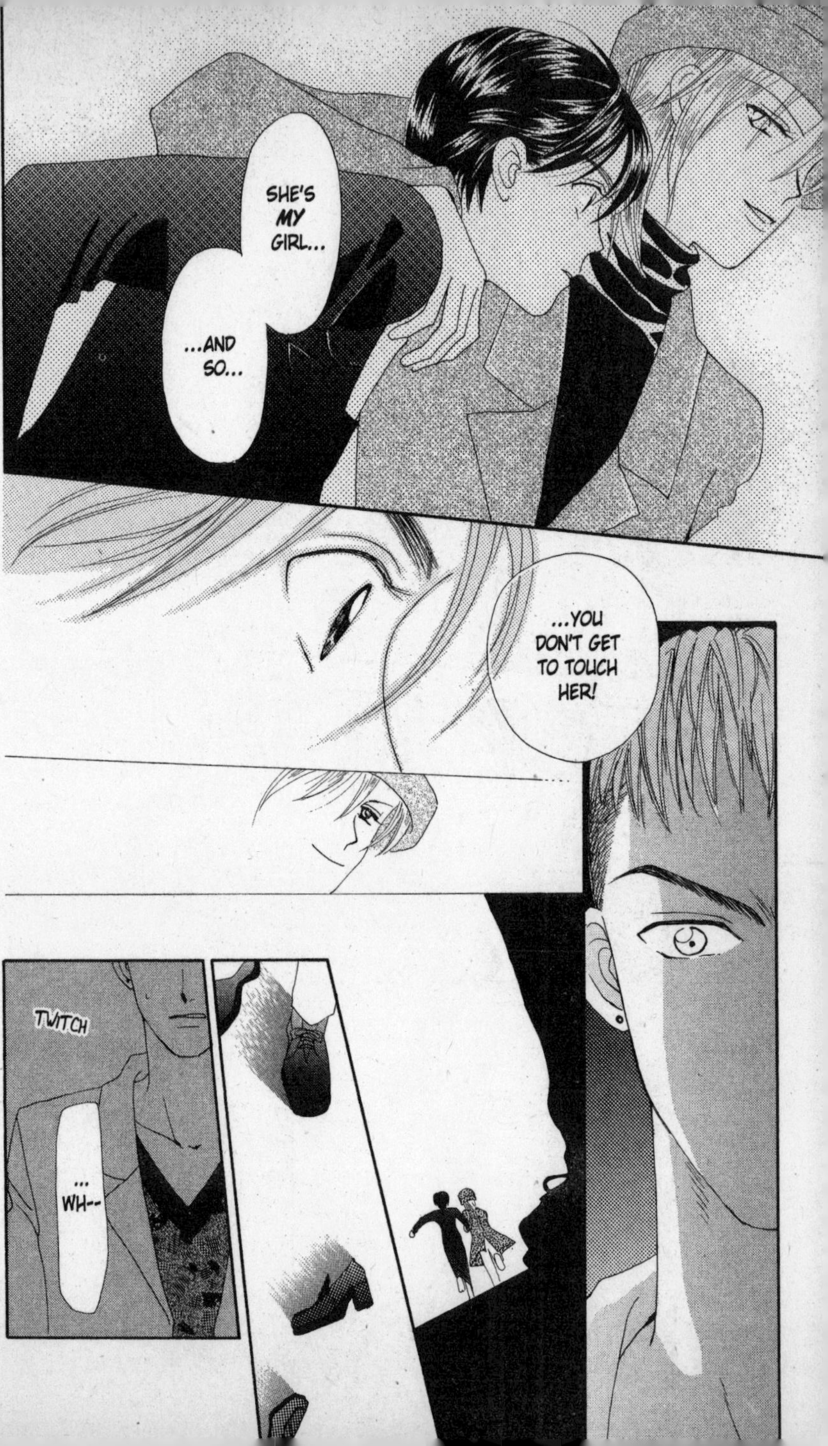
SHE'S MY GIRL...
...AND SO...
...YOU DON'T GET TO TOUCH HER!
...
TWITCH
... WH--

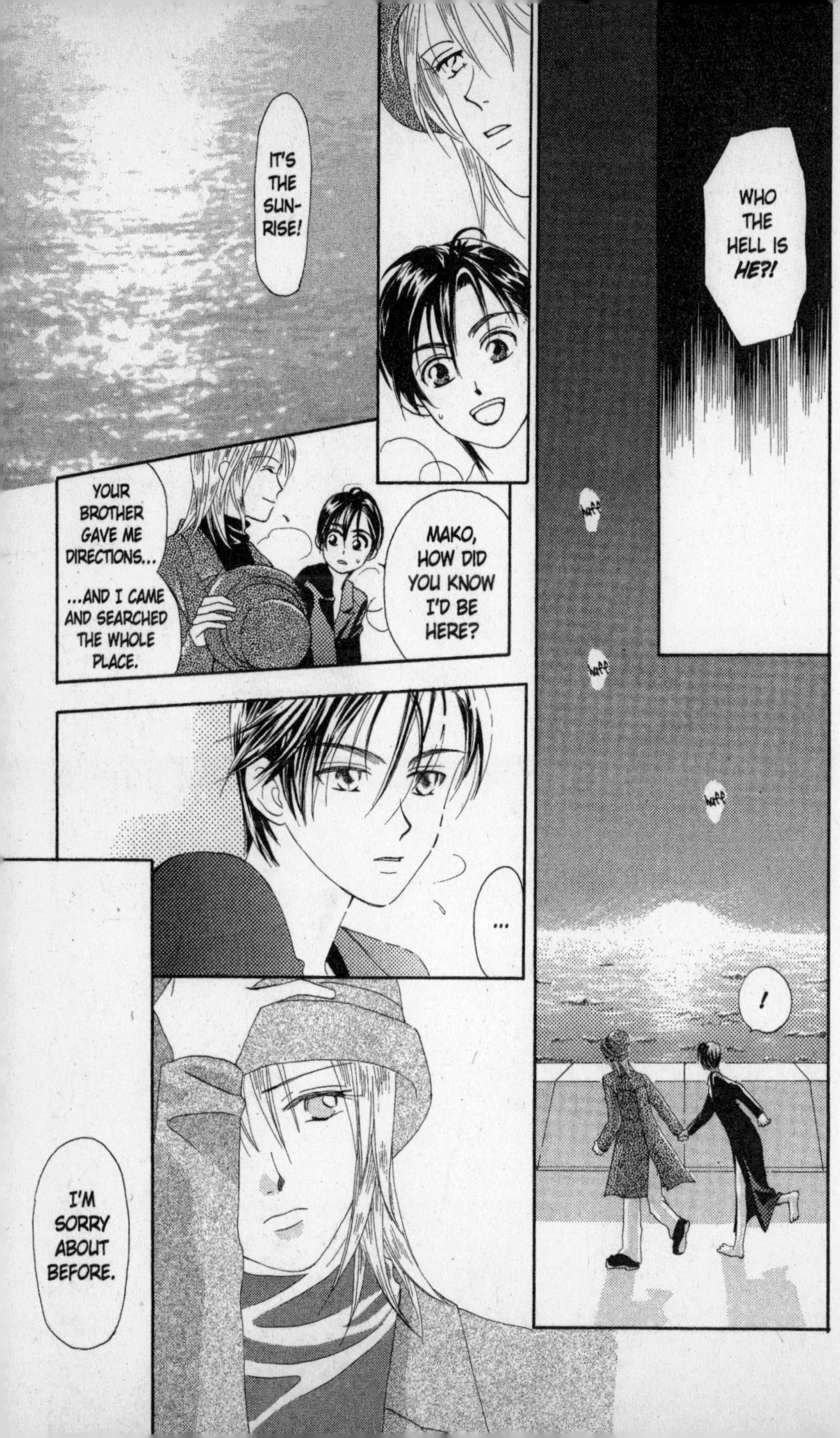
WHO THE HELL IS *HE?!*
huff
huff
huff
!
IT'S THE SUN-RISE!
MAKO, HOW DID YOU KNOW I'D BE HERE?
YOUR BROTHER GAVE ME DIRECTIONS...
...AND I CAME AND SEARCHED THE WHOLE PLACE.
...
I'M SORRY ABOUT BEFORE.

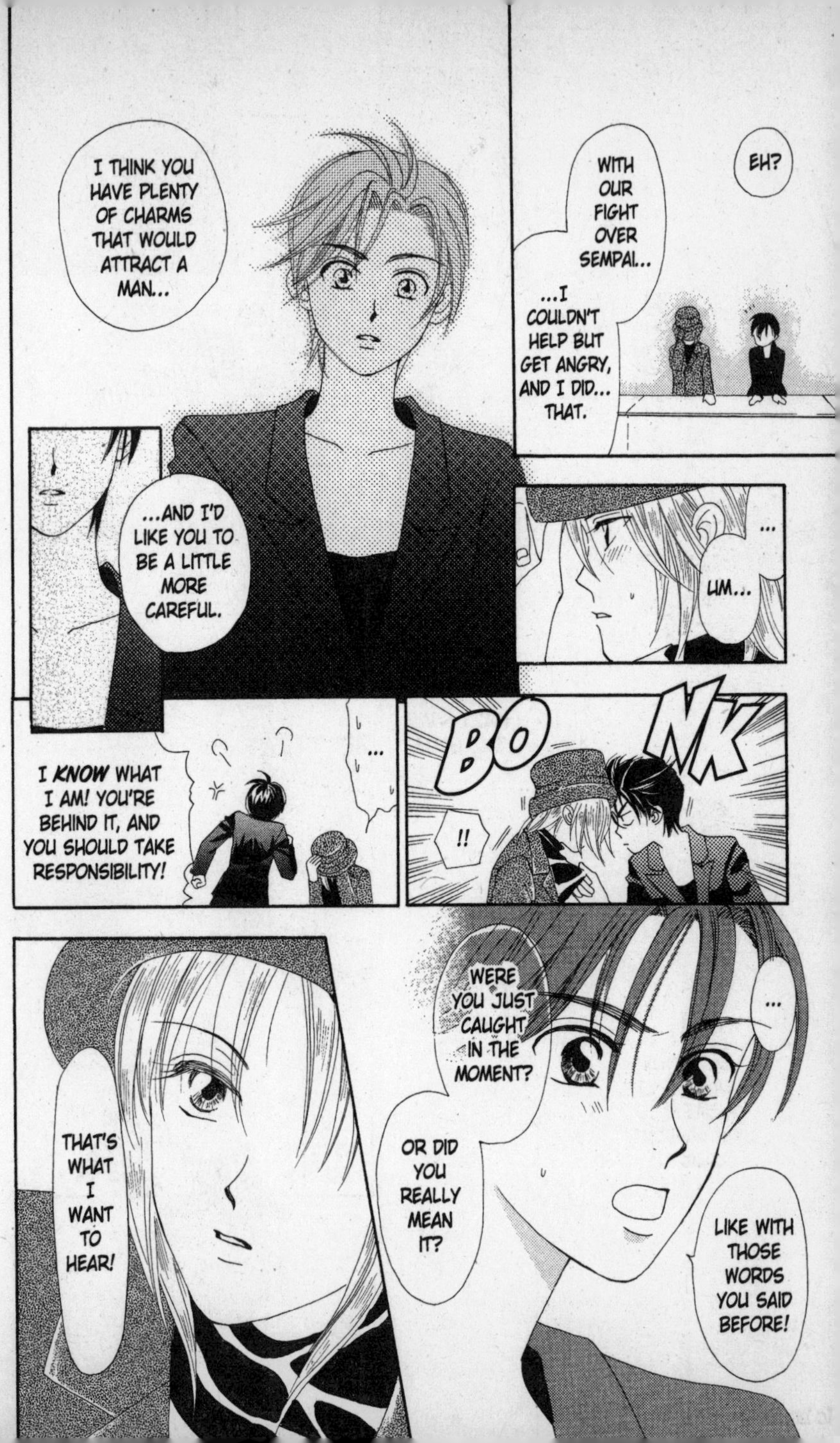
EH?
WITH OUR FIGHT OVER SEMPAI...
...I COULDN'T HELP BUT GET ANGRY, AND I DID... THAT.
...
UM...
I THINK YOU HAVE PLENTY OF CHARMS THAT WOULD ATTRACT A MAN...
...AND I'D LIKE YOU TO BE A LITTLE MORE CAREFUL.
BONK
!!
...
I *KNOW* WHAT I AM! YOU'RE BEHIND IT, AND YOU SHOULD TAKE RESPONSIBILITY!
...
WERE YOU JUST CAUGHT IN THE MOMENT?
OR DID YOU REALLY MEAN IT?
LIKE WITH THOSE WORDS YOU SAID BEFORE!
THAT'S WHAT I WANT TO HEAR!

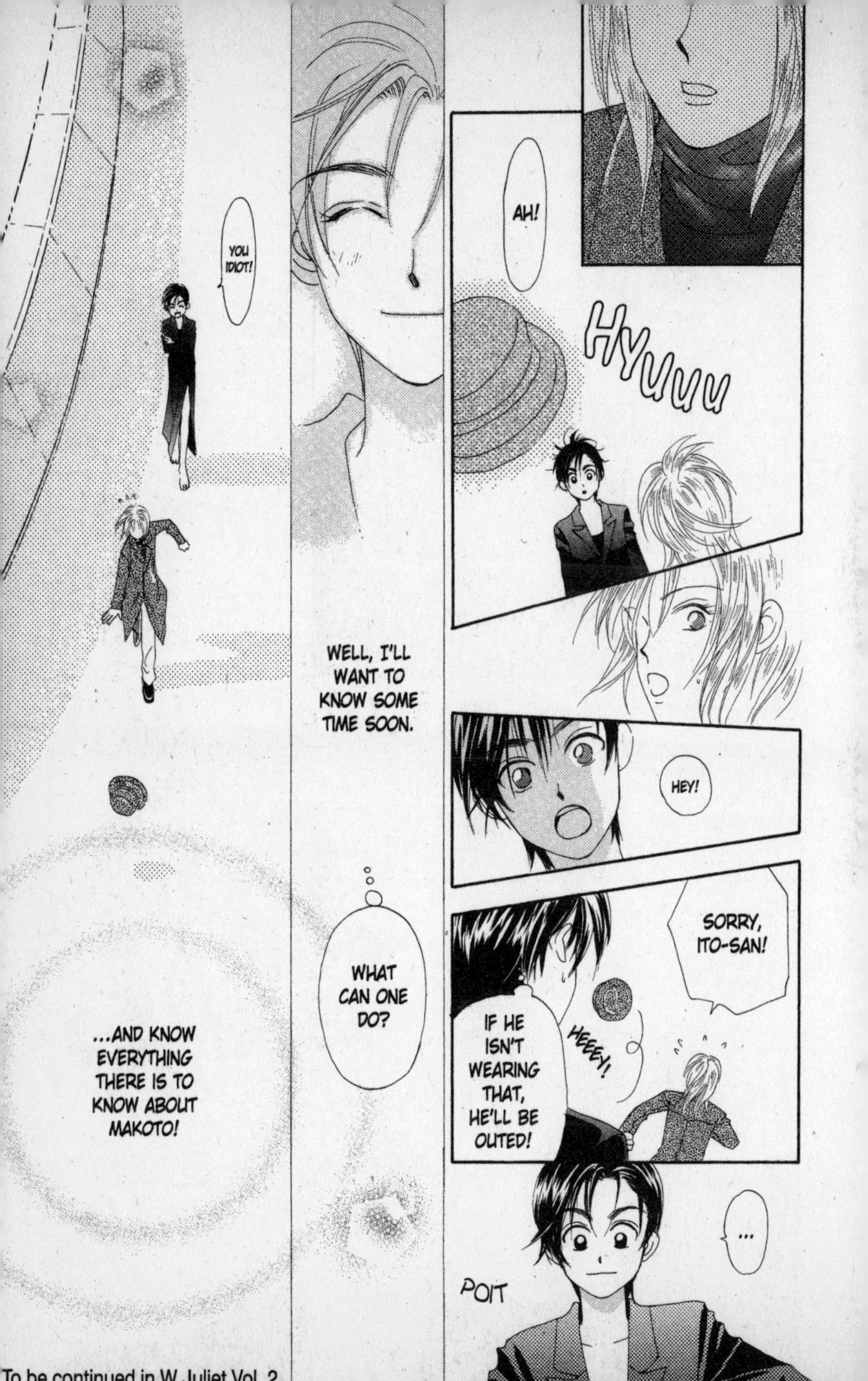
AH!
HYUUUU
HEY!
SORRY, ITO-SAN!
HEEEY!
IF HE ISN'T WEARING THAT, HE'LL BE OUTED!
...
POIT
WELL, I'LL WANT TO KNOW SOME TIME SOON.
WHAT CAN ONE DO?
YOU IDIOT!
...AND KNOW EVERYTHING THERE IS TO KNOW ABOUT MAKOTO!

To be continued in W Juliet Vol. 2.

THE VOLUME-ENDING AFTERWORD MANGA!

BEHIND THE SCENES

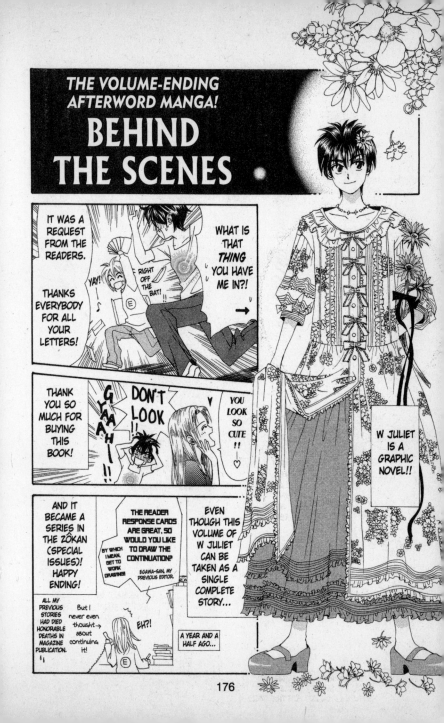

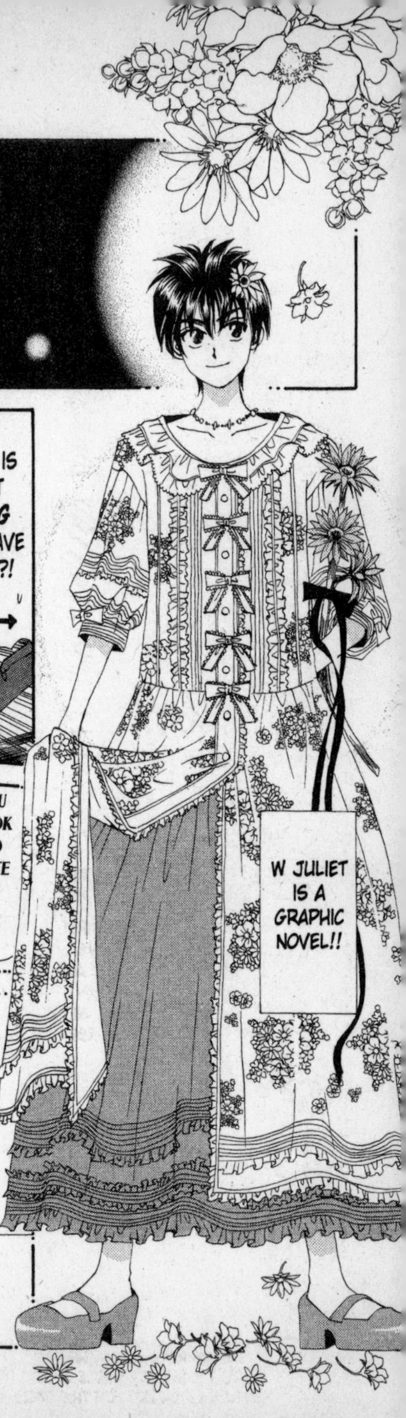
W JULIET IS A GRAPHIC NOVEL!!

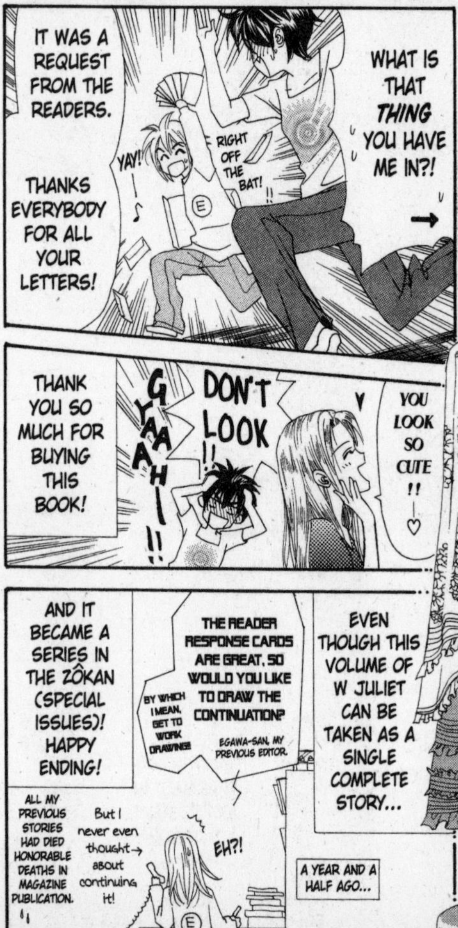
WHAT IS THAT THING YOU HAVE ME IN?!
RIGHT OFF THE BAT!
YAY!
IT WAS A REQUEST FROM THE READERS.
THANKS EVERYBODY FOR ALL YOUR LETTERS!
YOU LOOK SO CUTE!!
DON'T LOOK!!
GYAAAH!!
THANK YOU SO MUCH FOR BUYING THIS BOOK!
EVEN THOUGH THIS VOLUME OF W JULIET CAN BE TAKEN AS A SINGLE COMPLETE STORY...
A YEAR AND A HALF AGO...
THE READER RESPONSE CARDS ARE GREAT, SO WOULD YOU LIKE TO DRAW THE CONTINUATION?
BY WHICH I MEAN, GET TO WORK DRAWING!!
EGAWA-SAN, MY PREVIOUS EDITOR.
EH?!
But I never even thought about continuing it!
ALL MY PREVIOUS STORIES HAD DIED HONORABLE DEATHS IN MAGAZINE PUBLICATION.
AND IT BECAME A SERIES IN THE ZÔKAN (SPECIAL ISSUES)! HAPPY ENDING!

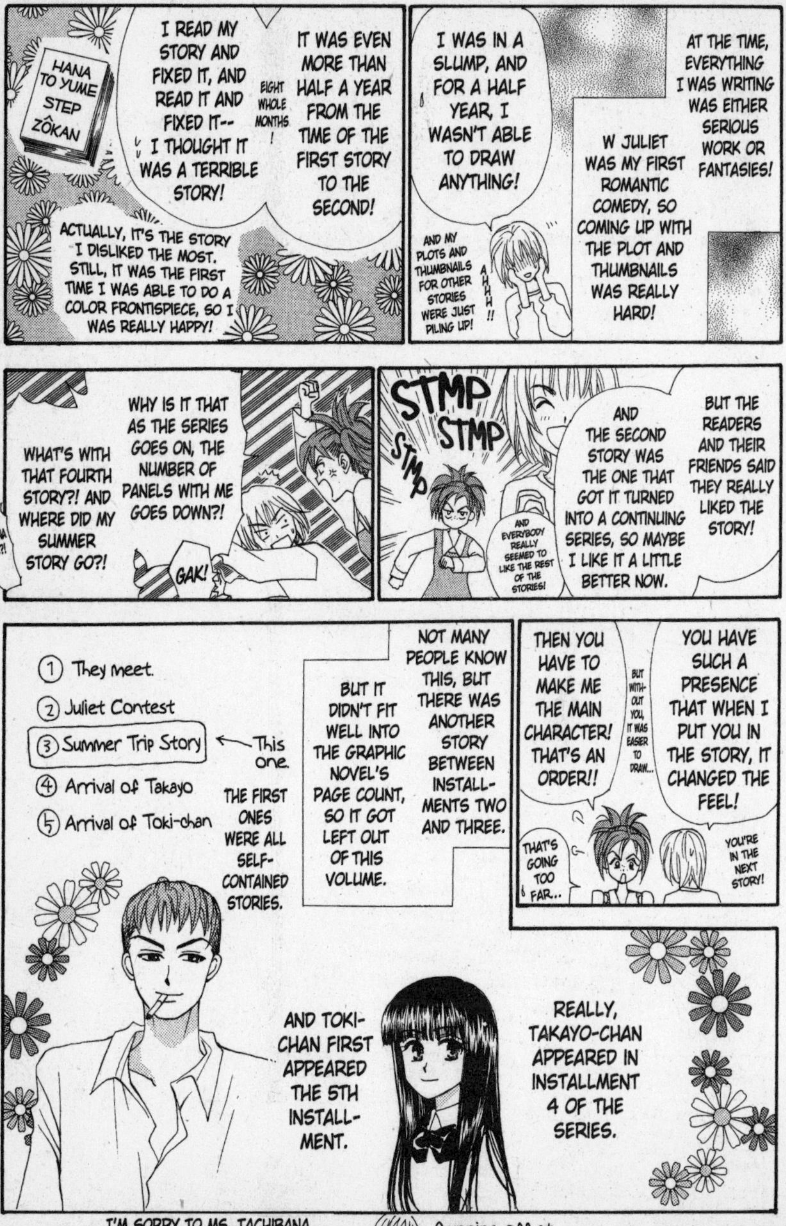
AT THE TIME, EVERYTHING I WAS WRITING WAS EITHER SERIOUS WORK OR FANTASIES!
I WAS IN A SLUMP, AND FOR A HALF YEAR, I WASN'T ABLE TO DRAW ANYTHING!
W JULIET WAS MY FIRST ROMANTIC COMEDY, SO COMING UP WITH THE PLOT AND THUMBNAILS WAS REALLY HARD!
AHHHH!!
AND MY PLOTS AND THUMBNAILS FOR OTHER STORIES WERE JUST PILING UP!
IT WAS EVEN MORE THAN HALF A YEAR FROM THE TIME OF THE FIRST STORY TO THE SECOND!
EIGHT WHOLE MONTHS!
I READ MY STORY AND FIXED IT, AND READ IT AND FIXED IT-- I THOUGHT IT WAS A TERRIBLE STORY!
HANA TO YUME STEP ZÔKAN
ACTUALLY, IT'S THE STORY I DISLIKED THE MOST. STILL, IT WAS THE FIRST TIME I WAS ABLE TO DO A COLOR FRONTISPIECE, SO I WAS REALLY HAPPY!
BUT THE READERS AND THEIR FRIENDS SAID THEY REALLY LIKED THE STORY!
AND THE SECOND STORY WAS THE ONE THAT GOT IT TURNED INTO A CONTINUING SERIES, SO MAYBE I LIKE IT A LITTLE BETTER NOW.
STMP STMP
STMP
AND EVERYBODY REALLY SEEMED TO LIKE THE REST OF THE STORIES!
WHY IS IT THAT AS THE SERIES GOES ON, THE NUMBER OF PANELS WITH ME GOES DOWN?!
WHAT'S WITH THAT FOURTH STORY?! AND WHERE DID MY SUMMER STORY GO?!
GAK!
YA WANNA DIE?!
YOU HAVE SUCH A PRESENCE THAT WHEN I PUT YOU IN THE STORY, IT CHANGED THE FEEL!
BUT WITHOUT YOU, IT WAS EASIER TO DRAW...
THEN YOU HAVE TO MAKE ME THE MAIN CHARACTER! THAT'S AN ORDER!!
YOU'RE IN THE NEXT STORY!
THAT'S GOING TOO FAR...
NOT MANY PEOPLE KNOW THIS, BUT THERE WAS ANOTHER STORY BETWEEN INSTALLMENTS TWO AND THREE.
BUT IT DIDN'T FIT WELL INTO THE GRAPHIC NOVEL'S PAGE COUNT, SO IT GOT LEFT OUT OF THIS VOLUME.
THE FIRST ONES WERE ALL SELF-CONTAINED STORIES.
① They meet.
② Juliet Contest
③ Summer Trip Story
This one.
④ Arrival of Takayo
⑤ Arrival of Toki-chan
REALLY, TAKAYO-CHAN APPEARED IN INSTALLMENT 4 OF THE SERIES.
AND TOKI-CHAN FIRST APPEARED THE 5TH INSTALLMENT.

I'M SORRY TO MS. TACHIBANA HIKUCHI, I WAS ONLY ABLE TO ADD TSUGUMI AS A GUIDE FOR THIS PAGE.

Running off at high speed!

CHAPTER 1

Yes, this is where they first meet. It took six months to be published, but before that, I was thinking the story over for about two years. Then one day, I saw the "Romeo and Juliet" with L. DiCaprio, and that's when I decided to draw it! But the story was completely different!!

And here's the scoop about their names... In the very first prototype story, they had the same name. Ito was Ito Miura, but Mako was Ito Amano!! And then I talked on the phone with my editor...

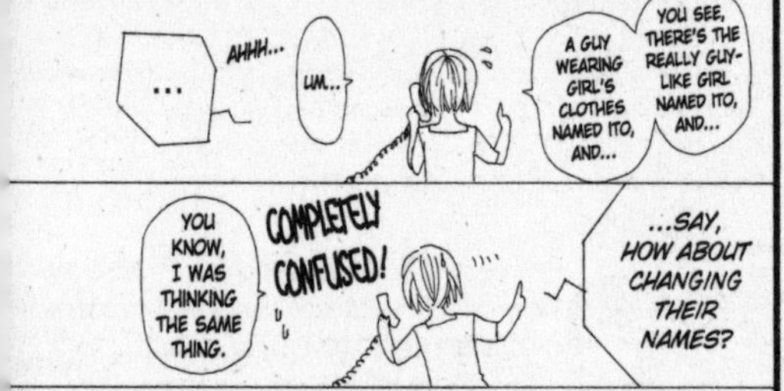
YOU SEE, THERE'S THE REALLY GUY-LIKE GIRL NAMED ITO, AND...
A GUY WEARING GIRL'S CLOTHES NAMED ITO, AND...
UM...
AHHH...
...
...SAY, HOW ABOUT CHANGING THEIR NAMES?
COMPLETELY CONFUSED!
YOU KNOW, I WAS THINKING THE SAME THING.

And thus, it was decided that Mako's name would be Makoto Amano. Oh, well...

Ah! But with the same name, the Double (W) part of the title has more meaning! Dammit! (Is it too late to change?) In any case, it was a story that was both interesting and fun to draw!

CHAPTER 2

The Juliet Contest/Pool story.

...yeah... I wrote about this on the other page, and I don't have much else to say... What a really stupid story I drew! Gaaaahhhhhh!!! (screams!) But it got a better response than the first story in the reader response cards! I just have all these conflicting thoughts about it. At first, I thought it was good. What was most difficult was Mako's character. At the time of the first story, all I did was tailor Mako's character to the events of the short story. Now that I got to this point, it was really hard to move the characters as a team! They just didn't want to move! Really! Maybe that's why the plot and thumbnails just never came together as a real story! If I did it now, the characters are more fleshed out, and I think I would have no problem...maybe.

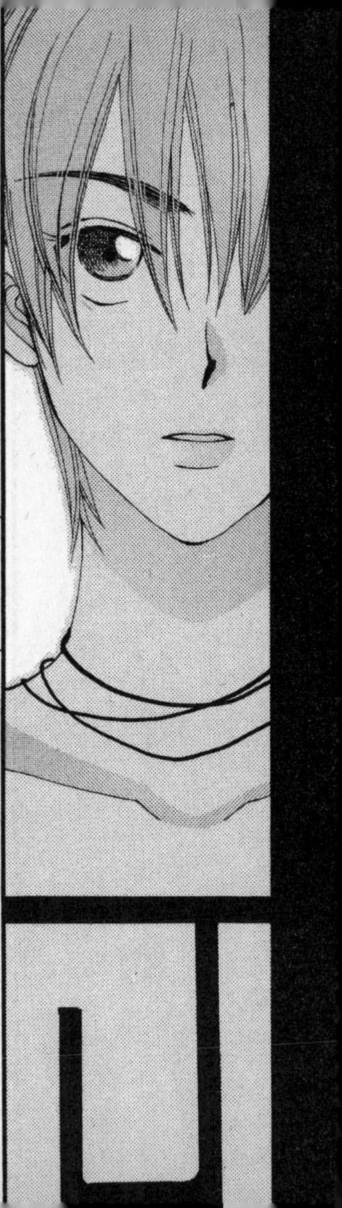

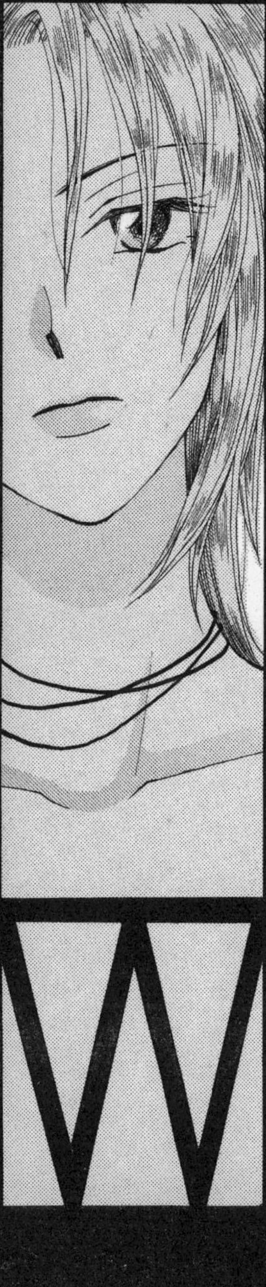

CHAPTER 3

The installment when Takayo-chan first appears, right? I get the feeling that this is the story where my art stabilized. Also it's the story I was doing when the response cards and fan letters broke onto the scene. Thank you for all the great letters!! I take care to read each and every one! ♡ I'm sorry that I don't seem to be able to respond too fast, and unless my luck changes very soon, I won't be able to mail the responses I have actually written. Please be as patient as you can be.

...now, back to the story... Umm... I know this is always the case, but the sheer number of panels in this episode made it really hard!! With my manga, it always seems like I don't have enough pages, even though I'm always crossing out sections! It's so sad! The prototype Takayo-chan at first had much more of a persecution complex, and was a nastier person! Forgive me, Takayo-chan! Now, after I have gotten farther into the series and things are clearer, she's gradually becoming a nicer person. In her place, her big brother Takashi has taken on the job of the bad guy. Actually Mr. Sister-Complex Takashi was supposed to be introduced in this installment, but I ran short on pages, and all the scenes were cut out. But he lives it up (?) later in the series!

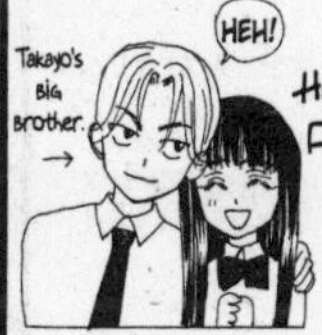
HEH!
Takayo's big brother. →

He's here!! The appearance of Toki-chan! For the sake of the magazine readers (the first people to read each installment), I was really psyched to do this chapter, but the thumbnails just didn't come together!

CHAPTER 4

And because of that, I feel that the artwork really suffered! So for its release in the comics (graphic novels), I did a whole lot of reworking of the art. The page count increased, and there were so many things that I still forgot to put in it! I got a lot of letters asking why Ito was barefoot at the end. Here is the answer... I forgot to draw her shoes!! (Bottom of Page 173.) What can I say? I really do realize just how much the magazine version wasn't ready to be published! And even this time, I wanted to work more on it, but I had no time!

The art-board pages that I'm doing for the magazine version are still way too white!

But because of these complete-in-one-story chapters, it was decided that I could do a continuing story! Thank you everybody! You're the ones who did it for me!

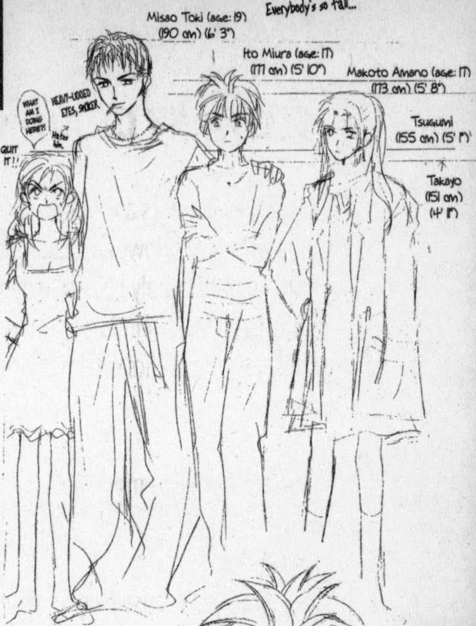

Everybody's so tall...
Misao Toki (age: 19) (190 cm) (6' 3")
Ito Miura (age: 17) (177 cm) (5' 10")
Makoto Amano (age: 17) (173 cm) (5' 8")
Tsugumi (155 cm) (5' 1")
Takayo (151 cm) (4' 11")
WHAT AM I DOING HERE?!
HEAVY-LIDDED EYES, SMOKER
QUIT IT!!

It's the last page!

Thank you so much for reading all of this! Actually this May (as of this writing), it will make exactly three years since my debut! Time really flies fast! Especially this year! It ended so fast, there were a whole lot of things that I still have yet to do! There's so much work! Everything you read in this book was stuff that I drew while I was doing a day job. (I was an hourly worker.) When it got close to my deadlines, I called in sick to finish up! To everybody at the confectioners' shop, sorry!!

- To the real Toki-chan, Takayo, and Amano-chan! Thanks for letting me borrow your names!
- Thanks, as always, to Yukino-san, who is always helping me with the artboards. To my little sister Sayaka, you're the person I should probably thank the most!
- Thanks to my mother who always makes the best food!
- To my brother and father who always give me rides in their cars, thank you!!♥
- To my editor, A-san! Sorry for giving you all of the headaches! Thank you!
- To my friend Yumi! ♥ Thanks for the birthday call! Happy Birthday 3-year-old Tatsuya! Same day as me!
- And to my friend ♥ Kaori!!

——— Congratulations on your wedding!! Become the happiest woman in the world, okay? And in the future, make me smile with your wild speeches again, huh? ——— ! (笑) But you guys are getting married too soon! (Yumi: 18, Kaori: 21)

- And most of all, to the readers, thank you so much!! If you receive this work warmly, it will make me very happy!

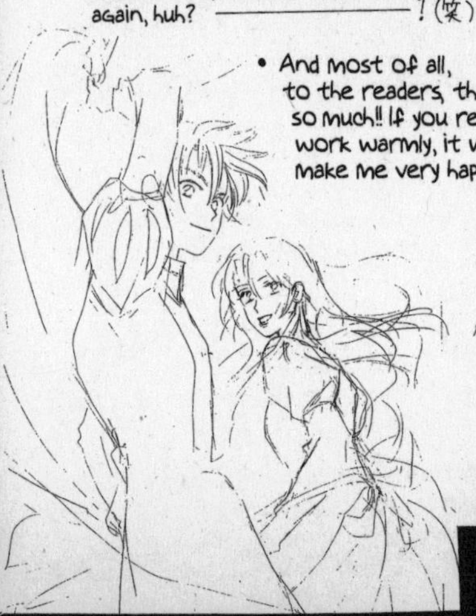

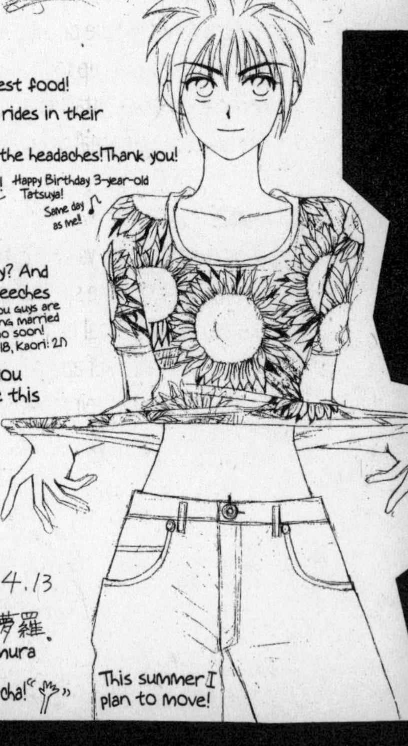

'99. 4. 13

絵夢羅。
Emura

Bye-cha!

This summer I plan to move!

GLOSSARY OF HONORIFIC TERMS

Japanese honorifics are roughly similar to the use of Mr., Ms., and other titles in English. However, Japanese honorifics have a few major differences from English, mainly having to do with relative status (higher or lower social status) and level of intimacy (more intimate or more distant personal relationships). Honorifics can be attached to either the family name or personal name.

Here are the terms most used:

-chan
A diminutive. It is used for young children, or to make a person's name seem more childlike or cute. It is most commonly found among groups of close friends, girls up to their mid twenties, and for "cute" men. This honorific is generally attached to personal names or shortened, "nickname" forms of the personal or family name.

-kun
Used mostly for boys of middle-school age until college age, and only when talking on the same social level or down. It can be used for girls' family names, but personal name plus *-chan* is more common. If an adult uses the term to someone of approximately the same age, odds are they've known each other since their school days.

-san
Used for all persons of higher status, of undetermined status, of equal status (for adults), of lower-but-respected status, or for people who are no closer to the speaker than acquaintances. Unless wildly inappropriate, the use of *-san* will go completely unnoticed by a Japanese listener. The use of any other honorific, or the lack of use, will be noted.

Note: Teachers generally refer to their students as *-kun* or *-chan* and infrequently *-san* for students up through college age. When the students are college age or older, they generally use *-san*. Teachers rarely leave off the honorific.

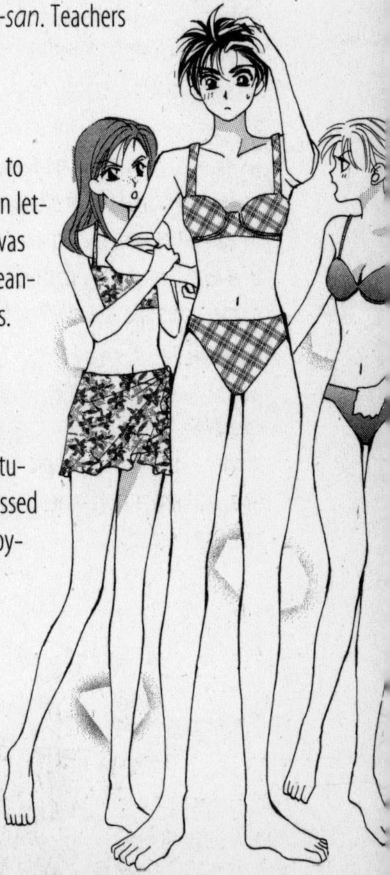

-sama
Mainly reserved for use in formal occasions, to address customers in a shop or restaurant, in letters, or in other formalized applications. It was an address for feudal superiors, and that meaning is held over for modern sarcasm or jokes.

-sempai
Used to address more senior members of an institutionalized organization. In a school, students senior to the speaker would be addressed with *-sempai*, as would more senior employees in a company.

yobisute (no suffix)
Leaving off the honorific (called *yobisute* in Japan) indicates intimacy

or superior status for the speaker. It is common to leave off the honorific for people lower than one in seniority, lower rank in the military, or among close friends. Higher status males addressing lower status females (assuming there is no intimate relationship) do not leave off the honorific. If a person asks someone they just met to leave off the honorific when addressing them (as in, "Just call me Taro!"), it indicates a very bold personality. Leaving off the honorific is mandatory when saying one's own name or when speaking of the members of one's immediate family to a third party outside the speaker's family group.

Note: Status among students is usually simple. Grades above are superior, same grade is equal, grades below are lower status. Students usually use -*san* or -*sempai* for students of higher grades,
-*san*, -*kun*, -*chan*, or no honorific for students of the same grade, and mainly no honorific for students of lower grades (although males will use -*chan* when addressing lower status females). When using no honorific, to sound commanding, the student will call the inferior by the family name. To sound friendly, the student will use the personal name.

-sensei
Reserved to address people of certain professions such as teachers, doctors, and artisans. (Sometimes used for people playing the role of a teacher, doctor, etc.)

-dono

Archaic. Similar meaning to -*sama*, but hardly ever used in modern Japan.

-sempai/kohai relationship

Since W Juliet takes place in a school club, the *sempai/kohai* relationship is a crucial aspect of the life of club members. It is much like the Western mentor/protégé relationship, but on a institution-wide scale. *Sempai*, the senior members, are expected to look after the interests of their *kohai* and guide them, help them with their problems, give them referrals, and be a counselor. *Kohai* are always expected respect their *sempai*, do chores or menial tasks, follow orders, and learn whatever the organization teaches.

Note: The *sempai/kohai* relationship is very strong among alumni of the same school. A *kohai* has a reason-able expectation that any *sempai* (even though they may never have met) who can assist will help in the *kohai*'s career. This is one of the reasons that some students are desperate to enter highly regarded schools. School *sempai* in high positions can jump-start a career. Members of the same club in the same school make the *sempai/kohai* obligation even stronger.

EDITOR'S RECOMMENDATIONS

If you enjoyed this volume of W Juliet then here's some more gender-bending manga you might be interested in.

HANA KIMI: FOR YOU IN FULL BLOSSOM ©Hisaya Nakajo 1996/ HAKUSENSHA, Inc.

Hana Kimi by Hisaya Nakajo: To be close to her idol, high jumper Izumi Sano, Japanese-American track-and-field star Mizuki has gotten herself a transfer to a boarding school in Japan...an all guy's high school! Now Mizuki, disguising herself as a boy, must learn how to keep her secret in the classroom, the locker room, and the dorm room!

©1988 Rumiko Takahashi/ Shogakukan, Inc.

Ranma 1/2 by Rumiko Takahashi: This Rumiko Takahashi classic is universally acknowledged as the masterpiece of the gender-bending kung-fu comedy genre. When Ranma and his father get splashed with cold water, papa turns into a giant panda and male Ranma becomes a buxom young woman! Hot water reverses the effect--but only until the next time!

© 1999 Hiroyuki Nishimori/ Shogakukan, Inc.

Cheeky Angel by Hiroyuki Nishimori: All young scamp Megumi ever wanted was to be "the manliest man on Earth," however, a hard-of-hearing genie misunderstood his wish and turned him into the "womanliest woman"! Six years later, Megumi is the hottest girl in school, but has stayed true to his/her tough talkin', punk stompin' ways...

In Dorm Life, Anything Goes!

When Kazuya's brother marries his love interest – and takes her home to live with them – he escapes to a prestigious all-boys' school. Little did he know that life at Ryokuto Academy's dorm (a.k.a. Greenwood) would be nuttier than his already chaotic existence!

Only $9.99!

shōjo

Here is
Greenwood.

story and art by **Yukie Nasu** vol.1

Here is Greenwood™

Start your graphic novel collection today!

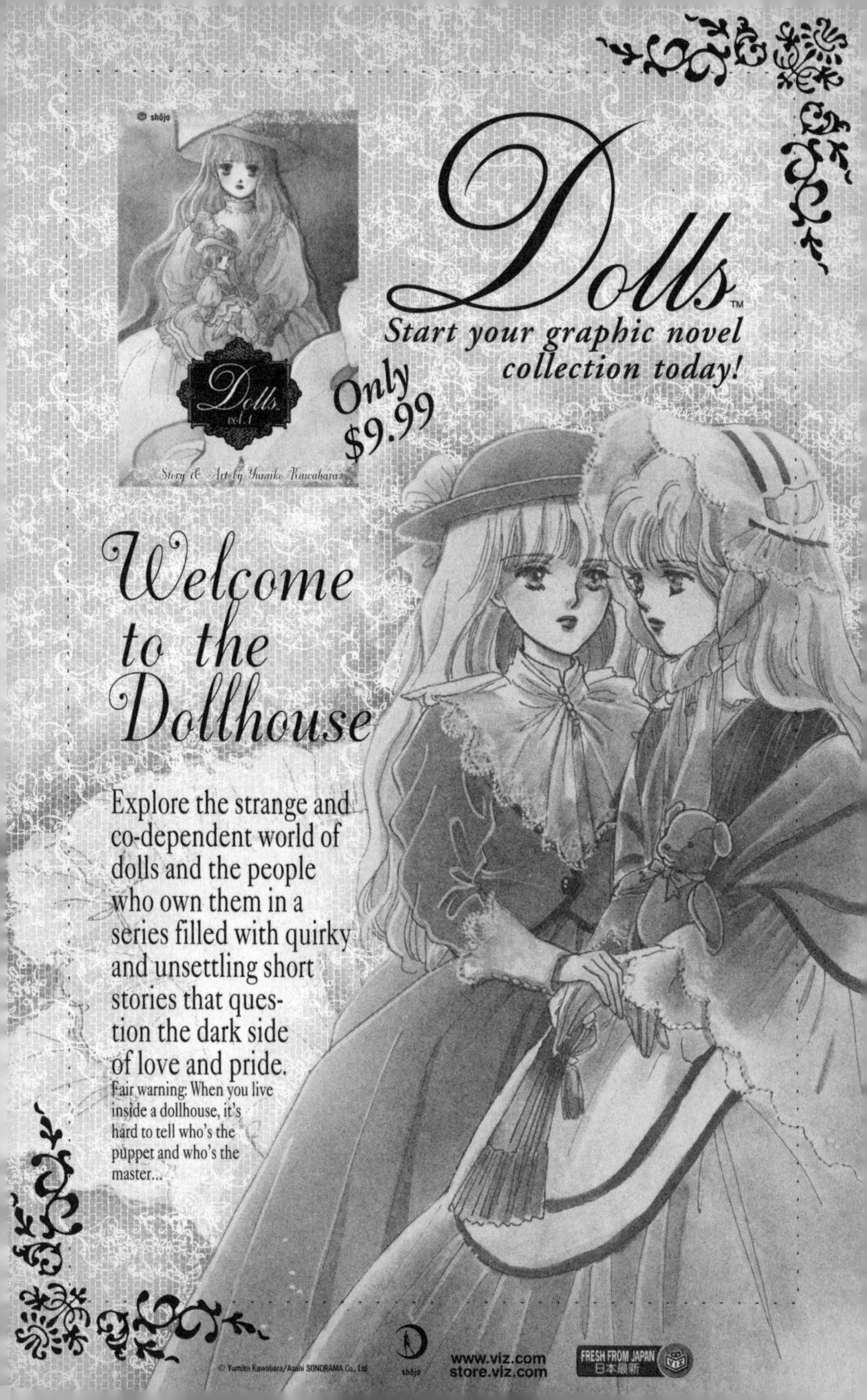
shōjo
Dolls vol.1
Story & Art by Yumiko Kawahara
Dolls™
Start your graphic novel collection today!
Only $9.99
Welcome to the Dollhouse
Explore the strange and co-dependent world of dolls and the people who own them in a series filled with quirky and unsettling short stories that question the dark side of love and pride.
Fair warning: When you live inside a dollhouse, it's hard to tell who's the puppet and who's the master...
© Yumiko Kawahara/Asahi SONORAMA Co., Ltd
shōjo
www.viz.com
store.viz.com
FRESH FROM JAPAN
日本最新
VIZ

COMPLETE OUR SURVEY AND LET US KNOW WHAT YOU THINK!

☐ Please do NOT send me information about VIZ products, news and events, special offers, or other information.

☐ Please do NOT send me information from VIZ's trusted business partners.

Name: _____

Address: _____

City: _____ **State:** _____ **Zip:** _____

E-mail: _____

☐ Male ☐ Female **Date of Birth** (mm/dd/yyyy): ___ / ___ / _____ (Under 13? Parental consent required)

What race/ethnicity do you consider yourself? (please check one)

☐ Asian/Pacific Islander   ☐ Black/African American   ☐ Hispanic/Latino

☐ Native American/Alaskan Native ☐ White/Caucasian   ☐ Other: _____

What VIZ product did you purchase? (check all that apply and indicate title purchased)

☐ DVD/VHS _____

☐ Graphic Novel _____

☐ Magazines _____

☐ Merchandise _____

Reason for purchase: (check all that apply)

☐ Special offer   ☐ Favorite title   ☐ Gift

☐ Recommendation   ☐ Other _____

Where did you make your purchase? (please check one)

☐ Comic store   ☐ Bookstore   ☐ Mass/Grocery Store

☐ Newsstand   ☐ Video/Video Game Store ☐ Other: _____

☐ Online (site: _____)

What other VIZ properties have you purchased/own? _____

_____

How many anime and/or manga titles have you purchased in the last year? How many were VIZ titles? (please check one from each column)

ANIME
☐ None
☐ 1-4
☐ 5-10
☐ 11+

MANGA
☐ None
☐ 1-4
☐ 5-10
☐ 11+

VIZ
☐ None
☐ 1-4
☐ 5-10
☐ 11+

I find the pricing of VIZ products to be: (please check one)
☐ Cheap   ☐ Reasonable   ☐ Expensive

What genre of manga and anime would you like to see from VIZ? (please check two)
☐ Adventure   ☐ Comic Strip   ☐ Science Fiction   ☐ Fighting
☐ Horror   ☐ Romance   ☐ Fantasy   ☐ Sports

What do you think of VIZ's new look?
☐ Love It   ☐ It's OK   ☐ Hate It   ☐ Didn't Notice   ☐ No Opinion

Which do you prefer? (please check one)
☐ Reading right-to-left
☐ Reading left-to-right

Which do you prefer? (please check one)
☐ Sound effects in English
☐ Sound effects in Japanese with English captions
☐ Sound effects in Japanese only with a glossary at the back

THANK YOU! Please send the completed form to:

VIZ Survey
42 Catharine St.
Poughkeepsie, NY 12601

All information provided will be used for internal purposes only. We promise not to sell or otherwise divulge your information.